Amsterdam

"All you've got to do is decide to go
and the hardest part is over.

So go!"

TONY WHEELER, COFOUNDER – LONELY PLANET

Catherine Le Nevez, Abigail Blasi

Contents

Plan Your Trip   4

Explore Amsterdam   60

Understand Amsterdam   223

Survival Guide   259

Amsterdam Maps   288

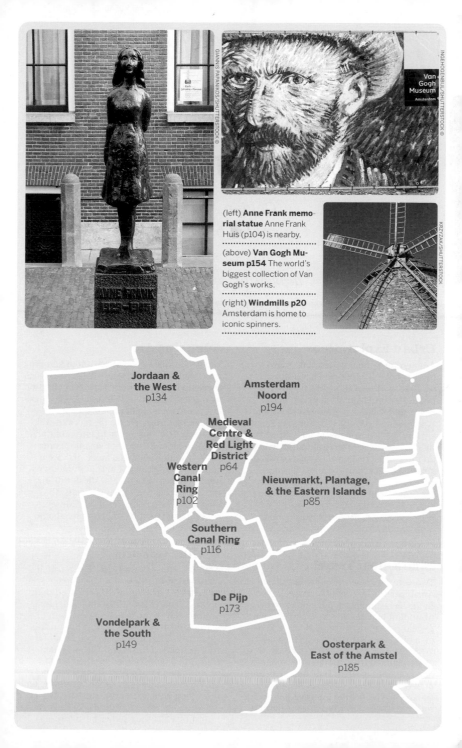

(left) **Anne Frank memorial statue** Anne Frank Huis (p104) is nearby.

(above) **Van Gogh Museum p154** The world's biggest collection of Van Gogh's works.

(right) **Windmills p20** Amsterdam is home to iconic spinners.

Jordaan & the West
p134

Amsterdam Noord
p194

Medieval Centre & Red Light District p64

Western Canal Ring
p102

Nieuwmarkt, Plantage, & the Eastern Islands
p85

Southern Canal Ring
p116

De Pijp
p173

Vondelpark & the South
p149

Oosterpark & East of the Amstel
p185

Welcome to Amsterdam

Golden Age canals lined by tilting gabled buildings are the backdrop for Amsterdam's treasure-packed museums, vintage shops and creative design, drinking and dining scenes.

Urban Explorations

Amsterdam's canal-woven core is crossed by atmospheric lanes. You never know what you'll find: a tiny hidden garden; a boutique selling Dutch-designed homewares and fashion; a jewel-box-like *jenever* (Dutch gin) distillery; a flower stall filled with tulips in a rainbow of hues; an old monastery-turned-classical-music-venue; an ultra-niche restaurant – an avocado or strawberry specialist or one reinventing age-old Dutch classics. Fringing the centre, post-industrial buildings in up-and-coming neighbourhoods now house creative enterprises, from galleries to breweries and cutting-edge tech start-ups, as well as some of Europe's hottest clubs.

Bike & Boat Travel

Two-wheeling is a way of life here. It's how Amsterdammers commute to work, go to the shop, and meet a date for dinner. Abundant bike-rental shops make it easy to gear up and take a spin. If locals aren't on a bike, they may well be on the water. With its canals and massive harbour, this city reclaimed from the sea offers countless opportunities to drift. Hop aboard a canal boat (preferably an open-air one) or one of the free ferries behind Centraal Station, or rent your own for a wind-in-your-hair ride.

Admiring Art

You can't walk a kilometre without bumping into a masterpiece in the city. The Van Gogh Museum hangs the world's largest collection by tortured native son Vincent. A few blocks away, Vermeers, Rembrandts and other Golden Age treasures fill the glorious Rijksmuseum. The Museum het Rembrandthuis offers more of Rembrandt via his etching-packed studio, while the Stedelijk Museum counts Matisses and Mondrians among its modern stock. And for blockbuster displays, the Hermitage Amsterdam delivers: the outpost of Russia's State Hermitage Museum sifts through its three-million-piece home trove to mount mega exhibitions.

Feeling Gezellig

Amsterdam is famously *gezellig,* a Dutch quality that translates roughly as 'convivial' or 'cosy'. It's more easily experienced than defined. There's a sense of time stopping, an intimacy of the here-and-now that leaves your troubles behind, at least until tomorrow. The easiest place to encounter this feeling is a *bruin café* (brown cafe; traditional pub). Named for their wood panelling and walls once stained by smoke, brown cafes have *gezelligheid* (cosiness) on tap, along with good beer. You can also feel *gezellig* lingering after dinner in snug restaurants while the candles burn low.

Why I Love Amsterdam

By Catherine Le Nevez, Writer

For me, and for countless other travellers over the centuries, Amsterdam has become a home away from home. Since the earliest seafarers set out to explore the world, Amsterdammers have had an open-minded global outlook and sense of adventure that still defines them today. While Amsterdam retains its Dutch heritage in its charming canal architecture, works by Old Masters, *jenever* tasting houses and candlelit brown cafes, I love that this free-spirited city is a multinational melting pot with an incredible diversity of cultures and cuisines in a compact, village-like setting.

For more about our writers, see p320

Above: Groenburgwal canal (p90) and the Zuiderkerk (p88)

Amsterdam's
Top 10

Rijksmuseum *(p151)*

1 The Netherlands' top treasure house does not disappoint. The crowds huddle around Rembrandt's humongous *Night Watch* and Vermeer's *Kitchen Maid* in the Gallery of Honour, but that just means the remaining 1.5km of rooms are free for browsing antique ship models, savage-looking swords, crystal goblets and magic lanterns. You could spend days gaping at the beautiful and curious collections tucked into the nooks and crannies. What's more, free sculpture-studded gardens surround the monumental building, which now also shelters a Michelin-starred restaurant, Rijks.

 *Vondelpark & the South*

Van Gogh Museum *(p154)*

2 Housing the world's largest collection by artist Vincent van Gogh, this museum is as much a tour through the driven painter's troubled mind as it is a tour through his body of work. More than 200 canvases are on display, from his dark, potato-filled early career in the Netherlands through to his later years in sunny France, where he produced his best-known work with its characteristic giddy colour. Paintings by contemporaries Gauguin, Toulouse-Lautrec, Monet and Bernard round out the retrospective.

⊙ *Vondelpark & the South*

Brown Cafes (p49)

3 For a quintessential Amsterdam experience, pull up a stool in one of the city's famed *bruin cafés* (brown cafes; traditional Dutch pubs) such as In 't Aepjen. The true specimen has been in business a while and gets its name from centuries' worth of smoke stains on the walls. Brown cafes have candle-topped tables, wooden floors and sometimes an affectionate house cat. Most importantly, brown cafes induce a cosy vibe that prompts friends to linger and chat for hours over drinks – the same enchantment the cafes have cast for centuries.

🍷 *Drinking & Nightlife*

Vondelpark (p157)

4 On a sunny day it seems the whole city converges on this sprawling urban oasis. Couples kiss on the grass, friends cradle beers at the outdoor cafes, while others trade songs on beat-up guitars. Street performers work the crowds, joggers and cyclists loop past, and kids romp in the playgrounds. It's all very democratic, and sublime for people-watching. The English-style layout offers an abundance of ponds, lawns, thickets, sculptures and winding footpaths that encourage visitors to get out and explore the free-wheeling scene.

👁 *Vondelpark & the South*

Jordaan (p134)

5 If Amsterdam's neighbourhoods held a 'best personality' contest, the Jordaan (once the workers quarter) would win. Its intimacy is contagious, with modest old homes, offbeat galleries and vintage shops peppering a grid of tiny lanes. This is the place for jovial bar singalongs and beery brown cafes, the neighbourhood where you could spend a week wandering the narrow streets and still not discover all the hidden courtyards and tucked-away eateries. By now you know the Dutch propensity for *gezelligheid* (conviviality); the Jordaan is a fount of it. ABOVE: 'T SMALLE BROWN CAFE (P143)

🍺 *Jordaan & the West*

Outdoor Markets *(p176)*

6 Amsterdam is market-mad, and its streets lay out spreads from silks and coins to organic cheeses and bike locks. The Albert Cuypmarkt in De Pijp is king of the lot. Here stalls hawk rice cookers, spices and Dutch snacks, such as sweet *stroopwafels* (syrup-filled waffles). Bulbs fill the Bloemenmarkt, while porcelain teapots and other bric-a-brac tempt at Waterlooplein Flea Market. The Oudemanhuis Book Market has been selling tomes for a few centuries. Then there's the antiques market, farmers market, art market... BELOW: DUTCH CHEESES, ALBERT CUYPMARKT (P176)

🛍 *Shopping*

Cycling *(p29)*

7 There are more bicycles in Amsterdam than cars. Everyone rides: young, old, club-goers, cops on duty, bankers in suits with ties flapping in the breeze. Pedal power is what moves the masses to work, to shop and to socialise at the city's brown cafes. Renting a bike not only puts you shoulder to shoulder with locals, it gives you easy access to the city's outer neighbourhoods and their cool architecture and museums, as well the windmill-dotted countryside and its time-warped villages.

🏃 *By Bike*

Canal Trips *(p35)*

8 Amsterdam has more canals than Venice and getting on the water is one of the best ways to feel the pulse of the city. You could catch the vibe by sitting canal-side and watching boatss glide by: myriad brown cafes seem purpose-built for this sport. Or you could stroll alongside the canals and check out some of the city's 3050-plus houseboats. Better yet, hop on a tour boat and cruise the curved passages. From this angle, you'll understand why Unesco named the waterways a World Heritage Site.

🏃 *Canals*

Anne Frank Huis *(p104)*

9 Seeing Anne Frank's melancholy bedroom and her diary, preserved alone in its glass case, is a powerful experience that draws over a million visitors annually. Step behind the bookcase that swings open to reveal the 'Secret Annexe' and go up the steep stairs into the living quarters. It was in this dark and airless space that the Franks hid, observing complete silence during the day, before being arrested by the Nazis and sent to concentration camps. Anne's father, Otto, was the only survivor.

◉ *Western Canal Ring*

King's Day *(p23)*

10 For decades it was Queen's Day, but since the investiture of King Willem-Alexander, it's King's Day (Koningsdag), now celebrated on his birthday, 27 April (unless it falls on a Sunday, in which case it takes place the day before). It's really just an excuse for a gigantic drinking fest throughout the city's streets and for everyone to wear ridiculous orange outfits, the country's national colour. There's also a free market citywide (where anyone can sell anything) and rollicking free concerts.

🎆 *Month by Month*

What's New

Amsterdam Noord

Above the happening former industrial area of Amsterdam Noord – with artist studios, vintage shops and a slew of new cafes and bars – revolving restaurant Moon, on the 19th floor of A'DAM Tower, offers a 360-degree panorama. (p197)

North–South Metro Line

Following a decade and a half of construction, the much-delayed Noord/Zuidlijn, linking Amsterdam Noord and the World Trade Centre in the south, is finally ready to roll from mid-2018. (p224)

Design Emporium

Dutch design has a new showcase with the opening of X Bank, a vast space in a one-time bank that now has changing displays of fashion and homewares, and a packed calendar of exhibitions, workshops, launches and lectures, along with a stunning new hotel, W Amsterdam. (p83)

All-hours Clubbing

Amsterdam's *nachtburgemeester* (night mayor) has revolutionised the city's after-dark scene. Some phenomenal clubs now open 24 hours, especially outside the centre in repurposed venues such as Warehouse Elementenstraat. (p53)

Modern Contemporary Museum

Already awash with museums, Museumplein now has another: the 'Modern Contemporary' Moco Museum occupies a 1904 villa and mounts high-profile exhibitions on the likes of Salvador Dalí and Banksy. (p158)

Baking Hub

In Amsterdam's up-and-coming *oost* (east) neighbourhood, Baking Lab revives the concept of a communal oven for bakers and also runs baking workshops for adults and kids. (p191)

Train Hostel

Backpackers can now stay in an ex-Zürich–Rome sleeper carriage at the train-housed hostel Train Lodge. It sits on the tracks at Sloterdijk train station, a six-minute metro ride to the centre. (p219)

Houthavens

Previously docklands, the Houthavens (Lumber Ports) area in Amsterdam's west is now seeing a flurry of construction with new apartment buildings and establishments. An early highlight is the gleaming glass Theater Amsterdam. (p146)

Dining Innovations

Amsterdam continues to embrace on-trend dining. Avocado Show, for instance, is the world's first eatery to focus solely on avocados – in everything from burgers (with avocado halves in place of buns) to cocktails. (p176)

Eurostar Direct Route

No more stopping to switch trains in Belgium. A regular direct London-to-Amsterdam Eurostar route is slated to be up and running in spring 2018, cutting travel time to just under four hours. (p265)

For more recommendations and reviews, see **lonelyplanet.com/amsterdam**

Need to Know

For more information, see Survival Guide (p259)

Currency
Euro (€)

Language
Dutch

Visas
Generally not required for stays up to three months. Some nationalities require a Schengen visa.

Money
ATMs widely available. Credit cards accepted in most hotels but not all restaurants. Non-European credit cards are sometimes rejected.

Mobile Phones
Local prepaid SIM cards are widely available and can be used in most unlocked phones.

Time
Central European Time (GMT/UTC plus one hour)

Tourist Information
The I Amsterdam Visitor Centre (☑020-702 60 00; www.iamsterdam.com; Stationsplein 10; ⊘9am-5pm Mon-Sat; 🚊1/2/4/5/9/13/16/17/24 Centraal Station), located outside Centraal Station, offers maps, guides, transit passes, accommodation booking services and ticket purchases for attractions.

Daily Costs
Budget: Less than €100
➡ Dorm bed: €25–60

➡ Supermarkets and lunchtime specials for food: €20

➡ Boom Chicago late-night show ticket: €15

➡ Bike rental per day: €12

Midrange: €100–250
➡ Double room: €150

➡ Three-course dinner in casual restaurant: €35

➡ Concertgebouw ticket: €40

➡ Canal Bus day pass: €21

Top end: More than €250
➡ Four-star hotel double room: from €250

➡ Five-course dinner in top restaurant: from €80

➡ Private canal-boat rental for two hours: from €90

Advance Planning
Four months before Book your accommodation, especially if you're visiting in summer or on a weekend.

Two months before Check club and performing-arts calendars and buy tickets for anything that looks appealing.

Two weeks before Make dinner reservations at your must-eat restaurants, reserve walking or cycling tours, and purchase tickets online to popular attractions like the Van Gogh Museum (p154), Anne Frank Huis (p104) and Rijksmuseum (p151).

Useful Websites
Lonely Planet (www.lonelyplanet.com/amsterdam) Destination information, hotel bookings, traveller forum and more.

I Amsterdam (www.iamsterdam.com) City-run portal packed with sightseeing, accommodation and event info.

Dutch News (www.dutchnews.nl) News titbits and event listings.

Overdose.am (www.overdose.am) Art, music and fashion to-dos.

WHEN TO GO

Summer (June to August) is peak tourist season, with warm weather and lots of daylight for cycling. March to May is tulip time.

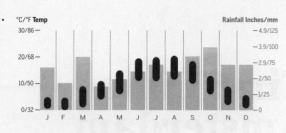

Arriving in Amsterdam

Schiphol Airport Trains to Centraal Station depart every 10 minutes or so from 6am to 12.30am, hourly at other times; the trip takes 15 minutes and costs €5.20; taxis cost €37.50.

Centraal Station In central Amsterdam with most tram lines connecting it to the rest of the city; taxis queue near the front entrance (toward the west side).

Bus Station Eurolines buses use Duivendrecht station, south of the centre, with an easy metro or train link to Centraal Station. FlixBus uses Sloterdijk station, west of the centre, with a fast metro or train link to Centraal.

For much more on **arrival** see p265

Getting Around

GVB passes in chip-card form are the most convenient option for public transport. Buy them at GVB ticket offices or visitor centres. Tickets aren't sold on board. Always wave your card at the pink machine when entering and departing.

➡ **Walking** Central Amsterdam is compact and very easy to cover by foot.

➡ **Bicycle** This is the locals' main mode of getting around. Rental companies are all over town; bikes cost about €12 per day.

➡ **Tram** Fast, frequent and ubiquitous, operating between 6am and 12.30am.

➡ **Bus and metro** Primarily serve the outer districts; not much use in the city centre.

➡ **Ferry** Free ferries depart for northern Amsterdam from docks behind Centraal Station.

➡ **Taxi** Expensive and not very speedy given Amsterdam's maze of streets.

For much more on **getting around** see p267

Sleeping

Rates and crowds peak during festivals, in summer (June to August) and on weekends at any time of the year. Book *well* ahead if you're travelling then. Prices are lowest from October to April (excluding Christmas, New Year and Easter).

Useful Websites

➡ **I Amsterdam** (www.iamsterdam.com) Wide range of options from the city's official website.

➡ **Hotels.nl** (www.hotels.nl) For deals on larger properties.

➡ **CityMundo** (amsterdam.citymundo.com) Reliable broker for apartment and houseboat rentals.

➡ **Lonely Planet** (lonelyplanet.com/the-netherlands/amsterdam/hotels) Recommendations and bookings.

For much more on **sleeping** see p211

First Time Amsterdam

For more information, see Survival Guide (p259)

Checklist

➡ Make sure your passport is valid for at least six months after your arrival date

➡ Inform your debit-/credit-card company of your travel

➡ Arrange appropriate travel insurance

➡ Call your mobile phone provider to enquire about roaming charges (abolished within the EU itself) or getting an international plan

What to Pack

➡ Good comfortable shoes – Amsterdam is best appreciated on foot or by bike

➡ Umbrella, because it can be rainy

➡ Netherlands electrical adaptor

➡ A small day pack (the smaller the better to avoid having to check it in when visiting museums)

Top Tips for Your Trip

➡ Plan your time – lengthy queues can add an hour or so to each museum visit. Wherever possible, pre-purchase tickets; most can be scanned from a phone.

➡ Make reservations for dinner at midrange and top-end eateries. Many restaurants are small and customers like to linger. Without a reservation, you might well miss out on your favourite spot.

➡ Walking is one of the best ways to get around this compact city – it's quick, free, and provides the opportunity to wander by hidden lanes and shops you might otherwise miss.

➡ Taking a cruise or renting a boat offers a different perspective on this watery city.

➡ Carry a mix of cash and cards; many establishments take only one or the other.

What to Wear

Locals dress stylishly, but practically. Most people wear jeans and hip boots for an evening out.

Pack layers of clothing, bearing in mind that the Dutch weather is notoriously fickle and there can be chilly spells even in summer. In spring, summer and autumn, a light trench coat or jacket and a small travel umbrella will mean you're prepared for the weather, but will still blend in with the crowd. In winter, bring a proper heavy coat, woolly hat, scarf and gloves to ward off the often-freezing temperatures (and you'll still want that umbrella).

Language

Dutch is the official language, but English is widely spoken. Most restaurants and cafes have menus in Dutch and English; most museums have information posted in both languages.

Taxes & Refunds

Value-added tax (BTW in Dutch) is levied on most goods and services at 6% for restaurants, hotels, books, transport, medicines and museum admissions, and 21% for most other items. It should already be included in stated prices.

Non-EU residents may be able to claim a refund on a minimum €50 spent per shop per day. The website www.belastingdienst.nl has details.

Tipping

➡ **Bars** Not expected.

➡ **Hotels** Tip €1 to €2 per bag for porters; not typical for cleaning staff.

➡ **Restaurants** Leave 5% to 10% for a cafe snack (if your bill comes to €9.50, you might round up to €10), 10% or so for a restaurant meal.

➡ **Taxis** Tip 5% to 10%, or round up to the nearest euro.

Getting Around

➡ **Bikes** Many rental bikes are branded; choose a hire company with no signs, such as Black Bikes (p29), to blend in.

➡ **Boats** Rent your own boat to take to the waterways like an Amsterdammer.

➡ **Tours** Get the inside track on the city on a local volunteer-led Mee In Mokum (p269) walking tour.

The magnificent Rijksmuseum (p155)

Etiquette

➡ **Greetings** Do give a firm handshake and a double or triple cheek kiss.

➡ **Marijuana & alcohol** Don't smoke dope or drink beer on the streets.

➡ **Smoking** Don't smoke (any substance) in bars or restaurants.

➡ **Bluntness** Don't take offence if locals give you a frank, unvarnished opinion. It's not considered impolite, rather it comes from the desire to be direct and honest.

➡ **Cycling paths** Don't walk in bike lanes (which are marked by white lines and bicycle symbols), and do look both ways before crossing a bike lane.

Be Forewarned

Amsterdam is a safe and manageable city and if you use your common sense you should have no problems.

➡ Be alert for pickpockets in tourist-heavy zones such as Centraal Station, the Bloemenmarkt and Red Light District.

➡ Avoid deserted streets in the Red Light District at night.

➡ It is forbidden to take photos of women in the Red Light District windows; this is strictly enforced.

➡ Be careful around the canals. Almost none of them have fences or barriers.

➡ Watch out for bicycles; never walk in bicycle lanes and always look carefully before you cross one.

Top Itineraries

Day One

Vondelpark & the South (p149)

 Begin with the biggies: tram to the Museum Quarter to ogle the masterpieces at the Van Gogh Museum (p154) and Rijksmuseum (p151). They'll be crowded, so make sure you've prebooked tickets. Modern-art buffs might want to swap the Stedelijk Museum (p156) for one of the others. They're all lined up in a walkable row.

> **Lunch** Slow Food favourite Gartine (p73) grows ingredients in its garden.

Medieval Centre (p64)

Spend the afternoon in the Medieval Centre. Explore the secret courtyard and gardens at the Begijnhof (p67). Walk up the street to the Dam (p69), where the Royal Palace (p66), Nieuwe Kerk (p72) and Nationaal Monument (p269) huddle and provide a dose of Dutch history. Bend over to sip your *jenever* (Dutch gin) like a local at Wynand Fockink (p79).

> **Dinner** Reinvented Dutch classics and cocktails at Lt Cornelis (p75).

Red Light District (p64)

 Venture into the Red Light District. A walk down Warmoesstraat or nearby Oudezijds Achterburgwal takes in an eye-popping array of fetish-gear shops, live sex shows, smoky coffeeshops and, of course, women in day-glo lingerie beckoning from crimson windows. Then settle in to a brown cafe (traditional Dutch pub), such as In 't Aepjen (p80), In de Olofspoort (p79) or 't Mandje (p81).

Day Two

De Pijp (p173)

 Browse the Albert Cuypmarkt (p176), Amsterdam's largest street bazaar, an international free-for-all of cheeses, fish, *stroopwafels* (syrup-filled waffles) and bargain-priced clothing. Then submit to the Heineken Experience (p175) to get shaken up, heated up and 'bottled' like the beer you'll drink at the end of the brewery tour.

> **Lunch** Brunch is De Pijp's forte; Bakers & Roasters (p180) does it best (all day).

Southern Canal Ring (p116)

Cross into the Southern Canal Ring and stroll along the grand Golden Bend. Visit Museum Van Loon (p119) for a peek into the opulent canal-house lifestyle, or get a dose of kitty quirk at the Kattenkabinet (p120). Browse the Bloemenmarkt (p119) and behold the wild array of bulbs.

> **Dinner** Organic dishes and canal views at Buffet van Odette (p123).

Southern Canal Ring (p116)

 When the sun sets, it's time to par-tee at hyperactive, neon-lit Leidseplein (p118). Paradiso (p131) and Melkweg (p131) host the coolest agendas. Otherwise, the good-time clubs and brown cafes, around the square beckon. Try beery Café de Spuyt (p130) or historic Eijlders (p127). For serious 24-hour clubbing, head out of the centre to venues like Warehouse Elementenstraat (p53).

Day Three

Vondelpark & the South (p149)

 Take a spin around beloved Vondelpark (p157). Long and narrow (about 1.5km long and 300m wide), it's easy to explore via a morning jaunt. All the better if you have a bicycle to zip by the ponds, gardens and sculptures.

> **Lunch** Enjoy timeless Dutch favourites at Bistro Bij Ons (p110).

Western Canal Ring (p102)

Immerse yourself in the Negen Straatjes (p113) (Nine Streets), a noughts-and-crosses board of speciality shops. The Anne Frank Huis (p104) is also in the neighbourhood, and it's a must. The claustrophobic rooms, their windows still covered with blackout screens, give an all-too-real feel for Anne's life in hiding. Seeing the diary itself – filled with her sunny writing tempered with quiet despair – is moving, plain and simple.

> **Dinner** Canal views and exceptional modern cuisine at De Belhamel (p110).

Jordaan (p134)

Spend the evening in the Jordaan, the chummy district embodying the Amsterdam of yore. Hoist a glass on a canal-side terrace at 't Smalle (p143), join the houseboat party at Café P 96 (p143), or quaff beers at heaps of other *gezellig* (cosy) haunts.

Day Four

Nieuwmarkt, Plantage & the Eastern Islands (p85)

 Mosey through Waterlooplein Flea Market (p100) in Nieuwmarkt. Rembrandt sure loved markets, if his nearby studio is any indication. Museum het Rembrandthuis (p87) gives a peek at the master's inner sanctum. Neighbouring Gassan Diamonds (p89) gives free tours. Or check out the intriguing Verzetsmuseum (p91), the Resistance Museum, or sea treasures at Het Scheepvaartmuseum (p92).

> **Lunch** Try a hot-spiced Surinamese sandwich at Tokoman (p93).

Amsterdam Noord (p194)

Hop on a free ferry to Noord, one of the city's coolest, most up-and-coming neighbourhoods. Check out the cinematic exhibits at the EYE Film Institute (p196) and the artists' studios in the sprawling Kunststad (Art City; p196) centre at former shipyards NDSM-werf (p196). Ascend A'DAM Tower (p196) for dazzling views across the IJ to the city centre.

> **Dinner** Views peak at Moon (p197), the restaurant atop A'DAM Tower.

Oosterpark & East of the Amstel (p185)

There are some fantastic nightlife venues in Noord; alternatively, back on the city side of the IJ, an evening spent on the terrace at De Ysbreeker (p191), looking out over the bustling, houseboat-strewn Amstel river, is a well deserved treat.

If You Like...

Art

Van Gogh Museum The world's largest collection of the tortured artist's paintings, from his early work to final pieces. (p154)

Rijksmuseum The Netherlands' mightiest museum displays Rembrandts, Vermeers and more in a dazzling neo-Gothic/Dutch Renaissance building. (p151)

Stedelijk Museum Bountiful modern trove that includes works by Picasso, Chagall, Mondrian, Warhol, Lichtenstein and the CoBrA cohort. (p156)

Museum het Rembrandthuis You almost expect to find the master himself still nipping around his old paint-spattered studio. (p87)

Hermitage Amsterdam This satellite of Russia's Hermitage Museum features one-off exhibitions, from Matisse cut-outs to Byzantine treasures. (p118)

Foam Changing exhibitions showcase world-renowned photographers such as Sir Cecil Beaton, Annie Leibovitz and Henri Cartier-Bresson. (p121)

Kunststad (Art City) Vast former shipbuilding warehouse now filled with artists' studios. (p196)

Windmills

De Gooyer It's hard to beat drinking freshly made organic beer at the foot of an 18th-century spinner. (p91)

Riekermolen Rembrandt used to sketch by this windmill, south of the city at Amstelpark's edge. (p160)

Windmills at Zaanse Schans (p210)

Zaanse Schans A whole village of blades turns in the North Sea breeze, a 20-minute train ride from the city. (p210)

National Windmill Day Here's your chance to peek inside some of the country's 1200 twirlers, including eight in Amsterdam. (p23)

Parks & Gardens

Vondelpark A mash-up of ponds, lawns, thickets and winding footpaths beloved by Amsterdammers of all ages. (p157)

Museumplein This festive green space draws a crowd for winter ice skating and summer lazing. (p158)

Oosterpark Sweeping park built for nouveau riche diamond traders a century ago. (p187)

Hortus Botanicus When Dutch ships sailed in the 1600s, the tropical seeds they brought back flourished here. (p90)

Amsterdamse Bos The Amsterdam Forest is criss-crossed with cycling and walking paths, and home to rowing ponds. (p158)

Westerpark Rambling, reedy wilderness abutting a former-gasworks-building-turned-edgy-cultural-centre. (p139)

Park Frankendael Seek out the formal garden that sits behind the Louis XIV–style mansion. (p187)

Sarphatipark De Pijp's fountain-filled park is an urban oasis. (p175)

Flevopark One of Amsterdam's wildest green spaces. (p187)

Active Endeavours

Cycling in Amsterdam Noord Ride into the countryside and spin by time-warp villages and cow-dotted pastures. (p198)

Mee in Mokum Lace up your shoes and see the sights with Mee in Mokum's local volunteer guides. (p269)

Canal Bike Explore the city from a different perspective with a pedal around the canals. (p38)

Ice Skating Museumplein's pond becomes Amsterdam's favourite wintertime rink, resembling the top of a wind-up jewellery box. (p158)

Friday Night Skate Strap on your skates for a 20km jaunt from Vondelpark through the city. (p172)

Hollandsche Manege Take a horse-riding lesson at this venerable riding school. (p172)

Sustainable Options

De Ridammerhoeve Feed the kids (both kinds) at the organic goat farm and cafe in Amsterdamse Bos. (p160)

De Kas Sit in a greenhouse and fork into ingredients grown just a few steps away. (p190)

Boerenmarkt This organic farmers market sets up on Saturdays at Noordermarkt and Nieuwmarkt at the Waag. (p100)

Instock This restaurant 'rescues' food that's about to reach its expiration date and transforms it into three-course meals. (p96)

Lot Sixty One Sniff out the roasting coffee beans from sustainable farms around the globe. (p167)

Marie-Stella-Maris A percentage of this skincare company's profits helps provide clean drinking water worldwide. (p114)

Conscious Hotel Vondelpark Sustainable materials at this green hotel include pressed-cardboard bathroom benchtops. (p220)

For more top Amsterdam spots, see the following:
➜ Eating (p43)
➜ Drinking & Nightlife (p48)
➜ Entertainment (p55)
➜ Shopping (p57)

Moer Restaurant with organic produce and Slow Food ethic adjoining the Tire Station hotel. (p166)

Architecture

Rijksmuseum Pierre Cuypers' magnificent 1875 design incorporates Renaissance ornaments carved in stone around the facade. (p151)

ARCAM Amsterdam's Centre for Architecture is a one-stop shop for architectural exhibits, guidebooks and maps. (p92)

NEMO Science Museum Renzo Piano's green-copper, ship-shaped museum is a modern classic. (p92)

Scheepvaarthuis This grand 1916 building is the first true Amsterdam School example. (p88)

Whale See this and other examples of cutting-edge Dutch architecture on the Eastern Islands. (p252)

Beurs van Berlage The 1903 financial exchange building is a temple to capitalism. (p69)

Museum Het Schip In the west, this 1920s housing project is the pinnacle of Amsterdam School style. (p139)

Offbeat Museums

Kattenkabinet Canal house filled with kitty-cat art from the likes of Picasso, Steinlen and Rembrandt. (p120)

Houseboat Museum Get a feel for the compact, watery lifestyle aboard a 23m-long sailing barge. (p137)

Tassenmuseum Hendrikje This entire museum is devoted to handbags, from 16th-century pouches to Madonna's modern arm candy. (p121)

Amsterdam Pipe Museum Chinese opium pipes, Turkish water pipes, 1500-year-old Ecuadorian pipes and more cram the cabinets. (p118)

Pianola Museum An extraordinary paean to the player piano, bursting with musical keys from the early 1900s. (p136)

Electric Ladyland The world's first museum of fluorescent art, glowing with psychedelic rocks, rice and rabbits. (p137)

History Lessons

Anne Frank Huis Anne's melancholy bedroom and her actual diary serve as poignant reminders of WWII. (p104)

Oude Kerk The senior citizen of Amsterdam's structures, now more than 700 years old. (p68)

Amsterdam Museum Intriguing multimedia exhibits take you through the twists and turns of Amsterdam's convoluted history. (p70)

Verzetsmuseum Learn about WWII Dutch Resistance fighters during the German occupation. (p91)

Stadsarchief The city's rich archives offer remarkable displays, including Anne Frank's stolen-bike report from 1942. (p120)

Mee in Mokum Local volunteer guides put the city's history into context on these walking tours. (p269)

Food & Drink

Hungry Birds Street Food Tours Work up an appetite on these food-focused walking tours (tastings included). (p269)

Reypenaer Cheese Tasting Guided tastings reveal the intricacies of Dutch cheeses. (p111)

Petit Gâteau Regular pastry-making courses are run by this wonderful patisserie. (p108)

Papabubble Watch sweets being made at this confectioner. (p147)

Baking Lab Baking workshops and a communal bread oven. (p191)

Brouwerij De Prael Tours at this Red Light District brewery are followed by tastings. (p72)

Brouwerij Troost Westergas Tour Troost's Westergas brewery, where it also distils its own gin. (p145)

Brouwerij ('t IJ Brewery tours here are made even more memorable by the adjacent 1725-built De Gooyer windmill. (p97)

Heineken Experience Fun interactive tours of Heineken's former brewery. (p175)

Wynand Fockink Distillery tours of this 1679 *jenever* (Dutch gin) distillery are accompanied by half-a-dozen tastings. (p79)

Hedonistic Pursuits

Dampkring This coffeeshop stalwart has a comprehensive, well-explained menu, a prize-winning product and a Hollywood-backdrop pedigree. (p78)

Condomerie Het Gulden Vlies Puts the 'pro' back in prophylactic with its tasteful setting and huge array of condoms for sale. (p84)

Kokopelli Magic truffles are the stock in trade at this classy, smart shop. (p84)

Prostitution Information Centre Get frank information about the women in the windows on the centre's walking tour. (p269)

Casa Rosso Jaw-dropping tricks with lit candles and more at the city's most popular sex show (a hen-night favourite). (p82)

Webers When you need a PVC catsuit with whip holster, this little shop can do the fitting. (p100)

Red Light Secrets See inside a Red Light room (including a dominatrix room). (p72)

Month By Month

January

While January is cold and dark, museum queues are nonexistent and there's more time to relax in a cosy *café* (bar, pub) in front of a crackling fireplace.

⭐ Amsterdam International Fashion Week

Amsterdam's fashion scene takes flight during Fashion Week (www.fashionweek.nl), with catwalk shows, parties, lectures and concerts. Many events – both free and ticketed – are open to the public. They take place in the city centre and at the Westergasfabriek (p145). There's also a July fashion week.

⭐ National Tulip Day

On 21 January, Tulpendag (www.tulpen.nl) marks the start of the tulip season, which runs to the end of April. Some 200,000 tulips are displayed on the Dam; in the afternoon everyone is encouraged to take one for free.

March

Early spring weather can be fickle (warm clothes are a must), but if it complies you can get a jump-start on tulip-viewing (and the crowds) at Keukenhof.

⭐ DGTL

Three-day techno and house festival DGTL takes place from Friday to Sunday over the Easter weekend at NDSM-werf (p196) in Amsterdam Noord.

April

Days are getting longer, temperatures are rising and flowers are in full bloom in the lead-up to the show-stopping King's Day party, the highlight of Amsterdam's annual calendar.

⭐ King's Day

One of the biggest – and arguably best – street parties in Europe, King's Day celebrates the birthday of King Willem-Alexander on 27 April. There's uproarious partying, music and *oranjekoorts* (orange fever), as well as a city-wide flea market.

May

Amsterdam follows Remembrance Day (4 May) observances with Liberation Day (5 May) festivities, and flourishing cafe terraces make this mild month a perfect time to linger in the city.

⊙ National Windmill Day

During the second weekend in May, many of the 1200 windmills (www.molens.nl) and watermills throughout the country welcome the public into their creaking innards. Look for mills flying a blue pennant.

June

Visitors start flocking to the city for the summer peak season. It's typically sunny and warm, prime for bicycle rides and drinks on canal-side patios.

☆ Holland Festival

Big-name theatre, dance and opera meet offbeat digital films and experimental music in the Netherlands' biggest performing-arts extravaganza, the Holland Festival (www.holland festival.nl). The month-long, highbrow/lowbrow mash-up happens at venues citywide.

☉ Open Garden Days

Open Tuinen Dagen (www. opentuinendagen.nl), on the third weekend in June, brings a unique opportunity to view some 25 private gardens along the canals.

July

The days are long, the sun is shining, so who cares if the crowds are clogging Amsterdam's streets and canals? It only adds to the party atmosphere.

☆ Amsterdam Roots Festival

A week-long roots festival (www.amsterdamroots. nl) programs world music in key venues around town in late June or early July. It culminates in the vibrant all-day Roots Open Air fest at Park Frankendael.

☆ Over het IJ Festival

Alternative venues at the NDSM-werf former shipyards in Amsterdam Noord host unconventional performing arts productions for 10 days in early July during this festival (www. overhetij.nl).

August

A welter of events takes place during Amsterdam's high summer, yet the city has less sweltering temperatures than many other European cultural capitals and relatively few summer closures.

☆ Amsterdam Gay Pride

The world's only waterborne Pride Parade, on the Prinsengracht and Amstel, is a highlight of the week-long Amsterdam Gay Pride (p261) fest, which is celebrated from late July to early August.

☆ Grachtenfestival

Classical musicians pop up in canal-side parks and hidden gardens during mid-August's 10-day Grachtenfestival (www. grachtenfestival.nl). The highlight of the festival is the free concert on a floating stage in the Prinsengracht.

☆ Uitmarkt

At the end of August, Amsterdam's cultural venues preview their upcoming season on outdoor stages during mega arts event Uitmarkt (p32). It's complemented by big concerts.

September

Summer may be technically over, but September is one of the best months to visit Amsterdam. There are some superb festivals along with fair weather and fewer crowds.

☆ Amsterdam City Swim

More than 2500 people jump into the canals for the City Swim (www. amsterdamcityswim.nl) in early September to help raise money for charity. Swimmers splash through the waters of the IJ, Amstel, Keizergracht and more on the 2km course.

October

Autumnal hues colour Amsterdam's parks and gardens, and while the weather may remain mild, low-season prices start to kick in and queues begin to thin out.

☆ Amsterdam Dance Event

Over five long, sweaty days and nights in late October, massive dance festival ADE (p53) sees 2200 DJs and artists and more than 300,000 clubbers attending 450 events at over 120 venues throughout the city.

November

Cultural events and reduced low-season rates make up for the shortening days and chilly nights, while the arrival of Sinterklaas heralds the start of the festive season.

☉ Museumnacht

On the first Saturday in November around 50 museums throughout the city stay open until 2am for Museum Night, scheduling live music, DJs and art-fuelled parties (www. museumnacht.amsterdam).

Top: Amsterdam Roots Festival
Bottom: Amsterdam Light Festival

⭐ Sinterklaas Intocht

St Nicholas arrives by boat from Spain for the Sinterklaas Intocht (www.sintinamsterdam.nl) in the second half of November, and parades on his white horse to the Dam and Leidseplein to the delight of the city's children.

☆ International Documentary Film Festival

Ten days in late November are dedicated to screening fascinating, true stories from all over the world (www.idfa.nl) at various venues within walking distance of Muntplein.

December

Winter magic blankets the city (as, some years, does snow), ice-skating rinks set up in open spaces and the city is a vision of twinkling lights.

⭐ Amsterdam Light Festival

The twin highlights of this six-week-long festival (www.amsterdamlightfestival.com) include a Boulevard Walk of Light along the Amstel, passing magnificently lit monuments, and a mid-December Christmas Canal Parade of illuminated boats floating along the canals.

⭐ New Year's Eve

Fireworks light up the skies in a spark-showering spectacle and countless parties take place around the city. Event locations vary annually; check with the I Amsterdam visitor centre (p267) to find out where to ring in the new year.

With Kids

Breathe easy: you've landed in one of Europe's most kid-friendly cities. The famous Dutch tolerance extends to children and Amsterdammers are cheerfully accommodating to them. You'll find that virtually all quarters of the city – except the Red Light District, of course – are fair game for the younger set.

Kids love *stroopwafels* (syrup-filled waffles)

IRYNA MELNYK/SHUTTERSTOCK ©

Outdoor Activities

Green spaces, parks and canals galore provide plenty of fresh-air fun for the little (and not so little) ones.

Parks & Playgrounds

A hot favourite with kids of all ages is the vast play space of the Vondelpark (p157), with leafy picnic spots and duck ponds, as well as cool space-age slides at its western end and a playground in the middle of the park. Westerpark (p139) also has a terrific playground, while Sarphatipark (p175) and Oosterpark (p187) shouldn't be overlooked as great open spaces to let the kids run free. Canoeing, a tree-climbing park, paddle boats and a goat farm are among the fun activities in the huge, forested Amsterdamse Bos (p158).

Winter Magic

Kids will love the skating rinks that spring up in public spaces such as the Museumplein (p158). Don't miss uniquely Dutch festive season treats such as *poffertjes* (small pancakes) and gingery-cinnamon *speculaas* (cookies), traditionally eaten around Sinterklaas (Saint Nicholas' Eve; 5 December), which are served up at rustic market stalls.

Canals

Take to the canals on a unique pedal-powered ride with Canal Bike (p38).

Artis Royal Zoo

The extrovert monkeys, big cats, shimmying fish and dazzling planetarium will keep young eyes shining for hours at Artis Royal Zoo (p93), while teenagers and adults will love the beautifully landscaped grounds. You can also peek inside Micropia, a building on the premises that is a 'zoo' for microbes. It's way more entertaining than you think, with exhibits that show how bacteria exchange when you kiss and what microbes live in the poop of anteaters, lions and other animals.

Museum Fun

Amsterdam has plenty of museums that are accessible, educational and, above all, fun.

NEMO Science Museum

A tailor-made, hands-on experience, NEMO Science Museum (p92) is useful for answering all those 'how' and 'why' questions.

Het Scheepvaartmuseum

The life-size ship moored beside the Maritime Museum (p92) lets kids fire a (replica!) cannon, hoist cargo and skedaddle around a reproduction Dutch East India Company vessel from 1749.

Tropenmuseum

The children's section devoted to exotic locations at the Tropenmuseum (p188) is a winner in any language.

Joods Historisch Museum

There is a great kids' display on Jewish life in Amsterdam at the Joods Historisch Museum (p89).

Verzetsmuseum

A section at the Verzetsmuseum (p91) known as the Verzetsmuseum Junior puts the Dutch Resistance into context for kids through the experiences of four children: Eva, Jan, Nelly and Henk.

Van Gogh Museum

The Van Gogh Museum (p154) provides a free treasure hunt for kids to search for items in the paintings and displays. A small prize awaits those who complete the hunt.

Beaches & Castles

City Beaches

Urban beaches pop up on Amsterdam's outskirts each summer around the IJ. While most cater to adults (complete with cocktails and DJs), some are more family-friendly – check with the tourist office for locations. The only one you can swim at is Blijburg (p192), which also has a watersports centre.

Muiden Castle

Just outside Amsterdam, the Muiderslot (p190) is a 700-year-old castle straight out of a fairy tale, with a drawbridge, moat, hulking towers and battlements. It offers special activities (like falconry) for kids on certain days. Combine it with a visit to the atmospheric fort on the nearby island of Pampus (p190).

Rainy-Day Ideas

It's prudent to have a rainy-day plan in your back pocket. In fact, it might be so much fun that kids will hope the sun doesn't come back out all day.

TunFun

Set 'em loose for a romp in the underground, all-round pleasure centre TunFun (p101).

Cinema

Kids can eat popcorn and watch new releases at the art-deco Pathé Tuschinskitheater (p130) or the intimate, atmospheric Movies (p146) while adults revel in the historic environs.

Indoor Pools & Saunas

The recreational Zuiderbad (p172) is a good place to take the kids swimming on a rainy day. Adults will enjoy the palatial vintage interior.

Centrale Bibliotheek Amsterdam

The city's stunning, contemporary OBA: Centrale Bibliotheek Amsterdam (p92)

NEED TO KNOW

Admission prices 'Child' is defined as under 18 years. But at many tourist sites, the cut-off age for free or reduced rates is 12. Some sights may only provide free entry to children under six.

Bike seats Most bike-rental shops rent bikes with baby or child seats.

Babysitting Many higher-end hotels arrange babysitting services for a fee.

OLDGENTLEMAN/SHUTTERSTOCK ©

Geological Museum in Artis Royal Zoo (p93)

has a whole floor dedicated to children's activities, including comfy reading lounges and the amazing Mouse Mansion, with 100 incredibly beautifully detailed rooms, designed by artist Karina Content. Check out the weekly story times (some in English) for younger visitors.

Kid-Friendly Cuisine

While Amsterdam's foodie scene continues to explode with adventurous and sophisticated offerings, you can still find plenty of fare that junior diners will enjoy.

Sandwich Shops

A *broodje* (filled bread roll) or *tosti* (toasted sandwich) always hits the spot. Scores of shops throughout the city specialise in these staples; try Broodje Bert (p75).

Pancakes

The city is full of these kid-pleasing delights. Top choices include Pancakes! (p110) and Pancake Bakery (p108).

For true pancake aficionados, a trip aboard De Pannenkoekenboot (www. pannenkoekenboot.nl), is definitely in order. Brunch and evening cruises depart from the NDSM-werf in Amsterdam Noord, reached by a free ferry.

Burgers

Gourmet burgers made from organic ingredients continue to go gangbusters in Amsterdam. Best burger bets are the Butcher (p177) and Geflipt (p177) in De Pijp.

Fries

Fries slathered in mayonnaise or other sauces are favourites with all ages. Local institutions include Vleminckx (p73) near the Spui and Wil Graanstra Friteshuis (p110) by the Anne Frank Huis. Frites uit Zuyd (p178) fires up crispy beauties in De Pijp.

Ice Cream

Try the chocolate-dipped waffle cones at Jordino (p140). IJsmolen (p95) has uniquely Dutch flavours such as *speculaas* (spicy Christmas biscuits) among its line-up. As a bonus, it's located by a windmill.

Cafes & Restaurants

Particularly kid-friendly cafes and restaurants include Moeders (p140), Het Groot Melkhuis (p168), Café Toussaint (p165) and NeL (p128). Café Noorderlicht (p199) has a big play area outside.

Markets

Kids love browsing the markets for both familiar and exotic treats. Try the Albert Cuypmarkt (p176) for *stroopwafels* (syrup-filled waffles), smoothies, sweets and fresh fruit. Or pick up ingredients here and take a picnic to the nearby Sarphatipark.

Kid-Friendly Shops

Dozens upon dozens of shops cater for children, who will adore deliberating over toys and sweet treats.

Check out Knuffels (p100) for stuffed-animal toys, Joe's Vliegerwinkel (p100) for kites, Mechanisch Speelgoed (p148) for nostalgic wind-up toys, and De Winkel van Nijntje (p171) for merchandise related to Dutch illustrator Dick Bruna's most famous character – the cute rabbit Miffy (Nijntje in Dutch).

Het Oud-Hollandsch Snoepwinkeltje (p147) has jar after jar of Dutch penny sweets.

By Bike

Bicycles are more common than cars in Amsterdam, and to roll like a local you'll need a two-wheeler. Rent one from the myriad outlets around town or your accommodation, and the whole city becomes your playground. Cycling is the quintessential activity while visiting.

MARK READ/LONELY PLANET ©

Exploring Noorderpark

Hiring a Bike

Many visitors rent a bike late in their stay and wish they'd done so sooner. Rental shops are everywhere; you'll have to show a passport or European national ID card and leave a credit-card imprint or pay a deposit (usually €50 to €100). Prices per 24-hour period for basic 'coaster-brake' bikes average €12. Bikes with gears and handbrakes cost more. Theft insurance costs around €3 to €5 extra per day but is strongly advised.

Ajax Bike (www.ajaxbike.nl; Gerard Doustraat 153; bike rental per 4/24hr from €6.50/9; ⊙10am-5.30pm Mon-Sat, noon-4pm Sun; 🚊4 Stadhouderskade) Off the beaten path in De Pijp, with bargain prices on city, kids', tandem and cargo bikes.

Bike City (www.bikecity.nl; Bloemgracht 68-70; bike rental per day from €14; ⊙9am-5.30pm; 🚊13/14/17 Westermarkt) Jordaan shop; bikes carry no advertising, so you'll look like a local.

Black Bikes (www.black-bikes.com; Nieuwezijds Voorburgwal 146; bike rental per 3/24hr from €9/13, electric bikes €24/37.50; ⊙8am-8pm Mon-Fri, 9am-7pm Sat & Sun; 🚊1/2/5/13/14/17 Raadhuisstraat) Signless company offering city, kids', tandem and cargo bikes at 10 shops, including this one in the centre.

Damstraat Rent-a-Bike (www.rentabike.nl; Damstraat 20-22; bike rental per 3/24hr from €7/9; ⊙9am-6pm; 🚊4/9/16/24 Dam) Rents bikes of all types from its shop near the Dam.

MacBike (www.macbike.nl; De Ruijterkade 34b; bike rental per 3/24hr from €11/14.75; ⊙9am-5.45pm; 🚊1/2/4/5/9/13/16/17/24 Centraal Station) Among the most touristy of companies (bikes are bright red, with logos), but has a convenient location at Centraal Station, plus others at Waterlooplein and Leidseplein. Big assortment of bikes available.

Bike Sharing & Apps

Donkey Republic (www.donkey.bike) Unlock/lock a bike via Bluetooth. Rates per 24 hour are €12. You'll need to return the bike to the same location, or pay €20 extra.

FlickBike (www.flickbike.nl) Locate bikes around town via this app; rental per 30 minutes costs €1. Scan the QR code to unlock/lock the bike. It can be returned to any Amsterdam bike rack.

Crossing Prinsengracht canal (p110)

MARK READY/LONELY PLANET ©

Spinlister (www.spinlister.com) Like Airbnb for bikes: rent a bike straight from an Amsterdammer. Prices vary.

Bike Tours

A bike tour is an ideal way to get to know Amsterdam. Bike rental is included in prices (tour companies also rent bikes). Be sure to reserve in advance. Great options include the following:

Orangebike (www.orange-bike.nl; Buiksloterweg 5c; tours €22.50-37.50, hire per hr/day from €5/11; ⊙9am-6pm; ⛴Buiksloterweg) Traditional city and countryside tours (including a beach tour), plus themed options such as food or architectural tours.

Mike's Bike Tours (www.mikesbike toursamsterdam.com; Prins Hendrikkade 176a; city tours per adult/13-18yr from €28/25, countryside from €32; ⊙office 9am-6pm Mar-Oct, from 10am Nov-Feb; ⛴16/24 Keizersgracht) Fantastic tours cover the city, harbour or windmill-dotted countryside.

Yellow Bike (www.yellowbike.nl; Nieuwezijds Kolk 29; city tours from €23.50, Waterland tour €33.50; ⊙Mar-Oct; ⛴1/2/5/13/17 Nieuwezijds Kolk) Choose from city jaunts or a spin through the bucolic Waterland region.

Road Rules

➡ Helmets aren't compulsory. Most Dutch cyclists don't use them and they don't come standard with rental.

➡ Amsterdam has 500km of bike paths. Use the bicycle lane on the road's right-hand side, marked by white lines and bike symbols.

➡ Cycle in the same direction as traffic and adhere to all traffic lights and signs.

➡ Hand signal when turning.

➡ A bell is mandatory.

➡ After dark, a white or yellow headlight and red tail light are required by law.

➡ Park only in bicycle racks near train and tram stations and in certain public squares (or risk the removal of your bike by the police).

➡ Cycling on footpaths is illegal.

Cycling Tips

➡ Most bikes come with two locks: one for the front wheel (attach it to the bike frame), the other for the back. One of these locks should also be attached to a fixed structure (preferably a bike rack).

➡ Cross tram rails at a sharp angle to avoid getting stuck.

➡ Watch out for vehicles, other bikes and oblivious pedestrians.

➡ Ring your bell as a warning as often as necessary.

➡ If your bike goes missing, call the **Fietsdepot** (Bike Depository) at ☎020-334 45 22 to see if it was removed by the city (perhaps for being parked in an unsafe spot). If not, call the **police** on ☎0900 88 44 or visit the local station to report it as stolen.

Online Journey Planners

Fietsersbond (www.routeplanner.fietsersbond. nl) Official route planner of the Dutch Cyclists' Union.

Holland Cycling (www.holland-cycling.com) Has a wealth of up-to-date info such as bicycle repair shops.

Routecraft (www.routecraft.com/ fietsrouteplanner-amsterdam.html) Calculates the best bike routes from point to point in the city.

Route You (www.routeyou.com) Good for scenic routes.

Like a Local

Hop on your bike, head to the nearest brown cafe and take a free course in Dutch culture by simply observing what goes on around you. While it's one thing to witness local life, it's even better to truly immerse yourself in it.

Hoppe brown cafe (p78)

WOODVALE/GETTY IMAGES ©

Embrace the Gezellig Culture

This particularly Dutch quality, which is most widely found in old brown cafes, is one of the best reasons to visit Amsterdam. It's variously translated as 'snug', 'friendly', 'cosy', 'informal' and 'convivial', but *gezelligheid* – the state of being *gezellig* – is more elemental. You'll feel this all-is-right-with-the-world vibe in many places and situations, often while nursing a brew with friends during *borrel* (an informal gathering over drinks). And nearly any low-lit, welcoming establishment qualifies.

Delve into Local Neighbourhoods

Beyond the tourist epicentres, Amsterdam's further-flung neighbourhoods are easy to reach and perfect places to engage with local life. Great starting points are the edgy galleries and post-industrial cafes, bars and restaurants of Amsterdam-Nood, the backstreets of villagey De Pijp (such as the tucked-away square Van der Helstplein, lined with cafes, pubs and bars), the rapidly gentrifying West (including another post-industrial hub, the former-gasworks-turned-cultural-centre Westergasfabriek) and the multicultural Oost (East).

Find Your Way Around

Navigate the Country

Holland is a popular synonym for the Netherlands, yet it only refers to the combined provinces of Noord (North) and Zuid (South) Holland. (Amsterdam is Noord-Holland's largest city; Haarlem is the provincial capital.) The rest of the country is not Holland, even if locals themselves often make the mistake.

Navigate the City

Amsterdam's concentric canals and similarly named streets make it all too easy to get lost. Some pointers: a *gracht* (canal), such as Egelantiersgracht, is distinct from a *straat* (street) such as Egelantiersstraat. A *dwarsstraat* (cross-street) that intersects a *straat* is often preceded by *eerste, tweede, derde* or *vierde* (first, second, third or fourth; marked 1e, 2e, 3e or 4e on maps). For example Eerste Egelantiersdwarsstraat is the first cross-street of Egelantiersstraat (ie the nearest cross-street to the city centre). Streets preceded by *lange* (long) and *korte* (short) simply mean the longer or shorter street. Be aware, too, that seemingly continuous streets regularly change name along their length.

Pedal Power

It takes spending all of five minutes in Amsterdam to realise that locals bike everywhere. Literally everywhere. They bike to the dentist, to work, to the opera and to brunch; they bike in snow, rain, sunshine and fog. So don't just rent a bike for a quick spin around the Vondelpark – get on the beaten path by biking everywhere too. Dressing up to bike to dinner and a show, or to drinks and a club, is a typical Dutch pastime that locals shrug off but visitors marvel over. Put on a suit or a cocktail dress and pedal away. No matter what you wear or where you're going, you'll fit right in (and have fun too).

Orange Fever

If you've ever attended a sporting event where the Dutch are playing, you'll already be familiar with *oranjegekte* (orange craze), also known as *oranjekoorts* (orange fever). The custom of wearing the traditional colour of the Dutch royal family, the House of Orange-Nassau, was originally limited to celebration days for the monarchy, such as Queen's Day (Koninginnedag), now King's Day (Koningsdag). But particularly since the 1974 FIFA World Cup, when tens of thousands of orange-clad football supporters cheered on every game, the ritual of wearing outlandish orange

get-ups – clothes, scarves, wigs, fake-fur top hats, face paint, feather boas, you name it – has become a Dutch phenomenon. To really celebrate like a local, you know what colour to wear.

Burning of the Christmas Trees

It's a strange Dutch tradition that makes even normally jaded adults positively wide-eyed: the burning of the Christmas trees. Think of it as a pagan version of Sinterklaas – a time when people of all ages take to the streets to create massive bonfires of festive trees past their prime, to usher in the new year without 'dead wood', so to speak. The event usually takes place about a week after New Year's. Museumplein is a good spot to check out the madness.

Join in the Festivities

Explore the unique character of Amsterdam's diverse neighbourhoods by partying with the locals at a neighbourhood festival.

Revel in the city's rich Surinamese and African heritage at the food-and-football **Kwaku** (www.kwakufestival.nl; 🚊Tulastraat) festival, held in Nelson Mandelapark most weekends from mid-July to early August.

Listen to classic Jordaan ballads during the Jordaan Festival (p141).

Or grab your platinum-blonde wig and platform shoes for the hysterically fun **Hartjesdagen Zeedijk** (Heart Day; www. stichtinghartjesdagen.nl; ☺late Aug) festival, held on the third Monday of August. Dating back to medieval times, it features street theatre, a parade and all kinds of costumed extroverts on and around Zeedijk.

Locals party like it's King's Day during the **Uitmarkt** (www.uitmarkt.nl; ☺late Aug) festival, which kicks off the cultural season in late August.

For Free

Although the costs of Amsterdam's accommodation and dining can mount up, there's a bright side. Not only is the entire Canal Ring a Unesco World Heritage Site (effectively a free living museum), but almost every day you'll find things to do and see that are free (or virtually free).

ae EYE Film Institute (p196) has pods screening free films

Free Sights

Civic Guard Gallery (p70) Stroll through the monumental collection of portraits, from Golden Age to modern.

Rijksmuseum Gardens (p151) Even many locals don't know that the Renaissance and baroque gardens, with rose bushes, hedges and statues, are free and open to the public (including occasional sculpture exhibitions).

Begijnhof (p67) Explore the 14th-century hidden courtyard and its clandestine churches.

Stadsarchief (p120) You never know what treasures you'll find in the vaults of the city's archives.

Gassan Diamonds (p89) Distinguish your princess from marquise, river from top cape.

Albert Cuypmarkt (p176) Amsterdam's busiest market; it and the city's many other bazaars are all free to browse.

ARCAM (p92) A fascinating look at Amsterdam's architecture – past, present and future.

Kunststad (p196) Wander through these vast artist studios in Amsterdam Noord.

NEMO Science Museum roof terrace (p92) One of the best views of Amsterdam extends from the roof of this landmark building.

Free Entertainment

For discounted same-day tickets, visit the Last Minute Ticket Shop (www.lastminuteticketshop.nl).

Concertgebouw (p168) Sharpen your elbows to get in for Wednesday's lunchtime concert (September to June), often a public rehearsal for tho porformanco lator that ovening.

NEED TO KNOW

➡ **Discount Cards** Various discount cards (p260) offer savings and freebies at numerous attractions, shops and restaurants.

➡ **Concessions** Students and seniors should bring ID and flash it at every opportunity for reduced admission lees.

➡ **Wi-fi** Visit www.wifi-amsterdam.nl to find free hotspots around town.

The peaceful enclave of Begijnhof (p67)

Muziektheater (p99) Free classical concerts fill the air during lunch most Tuesdays (September to May).

Bimhuis (p98) Jazz sessions hot up the revered venue on Tuesday nights.

Openluchttheater (p169) Vondelpark's outdoor theatre puts on concerts and kids' shows throughout summer.

EYE Film Institute (p196) Has pods in the basement where you can watch free films.

Mulligans (p130) Free music sessions and gigs at the city's best-known and loved Irish pub.

King's Day (p23) The ultimate party, this is one of many festivals and events that are totally free. (Well, you might want to bring some euros for beer and a cheap orange wig.)

Free Transport

Yellow Backie (www.yellowbackie.org) A program that lets visitors catch a free ride on the back of a local's bike. When you see someone cycling by with a bright-yellow luggage rack on the rear, yell 'Backie!' The rider will stop, let you hop on, and pedal you onward.

Ferries Free ferries depart behind Centraal Station to NDSM-werf, Amsterdam Noord's edgy art community 15 minutes up harbour; to the EYE Film Institute, five minutes across the river; and to IJ Plein, also a five-minute ride.

Locals take to Amsterdam's canals on King's Day (p23)

 Canals

Amsterdammers have always known their Canal Ring, built during the Golden Age, is extraordinary. Unesco made it official in 2010, when it listed the waterways as a World Heritage site. Today the city has 165 canals spanned by 1753 bridges — more than any other city in the world.

NEED TO KNOW

Canal Safety

➡ Virtually none of Amsterdam's canals have fences or barriers. Keep a close eye on young children to ensure they don't take an unexpected plunge.

Ice-skating Safety

➡ Drownings periodically occur; stay away from the ice unless you see large groups of people and be very careful at the edges and under bridges – areas with weak ice.

Boating Rules & Advice

➡ Stay on the waterways' right (starboard) side.

➡ Commercial traffic (including tour boats) has right of way, as do boats on your right-hand side.

➡ The speed limit is 7.5km/h (the top speed for many electric rental boats).

➡ Life jackets/vests aren't compulsory (but are strongly recommended).

➡ Drinking alcohol (or taking drugs) while in control of a boat is illegal.

➡ Shouting and amplified music is also illegal on board.

➡ Many bridges have low clearance (less than 2m).

➡ Docking is permitted anywhere in the city except beneath bridges, on narrow waterways, junctions or adjacent to rescue steps, or locations signposted as prohibited.

➡ Switch on your lights at dusk.

History

Far from being simply decorative or picturesque, or even waterways for transport, the canals were crucial to drain and reclaim the waterlogged land. They solved Amsterdam's essential problem: keeping the land and sea separate.

Names & Layout

In Dutch a canal is a *gracht* (pronounced 'khrakht') and the main canals form the central *grachtengordel* (canal ring). These beauties came to life in the early 1600s, after Amsterdam's population grew beyond its medieval walls and city planners put together an ambitious design for expansion. The concentric waterways they built are the same ones you see today.

CORE CANALS

Starting from the core, the major semicircular canals are the Singel, Herengracht, Keizersgracht and Prinsengracht. An easy way to remember them is that, apart from the singular **Singel** (which originally was a moat that defended Amsterdam's outer limits), these canals are in alphabetical order.

The **Herengracht** is where Amsterdam's wealthiest residents moved once the canals were completed. They built their mansions alongside it (particularly around the Golden Bend), hence its name, which translates to Gentlemen's Canal.

Almost as swanky was the **Keizersgracht** (Emperor's Canal), a nod to Holy Roman Emperor Maximilian I.

The **Prinsengracht** – named after William the Silent, Prince of Orange and the first Dutch royal – was designed as a slightly cheaper canal with smaller residences and warehouses. It also acted as a barrier against the working-class Jordaan beyond.

RADIAL CANALS

The canals that cut across the core canals like spokes on a bicycle wheel are known as radial canals. From west to east the major radial canals are Brouwersgracht, Leidsegracht and Reguliersgracht, and, like the core canals, they are in alphabetical order.

The **Brouwersgracht** (Brewers Canal) is one of Amsterdam's most beautiful waterways. It takes its name from the many breweries that lined the banks in the 16th and 17th centuries.

The **Leidsegracht** was named after the city of Leiden, to which it was the main water route.

Peaceful **Reguliersgracht** was named after an order of monks whose monastery was located nearby. Today it's often better known as the 'canal of seven bridges' and its iconic scenery isn't lost on canal-boat operators.

Bridges

Some truly striking bridges straddle the city's waterways.

Spanning the Singel, the Torensluis was built in 1648, making it Amsterdam's oldest bridge (also, at 39m, its widest). The

Blauwbrug (p121) crosses the Amstel river, with fish sculptures and imperial-crowned street lamps dotting the way. And you've probably seen the iconic Magere Brug (p121) in photos or appearing in films, stretching over the Amstel, glowing beneath the twinkle of 1200 tiny lights. In the Western Islands, look out for the narrow, charming Drieharingenbrug (p137).

Houseboats

Some 3050 houseboats line Amsterdam's canals. Living on the water became popular after WWII, when a surplus of old cargo ships helped fill the gap of a housing shortage on land. The Prinsengracht displays a particularly diverse mix of houseboats. You can climb aboard one and explore the cosy (ie cramped) interior at the Houseboat Museum (p137), or book to stay overnight on the water yourself in true Amsterdam style.

Greener Canals

While Amsterdam's canals certainly aren't crystal clear (around 12,000 to 15,000 bicycles are pulled from the canals each year), they're cleaner today than ever before in the city's history.

In part this is due to the locks, most of which close three times per week to allow fresh water to be pumped from the IJsselmeer. This creates a current that flushes the stagnant canal water out through open locks on the other side of the city and out to sea – check out the mighty Amstelsluizen (p122) on the Amstel in the Southern Canal Ring. What's more, the canals are regularly patrolled by specialised cleaning boats. And since 2005, houseboats have been required to connect to the city's sewerage system. Virtually all are now connected.

These efforts have made a significant difference, as evidenced by the wildlife the canals now attract. Some 20 fish and crab species now live happily below the water's surface. They, in turn, attract a wide variety of waterbirds such as gulls, herons, ducks, coots and cormorants. You might even see – or more likely, hear – neon-green ring-necked parakeets circling above. These, of course, aren't native; their presence in the city dates from 1976, when a pet-shop owner, tormented by a pair of parakeets screeching in store, high-tailed them to the Vondelpark and let them loose. The birds soon bred, and now more than 6000 parakeets shriek around town.

As part of its comprehensive sustainability plan, Amsterdam now only allows electric tour boats on its central canals. It's also considering a one-way boat-traffic system to further reduce emissions and noise pollution and keep the waterways as pristine as possible.

Ice Skating

Ice skating was part of the Dutch psyche long before scarfed figures appeared in Golden Age winterscapes. The first skates were made from cow shanks and ribs, had hand-drilled holes and were tied to the feet. When canals and ponds freeze over, everyone takes to the ice.

Boat Tours

Sure they're touristy, but canal cruises are also a delightful way to see the city. Several operators depart from moorings at Centraal Station, Damrak, Rokin and opposite the Rijksmuseum. Costs are similar. To avoid the steamed-up-glass-window effect, look for a boat with an open seating area. On a night tour you'll see the bridges lit up (though these tours usually cost a bit more).

Those Dam Boat Guys Map p308 (www.thosedamboatguys.com; ☑06 1885 5219; tours €25; ☺11am, 1pm, 3pm, 5pm & 7pm Mar-Sep; ☐13/14/17 Westermarkt) Here's your least-touristy canal-cruise option. The guys offer cheeky small tours (no more than 10 people) on electric boats. Feel free to bring food, beer, smoking material and whatever else you want for the 90-minute jaunt.

Canal Bus (www.canal.nl; ☑02 0217 0501; hop-on, hop-off day pass €21, cruises €15-20; ☺10am-6pm) Offers a handy hop-on, hop-off service. Its 20 docks around the city are located near the big museums and landmarks.

Blue Boat Company Map p312 (www.blueboat.nl; ☑02 0679 1370; Stadhouderskade 30; 75min tour adult/child €17/8.50, 90min evening tour adult/child €19.50/15.50; ☺half-hourly 10am-6pm Mar-Oct, hourly Nov-Feb; ☐1/2/5/7/10 Leidseplein) Blue Boat's 75-minute main tour glides by the top sights. Other cruises include a children's pirate-themed tour, a dinner cruise and a tour in a smaller, open-top boat.

Wetlands Safari Map p290 (www.wetlandssafari.nl; ☑06 5355 2669; incl transport & picnic adult/child €59/33; ☺9.30am Mon-Fri, 10am Sat

Canals by Neighbourhood

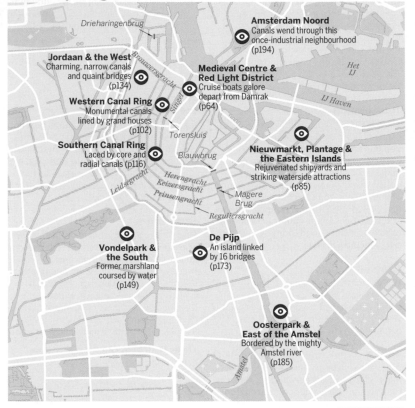

Amsterdam Noord
Canals wend through this once-industrial neighbourhood (p194)

Jordaan & the West
Charming, narrow canals and quaint bridges (p134)

Medieval Centre & Red Light District
Cruise boats galore depart from Damrak (p64)

Western Canal Ring
Monumental canals lined by grand houses (p102)

Southern Canal Ring
Laced by core and radial canals (p116)

Nieuwmarkt, Plantage & the Eastern Islands
Rejuvenated shipyards and striking waterside attractions (p85)

Vondelpark & the South
Former marshland coursed by water (p149)

De Pijp
An island linked by 16 bridges (p173)

Oosterpark & East of the Amstel
Bordered by the mighty Amstel river (p185)

Drieharingenbrug
Brouwersgracht
Singel
Het IJ
IJ Haven
Torensluis
Blauwbrug
Herengracht
Keizersgracht
Prinsengracht
Leidsegracht
Magere Brug
Reguliersgracht
Amstel

& Sun early Apr–late Sep) OK, so it's not a canal tour, but it is an exceptional five-hour boat trip canoeing through wetlands and past windmills and 17th-century villages.

Boat Rentals

If you'd like to explore under your own steam, several companies hire boats; a boat licence isn't required for boats under 15m in length or with a top speed of under 20km/h. Operators provide instruction before you set sail and usually have waterproof maps of the waterways. Other options for getting out on the water include kayaking.

Canal Bike (www.canal.nl; per person per hr €8; ☉10am-6pm Apr-Oct) These pedal boats allow you to splash around the canals at your own speed. Landing stages are by the Rijksmuseum, Leidseplein and Anne Frank Huis.

Boaty (www.boaty.nl; Jozef Israëlskade; boat rental per 3hr/full day from €79/179; 9am-30min before sunset early Mar-Oct; ☑12 Scheldestraat) Boaty's location on the peaceful Amstelkanaal makes it an ideal launching pad for exploring the waterways before approaching the crowded city-centre canals.

Kanoschool (www.kanoschool.nl; Admiralengracht 60; rental per hr €10; ☉hours vary) Hires one- and two-person kayaks for paddling along the canals as well as stand up paddleboards (SUPs).

Canal Motorboats Map p303 (www.canal motorboats.com; ☑02 0422 7007; Zandhoek 10a; rental 1st/2nd/3rd/4th hour €50/40/30/20, subsequent hours €20; ☉10am-10pm; ☑48 Barentszplein) Small, silent electric aluminium boats (maximum seven passengers) from Canal Motorboats are eco-friendly and easy to drive.

Lonely Planet's Top Choices

Prinsengracht (p110) The liveliest of Amsterdam's inner canals, with cafes, shops and houseboats lining the quays.

Reguliersgracht (p121) From here you can peer through the arches of seven bridges.

Brouwersgracht (p136) Amsterdammers swear this is the city's most beautiful canal, though it has some seriously tough competition.

Herengracht (p106) Amsterdam's stateliest canal takes in the city's most prestigious real estate along the Golden Bend.

Bloemgracht (p137) This gorgeous canal is home to a large number of fine, gabled houses.

Egelantiersgracht (p137) An elegant and serene canal that feels like you have it (practically) to yourself.

Best Canal Museums

Houseboat Museum (p137) Discover how *gezellig* (convivial, cosy) houseboat living can be aboard this 1914 barge-turned-museum.

Het Grachtenhuis (p106) Inventive multimedia displays explain how the Canal Ring and its amazing houses were built.

Museum Van Loon (p119) Magnificent Golden Age canal house.

Museum Willet-Holthuysen (p120) Sumptuous canal-side property.

Kattenkabinet (p120) Occupies the only canal house on the Golden Bend that's open to the public.

Best Canal Festivals & Events

King's Day (p23) During one of Europe's biggest street parties, plenty of action takes place around the city's famous waterways.

Grachtenfestival (p24) Sees classical musicians play alongside and on the water aboard a barge.

Amsterdam Gay Pride (p261) Amsterdam proudly hosts the only water-borne gay pride festival in the world.

Open Tuinen Dagen (p24) Open Garden Days offer the opportunity to view dozens of private gardens along the canals.

Sinterklaas Intocht (p25) Even St Nicholas sails into town; his arrival by boat heralds the Christmas season.

Amsterdam Light Festival (p25) Highlights include a magical, mid-December Christmas Canal Parade of illuminated boats floating along the waterways.

Amsterdam City Swim (p24) Locals kick and splash through the canals to raise money for charity.

Best Houseboat Accommodation

Houseboat Ms Luctor (p218) A beautiful 1913-built self-contained boat with mahogany panelling, moored in a quiet location near Centraal Station.

De Dageraad (p215) Eastern Docklands hospitality in an eco-friendly B&B boat that dates from 1929.

Little Amstel (p221) Two-room B&B with a prime position on the Amstel.

Best Canal-Side Dining

De Belhamel (p110) At the head of the Herengracht, this superb restaurant's canal-side tables are an aphrodisiac.

Buffet van Odette (p123) Simple, creative cooking overlooking the Prinsengracht's crooked canal houses.

Gebr Hartering (p95) Exquisitely presented modern Dutch dishes compete with an impossibly romantic canal-side location.

De Prins (p141) This brown cafe (traditional Dutch pub) serves delicious fondue at tables sprinkled along the Prinsengracht.

Best Canal-Side Drinking

't Smalle (p143) Dock right by the stone terrace of the 18th-century former *jenever* (Dutch gin) distillery.

Café P 96 (p143) The summertime terrace of this late-night watering hole is aboard a houseboat.

Café Papeneiland (p143) A 1642 gem on the corner of the Prinsengracht and Brouwersgracht canals.

Café Binnen Buiten (p182) The best canal-side terrace in Amsterdam's 'Latin Quarter', De Pijp.

Edel (p166) Fairy-light-draped charmer at the junction of two canals.

Café de Ceuvel (p197) Canal-side hotspot over the IJ river in Amsterdam Noord.

NEMO Science Museum (p92)

Museums & Galleries

Amsterdam's world-class museums draw millions of visitors each year. The art collections take pride of place – you can't walk a kilometre here without bumping into a masterpiece. Canal-house museums are another local speciality. And, of course, the free-wheeling city has a fine assortment of oddball museums dedicated to everything from hash to houseboats.

All the Art

The Dutch Masters helped spawn the prolific art collections around town. You've probably heard of a few of these guys: Johannes Vermeer, Frans Hals and Rembrandt van Rijn. They came along during the Golden Age when a new, bourgeois society of merchants and shopkeepers were spending money to brighten up their homes and workplaces with fresh paintings. The masters were there to meet the need, and their output from the era now fills the city's top museums.

Other Treasures

The Netherlands' maritime prowess during the Golden Age also filled the coffers of local institutions. Silver, porcelain and colonial knick-knacks picked up on distant voyages form the basis of collections in the Rijksmuseum (p151), Amsterdam Museum (p70), Het Scheepvaartmuseum (p92) and Tropenmuseum (p188).

Canal-House Museums

There are two kinds: the first preserves the house as a living space, with sumptuous interiors that show how the richest locals lived once upon a time, as at Museum Van Loon (p119). The other type uses the elegant structure as a backdrop for unique collections, such as the Kattenkabinet (p120) for cat art.

Contemporary Galleries

Van Gogh and the Golden Age masters grab all the glory, but Amsterdam's art scene goes well beyond them. Several contemporary galleries dot the city, providing outlets for avant-garde and emerging artists. Many galleries, such as W139 (p73) in the Red Light District, began as squats and then moved into the mainstream over the years. Gallery-dense neighbourhoods include the Jordaan and the Southern Canal Ring.

How to Beat the Crowds

Queues at the Van Gogh Museum, Rijksmuseum, Anne Frank Huis and others can easily reach an hour, particularly in summer. Want to avoid the mobs? Here are some strategies:

Take advantage of e-tickets Most sights sell them and there's little to no surcharge. They typically allow you to enter via a separate, faster queue. In some cases, you need to be able to print the tickets (though scannable mobile phone tickets are becoming increasingly common).

Go late Queues are shortest during late afternoon and evening. Visit after 3pm for the Rijksmuseum and Van Gogh Museum (also open Friday nights), and after 6pm for the Anne Frank Huis (open late nightly in summer).

Try tourist offices You can often buy advance tickets at visitor info centres, but the queues there can be as lengthy as the ones at the sights.

Buy a discount card In addition to saving on entrance fees, discount cards commonly provide fast-track entry.

Museums & Galleries by Neighbourhood

➡ **Medieval Centre & Red Light District** Spans the sacred (several church museums) to the profane (Sexmuseum; Hash, Marijuana & Hemp Museum).

➡ **Nieuwmarkt, Plantage & the Eastern Islands** Museum Het Rembrandthuis, NEMO Science Museum, Het Scheepvaartmuseum and the Verzetsmuseum are scattered around the neighbourhood.

➡ **Western Canal Ring** Anne Frank Huis draws the mega-crowds; smaller, canal-focused museums pop up too.

➡ **Southern Canal Ring** Home to the Hermitage Amsterdam plus several quirky museums.

➡ **Jordaan & the West** Off-the-beaten-path collections from tulips to houseboats to fluorescent art.

NEED TO KNOW

Opening Hours

➡ Most museums open 10am to 5pm, some close on Monday.

➡ The Van Gogh Museum stays open to 10pm on Friday.

➡ The Anne Frank Huis stays open to 10pm daily from April to October and to 9pm Saturday November to March.

Costs

➡ Tickets are typically €8–€18.

➡ Kids under 13 often get in for free or half-price.

➡ Audio guides are around €5.

Top Tips

➡ Pre-book tickets for the big museums.

➡ Queues are shortest during late afternoon and evening.

➡ Friday, Saturday and Sunday are the busiest days.

➡ Many hotels sell surcharge-free tickets to the big museums as a service to guests; be sure to ask your front-desk staff.

Advance-Purchase Recommendations

Van Gogh Museum & Rijksmuseum Puts you in a faster queue.

Anne Frank Huis E-tickets with set entry times compulsory before 3.30pm.

Stedelijk Museum Lets you bypass the queue.

Heineken Experience E-tickets provide a small discount and faster queue.

Het Grachtenhuis E-tickets ensure access for the limited-space tours.

➡ **Vondelpark & the South** Holds the Museum Quarter and its big three: Van Gogh Museum, Rijksmuseum and Stedelijk Museum.

➡ **De Pijp** Crowds amass to learn about brewing at the Heineken Experience.

➡ **Oosterpark & East of the Amstel** Colonial trinkets at Tropenmuseum.

➡ **Amsterdam Noord** Kunststad (Art City) has 175 artists working in its studios.

Lonely Planet's Top Choices

Van Gogh Museum (p154) Hangs the world's largest collection of the tormented artist's vivid swirls.

Rijksmuseum (p151) Rembrandts, Vermeers, crystal goblets and magic lanterns pack the nation's sprawling treasure chest.

Anne Frank Huis (p104) The Secret Annexe and Anne's claustrophobic bedroom provide an unnerving insight into life during WWII.

Pianola Museum (p136) Listen to rare jazz and classical tunes unrolling on vintage player pianos.

Best Art Museums

Museum het Rembrandthuis (p87) Immerse yourself in the old master's paint-spattered studio and handsome home.

Stedelijk Museum (p156) Renowned modern art from Picasso to Mondrian to Warhol fills the newly revamped building.

Hermitage Amsterdam (p118) The outpost of Russia's Hermitage Museum picks from its rich home trove to mount mega exhibits.

Foam (p121) Hip photography museum with changing exhibits by famous shutterbugs.

Best History Museums

Amsterdam Museum (p70) Whiz-bang exhibits take you through seven centuries of the city's intriguing history.

Verzetsmuseum (p91) Find out how the Dutch Resistance

operated when the Germans occupied the country during WWII.

Het Grachtenhuis (p106) Covers the history of Amsterdam's canals.

Best Unusual Museums

Tassenmuseum Hendrikje (p121) A museum of handbags and purses throughout history, with lots of sparkling celebrity clutches.

Sexmuseum Amsterdam (p69) The naughty art and artefacts make for a fun, silly browse.

Electric Ladyland (p137) The world's first museum of fluorescent art offers a trippy glow-in-the-dark experience.

Torture Museum (p71) Eerie galleries show branding tongs, skull crackers, a guillotine and the Iron Maiden of Nuremberg.

Best Canal-House Museums

Museum Van Loon (p119) This opulent old manor whispers family secrets in its shadowy rooms.

Museum Willet-Holthuysen (p120) Peruse sumptuous paintings, china and a French-style garden with sundial.

Kattenkabinet (p120) Art devoted to cats (including works by Picasso and Rembrandt) fills a rambling old canal house on the Golden Bend.

Best Underappreciated Museums

Tropenmuseum (p188) Contains a whopping collection of ritual masks, spiky spears and other colonial booty.

Het Scheepvaartmuseum (p92) The Maritime Museum features ancient globes, spooky ship figureheads and a replica schooner to climb.

Museum Ons' Lieve Heer op Solder (p74) Looks like an ordinary canal house, but hides a relic-rich 17th-century church inside.

Best Galleries & Arts Centres

Walls Gallery (p133) Edgy space in a former garage that shows up-and-coming artists.

W139 (p73) Ponder political, hot-button multimedia works in the thick of the Red Light District.

Civic Guard Gallery (p70) Check out the collection of enormous portraits, from Golden Age to modern day.

KochxBos (p136) Peculiar pop surrealism and underground art brighten a corner in the Jordaan.

Kunststad (p196) Creative studios in former shipbuilding yards.

Best for Kids

NEMO Science Museum (p92) Kid-focused, hands-on science labs inside and a terrace with a splashy summer water feature on the roof.

Joods Historisch Museum (p89) The children's section replicates a Jewish home, with a hands-on music room and kitchen for baking.

Madame Tussauds Amsterdam (p69) Youth get excited to see their favourite celebrities and heroes up close (albeit in wax).

Micropia (p93) The world's first microbe museum has a wall of poop, kissing meter and other inventive exhibits.

Hotel de Goudfazant (p197)

 # Eating

Amsterdam's sizzling-hot foodie scene spans classic Dutch snacks to reinvented traditional recipes at contemporary restaurants, on-trend establishments pioneering world-first concepts, a wave of new, ultra-healthy, often vegetarian or vegan eateries, and an increasing focus on wine, cocktail and craft beer pairings. And this multinational city has a cornucopia of cuisines from all over the globe.

NEED TO KNOW

Opening Hours
Most restaurants open 11am to 2.30pm for lunch and 6pm to 10pm for dinner.

Price Ranges
Prices are for the cost of a main dish at dinner:

€ less than €12

€€ €12–25

€€€ more than €25

Reservations
Phone ahead to make a reservation for eateries in the middle and upper price brackets. Nearly everyone speaks English. Many places offer online booking options.

Cash & Cards
Many restaurants, even top-end ones, don't accept credit cards. Or if they do, there's often a 5% surcharge. Conversely, some places accept cards only. Check first.

Saving Money
Dagschotel is dish of the day; heartier appetites might go for a *dagmenu* (a set menu of three or more courses).

Tipping
Diners do tip, but modestly. Leave 5% to 10% for a cafe snack (if your bill comes to €9.50, you might round up to €10), leave 10% to 15% for a restaurant meal (the higher end for particularly good service).

Best Websites
➜ **Amsterdam Foodie** (www.amsterdamfoodie.nl) Restaurant reviews galore.

➜ **IENS** (www.iens.nl) Everyday eaters give their restaurant opinions; in Dutch.

➜ **Your Little Black Book** (www.yourlittleblackbook.me) What's new and hot in the city.

New Trends

Concept restaurants are popping up all over the city, with kitchens often zeroing in on a single item, such as strawberries or avocados. Other current trends include gourmet street food (*poké* bowls, ramen, tacos, hot dogs...) as well as all-day brunch. Contemporary Dutch cuisine is also rapidly on the rise.

Amsterdam is a major start-up hub, which extends to its dining landscape. All over the city you'll find expanding mini-chains of home-grown eateries. Popular ones include Stach (gourmet sandwiches and deli items), SLA (design-your-own salads), De Bakkerswinkel (baked goods), De Pizzabakkers (pizza and Prosecco) and the Butcher (burgers); there are countless others.

Foodhallen (p161), in the De Hallen tram-depot-turned-cultural-complex, has a host of eateries under one roof, and is a fantastic place to take the city's dining temperature. Festivals, such as food-truck extravaganza **Rollende Keukens** (Rolling Kitchens; www.rollendekeukens.amsterdam; ☉late May; 🚊10 Van Limburg Stirumstraat), are also great for tapping into the Zeitgeist. The Sunday Market (p145) is another good bet for discovering new food directions.

Specialities
TRADITIONAL DUTCH
Traditional Dutch cuisine revolves around meat, potatoes and vegetables. Typical dishes include *stamppot* (mashed pot) – potatoes mashed with another vegetable (usually kale or endive) and served with smoked sausage and strips of bacon – and *erwtensoep* – a thick pea soup with smoked sausage and bacon that's usually served in winter.

Pannenkoeken translates to pancakes; the Dutch variety is huge, served one to a plate and topped with sweet or savoury ingredients. The mini version, covered in sugar or syrup, is *poffertjes*. You can often find these being cooked fresh at markets.

Many snack bars and pubs serve *appeltaart* (apple pie) accompanied by *slagroom* (whipped cream). For breakfast it's common to eat *hagelslag* (chocolate sprinkles) on buttered bread.

CONTEMPORARY DUTCH
Fresh winds are blowing through the Dutch traditional kitchen, breathing new life into centuries-old recipes by giving them a contemporary twist. Creative Dutch chefs are also taking concepts from the rest the world and melding them with locally sourced meats, seafood and vegetables. Amsterdam is ground zero for contemporary Dutch fare.

INDONESIAN & SURINAMESE
The Netherlands' historical ties with Indonesia and Suriname means there are loads of places to try these two cuisines.

The most famous Indonesian dish is a rijsttafel (Indonesian banquet): a dozen or more tiny dishes such as braised beef, pork satay and ribs served with white rice. Other popular dishes are *nasi goreng* – fried rice with onion, pork, shrimp and spices, often topped with a fried egg or shredded omelette – and *bami goreng,* the same thing, but with noodles in place of rice. Indonesian food is usually served mild for Western palates. If you want it hot (*pedis,* pronounced 'p-*dis*'), say so, but be prepared for the ride of a lifetime.

Surinamese Caribbean–style cuisine prominently features curries (chicken, lamb or beef). Roti are burrito-like flatbread wraps stuffed with curried meat or veg; they're delicious, filling and cheap.

Snacks

Vlaamse frites/patat The iconic 'Flemish fries' are cut from whole potatoes and smothered in mayonnaise or myriad other sauces.

Kroketten Croquettes are dough balls with various fillings that are crumbed and deep-fried; the meat-filled variety called *bitterballen* are a popular brown-cafe snack served with mustard.

Haring Herring is a Dutch institution, sold at stalls around the city. It's prepared with salt or pickled, but never cooked, and served with diced onion and sometimes sweet-pickle chips.

Quick Eats

Besides restaurants and *eetcafés* (pub-like eateries serving affordable meals), there are several quick options.

Broodjeszaken (sandwich shops) are everywhere. Stroll up to the counter and pick the meat and/or cheese to go on a fluffy white or wheat roll for a few euros.

Snack bars are also ubiquitous; FEBO is the most well-known, with its long rows of coin-operated yellow windows from which you pluck out a deep-fried treat. Branches arc open into the wee hours, and stopping by for a greasy snack after a hard night of drinking is a Dutch tradition.

Cheese

Locals love their *kaas* (cheese). Nearly two-thirds of all cheese sold is Gouda. The tastiest varieties have strong, complex flavours. Try some *oud* (old) Gouda, hard and rich in flavour and a popular bar snack with mustard. Edam is similar to Gouda, but slightly drier and less crumbly. Round or Leiden cheese is another export hit, laced with cumin or caraway seed and light in flavour.

Sweets

The most famous candy is *drop,* sweet or salty liquorice sold in a bewildering variety of flavours. It's definitely an acquired taste. *Stroopwafels* hide their caramel syrup filling inside two cookie-esque waffles.

Eating by Neighbourhood

➡ **Medieval Centre & Red Light District** (p73) Everything from elegant Dutch to Zeedijk's Asian restaurants to alley-side sandwich shops.

➡ **Nieuwmarkt, Plantage & the Eastern Islands** (p93) Outdoor terraces and dramatic waterfront settings.

➡ **Western Canal Ring** (p108) Cute cafes and small restaurants surround the Negen Straatjes.

➡ **Southern Canal Ring** (p122) Cheap and cheerful around Leidseplein; diverse, quality options on Utrechtsestraat.

➡ **Jordaan & the West** (p139) Convivial little spots are the Jordaan's hallmark; scenester eats dot Westergasfabriek.

➡ **Vondelpark & the South** (p161) From squats serving organic fare to cool-cat international restaurants to the big, airy Foodhallen.

➡ **De Pijp** (p176) Grazing galore in the Albert Cuypmarkt; ethnic places and brunch spots everywhere.

➡ **Oosterpark & East of the Amstel** (p188) Indonesian, Moroccan, Turkish and Surinamese abounds.

➡ **Amsterdam Noord** (p197) Stunning post-industrial and/or waterside settings for creative cuisine.

Local Eat Streets

Jan Pieter Heijestraat Sociable spots keep popping up on this artery between Vondelpark and De Hallen cultural complex.

Amstelveenseweg Loads of international options along the western edge of Vondelpark.

Utrechtsestraat Chock-a-block with cafes where cool young Amsterdammers hang out; in the Southern Canal Ring.

Haarlemmerstraat and Haarlemmerdijk Adjoining streets spanning the Western Canal Ring and Jordaan that burst with trendy spots.

2e luindwarsstraat Cosy restaurants, including many Italian spots, congregate on and around this narrow Jordaan backstreet.

Lonely Planet's Top Choices

Rijks (p165) Michelin-starred dining in the magnificent Rijksmuseum.

D'Vijff Vlieghen (p75) A treasure rambling through five 17th-century canal houses.

Ron Gastrobar (p163) Dutch-style tapas from the city's top chef.

Greetje (p96) Resurrects and re-creates Dutch classics, with mouthwatering results.

De Kas (p190) Dine in the greenhouse that grew your meal's ingredients.

Lt Cornelis (p75) Cutting-edge Dutch cooking and craft cocktails.

Best By Budget

€

Avocado Show (p176) Avocados feature in everything from salad bowls to ice cream and cocktails.

Fat Dog (p177) Ultra-gourmet hot dogs by star chef Ron Blaauw.

Gartine (p73) Slow Food sandwiches and a dazzling high tea hide in the Medieval Centre.

Braai BBQ Bar (p161) Street-food-style hot spot barbecuing tangy ribs.

Sterk Staaltje (p93) Greengrocer-like shop filled with ready-to-eat savoury treats.

De Laatste Kruimel (p73) Munch fab sandwiches and quiches amid vintage and upcycled decor.

€€

Mossel En Gin (p142) G&T-battered fish and chips are among the creative gin-infused dishes at this Westergasfabriek stunner.

Balthazar's Keuken (p140) Ever-changing, Mediterranean-tinged dishes served in a revamped blacksmith's forge.

Buffet van Odette (p123) Airy, canal-side terrace for creative pastas and sandwiches.

€€€

Wolf Atelier (p141) Ground-breaking gastronomy atop a disused railway bridge.

Graham's Kitchen (p181) Ingredients at this diamond find are sourced from the Amsterdam area.

Marius (p142) The chef whips up a four-course menu from his daily market finds.

Ciel Bleu (p181) Two-Michelin-starred haute cuisine with 23rd-floor views over Amsterdam.

Blauw aan de Wal (p76) A 17th-century warehouse-turned-romantic-restaurant in the Red Light District.

Best By Cuisine

Traditional Dutch

Bistro Bij Ons (p110) Honest-to-goodness Dutch classics

Letting (p108) Start the day with authentic Dutch breakfast dishes.

La Falote (p165) Stewed fish, meatballs with endives, and other daily specials of home-style cooking.

Pantry (p124) A *gezellig* (cosy, convivial) atmosphere and classic Dutch fare.

Van Dobben (p122) Meaty goodness diner-style.

Contemporary Dutch

Lt Cornelis (p75) A new spin on age-old Dutch recipes.

Wilde Zwijnen (p189) The Oost's rustic gem reaps praise for bold, eclectic seasonal fare.

Gebr Hartering (p95) In a seductive canal-side location, the menu changes daily, but is unfailingly delicious.

Hemelse Modder (p94) North Sea fish followed by a heavenly mousse for dessert.

Indonesian

Dèsa (p179) Hugely popular for its rijsttafel.

Restaurant Blauw (p166) Feted Indonesian fare in contemporary surrounds.

Café Kadijk (p95) Does a mini rijsttafel.

Surinamese

Tokoman (p93) Crowds queue for the hot-spiced Surinamese sandwiches.

Spang Makandra (p178) Fabulous array of astonishingly cheap dishes served in cosy surrounds.

Roopram Roti (p189) No-frills spot for flaky roti and fiery hot sauce.

Best Bakeries & Sweets

Patisserie Holtkamp (p126) You're in good company, as the gilded, royal coat of arms outside attests.

Baking Lab (p191) A communal oven, baking classes and heavenly breads.

Firma Stroop (p73) Charming *stroopwafel* specialist.

Petit Gâteau (p108) Row upon row of gorgeous mini tarts.

Arti Choc (p161) Original and custom-made chocolate creations.

Van Stapele (p75) Insanely addictive dark-chocolate cookies.

Best Vegetarian

Alchemist Garden (p162) Vegan heaven, serving delicious gluten- and lactose-free dishes.

Moer (p166) Extensive vegetarian choices.

SLA (p178) Super-chic organic salads.

Mastino V (p142) Only serves vegan pizza.

Venkel (p178) Dishes are served on planks made from a fallen Vondelpark tree.

Best Neighbourhood Gems

Dikke Graaf (p163) Cooking so delicious the aromas lure you in from the street.

Café Modern (p197) An Amsterdam Noord favourite.

Volt (p180) Lively locals' local with luscious tapas and Mediterranean mains; in De Pijp.

Éénvistwéévis (p96) Locals fork into fresh seafood from nearby waters; in the Plantage.

Best Views

Moon (p197) Take in 360-degree views from A'DAM Tower's revolving restaurant.

REM Eiland (p142) There's nothing like this 22m former pirate-radio tower.

Pont 13 (p142) Moored vintage car ferry with a superb Mediterranean-inspired menu.

Café-Restaurant Stork (p197) Seafood specialist on the IJ.

Hotel de Goudfazant (p197) Watch river boats while dining on punk French fare in Amsterdam Noord.

Best Brunch

Bakers & Roasters (p180) Banana nutbread French toast and Bloody Marys at Amsterdam's brunch specialist.

Breakfast Club (p162) British, US and Mexican brunch dishes.

Scandinavian Embassy (p180) Goat's milk yoghurt, salmon on Danish rye bread, and more dishes from northern lands.

CT Coffee & Coconuts (p180) Soaring art-deco space for coconut-buckwheat pancakes, eggs and avocado toast.

Little Collins (p180) Hip little hang-out with extraordinarily good, globe-spanning brunches.

Best Frites

Vleminckx (p73) To slather your golden potatoes in mayonnaise, curry or one of the myriad other sauces?

Wil Graanstra Friteshuis (p110) This family-run stand has served cones of fries near Anne Frank's house for decades.

Frites uit Zuyd (p178) Munch Flemish frites in the hall has out front.

Best Ice Cream

IJsmolen (p95) Lick uniquely Dutch flavours near the De Gooyer windmill.

Massimo (p176) Handmade in De Pijp by a fourth-generation gelato maker.

Banketbakkerij Van der Linde (p75) The creamiest vanilla you'll ever taste.

Monte Pelmo (p139) Inventive flavours draw loads of locals.

Best Sandwiches

Vinnies Deli (p108) Puts inventive all-organic combinations like smoked fish and rhubarb chutney between bread slices.

Rob Wigboldus Vishandel (p75) Great spot to get your herring on.

Loekie (p123) Choose from the lengthy menu of lip-smacking ingredients.

Broodje Bert (p75) It's tough to beat house-special lamb meatballs.

Best Pizza

Pazzi (p139) Perfectly charred crust cradles fresh mozzarella.

Yam Yam (p140) Many Amsterdammers swear this contemporary trattoria makes the city's best pizza.

Deegrollers (p162) Cordial neighbourhood spot for wood-fired pies.

Lo Stivale d'Oro (p124) The Italian owner fires up a mighty fine disc of goodness.

Sugo (p177) Sublime pizzas by the slice.

Friday cocktails at the Van Gogh Museum (p154)

Drinking & Nightlife

Amsterdam is one of the wildest nightlife cities in Europe and the world. Beyond the Red Light District and hotspots around Leidseplein and Rembrandtplein, the clubbing scene is also rapidly expanding thanks to 24-hour-licensed venues. Yet you can easily avoid a hardcore party scene: Amsterdam remains a café (pub) society where the pursuit of pleasure centres on cosiness and charm.

Cafés

Cafés When the Dutch say *café* they mean a pub, and there are more than 1000 throughout Amsterdam. In a city that values socialising and conversation more than the art of drinking itself, *cafés* aren't just about consuming alcohol: they're places to hang out for hours of contemplation or camaraderie. Scores of *cafés* have outside seating on *terrassen* (terraces), which are glorious in summer and sometimes covered and heated in winter. Most serve food as well, ranging from snacks and sandwiches to excellent meals.

Bruin Cafés Amsterdam is famed for its historic *bruin cafés* (brown cafes; traditional drinking establishments). The name comes from the nicotine stains from centuries of use (although recent aspirants slap on brown paint to catch up). Occasionally you'll find sand on the wooden floor to soak up spilt beer. Most importantly, the city's brown cafes provide an atmosphere conducive to conversation – and the nirvana of *gezelligheid* (conviviality, cosiness).

Grand Cafés These are spacious, have comfortable furniture and are, well, grand. They all have food menus, some quite elaborate. Despite the name, there's no need to dress up for a visit to a *grand café*.

Theatre Cafés Often similar to *grand cafés*, these are normally attached or adjacent to theatres, serving meals before and drinks after performances. Generally they're good places to catch performers after the show, though they're lovely any time of day.

Drinks

BEER

In stiff competition with a few of their European cohorts – the Belgians, Germans, Irish and Czechs – the Dutch take their beer very seriously (although they drink less per capita than any of them).

Lager is the staple, served cool and topped by a two-finger-thick head of froth to trap the flavour. *Een bier, een pils* or *een vaasje* will get you a normal glass of beer; *een kleintje pils* is a small glass and *een fluitje* is a small, thin, Cologne-style glass. Many places also serve *een grote pils* (a half-litre mug of beer) to please tourists, but it goes flat if you don't drink it quickly.

Local brands include Heineken, Amstel, Grolsch, Oranjeboom, Dommelsch and Bavaria (which, despite its name, isn't German but Dutch). Stronger Belgian beers, such as Duvel and Westmalle Triple, are also very

popular. *Witbier* (white beer) is a cloudy wheat beer drunk in summer with a slice of lemon. Dark, sweet *bokbier* comes out in the autumn.

Amsterdam's craft beer scene has exploded in recent years. Alongside long-standing microbreweries like Brouwerij 't IJ and Brouwerij de Prael, whose beers you'll find around town as well as at the breweries, are newer ones such as Brouwerij Troost, Oedipus and Butcher's Tears. You'll also find numerous craft-beer specialist bars and/or shops.

WINE & SPIRITS

It's not just beer here: the Dutch also make the hard stuff. *Jenever* (ye-*nay*-ver; Dutch gin; also spelt *genever*) is made from juniper berries and is drunk chilled. It arrives in a tulip-shaped shot glass filled to the brim – tradition dictates that you bend over the bar, with your hands behind your back, and take a deep sip. Most people prefer *jonge* (young) *jenever*, which is smooth and

Above: Ornate Café Papeneiland (p143)

Left: Amsterdam's merchants introduced coffee to Europe

Drinking & Nightlife by Neighbourhood

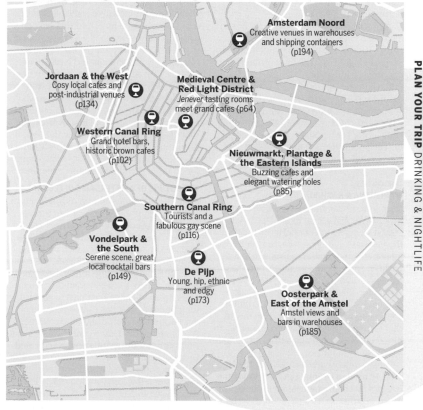

Amsterdam Noord
Creative venues in warehouses
and shipping containers
(p194)

Jordaan & the West
Cosy local cafes and
post-industrial venues
(p134)

**Medieval Centre &
Red Light District**
Jenever tasting rooms
meet grand cafes (p64)

Western Canal Ring
Grand hotel bars,
historic brown cafes
(p102)

**Nieuwmarkt, Plantage &
the Eastern Islands**
Buzzing cafes and
elegant watering holes
(p85)

Southern Canal Ring
Tourists and a
fabulous gay scene
(p116)

**Vondelpark &
the South**
Serene scene, great
local cocktail bars
(p149)

De Pijp
Young, hip, ethnic
and edgy
(p173)

**Oosterpark &
East of the Amstel**
Amstel views and
bars in warehouses
(p185)

relatively easy to drink; *oude* (old) *jenever* has a strong juniper flavour and can be an acquired taste.

A common combination, known as a *kopstoot* (head butt), is a glass of *jenever* with a beer chaser – few people can handle more than two or three of these. There are plenty of indigenous liqueurs, including *advocaat* (a kind of eggnog) and the herb-based Beerenburg, a Frisian schnapps.

More Dutch people are drinking wine than ever before, and wine bars are opening all over the city, although almost all wine here is imported from elsewhere in Europe and beyond.

COFFEE

Amsterdam's merchants introduced coffee to Europe and it's still the hot drink of choice. Traditionally, if you simply order *koffie* you'll get a sizeable cup of java with a small, airline-style container of *koffiemelk*, similar to unsweetened condensed milk. Caffe latte–like *koffie verkeerd* (wrong coffee) comes in a bigger cup or mug with plenty of real milk.

Roasteries and micro-roasteries are springing up around the city, and cafe baristas are increasingly using connoisseur styles of drip coffee.

BORREL

Borrel in Dutch means, quite simply, 'drink' – as in a glass of spirits, traditionally *jenever* (Dutch gin). But in social parlance, to be invited to *borrel* means to take part in an informal gathering for drinks, conversation and fun. It usually incorporates food too, especially *borrelhapjes* (bar snacks) like *bopwolpoatjeo* (peanuts encased in a crisp, spicy outer shell), and *kroketten* (croquettes) including *bitterballen* (small, round meat croquettes) – the name comes from the tradition of serving them with bitters, namely *jenever*.

Any occasion can be a reason for *borrel*: a birthday, a beautiful sunset that invites patio sitting or the end of a work day (*vrijdagmiddagborrel*, usually shortened to *vrijmibo* or just *vrimibo*, is specifically Friday-afternoon work drinks with colleagues). When you see a group of locals spilling out of a brown cafe onto the street with a glass of beer in hand? That's *borrel*. Grab a beer (or buy someone one) and join in. The famously tolerant and open Dutch rarely mind an addition to the party.

Smoking
MARIJUANA & HASHISH

Despite what you may have heard, cannabis is not *technically* legal in the Netherlands – yet it is widely tolerated. Here's the deal: the purchase and possession of small amounts (5g) of 'soft drugs' (ie marijuana, hashish, space cakes and mushroom-based truffles) is allowed and users won't be prosecuted for smoking or carrying this amount (although authorities do have the right to confiscate it, but this is rare). This means that coffeeshops are actually conducting an illegal business – but again, this is tolerated to a certain extent.

Most cannabis products sold in the Netherlands used to be imported, but today the country has high-grade home produce, so-called *nederwiet*. It's a particularly strong product – the most potent varieties contain 15% tetrahydrocannabinol (THC), the active substance that gets people high (since

2011, anything above 15% is classified as a hard drug and therefore illegal). In a nutshell, Dutch weed will literally blow your mind – perhaps to an extent that isn't altogether pleasant, which is why many native smokers have sworn off the local product. Newbies to smoking pot and hash should exercise caution; even many regular smokers can't stomach the home-grown stuff.

Space cakes and cookies (baked goods made with hash or marijuana) are sold in a rather low-key fashion, mainly because tourists often have problems with them. If people are unused to the time they can take to kick in and the effects, they could be in for an intense and long-lasting experience.

THE FUTURE OF AMSTERDAM COFFEESHOPS

Since the decriminalisation of soft drugs in 1976, the 'right to smoke' was not threatened in Amsterdam until relatively recently. Amsterdam currently has 173 coffeeshops (30% of the Netherlands' total), which is down from a high of 350 in 1995.

In 2011 the government proposed banning foreigners from cafes selling cannabis and requiring Dutch residents to sign up for a one-year *wietpas* ('weed pass') in order to purchase 'soft drugs' at a coffeeshop. Although the top Dutch court declared that such legislation was unlawful, it indicated that restricting tourists and foreigners from entering coffeeshops would not necessarily be considered unconstitutional. The law was passed in 2012; however, Amsterdam's councillors declared their opposition to it – on the grounds of increased crime, street dealing and antisocial behaviour – and coffeeshops have turned a blind eye.

COFFEESHOP & SMART SHOP DOS & DON'TS

➡ Do ask coffeeshop staff for advice on what and how to consume, and heed it, even if nothing happens after an hour.

➡ Don't ask for hard (illegal) drugs.

➡ Do ask staff for the menu of products on offer. Most shops offer rolling papers, pipes or bongs to use; you can also buy ready-made joints.

➡ Don't drink alcohol – it's illegal in coffeeshops.

➡ Don't smoke tobacco, whether mixed with marijuana or on its own; it is forbidden inside all bars and restaurants, in accordance with the Netherlands' laws.

➡ 'Herbal ecstasy' – usually a mix of herbs, vitamins and caffeine – is sold in smart shops; do ask staff what they recommend, as some varieties can have unpleasant side effects.

➡ Psilocybin mushrooms (aka magic mushrooms) are now illegal in the Netherlands, but many smart shops sell mushroom truffles, which have a similar effect.

If you're travelling further afield, be aware that elsewhere in the Netherlands, a number of regional councils are still trying the *wietpas* system, though some coffeeshops in these areas are pursuing this in court, so the outcome is uncertain – ask locally what the situation is when you visit.

Despite the 2014 commencement of the Dutch law dictating that coffeeshops must not operate within 250m of primary schools and 350m of secondary schools in Amsterdam, authorities are also in disagreement, arguing that minors are already forbidden, coffeeshops are monitored and that there are more effective ways to combat youth drug use, such as education. The law has, however, resulted in some 20 coffeeshops closing to date.

For now, Amsterdam's coffeeshops remain accessible to anyone (foreigners or locals) aged 18 and above. Coffeeshops are banned from advertising, and can sell up to 5g of cannabis per day, per customer. But their longer-term future remains a wait-and-see situation.

Clubbing

Amsterdam is banging on Berlin's door to claim the mantle of Europe's clubbing capital. The electronic music extravaganza **Amsterdam Dance Event** (ADE; www.amsterdam-dance-event.nl; ⊘late Oct) is a fixture on the city's calendar, and in 2012, nightclub promoter Mirik Milan became Amsterdam's (and the world's) inaugural *nachtburgemeester* (night mayor), representing and encouraging the city's nightlife and economy.

Inner-city clubs are integrating into the social fabric, and epic venues (including some with new 24-hour licences) are opening in repurposed buildings outside the city centre to avoid noise, and are reachable by public transport. In addition to club nights, they mount multi-genre art exhibitions, markets and other diverse cultural offerings.

Some of the best beats are to the west, at venues such as **Warehouse Elementenstraat** (www.elementenstraat.nl; Elementenstraat 25; ⊘hours vary; 🛜; ☐748 Contactweg, Ⓜ Isolatorweg), in a vast warehouse; **De School** (☑020-737 31 97; www.deschoolamsterdam.nl; Dr Jan van Breemenstraat 1; ⊘usually Thu-Sat; 🛜; ☐752, ☐13 Admiraal Helfrichstraat), in an ex–technical school; and **De Marktkantine** (☑020-788 44 66; http://marktkantine.nl; Jan van Galenstraat 6; ⊘usually Thu-Sun; 🛜; ☐18, night bus 752 Markthallen), in a market workers' canteen. To the southwest is **Radion** (☑020-452 47 09; www.radionamsterdam.nl; Louwesweg 1; ⊘hours vary; 🛜; ☐758, ☐2 Louwesweg), in a former dentistry academy. South of the city in the old newspaper district, the Volkshotel has an awesome club, Canvas (p191), on the premises. The red-hot, post-industrial neighbourhood of Amsterdam Noord is also fertile ground for clubs such as Shelter, buried beneath A'DAM Tower (p196); the radical 'political dance event' Progress Bar at Tolhuistuin (p199); and Sexyland (p196), with wildly disparate contributions from its 365 members, who each host their own annual event.

Amsterdam's Gay & Lesbian Scene

The Netherlands was the first country to legalise same-sex marriage (in 2001), so it's no surprise that Amsterdam's queer scene is one the largest in the world. Local gay and lesbian organisations (p261) can help you tap into the city's scene.

Five hubs party hardest:

Warmoesstraat In the Red Light District (between the Dam and Centraal Station); hosts the infamous, kink-filled leather and fetish bars.

Zeedijk Near Warmoesstraat, crowds spill onto laid-back bar terraces.

Rembrandtplein In the Southern Canal Ring, this area has traditional pubs and brown cafes, some with a campy bent, and several popular lesbian hangouts.

Leidseplein A smattering of trendy venues along Kerkstraat.

Reguliersdwarsstraat Draws the beautiful crowd.

Lonely Planet's Top Choices

't Smalle (p143) Amsterdam's most intimate canal-side drinking, with a gorgeous historic interior.

Warehouse Elementenstraat (p53) One of Europe's hottest 24-hour clubs.

Amsterdam Roest (p98) Artist collective/bar/urban beach on the site of abandoned shipyards.

Wynand Fockink (p79) This 1679 tasting house pours glorious *jenevers* (gins).

Pllek (p199) Hip bar made out of old shipping containers with an artificial beach.

SkyLounge (p97) A pinch-yourself, 360-degree city panorama extends from this 11th-floor bar and vast terrace.

Best Brown Cafes

In 't Aepjen (p80) Candles burn all day long in the time-warped, 500-year-old house.

Hoppe (p78) An icon of drinking history beloved by journalists, bums and raconteurs.

De Sluyswacht (p97) Swig in the lock-keeper's quarters across from Rembrandt's house.

Café Pieper (p143) Antique beer mugs hang from the bar at this low-ceilinged gem.

Café de Dokter (p78) Amsterdam's teeniest pub wafts old jazz records and pours whiskeys galore.

Eijlders (p127) Stained-glass artists' favourite with a lingering Resistance spirit.

Best Beer

Brouwerij 't IJ (p97) Wonderful independent brewery at the foot of the De Gooyer windmill.

Brouwerij Troost Westergas (p145) Sip frothy house-made suds and gin.

Brouwerij De Prael (p269) Socially minded brewery that makes strong organic beers.

Oedipus Brewery & Tap Room (p199) Brilliant brewery in Amsterdam Noord.

Bierfabriek (p81) Right in the city centre, this microbrewery also does great food.

Best Cocktail Bars

Tales & Spirits (p78) House infusions and vintage glasses.

Dum Dum Palace (p80) Classic cocktails with Asian twists, a secret bar and a kitchen dishing up dumplings.

Canvas (p191) Edgy, artsy bar with great views atop the *Volkskrant* newspaper building (now a flash hotel).

Twenty Third Bar (p182) Aerial 23rd-floor views, sublime champagne cocktails and two-Michelin-star bar snacks.

Door 74 (p126) Speakeasy-style bar mixing some of Amsterdam's wildest cocktails.

Tunes Bar (p167) Sleek bar inside the stunning Conservatorium Hotel, specialising in G&Ts.

Best Coffeeshops

Dampkring (p78) Hollywood made the hobbit-like decor and prize-winning product famous.

Abraxas (p79) A haven of mellow music and comfy sofas spread over three floors.

Greenhouse (p81) Psychedelic mosaics and stained glass plus a big menu for munchies.

La Tertulia (p144) Cool Van Gogh murals mark this quiet spot on the Prinsengracht.

Betty Boop (p127) Gay favourite.

Best Gay & Lesbian Hangouts

't Mandje (p81) Amsterdam's oldest gay bar is a trinket-covered beauty.

Getto (p82) A younger crowd piles in for cheap food and Red Light District people-watching.

Montmartre (p129) Legendary bar where Dutch ballads and old top-40 hits tear the roof off.

De Trut (p145) A Sunday fixture on the scene.

Best Coffee

Monks Coffee Roasters (p145) Unmissable house blend.

Lot Sixty One (p167) Red-hot Amsterdam roastery.

Scandinavian Embassy (p180) Coffee sourced from Scandinavian micro-roasteries.

Sweet Cup (p129) Micro-roastery with five espresso styles and five slow brews.

Koffiehuis De Hoek (p112) Charming old-fashioned coffeehouse experience.

Best Wine Bars

Worst Wijncafe (p141) Chequerboard-tiled wine bar with superb sausage tapas dishes.

Glouglou (p182) All-natural, by-the-glass wines.

Vyne (p113) Slick wine bar with blonde-wood surrounds.

Pata Negra (p128) Wonderfully rustic Spanish-style bodega.

Entertainment

Amsterdam supports a flourishing arts scene, with loads of big concert halls, theatres, cinemas, comedy clubs and other performance venues filled on a regular basis. Music fans are superbly catered for here, and there is a fervent subculture for just about every genre, especially jazz, classical, rock and avant-garde beats.

Music

JAZZ

Jazz is extremely popular, from far-out, improvisational stylings to more traditional notes. The grand Bimhuis (p98) is the big game in town, drawing visiting musicians from around the globe, though its vibe is more that of a funky little club. Smaller jazz venues abound and it's easy to find a live combo.

CLASSICAL

Amsterdam's classical-music scene, with top international orchestras, conductors and soloists crowding the agenda, is the envy of many European cities. Choose between the flawless Concertgebouw (p168) or dramatic Muziekgebouw aan 't IJ (p98) for the main shows.

ROCK

Many of the city's clubs also host live rock bands. Huge touring names often play smallish venues such as the Melkweg (p131) and Paradiso (p131); it's a real treat to catch one of your favourites here.

Comedy & Theatre

Given that the Dutch are fine linguists and have a keen sense of humour, English-language comedy thrives in Amsterdam, especially around the Jordaan. Local theatre tends towards the edgy and experimental.

Cinema

Go to the movies on holiday? Actually, Amsterdam's weather is fickle, and let's face it,

even art lovers can overdose on museums. Luckily this town is a cinephile's favourite, with oodles of art-house cinemas.

Entertainment by Neighbourhood

➡ **Medieval Centre & Red Light District** (p82) Several young rock/DJ clubs thrash throughout the 'hood, while avant-garde theatres line Nes.

➡ **Nieuwmarkt, Plantage & the Eastern Islands** (p98) Classical venues include the Muziekgebouw aan 't IJ, Bimhuis and Conservatorium.

➡ **Western Canal Ring** (p113) Limited options until the Felix Meritis cultural centre reopens in late 2018.

➡ **Southern Canal Ring** (p130) Clubs and live-music venues fan out around Leidseplein.

➡ **Jordaan & the West** (p146) Venues for comedy, blues and cult films, plus the Westergasfabriek complex.

➡ **Vondelpark & the South** (p168) Home to the world-renowned Concertgebouw, free theatre in the park and squats-turned-culture-centres.

➡ **De Pijp** (p183) Great cinema, a smattering of jazz and buskers.

➡ **Oosterpark & East of the Amstel** (p193) Mega-venues and Amsterdam's beloved football team entertain here.

➡ **Amsterdam Noord** (p199) Live music plays regularly at venues like Café Noorderlicht and Pllek.

NEED TO KNOW

Opening Hours

➔ Entertainment in Amsterdam can range from afternoon matinees to three-day-long raves, so opening hours are as sporadic and diverse as the delights on offer. Check individual venues for full details.

Discounted Tickets

➔ The Last Minute Ticket Shop (www. lastminuteticketshop.nl) sells half-price seats on the day of performance. Available shows are announced daily on the website at 10am. Events are handily marked 'LNP' (language no problem) if understanding Dutch isn't vital. There's a maximum of two tickets per transaction.

Resources

I Amsterdam (www. iamsterdam.com) Events listings.

Film Ladder (www.film ladder.nl/amsterdam) Movie listings.

A-Mag Magazine covering the local scene, published every two months and available at the visitor centre, local newsagents and various hotels..

Lonely Planet's Top Choices

Melkweg (p131) A galaxy of diverse music, cinema and theatre in a former dairy.

Muziekgebouw aan 't IJ (p98) Acoustically and visually stunning performing-arts venue on the IJ.

Westergasfabriek (p145) Options abound in this post-industrial former-gasworks-turned-cultural-complex.

Paradiso (p131) One-time church that preaches a gospel of rock and roll.

Studio K (p193) Diverse venue in Oost.

Best Classical & Opera

Concertgebouw (p168) World-renowned concert hall with superb acoustics.

Conservatorium van Amsterdam (p99) Catch recitals by students at Amsterdam's snazzy conservatory of music.

Orgelpark (p169) Listen to organ music in a lovely restored church on the edge of the Vondelpark.

Best Jazz & Blues

Bimhuis (p98) The beating jazz heart of the Netherlands, inside the Muziekgebouw aan 't IJ.

Jazz Café Alto (p131) Excellent little club where you're practically on stage with the musicians.

Maloe Melo (p146) All sub-genres of blues get a run at this good-time venue.

Bourbon Street Jazz & Blues Club (p131) Jam sessions regularly take place here.

Best Rock

Pacific Parc (p146) Westergasfabriek venue with regular gigs and a rock-and-roll spirit.

De Nieuwe Anita (p146) Rock out by the stage behind the bookcase-concealed door.

Cave (p131) Basement venue hosting live hard rock and metal.

Best Cinemas

EYE Film Institute (p196) New, old, foreign, domestic: the Netherlands' uber-mod film centre shows quality films of all kinds.

Pathé Tuschinskitheater (p130) Amsterdam's most famous cinema, with a sumptuous art-deco/Amsterdam School interior.

Movies (p146) Amsterdam's oldest cinema dates from 1912.

Best Theatre & Comedy

Boom Chicago (p146) Laugh-out-loud improv-style comedy in the Jordaan.

Stadsschouwburg (p131) Large-scale plays, operettas and festivals right on Leidseplein.

Theater Amsterdam (p146) Gleaming glass theatre with a multilingual translation system.

Best Free or Cheap

Openluchttheater (p169) Open-air summertime performances in the Vondelpark.

Muziektheater (p99) Classical freebies fill the air Tuesdays at lunchtime.

Concertgebouw (p168) Wednesday's free lunchtime concerts are often rehearsals for the evening's big show.

Best For Kids

Amsterdams Marionetten Theater (p99) Fairytale stage sets and stringed puppets bring operas to life.

Kriterion (p99) Lots of films for kids.

Filmhallen (p169) New-release children's films and a retro caravan selling popcorn.

Shopping

During the Golden Age, Amsterdam was the world's warehouse, stuffed with riches from the far corners of the earth. The capital's cupboards are still stocked with all kinds of exotica (just look at that Red Light gear!), but the real pleasure here is finding some odd, tiny shop selling something you wouldn't find anywhere else.

Specialities

Dutch fashion Locals have mastered the art of casual style. The result is hip, practical designs – such as floaty, layered separates and tailored denim (that don't get caught in bike spokes).

Dutch-designed homewares Dutch designers have shown a singular knack for bringing a creative, stylish touch to everyday objects. Items are colourful and sensible, with vintage and humorous twists mixed in.

Antiques and art Stores selling gorgeous antiques pop up all around the city. The Spiegel Quarter offers a long line of shops along Spiegelgracht and Nieuwe Spiegelstraat.

Delftware The Dutch have been firing up the iconic blue-and-white pottery since the 1600s. A few shops in Amsterdam sell the real deal, but it's much more common (and affordable) to buy replica pottery.

Flower bulbs Exotic tulip bulbs and other flower seeds are popular gifts. Check customs regulations, since bringing bulbs into your home country can be prohibited.

Cheese Famed Dutch *kaas* (such as Gouda and Edam) makes a great economical souvenir. Again, check customs (and packaging) regulations.

Alcohol *Jenever* (Dutch gin) is a distinctive souvenir.

Bongs, pot-leaf-logoed T-shirts and sex toys This is Amsterdam after all, so it's no surprise that these items are legion in Red Light District shops.

Boutiques & Shopping Streets

Stumbling across offbeat little boutiques is one of the great joys of shopping in Amsterdam. A teeny store selling only antique eyeglass frames or juggling supplies or doll parts? They're here. The best areas for such finds are the nexus of the Western Canal Ring and Jordaan, along Haarlemmerstraat and Haarlemmerdijk, which are lined with hip boutiques and food shops. To the south the Negen Straatjes (Nine Streets) offers a satisfying browse among its pint-sized, one-of-a-kind shops. Staalstraat in Nieuwmarkt is another bountiful vein.

The busiest shopping streets are Kalverstraat by the Dam and Leidsestraat, which leads into Leidseplein. Both are lined with clothing and department stores.

Near Vondelpark, stylish fashion boutiques line Cornelis Schuytstraat and Willemsparkweg. Close by, PC Hooftstraat queues up Chanel, Diesel, Gucci and other luxury brands along its length.

Markets

No visit to Amsterdam is complete if you haven't experienced one of its lively outdoor markets.

Check dates for the food- and craft-oriented Sunday Market (p145), at various locations, and IJ Hallen (p199) flea market, in Amsterdam Noord.

NEED TO KNOW

Opening Hours

➡ Department stores and large shops: 9am or 10am to 6pm Monday to Saturday, noon to 6pm Sunday.

➡ Smaller shops: 10am or noon to 6pm Tuesday to Friday; 10am to 5pm Saturday (and Sunday if open at all); from noon or 1pm to 5pm or 6pm Monday (if open at all).

➡ Many shops stay open late (to 9pm) Thursday.

Taxes

➡ Non-EU residents are entitled to a tax refund on purchases over €50 if the store has the proper paperwork (request it when paying).

➡ At the airport, present your goods, receipts and passport, get your refund cheque stamped and take it to the Global Refund office. Allow ample time.

The website www.belastingdienst.nl has details.

Cash & Cards

A surprising number of stores do not accept credit cards. Conversely, some shops only accept Dutch PIN debit cards, not credit cards or cash (there will be a sign on the window or door).

Bargaining

For a nation of born traders, the Dutch don't haggle much – if only because most retailers aren't set up for it. Flea markets, art galleries and antique shops are among the few places where you can try.

Shopping App

The nifty app AMS NXT (www.amsterdam next.com) guides you from long-standing classics to hot new design stores and temporary pop-up concept stores.

DAILY MARKETS

Amsterdam's daily markets are open every day except Sunday.

➡ **Albert Cuypmarkt** (p176) Food, clothing and everything else.

➡ **Dappermarkt** (p187) Similar but smaller.

➡ **Waterlooplein Flea Market** (p100) Bric-a-brac galore.

➡ **Ten Katemarkt** (p171) Adjoins the cultural and design complex De Hallen, with fresh food, flowers and more.

➡ **Bloemenmarkt** (p119) Specialises in bulbs (and kitsch souvenirs); open *every* day.

➡ **Oudemanhuispoort Book Market** (p83) Old tomes, maps and sheet music.

WEEKLY MARKETS

➡ **Westermarkt** (p148) Clothing; held on Monday.

➡ **Noordermarkt** (p148) Flea-market wares; held on Monday.

➡ **Postzegelmarkt** (p84) Stamps and coins; held on Wednesdays and Saturdays.

➡ **Lindengracht Market** (p148) Food, arts, crafts and trinkets; held on Saturday.

➡ **Boerenmarkt** (p100) Farmers market in Nieuwmarkt and in the Jordaan; held on Saturday.

➡ **Antiques Market** (p100) Held on Sunday May to September.

➡ **Art Market** (p84) Held on Sunday March to December.

Shopping by Neighbourhood

➡ **Medieval Centre & Red Light District** (p82) From adult shops to bookshops and design emporiums.

➡ **Nieuwmarkt, Plantage & the Eastern Islands** (p99) Waterlooplein Flea Market is a key draw, along with eccentric local shops on Staalstraat.

➡ **Western Canal Ring** (p113) The Negen Straatjes hold the mother lode of teensy, quirky speciality shops.

➡ **Southern Canal Ring** (p132) Hunt for art and antiques in the Spiegel Quarter, and fashion, music and homewares nearby.

➡ **Jordaan & the West** (p147) Jordaan shops are artsy and eclectic; Haarlemmerdijk has the newest, coolest boutiques.

➡ **Vondelpark & the South** (p170) Stylish boutiques on Cornelis Schuytstraat and Willemsparkweg and ultra-luxe labels on PC Hooftstraat.

➡ **De Pijp** (p183) Beyond Albert Cuypmarkt are quirky shops, galleries, and vintage and designer fashion boutiques.

➡ **Oosterpark & East of the Amstel** (p193) Trawl the ethnically diverse Dappermarkt.

➡ **Amsterdam Noord** (p199) Vintage finds and cool homewares in industrial surrounds.

Lonely Planet's Top Choices

X Bank (p83) Stunning Dutch design showcase.

Pied à Terre (p170) Europe's largest travel bookshop will make anyone's feet itch.

Condomerie Het Gulden Vlies (p84) Fun setting with a wild array of condoms for sale.

De Kaaskamer (p114) This 'cheese room' is stacked to the rafters with goodness.

PGC Hajenius (p83) Gilded, art-deco tobacco emporium where the royal family has its humidor.

Neef Louis Design (p199) Vintage and designer finds in a warehouse setting.

Best Markets

Albert Cuypmarkt (p176) Vibrant street market spilling over with food, fashion and bargain finds.

Waterlooplein Flea Market (p100) Piles of curios for treasure hunters.

Westermarkt (p148) Bargain-priced clothing and fabrics at scores of stalls.

Lindengracht Market (p148) Wonderfully authentic local affair, with bushels of fresh produce.

IJ Hallen (p199) Enormous monthly flea market at NDSM-werf.

Dappermarkt (p187) Multi-ethnic food, clothing and homewares.

Best Books

Mendo (p115) Sleek bookshop specialising in art, design, architecture, fashion and photography.

Oudemanhuispoort Book Market (p83) Covered alleyway lined with second-hand book stalls.

American Book Center (p84) English-language books of all kinds sprawl across three floors.

Best Fashion

Young Designers United (p132) Tomorrow's big names jam the racks here.

By AMFI (p83) Students and alumni of the Amsterdam Fashion Institute sell their wares.

Amatør (p114) Local Amsterdam label.

VLVT (p171) Up-and-coming Dutch-designed women's fashion on chic Cornelis Schuytstraat.

Good Genes (p183) De Pijp–designed jeans.

Best Souvenirs

Bloemenmarkt (p119) Bulbs, bulbs and more bulbs fill Amsterdam's 'floating' flower market.

Galleria d'Arte Rinascimento (p148) Royal Delftware ceramics (both antique and new).

Mark Raven Grafiek (p83) Artsy, beyond-the-norm T-shirts and prints of the city.

Museum Shop at the Museumplein (p171) The one-stop shop for all your Rembrandt, Vermeer and Van Gogh items.

Best Dutch Design

Droog (p99) The famed collective is known for sly, playful, repurposed and reinvented homewares.

Frozen Fountain (p114) Amsterdam's best-known showcase of Dutch-designed furniture and homewares.

Local Goods Store (p170) Inspired fashion and homewares by Dutch designers inside cultural complex De Hallen.

Hutspot (p183) Funky store giving emerging designers an opportunity to sell their work.

Mobilia (p133) Dutch design is stunningly showcased at this three-storey 'lifestyle studio'.

X Bank (p83) Dazzling, monthly-changing displays.

Best Food & Drink

Hart's Wijnhandel (p133) Historic shop selling tipples, including *jenever*.

Het Oud-Hollandsch Snoepwinkeltje (p147) All kinds of Dutch candies, including sweet and salty *drop* (Dutch liquorice).

Papabubble (p147) Sweet, sugary, made-in-front-of-you creations.

Beer Baum (p170) Craft beers from over 25 different countries.

't Kaasboertje (p184) Cheeses galore.

Best Antiques & Vintage

Antiekcentrum Amsterdam (p148) Quirky indoor mall with stalls offering anything from 1940s dresses to 1970s Swedish porn.

Marbles Vintage (p100) Awesome selection of classic skirts, dresses and coats.

Gastronomie Nolstalgie (p83) Beautiful old china, goblets, candlesticks and other tableware from far-flung auctions.

360 Volt (p114) Reconditioned industrial light fittings.

Explore Amsterdam

AMSTERDAM'S
TOP SIGHTS

Neighbourhoods at a Glance

❶ Medieval Centre & Red Light District p64

Amsterdam's oldest quarter is remarkably preserved, looking much as it did in its Golden Age heyday. It's the busiest part of town for visitors. While some come to see the Royal Palace and Oude Kerk, others make a beeline for the coffeeshops and Red Light District.

❷ Nieuwmarkt, Plantage & the Eastern Islands p85

Buzzing Nieuwmarkt is sewn through with rich seams of history. Alongside, leafy Plantage takes it down a gear, with the sprawling zoo and botanical gardens. It segues into the Eastern Islands, with a completely different atmosphere involving ex-warehouses turned funkfest bars, and flagship modern Dutch architecture.

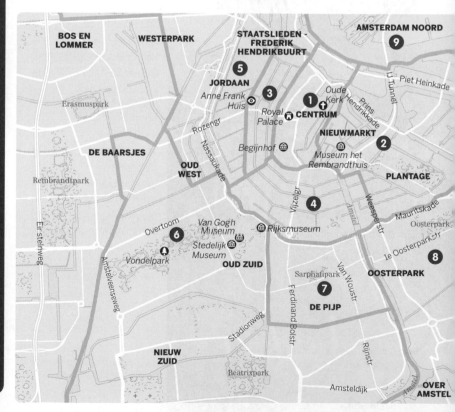

❸ Western Canal Ring p102

Grand old mansions and tiny, charming speciality shops line the glinting waterways of the Western Canal Ring, one of Amsterdam's most gorgeous areas. Roaming around them can cause days to vanish. But most people come here for a singular reason: to visit Anne Frank's house and see her famous diary.

❹ Southern Canal Ring p116

The Southern Canal Ring is a horseshoe-shaped loop of parallel canals. It's home to the nightlife hubs of Leidseplein (p118) and Rembrandtplein (p121), with bars, clubs and restaurants clustered around large squares. Between these two districts, the canals are lined by some of the city's most elegant houses; the area also encompasses many fine museums, a flower market and waterside restaurants and bars.

❺ Jordaan & the West p134

The Jordaan teems with cosy pubs, galleries and markets crammed into a grid of tiny lanes. It's short on conventional sights, but it's a wonderfully atmospheric place for an aimless stroll. It abuts the West, industrial badlands that have transformed into an avant-garde cultural hub.

❻ Vondelpark & the South p149

Vondelpark has a special place in Amsterdam's heart, a lush green egalitarian space where everyone hangs out at some point. Close to the park, the wealth-laden Old South holds the Van Gogh, Stedelijk and Rijksmuseum collections. Head further south still, and there's the lush Amsterdamse Bos (Amsterdam Forest) and the Cobra Museum.

❼ De Pijp p173

A hotbed of creativity, village-like De Pijp is home to a diverse mix of labourers, immigrants, intellectuals, prostitutes and young urbanites. Marvel at the scene at Amsterdam's largest street market, the colourful Albert Cuypmarkt, and the outstanding eateries and free-spirited *cafés* (pubs) that surround it.

❽ Oosterpark & East of the Amstel p185

Oost (East) is one of Amsterdam's most culturally diverse neighbourhoods. It's an area that grew up in the 19th century, with grand buildings and wide boulevards. The large English-style Oosterpark was laid out in 1861, while lush Flevopark, further east, dates from when this area was a country retreat. Beyond this is Amsterdam's newest neighbourhood, the IJburg, built across several islands, with the city beach.

❾ Amsterdam Noord p194

Amsterdam Noord encompasses fields, horses and the odd windmill, minutes away from ex-industrial areas, cutting-edge architecture, and hangars turned hipster hangouts whose walls burst with street art. Long neglected, the area has been reinvented as the city's hippest neighbourhood, where it's great to roam around by bike, and to eat and drink in its out-there venues.

Medieval Centre & Red Light District

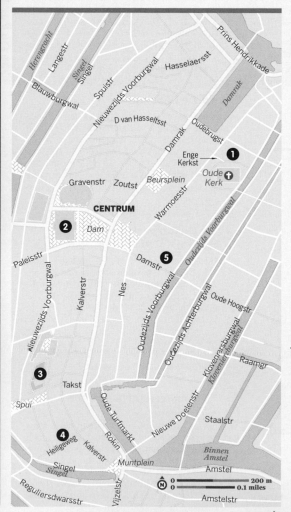

Neighbourhood Top Five

1 **Prostitution Information Centre Red Light District Tour** (p269) Getting a behind-the-scenes look at the infamous Red Light District and the 'world's oldest profession' on an illuminating guided tour.

2 **Royal Palace** (p66) Marvelling at the chandeliered opulence and taking a Dutch history lesson at the city's landmark palace.

3 **Begijnhof** (p67) Pushing open the door and discovering this tranquil courtyard's hidden gardens and churches.

4 **Vleminckx** (p73) Biting into crisp golden *frites* (fries) slathered in mayonnaise, curry or peanut sauce from Amsterdam's best *frites* stand.

5 **Wynand Fockink** (p79) Bowling up to this 17th-century tasting house to knock back a *jenever* (Dutch gin) or taking a pre-booked weekend tour.

For more detail of this area see Map p290 and p294 ➡

Explore Medieval Centre & Red Light District

Amsterdam's heart beats in its medieval core and centuries-old Red Light District. All visitors end up here at some point. Centraal Station (p70) is the main landmark; Damrak slices south from the station to the Dam – Amsterdam's central square and home to the Royal Palace.

There are several intriguing sights, but the big-ticket museums lie elsewhere. The main thing to do here is wander. The compact area is laced with atmospheric lanes, and 17th-century tasting rooms, *bruin cafés* (pubs), hidden courtyards and tiny speciality shops are the prizes for those who venture off the main drags.

While the infamous Red Light District can get rowdy at night, it has some beautiful historic bars, as well as the stunning Oude Kerk (p68), the city's oldest church.

The area's layout has changed little since the 17th century and certain vistas look like they belong in a Golden Age landscape. You could easily spend your entire trip here, so remember: there are more neighbourhoods beyond.

Local Life

➡**Bikes** The four-storey bike-parking station to the west of Centraal Station, jam-packed with 2500-plus bikes, demonstrates how integral cycling is to Amsterdam life. Plans are now under way to create a 4000-capacity bike station beneath the IJ.

➡**Beers & books** Inviting *cafés* and bookshops ring the Spui (p69), a favoured haunt of academics and journalists.

➡**Dam** A fair, a protest, a speech by the monarch – there's always something drawing people to Amsterdam's main square (p69).

Getting There & Away

➡**Tram** The majority of the city's 15 tram lines go through the neighbourhood en route to Centraal Station. Useful lines include trams 1, 2, 5, 13 and 17, which travel to the station's west side, and trams 4, 9, 16 and 24, which travel to the east side.

➡**Metro** Metros travel from Centraal to Amsterdam's outer neighbourhoods and, as of mid-2018, to Amsterdam Noord and Station Zuid, with a stop in the Medieval Centre at Rokin.

➡**Boat** Free ferries run to NDSM-werf and elsewhere in Amsterdam Noord, departing from the piers (Map p250, De Ruijterkade) behind Centraal Station.

Lonely Planet's Top Tip

If you're searching for somewhere to drink and/or dine around Centraal Station, you'll find some of the best-quality, least-crowded options on the revitalised northern side alongside the IJ near the docks for the free ferries to Amsterdam Noord.

MEDIEVAL CENTRE & RED LIGHT DISTRICT

✗ Best Places to Eat

➡ Lt Cornelis (p75)
➡ D'Vijff Vlieghen (p76)
➡ Vleminckx (p73)
➡ Firma Stroop (p73)
➡ Gartine (p73)

For reviews, see p73 ➡

☕ Best Places to Drink

➡ In 't Aepjen (p80)
➡ Cut Throat (p78)
➡ Wynand Fockink (p79)
➡ Tales & Spirits (p78)
➡ Proeflokaal de Ooievaar (p79)

For reviews, see p78 ➡

🔒 Best Places to Shop

➡ X Bank (p83)
➡ Locals (p83)
➡ Mark Raven Grafiek (p83)
➡ Condomerie Het Gulden Vlies (p84)
➡ Oudemanhuispoort Book Market (p83)
➡ Hempstory (p84)

For reviews, see p82 ➡

TOP SIGHT
ROYAL PALACE (KONINKLIJK PALEIS)

Today's Royal Palace began life as a glorified town hall and was completed in 1665. Its architect, Jacob van Campen, spared no expense to display Amsterdam's wealth in a way that rivalled the grandest European buildings of the day. The result is opulence on a big scale. It's worth seeing the exterior at night, when the palace is dramatically floodlit.

Officially the Dutch king, King Willem-Alexander, lives in this landmark palace and pays a symbolic rent, though his actual residence is in Den Haag. If he's not here in Amsterdam, visitors have the opportunity to come in and wander around the monumental building.

Most of the rooms spread over the 1st floor, which is awash in chandeliers (51 shiners in total), along with damasks, gilded clocks, and some spectacular paintings by artists including Ferdinand Bol and Jacob de Wit.

The great *burgerzaal* (citizens' hall) that occupies the heart of the building was envisioned as a schematic of the world, with Amsterdam as its centre. Check out the maps inlaid in the floor; they show the eastern and western hemispheres, with a 1654 celestial map in the middle.

In 1808 the building became the palace of King Louis, Napoleon Bonaparte's brother. In a classic slip-up in the new lingo, French-born Louis told his subjects here that he was the 'rabbit' (*konijn*) of Holland, when he actually meant 'king' (*koning*, which had the old spelling variation *konink*). Napoleon dismissed him two years later.

Louis left behind about 1000 pieces of Empire-style furniture and decorative artworks. As a result, the palace now holds one of the world's largest collections from the period.

DON'T MISS

➡ Chandeliers (all 51 of them)
➡ The *burgerzaal*
➡ Paintings by Ferdinand Bol and Jacob de Wit
➡ Empire-style decor

PRACTICALITIES

➡ Koninklijk Paleis
➡ Map p294, C1
➡ 020-522 61 61
➡ www.paleis amsterdam.nl
➡ Dam
➡ adult/child €10/free
➡ 10am-5pm
➡ 4/9/16/24 Dam

TOP SIGHT
BEGIJNHOF

It feels like something out of a story book. You walk up to the unassuming door, push it open and voila – a hidden courtyard of tiny houses and gardens opens up before you. The 14th-century Begijnhof is not a secret these days, but somehow it remains a surreal oasis of peace in the city's midst.

The Beguines were a Catholic order of unmarried or widowed women who lived a religious life without taking monastic vows. The Begijnhof was their convent of sorts. The last true Beguine died in 1971.

One of two churches hidden in the *hof* (courtyard), the 1671 **Begijnhof Kapel** (☺1-6.30pm Mon, 9am-6.30pm Tue-Fri, 9am-6pm Sat & Sun) is a 'clandestine' chapel where the Beguines were forced to worship after the Calvinists took away their Gothic church. Go through the dog-leg entrance to find marble columns, stained-glass windows and murals commemorating the Miracle of Amsterdam. (In short: In 1345 the final sacrament was administered to a dying man, but he was unable to keep down the communion wafer and brought it back up. Here's the miracle part: when the vomit was thrown on the fire, the wafer would not burn. Yes, it's all depicted in wall paintings.)

The other church is known as the **Engelse Kerk** (English Church; www.ercadam.nl; ☺9am-5pm), built around 1392. It was eventually rented out to the local community of English and Scottish Presbyterian refugees – including the Pilgrim Fathers – and it still serves as the city's Presbyterian church. Look for pulpit panels by Piet Mondrian, in a figurative phase. Note that as this church is still in frequent use, it's sometimes closed to visitors.

Look out, too, for the **Houten Huis** (Wooden House) at No 34. It dates from around 1425, making it the oldest preserved wooden house in the Netherlands.

DON'T MISS
➡ Begijnhof Kapel
➡ Engelse Kerk
➡ Houten Huis
➡ Miracle of Amsterdam paintings

PRACTICALITIES
➡ Map p294, B5
➡ www.nicolaas-parochie.nl
➡ admission free
➡ ☺9am-5pm
➡ 🚊1/2/5 Spui

TOP SIGHT
OUDE KERK (OLD CHURCH)

Amsterdam's oldest building, the Oude Kerk dates to around 1306. Originally Catholic and now Protestant, the Gothic-style structure holds the city's oldest church bell (1450), a stunning Vater-Müller organ (1726/1742) and 15th-century choir stalls with surprisingly naughty carvings.

Many famous Amsterdammers are buried under the worn tombstones set in the floor, including Rembrandt's wife, Saskia van Uylenburgh. Each year on 9 March at 8.39am, a beam of light touches her grave and special events take place. Other notable graves are those of diamond dealer Killiaen van Rensselaer, naval hero Jacob van Heemskerck, organist Jan Pieterszoon Sweelinck, and the family tomb of Cornelis de Graeff. Some 10,000 citizens in all lie beneath the church. Ask for a map when you enter.

Art exhibitions regularly take place here, along with concerts and services featuring the church's four organs. As well as the Vater-Müller organ, the Oude Kerk has a 1965 transept organ, an Italian organ and a cabinet organ, all of which can be heard during concerts and church services.

Those who don't mind climbing narrow stairs can go on a half-hour guided tour of the 67m-high **tower** (www.westertorenamsterdam.nl; tour €8; ⊙1-7pm Mon-Sat Apr-Oct) for a sweeping view of the low-rise city's gabled rooflines. Tower tours depart every half-hour.

Fresh from extensive renovation works, the church is incongruously situated in full view of the Red Light District, with passers-by getting chatted up by ladies in windows a stone's throw from the holy walls. Outside on Oudekerksplein is the **statue of Belle**, erected in 2007 as a nod to sex-industry workers worldwide. The cobblestones nearby (by the church's main entrance) contain another bold statement: a **golden torso** of a naked woman held by a padlocked hand. The torso mysteriously appeared one day, was removed by police and then put back as most people seemed to like it.

DON'T MISS

➡ Floor tombstones, including Rembrandt's wife Saskia

➡ Choir-stall carvings

➡ Golden torso

➡ Surrounding Red Light ambience

➡ Tower tour

PRACTICALITIES

➡ Old Church

➡ Map p290, E7

➡ 020-625 82 84

➡ www.oudekerk.nl

➡ adult/child €10/free

➡ ⊙10am-6pm Mon-Sat, 1-5:30pm Sun

➡ 4/9/16/24 Dam

⊙ SIGHTS

⊙ Medieval Centre

ROYAL PALACE
PALACE

See p66.

DAM
SQUARE

Map p294 (🚋4/9/16/24 Dam) This square is the very spot where Amsterdam was founded around 1270. Today pigeons, tourists, buskers and the occasional funfair complete with Ferris wheel take over the grounds. It's still a national gathering spot, and if there's a major speech or demonstration it's held here.

Long before it hosted fun and games, the square was split into two sections: Vissersdam, a fish market where the Bijenkorf department store (p83) now stands, and Vijgendam, probably named for the figs and other exotic fruits unloaded from ships. Various markets and events have been held here through the ages, including executions – you can still see holes on the front of the Royal Palace where the wooden gallows were affixed.

NATIONAAL MONUMENT
MONUMENT

Map p294 (Dam; 🚋4/9/16/24 Dam) The obelisk on the Dam's eastern side was built in 1956 to commemorate WWII's fallen. Fronted by two lions, its pedestal has a number of symbolic statues: four males (war), a woman with child (peace) and men with dogs (resistance). The 12 urns at the rear hold earth from war cemeteries of the 11 provinces and the Dutch East Indies. The war dead are still honoured here at a ceremony every 4 May.

MADAME TUSSAUDS AMSTERDAM
MUSEUM

Map p294 (www.madametussauds.com/amsterdam; Dam 20; adult/child €23.50/19.50; ⊙9am-10pm Jul & Aug, 10am-10pm Sep-Jun; 🚋4/9/16/24 Dam) Sure, Madame Tussauds wax museum is overpriced and cheesy, but its focus on local culture makes it fun: 'meet' the Dutch royals, politicians, painters and pop stars, along with global celebs (Justin Bieber et al). Kids love it. Buying tickets online will save you a few euros and get you into the fast-track queue. Prepurchasing tickets online for earlier than 11.30am and after 6pm nets further discounts. Hours can vary; check the calendar online.

BEURS VAN BERLAGE
HISTORIC BUILDING

Map p290 (☎020-530 41 41; www.beursvan berlage.com; Damrak 243; tour €14.50; ⊙tours by reservation; 🚋4/9/16/24 Dam) Master architect and ardent socialist HP Berlage (1856–1934) built Amsterdam's financial exchange in 1903. He filled the temple of capitalism with decorations that venerate labour – look inside the **cafe** (⊙10am-6pm Mon-Sat, 11am-6pm Sun) to see tile murals of the well-muscled proletariat of the past, present and future. Within two decades trading had outgrown the building and relocated. The building now hosts conferences and art exhibitions. Tours lasting one hour detail its history and take you up into the bell tower for panoramic views.

SEXMUSEUM AMSTERDAM
MUSEUM

Map p290 (www.sexmuseumamsterdam.nl; Damrak 18; €5; ⊙9.30am-11.30pm; 🚋1/2/4/5/9/13/16/17/24 Centraal Station) The Sexmuseum is good for a giggle. You'll find replicas of pornographic Pompeian plates, erotic 14th-century Viennese bronzes, some of the world's earliest nude photographs, an automated farting flasher in a trench coat, and a music box that plays 'Edelweiss' and purports to show a couple in flagrante delicto. It's sillier and more fun than other erotic museums in the Red Light District. Minimum age for entry is 16.

PAPEGAAI
CHURCH

Map p294 (www.nicolaas-parochie.nl; Kalverstraat 58; ⊙10am-4pm; 🚋4/9/16/24 Dam) An unexpected oasis in the sea of consumerism on Kalverstraat, the curious Petrus en Pauluskerk, aka Papegaai, is a Catholic church from the 17th century that was a clandestine house of worship. Note the *papegaai* (parrot) over the door that gave the church its name. The slogan you'll see upon entering: '15 minutes for God'.

BEGIJNHOF
COURTYARD

See p67.

SPUI
SQUARE

Map p294 (🚋1/2/5 Spui) Inviting *cafés* (pubs) and brainy bookshops ring the Spui, a favoured haunt of academics, students and journalists. On Friday (weather permitting) a small book market sets up on the square; on Sunday it's an art market (p84). And just so you know, it's pronounced 'spow' (rhymes with 'now').

CENTRAAL STATION
NOTABLE BUILDING

Map p290 (Stationsplein; 🚊1/2/4/5/9/13/16/17/24 Centraal Station) Beyond being a transport hub, Centraal Station is a sight in itself. The turreted marvel dates from 1889. One of the architects, PJ Cuypers, also designed the Rijksmuseum (p151), and you can see the similarities in the faux-Gothic towers, the fine red brick and the abundant reliefs (for sailing, trade and industry).

Built on an artificial island, the station was designed as a neo-Renaissance 'curtain', a controversial plan that effectively cut off Amsterdam from the IJ river. The garage in the right-hand wing was built to shelter the Dutch royal carriage, but it's rarely there (read: never). The area around the station always has loads of construction going on.

ST NICOLAASKERK
CHURCH

Map p290 (www.nicolaas-parochie.nl; Prins Hendrikkade 73; ⊙11am-4pm; 🚊1/2/4/5/9/13/16/17/24 Centraal Station) In plain view from Centraal Station, the magnificent cupola and neo-Renaissance towers belong to the city's main Catholic church, the first to be built (between 1884 and 1887) after Catholic worship became legal again in the 19th century. As St Nicholas is the patron saint of seafarers, the church became an important symbol for Amsterdam.

The interior is notable for its high altar, the theatrical crown of Emperor Maximilian I and depictions of the Stations of the Cross, on which tireless painter Jan Dunselman laboured for 40 years.

SCHREIERSTOREN
HISTORIC BUILDING

Map p290 (www.schreierstoren.nl; Prins Hendrikkade 95; 🚊1/2/4/5/9/13/16/17/24 Centraal Station) Built around 1480 as part of the city's defences, this tower is where Henry Hudson set sail for the New World in 1609; a plaque outside marks the spot. It's called the 'weeping tower' in lore – as it was where women waved farewell to sailors' ships – but the name actually comes from the word 'sharp' (for the way the corner jutted into the bay). Step into the **VOC Café** (🅙020-428 82 91; ⊙10am-1am Sun-Thu, to 2.30am Fri & Sat) to see inside the tower.

TOP SIGHT
AMSTERDAM MUSEUM

Amsterdam's history museum is a spiffy place to learn about what makes the city tick. Start with the multimedia DNA exhibit, which breaks down Amsterdam's 1000-year history across entrepreneurship, free thinking, citizenship and creativity into seven whiz-bang time periods. At the Revolt Against the King and Church display, you can even 'dress' as a civic guard (ruffled collar!) and have a photo taken; it goes to the museum's Flickr page.

Afterwards, plunge into the maze-like lower floors to see troves of religious artefacts, porcelains and paintings. There are also displays on the world wars and the spread of bicycle use, and a re-creation of the original Café 't Mandje, a touchstone in the gay-rights movement.

The museum building used to be Amsterdam's civic orphanage. While you're in the courtyard, note the cupboards (now filled with art) in which the orphans stored their possessions. An exhibition specifically for children covers 17th-century orphanage life, with displays of dormitories, classrooms, bathrooms and kitchens.

Grand Golden Age paintings line the free **Civic Guard Gallery** (⊙10am-5pm) **FREE** in the arcade next door.

DON'T MISS

➔ Café 't Mandje re-creation

➔ Civic Guard Gallery paintings

➔ Orphans' cupboards

PRACTICALITIES

➔ Map p294, B4

➔ 🅙020-523 18 22

➔ www.amsterdam museum.nl

➔ Gedempte Begijnensloot

➔ adult/child €12.50/6.50

➔ ⊙10am-5pm

➔ 🚊1/2/5 Spui

RONDE LUTHERSE
KERK NOTABLE BUILDING
Map p290 (Round Lutheran Church; ☑020-6212
23; www.koepelkerk.com; Singel 11; ⊘by appointment; ☒1/2/5/13/17 Nieuwezijds Kolk) Built
between 1668 and 1671, this domed church
has the curious distinction of being the
only round Protestant church in the country. Falling attendance forced its closure in
1936. Although it's not open to the public
(other than for conferences, trade fairs and
events), it's connected by a tunnel to the
neighbouring Amsterdam Renaissance
Hotel, which you can contact about visiting
if it's not in use.

Ironically, the old church on the Spui,
which the Ronde Lutherse Kerk was
designed to replace, is still in use.

ALLARD PIERSON MUSEUM MUSEUM
Map p294 (www.allardpiersonmuseum.nl; Oude
Turfmarkt 127; adult/child €10/5; ⊘10am-5pm
Tue-Fri, 1-5pm Sat & Sun; ☒4/9/14/16/24
Spui/Rokin) Run by the University of
Amsterdam, this museum contains a rich
archaeological collection made acces-
sible by its manageable scale. You'll find
an actual mummy, vases from ancient
Greece and Mesopotamia, a very cool
wagon from the royal tombs at Salamis
(Cyprus), and galleries full of other items
providing insight into daily life in ancient
times. There are detailed descriptions in
Dutch and English.

TORTURE MUSEUM MUSEUM
Map p294 (www.torturemuseum.nl; Singel 449;
adult/child €7.50/4; ⊘10am-11pm; ☒1/2/5
Koningsplein) It's dilapidated and so dimly
lit inside that you can barely read the
placards, but fans of kitsch and oddball
lore will enjoy learning about devices like
the Flute of Shame for bad musicians (the
finger screws tighten), the Neck Violin for
quarrelling women (a shackle locked the
two face to face), branding tongs, skull
crackers, a guillotine and the Iron Maiden
of Nuremberg (use your imagination).

◉ Red Light District

OUDE KERK CHURCH
See p68.

RED LIGHT DISTRICT
FACTS & FIGURES
••
➡ Year prostitution officially legalised
in the Netherlands: 2000
➡ Number of people working as
prostitutes in Amsterdam: approximately 6000, though estimates range
between 5000 and 8000
➡ Minimum legal age to work as a
prostitute in the Netherlands: 21

PROSTITUTION
INFORMATION CENTRE LIBRARY
Map p290 (PIC; ☑020-420 73 28; www.pic-ams
terdam.com; Enge Kerksteeg 3; ⊘noon-5pm
Wed-Fri, to 7pm Sat; ☒4/9/16/24 Dam) Established by a former prostitute, the PIC
provides frank information about the
industry to sex workers, their customers
and curious tourists. It has a small on-
site shop selling enlightening reading
material and souvenirs, and it runs eye-
opening walking tours (p269).

TROMPETTERSTEEG STREET
Map p290 (☒4/9/16/24 Dam) An intriguing place to view the Red Light action
is Trompettersteeg, a teeny alley where
the women in the windows charge some
of the highest prices. Claustrophobes,
beware: it's only 1m wide and always
busy. Look for the entrance in the block
south of the Oude Kerk.

KUAN YIN SHRINE BUDDHIST TEMPLE
Map p290 (Fo Guang Shan He Hua Temple;
www.ibps.nl; Zeedijk 106-118; ⊘noon-5pm
Tue-Sat, 10am-5pm Sun; Ⓜ Nieuwmarkt)
Europe's largest Chinese Imperial–style
Buddhist temple, built in 2000, is dedicated to Kuan Yin, the Buddhist goddess
of mercy. Enter through the side gates
(as is customary; the main gates are
reserved for monks and nuns), make a
donation, light an incense stick and ponder the thousand eyes and hands of the
bodhisattva statue.

The ornate 'mountain gate' – an intriguing concept in the narrow confines of the
Zeedijk – refers to the traditional setting
of Buddhist monasteries. The middle section not back from the street was designed
along principles of feng shui.

CANNABIS COLLEGE CULTURAL CENTRE
Map p294 (☑020-423 44 20; www.cannabis
college.com; Oudezijds Achterburgwal 124;
☺11am-7pm; 🛜; 🚊4/9/16/24 Dam) This non-
profit centre offers visitors tips and tricks
for having a positive smoking experience
and provides the low-down on local cannabis laws. There are educational displays
and a library. Staff can provide maps and
advice on where to find coffeeshops that
sell organic weed and shops that are good
for newbies. T-shirts, stickers, postcards
and a few other trinkets with the logo are
for sale too.

**HASH, MARIJUANA
& HEMP MUSEUM** MUSEUM
Map p294 (☑020-624 89 26; www.hash
museum.com; Oudezijds Achterburgwal 148;
€9; ☺10am-10pm; 🚊4/9/16/24 Dam) Simple exhibits here cover dope botany and
the relationship between cannabis and
religion. Highlights include an impressive pipe collection, an interactive
vaporiser and a kiosk where you can create an e-postcard of yourself in a marijuana field. Admission also includes the
Hemp Gallery, filled with hemp art and

historical items, in a separate building
30m north.

The Sensi Seeds company (conveniently
attached to the museum) owns the whole
thing, so it's no surprise you get to peek
at a roomful of growing plants as part of
the deal.

RED LIGHT SECRETS MUSEUM
Map p290 (Museum of Prostitution; ☑020-846
70 20; www.redlightsecrets.com; Oudezijds
Achterburgwal 60h; €10; ☺11am-midnight;
🚊4/9/16/24 Dam) Inside a former brothel
in a 17th-century canal house, this
museum fills a gap by showing curious
visitors what a Red Light room looks like
and answering basic questions about the
industry. There's a short film as well as
photo opportunities aplenty (ahem, dominatrix room). The venue takes less than
an hour to tour. Tickets are €2 cheaper
online.

BROUWERIJ DE PRAEL BREWERY
Map p290 (☑020-408 44 70; www.deprael.nl;
Oudezijds Voorburgwal 30; tour with 1/4 beers
€8.50/17.50; ☺tours hourly 1-6pm Mon-Fri,
1-5pm Sat, 2-5pm Sun; 🚊1/2/4/5/9/13/16/17/24

⊙ TOP SIGHT
NIEUWE KERK

Don't let the 'New Church' name fool you – the structure dates from 1408 (though it is a good century
fresher than its neighbour, the Oude Kerk). Located
right on the Dam, this basilica is the historic stage for
royal weddings and the investiture of Dutch monarchs.
The stained glass over the main entrance recalls Queen
Wilhelmina, who ascended the throne in 1898, aged 18.
Most recently, the investiture of King Willem-Alexander
took place here in 2013. Other than for such ceremo-
nies, the building no longer functions as a church but
rather a hall for multimedia exhibitions and organ
concerts.

The interior is plain, but several key furnishings – the
magnificent oak chancel, the bronze choir screen and
the massive gilded organ (1645) – justify a look. Naval
hero Admiral Michiel de Ruyter and poets Joost van den
Vondel and Pieter Corneliszoon Hooft are among the
luminaries buried here.

It's possible to walk in and take a free peek, but you'll
have to pay the admission fee to get up close. Pick up a
'welcome' brochure, which maps out the highlights, at
the entrance. Opening times and admission fees can
vary depending on what's going on.

DON'T MISS

➡ Window for Queen
Wilhelmina's inaugu-
ration

➡ Main organ

➡ Monuments to
de Ruyter, Van den
Vondel and Hooft

➡ Oak chancel

PRACTICALITIES

➡ New Church

➡ Map p290, B7

➡ ☑638 69 09

➡ www.nieuwekerk.nl

➡ Dam

➡ admission €8-16

➡ ☺10am-6pm

➡ 🚊1/2/5/13/14/17
Dam

Centraal Station) Brouwerij De Prael offers engaging behind-the-scenes tours of its brewery. Tours depart on the hour and last 40 minutes, followed by a sample (or four). The tasting room (p80) is a great place to try more of its wares. De Prael also makes liqueurs that you can buy at the brewery's attached shop.

W139 GALLERY
Map p290 (www.w139.nl; Warmoesstraat 139; ⊙noon-6pm; 🚊4/9/16/24 Dam) `FREE` Duck into this contemporary arts centre and ponder the multimedia exhibits, which often have an edgy political angle. Check the website for frequent artist talks.

✖️ EATING

Snack stands and cafes abound for quick, inexpensive dishes, and numerous pubs serve food. Amsterdam's small Chinatown, with pan-Asian restaurants, centres on Zeedijk. Throughout the neighbourhood, however, an increasing number of places offering refined, often highly creative dining are flourishing.

✖️ Medieval Centre

★VLEMINCKX FAST FOOD €
Map p294 (http://vleminckxdesausmeester.nl; Voetboogstraat 33; fries €3-5, sauces €0.70; ⊙noon-7pm Sun & Mon, 11am-7pm Tue, Wed, Fri & Sat, to 8pm Thu; 🚊1/2/5 Koningsplein) Frying up *frites* (fries) since 1887, Amsterdam's best *friterie* has been based at this hole-in-the-wall takeaway shack near the Spui since 1957. The standard order of perfectly cooked crispy, fluffy *frites* is smothered in mayonnaise, though its 28 sauces also include apple, green pepper, ketchup, peanut, sambal and mustard. Queues almost always stretch down the block, but they move fast.

★DE LAATSTE KRUIMEL CAFE, BAKERY €
Map p294 (📞020-423 04 99; www.delaatste kruimel.nl; Langebrugsteeg 4; dishes €3-8; ⊙8am-8pm Mon-Sat, 9am-8pm Sun; 🚊4/9/14/16/24 Spui) Decorated with vintage finds from the Noordermarkt and wooden pallets upcycled as furniture, and opening to a tiny canal-side terrace, the 'Last Crumb' has glass display cases piled

high with pies, quiches, breads, cakes and lemon-and-poppy-seed scones. Grandmothers, children, couples on dates and just about everyone else crowds in for sweet treats and fantastic organic sandwiches.

★GARTINE CAFE €
Map p294 (📞020-320 41 32; www.gartine.nl; Taksteeg 7; dishes €6-12, high tea €17-25; ⊙10am-6pm Wed-Sat; 🍴; 🚊4/9/14/16/24 Spui/Rokin) 🌱 Gartine is magical, from its covert location in an alley off busy Kalverstraat to its mismatched antique tableware and its sublime breakfast pastries, sandwiches and salads (made from produce grown in its garden plot and eggs from its chickens). The sweet-and-savoury high tea, from 2pm to 5pm, is a treat.

★FIRMA STROOP BAKERY €
Map p290 (Molsteeg 11; dishes €3-5; ⊙10am-6pm; 🚊1/2/5/13/14/17 Dam) A working cash register from 1904 stands on the counter of this *stroopwafel* specialist. Along with classic caramel-filled, wafer-thin waffles, it bakes various other twists on this quintessential Dutch treat, such as chocolate-dipped *stroopwafels* with hazelnuts, and *stroopwafels* covered in coconut flakes or icing made from fresh strawberries. There's no on-site seating, but you'll find plenty of canal-side benches nearby.

AARDBEI AMSTERDAM CAFE €

Map p290 (www.aardbeiamsterdam.nl; Spuistraat 106; dishes €2-9; ◷8.30am-6pm Tue-Fri, 10am-8pm Sat, 10am-6pm Sun; ◲; ▣1/2/5/13/14/17 Dam/Raadhuisstraat) *Aardbei* is Dutch for 'strawberry', which is the star of every dish at this light, bright crowd-funded cafe. Strawberries come in cups or waffle cones or on sticks (plain or choc-dipped), as well as in smoothies, frozen yoghurt, jams, cakes, pies, tarts, muffins and popcorn. Items to take home range from strawberry wine and Prosecco to strawberry-printed socks.

CRÊPERIE BRETONNE COCOTTE CRÊPES €

Map p290 (Spuistraat 127; crêpes €6-8, galettes €8-13; ◷9am-9pm Sun-Thu, to 10pm Fri & Sat; ▣1/2/5/13/14/17 Dam) Savoury *galettes* (made with organic, gluten-free buckwheat flour from Brittany's oldest mill) come with scrumptious fillings such as Breton sardines and sautéed sliced apples, or an Amsterdam version with smoked herring, potatoes and crème fraîche. Sweet crêpes include salted caramel with almonds. Inside a charming gabled canal house, the split-level space has soaring brick walls, recycled timbers and mezzanine seating.

BURGERIJ BURGERS €

Map p290 (www.burgerij.nl; De Ruijterkade 42b; mains €9-16; ◷7am-11pm; ◲▣; ▣1/2/4/5/9/13/16/17/24 Centraal Station) Bypass Centraal Station's fast-food mega-chains and head to this contemporary spot for outstanding burgers. Its 14 varieties include a towering beef Double Decker with tangy barbecue sauce, plus vegie and fish options; sides span fluffy triple-cooked *frites* (fries) to corn on the cob and salads. A kids' menu, high chairs and an indoor play area make it ideal for families.

GEBR NIEMEIJER CAFE, BAKERY €

Map p290 (www.gebroedersniemeijer.nl; Nieuwendijk 35; dishes €5-11, high tea €16-20; ◷8.15am-5.30pm Tue-Fri, to 4.30pm Sat, 9am-4.30pm Sun; ◲; ▣1/2/4/5/9/13/16/17/24 Centraal Station) This French bakery is a real find near Centraal Station. Take a seat at one of the sturdy wooden tables beneath the art-deco ceiling to linger over flaky croissants at breakfast or sandwiches made with breads such as house-speciality sourdough

---

◉ TOP SIGHT
MUSEUM ONS' LIEVE HEER OP SOLDER

The Museum Ons' Lieve Heer op Solder is one of those 'secret' Amsterdam places. What looks like an ordinary canal house in the Red Light District turns out to have an entire Catholic church stashed inside, with room for 150 worshippers.

Ons' Lieve Heer op Solder (Our Dear Lord in the Attic) was founded in the mid-1600s, when local merchant Jan Hartman decided to build a covert church in his house so his son could study to be a priest. At the time, the country's Calvinist rulers had outlawed public worship of Catholicism.

So, as you wander through, you get to see not only the city's richest collection of Catholic art but also period pieces from 17th-century canal-house life. There's a fantastic labyrinth of staircases, cubby-hole quarters, heavy oak furniture and a porcelain-tiled kitchen.

Once you're upstairs – in the attic, so to speak – you'll see that the church itself is unexpectedly grand, with a marble-columned altar and a painting by Jacob de Wit, a steep gallery and an impressive organ.

DON'T MISS

➡ Altar
➡ Jacob de Wit painting
➡ Kitchen and other 17th-century restored rooms

PRACTICALITIES

➡ Map p290, F6
➡ ☑020-624 66 04
➡ www.opsolder.nl
➡ Oudezijds Voorburgwal 38
➡ adult/child €10/5
➡ ◷10am-6pm Mon-Sat, 1-6pm Sun
➡ ▣4/9/16/24 Dam

or walnut bread with fillings like lamb sausage, Gruyère cheese and fig jam at lunch.

LANSKROON
BAKERY, TEAHOUSE €

Map p294 (www.lanskroon.nl; Singel 385; dishes €2-6; ⏰8am-7pm Mon-Fri, 9am-7pm Sat, 10am-7pm Sun Apr-Sep, to 5.30pm Oct-Mar; 🚇; 🚊1/2/5 Spui) Fourth-generation-run Lanskroon is famed for its *stroopwafels* – crispy, big as a dessert plate and slathered with caramel, honey or fig paste. In winter, locals come for spiced *speculaas* cookies and other Christmas treats, and in summer the thick nut- or fruit-swirled ice cream is a kid favourite.

PANNENKOEKENHUIS
UPSTAIRS
DUTCH €

Map p294 (☏020-626 56 03; www.upstairs pannenkoeken.nl; Grimburgwal 2; mains €7-12; ⏰noon-6pm Wed-Sat, to 5pm Sun; 🚊4/9/14/16/24 Rokin) Climb some of Amsterdam's steepest stairs inside a 1539 building to reach this small-as-a-postage-stamp restaurant with 100-plus teapots hanging from the ceiling, portraits of the Dutch royals and paintings of old Amsterdam. Traditional Dutch pancakes, such as bacon, cheese and ginger, are served. It's a two-person show, so things happen at their own pace; opening hours can be erratic. Cash only.

BANKETBAKKERIJ
VAN DER LINDE
ICE CREAM €

Map p290 (Nieuwendijk 183; ice creams small/medium/large from €0.95/1.10/1.50; ⏰1-5pm Mon, 11am-5.45pm Tue-Thu, 9am-5.45pm Fri, 9am-5pm Sat, noon-5pm Sun; 🚊4/9/16/24 Dam) A long line regularly snakes out the door of this narrow, generations-old shop where everyone is queuing for – wait for it – vanilla ice cream. That's the only flavour! Only this vanilla is unlike any other: a soft, velvety sugar cloud almost like whipped cream in texture. Choose from cones, cups or waffle ice-cream sandwiches, each in three sizes.

BROODJE BERT
SANDWICHES €

Map p294 (Singel 321; sandwiches €5-8; ⏰8am-5pm; 🚊1/2/5 Spui) Join the locals sitting on wooden chairs in the sun (or on the window seats inside) at this fabulous little sandwich shop in a winning canal-side location. In addition to huge sandwiches, such as marinated grilled chicken or the signature house special 'Broodje Bert' (lamb meatballs on Turkish bread), there are burgers and omelettes made to order. Cash only.

VAN STAPELE
BAKERY €

Map p294 (www.vanstapele.com; Heisteeg 4; 1/6 cookies €2/10; ⏰noon-6pm Mon, 10am-6pm Tue-Fri, 11am-6pm Sat & Sun; 🚊1/2/5 Spui) Teensy Van Stapele is a true specialist, baking just one thing and baking it well: chocolate cookies. Specifically, it's a Valrhona dark-chocolate cookie on the outside, filled with melted white chocolate inside. The disc of gorgeous sweetness is served soft and warm straight from the oven (it bakes 46 every 10 minutes).

ROB WIGBOLDUS
VISHANDEL
SANDWICHES €

Map p290 (Zoutsteeg 6; sandwiches €2-6; ⏰9am-5pm Tue-Sat; 🚊4/9/16/24 Dam) A wee three-table oasis in a narrow alleyway just off the touristy Damrak, this fish shop serves excellent herring sandwiches on a choice of crusty white or brown rolls. Other sandwich fillings include smoked eel, Dutch prawns and fried whitefish.

★ LT CORNELIS
DUTCH €€

Map p294 (☏020-261 48 63; Voetboogstraat 13; mains €17-23, 3-/4-/5-course menus €35/42/47, with paired wines €54/68/81; 🚊1/2/5 Spui) Blending Golden Age and contemporary elements, Lt Cornelis' downstairs bar crafts signature cocktails like *drop* (liquorice), caramel *stroopwafel* and apple pie with cinnamon. Upstairs, the stunning art-gallery-like dining room has framed Dutch paintings on marine-blue walls and reinvents classic recipes such as salted herring with apple and beetroot carpaccio, and lamb with white asparagus, sea vegetables and liquorice sauce.

TOMAZ
DUTCH €€

Map p294 (☏020-320 64 89; www.tomaz.nl; Begijnensteeg 6-8; mains lunch €8-17, dinner €15-33; ⏰noon-10pm; 🚊1/2/5 Spui) Charming little Tomaz hides near the Begijnhof (p67) and is a fine spot for a light lunch or an informal dinner. Staples include a daily *stamppot* (potato mashed with other vegetables), veal croquettes, IJsselmeer mussels and Dutch sausages. A vegetarian special is always available. Linger for a while over a game of chess.

★ D VIJFF VLIEGHEN
DUTCH €€€

Map p294 (☏020-530 40 60; www.vijffvlieghen.nl; Spuistraat 294-302; mains €23-29; ⏰6-10pm; 🚊1/2/5 Spui) Spread across five 17th-century canal houses, the 'Five Flies' is a jewel. Old-wood dining rooms overflow with character, featuring Delft-blue tiles and original works by Rembrandt; chairs have copper plates inscribed with the names of famous guests (Walt Disney, Mick Jagger...). Exquisite dishes range from goose breast with apple, sauerkraut and smoked butter to candied haddock with liquorice sauce.

✖ Red Light District

IVY & BROS
CAFE €

Map p290 (Oudezijds Voorburgwal 96; dishes €4-11; ⊘10am-7pm; 🗟🖉; 🚊4/9/24 Damrak) Except for the life-size replica megalodon shark jaws suspended above the open kitchen, all of the artwork at this hip cafe is for sale, as is the furniture and crockery. Most of its hot dishes, sandwiches and salads such as homemade cottage cheese and pomegranate are vegetarian, with some vegan options. Coffees come etched with extraordinarily intricate designs.

KOFFIESCHENKERIJ
CAFE €

Map p290 (Oudekerksplein 27; dishes €3-7; ⊘10am-6pm Mon-Sat, to 5pm Sun; 🗟; 🚊4/9/16/24 Dam) Freshly made sandwiches such as brie with sweet pepper, rocket (arugula) and mustard mayo or smoked salmon and cream cheese, a soup of the day, and sweets like spiced carrot cake or apple pie are served at this delightful cafe attached to the Oude Kerk. In fine weather, take a seat in the courtyard garden, blooming with tulips in spring.

BIRD SNACKBAR
THAI €€

Map p290 (☑020-420 62 89; www.thaibird.nl; Zeedijk 77; mains €10-16; ⊘1-10pm Mon-Wed, to 10.30pm Thu-Sun; 🚊1/2/4/5/9/13/16/17/24 Centraal Station) Bird has some of the best Asian food on the Zeedijk – the cooks, wedged in a tiny kitchen, don't skimp on lemongrass, fish sauce or chilli. The resulting curries and basil-laden meat and seafood dishes will knock your socks off. There's a bit more room to spread out in the (slightly pricier) restaurant across the street (No 72).

NAM KEE
CANTONESE €€

Map p290 (☑020-624 34 70; www.namkee.nl; Zeedijk 111-113; mains €11-21; ⊘noon-11pm; ⓜNieuwmarkt) It won't win any design awards, but year in, year out, Nam Kee, serving Cantonese classics, is the most popular Chinese spot in town. The steamed oysters and black-bean sauce are legendary. If you want to avoid the fluorescent-light ambience, try Nam Kee's nearby branch (p94) in Nieuwmarkt, which is fancier.

NEW KING
CHINESE €€

Map p290 (☑020-625 21 80; www.newking.nl; Zeedijk 115-117; mains €12-20; ⊘11am-11.30pm; 🖉; ⓜNieuwmarkt) Spread over several levels and adjoining buildings, this classy, low-lit restaurant is one of Chinatown's most beloved, so book ahead or plan to wait at busy times. Its signature dish is its black-bean steamed oysters; other standouts include salt-and-pepper prawns, whole Peking duck and numerous vegetarian choices including a delectable tofu and aubergine hotpot. Welcoming staff are ultra-efficient.

BRIDGES
SEAFOOD €€€

Map p294 (☑020-555 35 60; www.bridges restaurant.nl; Oudezijds Voorburgwal 197; 2-/3-course lunch menus €29.50/39.50, 4-/5-/6-course dinner menus €64/79/89, mains €29-35; ⊘noon-2.30pm & 6.30-10.30pm Tue-Fri, 1-3pm & 6.30-11.30pm Sat & Sun; 🚊4/9/14/24 Rokin) Celebrated Amsterdam chef Ron Blaauw is one of the gastronomic heavyweights behind this Michelin-starred restaurant in a historic setting on Amsterdam's oldest canal. Seafood is the speciality – from caviar and oysters to starters such as sesame cylinders filled with tuna and wasabi cream, and mains like salt-crusted sea bass or red mullet with langoustines and Pata Negra ham. Wine pairings are available.

BLAUW AAN DE WAL
EUROPEAN €€€

Map p294 (☑020-330 22 57; www.blauw aandewal.com; Oudezijds Achterburgwal 99, 3-/4-/5-course menu €39/52/65; ⊘6-11.30pm Mon-Sat; 🚊4/9/16/24 Dam) Refined Blauw aan de Wal is a rose among thorns. A long, often-graffiti-covered laneway off Oudezijds Achterburgwal 99 in the middle of the Red Light District leads to this 17th-century former herb warehouse where the whitewashed, exposed-brick, multilevel space features old steel weights, and tables fill the romantic garden in summer. Seasonally changing menus are artistically presented; service is first rate.

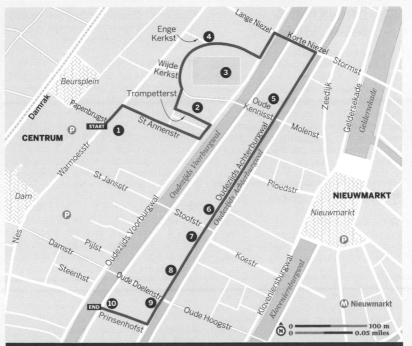

Neighbourhood Walk
Red Light District Stroll

START CONDOMERIE HET GULDEN VLIES
END GREENHOUSE
LENGTH 1.25KM; 25 MINUTES

Amsterdam's oldest quarter isn't all about the world's oldest profession – as this short saunter through the sinful side of the city shows.

What better way to set the mood than at **1 Condomerie Het Gulden Vlies** (p84)? Cherry red, hypoallergenic, cartoon character embodiments – the shop is a shrine to condom art, selling all sizes and colours.

It's easy to walk right by the teeny alley **2 Trompettersteeg** (p71). After turning onto Oudezijds Voorburgwal from St Annenstraat, it'll be the second little street you come to en route to the church. Claustrophobes beware: the medieval alley is only 1m wide, and the red-light windows keep it busy.

A contradiction if ever there was one: the 14th-century **3 Oude Kerk** (p68) is Amsterdam's oldest building, but the surrounding square has long been ground-zero for prostitution. Look near the entrance for the 'golden torso' pavement plaque, with a hand groping a breast.

Just northwest of the church, the **4 Prostitution Information Centre** (p71) dispenses forthright facts to sex workers and visitors alike.

Cross the canal onto Korte Niezel and turn right down Oudezijds Achterburgwal, where bondage exhibits and dildo bikes 'educate' visitors in the Erotic Museum. For further browsing, multiple **5 shops** around here offer 'nonstop hard porno' and trinkets such as whips, masks and spiked collars.

It's rapid-fire vice as you continue down Oudezijds Achterburgwal: live sex shows at **6 Casa Rosso** (p82), smoky vaporisers at the **7 Cannabis College** (p72), botany lessons at the **8 Hash, Marijuana & Hemp Museum** (p76), and 'Big Bud' at the **9 Sensi Seeds Shop**.

Turn right along Prinsenhofstraat towards Oudezijds Voorburgwal. At the corner of Prinsenhofstraat and Oudezijds Voorburgwal, popular coffeeshop **10 Greenhouse** (p85), is renowned for its high-quality cannabis and serves up good food and funky music. There are many places for actual coffee in the district too.

🍷 DRINKING & NIGHTLIFE

This area is renowned for its wild pubs and bars as well as its coffeeshops (cannabis cafes), but choices here are surprisingly diverse, taking in genteel *jenever* distillery tasting houses, unchanged-in-decades brown cafes, breweries, and on-trend addresses such as a combined craft-beer bar and barber shop. Zeedijk and Warmoesstraat are the twin hubs of the area's gay scene.

📍 Medieval Centre

⭐ TALES & SPIRITS   COCKTAIL BAR

Map p290 (www.talesandspirits.com; Lijnbaanssteeg 5-7; ⊙5.30pm-1am Tue-Thu & Sun, to 3am Fri & Sat; 🚊1/2/5/13/17 Nieuwezijds Kolk) Chandeliers glitter beneath wooden beams at Tales & Spirits, which creates its own house infusions, syrups and vinegar-based shrubs. Craft cocktails such as Floats Like a Butterfly (orange vodka, peach liqueur, saffron honey and lemon sorbet) and Stings Like a Bee (Dijon gin, cognac, maple syrup and soda water) are served in vintage and one-of-a-kind glasses. Minimum age is 21.

⭐ HOPPE   BROWN CAFE

Map p294 (www.cafehoppe.com; Spui 18-20; ⊙8am-1am Sun-Thu, to 2am Fri & Sat; 🚊1/2/5 Spui) An Amsterdam institution, Hoppe has been filling glasses since 1670. Barflies and raconteurs toss back brews amid the ancient wood panelling of the brown cafe at No 18 and the more modern, early-20th-century pub at No 20. In all but the iciest weather, the energetic crowd spills out from the dark interior and onto the Spui.

⭐ CUT THROAT   BAR

Map p290 (📞06 2534 3769; www.cutthroatbarber.nl; Beursplein 5; ⊙bar 9.30am-1am Sun-Thu, to 3am Fri & Sat, barber 11am-8pm Mon-Thu, 11am-7pm Fri, 10am-6pm Sat, noon-6pm Sun; 🖥; 🚊4/9/24 Rokin) Beneath 1930s arched brick ceilings, Cut Throat ingeniously combines a men's barbering service (book ahead) with a happening bar serving international craft beers, cocktails including infused G&Ts (such as blueberry and thyme or mandarin and rosemary), 'spiked' milkshakes, and coffee from Amsterdam roastery De

Wasserette. Brunch stretches to 4pm daily; all-day dishes span fried chicken and waffles, and surf-and-turf burgers.

⭐ CAFÉ BELGIQUE   BEER CAFE

Map p290 (www.cafe-belgique.nl; Gravenstraat 2; ⊙3pm-1am Mon-Wed, 1pm-1am Thu & Sun, 1pm-3am Sat; 🚊4/9/16/24 Dam) Pull up a stool at the carved wooden bar and choose from the glinting brass taps. It's all about Belgian beers here: eight flow from the spouts, and 50 or so more are available in bottles. The ambience is quintessentially *gezellig* (cosy, convivial) and draws lots of chilled-out locals. Live music or DJs play some nights.

⭐ CAFÉ DE DOKTER   BROWN CAFE

Map p294 (www.cafe-de-dokter.nl; Rozenboomsteeg 4; ⊙4pm-1am Wed-Sat; 🚊1/2/5 Spui) Candles flicker on the tables, old jazz records play in the background, and chandeliers and a birdcage hang from the ceiling at atmospheric Café de Dokter, which is said to be Amsterdam's smallest pub. Whiskies and smoked beef sausage are the specialities. A surgeon opened the bar in 1798, hence the name. His descendants still run it.

DE BLAUWE PARADE   BAR

Map p290 (www.deblauweparade.com; Nieuwezijds Voorburgwal 178; ⊙noon-midnight; 🖥; 🚊1/2/5/13/14/17 Dam) A frieze of Delft blue-and-white tiles – the world's largest Delft-tile tableau – wraps around the walls above beautiful wood panelling at this exquisite bar (a listed monument) within the Die Port van Cleve (p215) hotel. Regular events include tasting sessions of liqueurs on Monday and *jenevers* (gins) on Wednesday (both from 7pm), where you pay by the glass.

LITTLE DELIRIUM   CRAFT BEER

Map p290 (www.littledelirium.nl; De Ruijterkade 42a; ⊙10am-11pm; 🖥; 🚊1/2/4/5/9/13/16/17/24 Centraal Station) Its location by the IJ at the northern end of Centraal Station makes this beer specialist ideal while waiting for a train or to pick up bottles to drink aboard, but the sensational craft-beer selection – 20 on tap, including five of its own brews, and more than 80 by the bottle – justifies a visit even if you're not in transit.

DAMPKRING   COFFEESHOP

Map p294 (www.dampkring-coffeeshop-amsterdam.nl; Handboogstraat 29; ⊙8am-1am;

🕾; 🚊1/2/5 Koningsplein) With an interior that resembles a larger-than-life lava lamp, Dampkring is famed for having one of Amsterdam's most comprehensive coffeeshop menus, with details about aroma, taste and effect. Its name references the ring of the earth's atmosphere where smaller items combust.

ABRAXAS
COFFEESHOP

Map p294 (www.abraxas.tv; Jonge Roelensteeg 12; ⊙8am-1am; @🕾; 🚊1/2/5/14 Dam/Paleisstraat) Mellow music, comfy sofas, thick milkshakes and rooms with different energy levels spread across Abraxas' floors (connected by a spindly spiral staircase). The considerate staff make it a great place for coffeeshop newbies (though the fairytale artwork can get a bit intense).

CAFÉ HET SCHUIM
BAR

Map p294 (Spuistraat 189; ⊙11am-1am Mon-Thu, to 3am Fri & Sat, noon-1am Sun; 🕾; 🚊1/2/5/14 Dam) *Schuim* means 'foam' (on beer) and this grungy, arty bar is extraordinarily popular with beer-swigging locals day or night. Art rotates on the walls every couple of months; DJs spin most weekends. The pavement terrace is great for people-watching.

OPORTO
BROWN CAFE

Map p290 (Zoutsteeg 1; ⊙11am-1am Sun-Thu, to 3am Fri & Sat; 🚊4/9/16/24 Dam) With a decor untouched in decades, this tiny brown cafe is worth visiting for its inlaid woodwork behind the bar (check out the zodiac signs) and wrought-iron-and-parchment lighting fixtures.

TASTING HOUSES
∙∙

Tasting houses hide among the Medieval Centre's streets, offering a prime opportunity to try *jenever* and other local liqueurs. Most have been pouring their wares for two to three centuries.

Look out for the following:

Wynand Fockink (Map p294; 🕿020-639 26 95; www.wynand-fockink.nl; Pijlsteeg 31; tours €17.50; ⊙tasting tavern 3-9pm daily, tours 3pm, 4.30pm, 6pm & 7.30pm Sat & Sun; 🚊4/9/16/24 Dam) Dating from 1679, this small tasting house in an arcade behind Grand Hotel Krasnapolsky serves scores of *jenevers* (Dutch gins) and liqueurs. Although there's no seating, it's an intimate place to knock back a shot glass or two. At weekends, guides give 45-minute distillery tours (in English) that are followed by six tastings; reserve online.

If you're deliberating over flavours, try the house speciality *boswandeling* (secret of the forest), a vivacious combination of young *jenever*, herb bitters and orange liqueur – the result tastes like cloves.

Proeflokaal de Ooievaar (Map p290; www.proeflokaaldeooievaar.nl; St Olofspoort 1; ⊙noon-midnight; 🚊1/2/4/5/9/13/16/17/24 Centraal Station) Not much bigger than a vat of *jenever*, this magnificent little tasting house has been going strong since 1782. On offer are 14 *jenevers* and liqueurs (such as Bride's Tears with gold and silver leaf) from De Ooievaar distillery, still located in the Jordaan. Despite appearances, the house has not subsided but was built leaning over.

In de Olofspoort (Map p290; www.olofspoort.com; Nieuwebrugsteeg 13; ⊙4pm-12.30am Tue-Thu, 3pm-1.30am Fri & Sat, 3-10pm Sun; 🚊4/9/16/24 Centraal Station) The door of this brown cafe–tasting room dating from 1618 was once the city gate. It stocks over 200 *jenevers* (Dutch gins), liqueurs and bitters; check out the extraordinary selection behind the back-room bar. You can also buy its unique tipples at its on-site shop, which opens until 10pm. Occasional singalongs add to the spirited atmosphere.

De Drie Fleschjes (Map p290; www.dedriefleschjes.nl; Gravenstraat 18; ⊙4-8.30pm Mon-Wed, 2-8.30pm Thu-Sat, 3-7pm Sun; 🚊1/2/5/13/14/17 Dam) A treasure dating from 1650, with a wall of barrels made by master shipbuilders, the tasting room of distiller Bootz specialises in liqueurs, including its signature almond-flavoured *bitterkoekje* (Dutch-style macaroon) liqueur, as well as superb *jenever*. Take a peek at the collection of *kalkoentjes* (small bottles with hand-painted portraits of former mayors).

PUT OUT THE RED LIGHT?

Since 2007 city officials have been reducing the number of Red Light windows in an effort to clean up the district. They claim it's not about morals but about crime: pimps, traffickers and money launderers have entered the scene and set the neighbourhood on a downward spiral. Opponents point to a growing conservatism and say the government is using crime as an excuse, because it doesn't like Amsterdam's current reputation for sin.

As the window tally has decreased, fashion studios, art galleries and trendy cafes have moved in to reclaim the deserted spaces, thanks to a program of low-cost rent and other business incentives. It's called Project 1012, after the area's postal code.

To date, 300 windows remain, down from 482. Scores of prostitutes and their supporters have taken to the streets to protest the closures: the concern is that closing the windows simply forces prostitutes to relocate to less safe environments. The city is now rethinking its plan to buy back many more of the windows. In the meantime, other initiatives for changing the face of the area include the introduction of festivals such as the **Red Light Jazz Festival** (www.redlightjazz.com; ☺early Jun).

CAFÉ THE MINDS   BAR
Map p294 (www.theminds.nl; Spuistraat 245; ☺9pm-3am Sun-Thu, to 4am Fri & Sat; ☒1/2/5 Spui) Don't let the word 'cafe' in the name fool you – this is a hard-core (but very friendly) punk bar (Amsterdam's last remaining one) where the beer's cheap, the music's loud and the party's rockin'. It's smack in the middle of a little strip of the Spui that's home to a few squats and plenty of graffiti.

BEERTEMPLE   CRAFT BEER
Map p294 (☎020-627 14 27; www.beertemple.nl; Nieuwezijds Voorburgwal 250; ☺noon-midnight Sun-Thu, to 2am Fri & Sat; ☒1/2/5/14 Dam) BeerTemple's taps, with 35 rotating draught beers, feature mainly American varieties that you'll be hard-pushed to find elsewhere in the Dutch capital, as well as its own house brew, Tempelbier. Another 200 beers are available by the bottle. Reserve for tastings (€20) on Saturday at 12.30pm. Coasters cover the walls of the grungy interior.

PRIK   GAY
Map p290 (www.prikamsterdam.nl; Spuistraat 109; ☺4pm-1am Mon-Thu, to 3am Fri & Sat, 3pm-1am Sun; ☒1/2/5/13/14/17 Dam) 'Lovely liquids, sexy snacks and twisted tunes' is the siren call of this hyper-retro bar with cocktails galore and Prosecco on tap. DJs spin pop, house and dance tunes on Friday and Saturday.

🍷 Red Light District

★IN 'T AEPJEN   BROWN CAFE
Map p290 (Zeedijk 1; ☺noon-1am Mon-Thu, to 3am Fri & Sat; ☒1/2/4/5/9/13/16/17/24 Centraal Station) Candles burn even during the day in this 15th-century building – one of two remaining wooden buildings in the city – which has been a tavern since 1519: in the 16th and 17th centuries it served as an inn for sailors from the Far East, who often brought *aapjes* (monkeys) to trade for lodging. Vintage jazz on the stereo enhances the time-warp feel.

★DUM DUM PALACE   COCKTAIL BAR
Map p290 (www.dumdum.nl; Zeedijk 37; ☺11am-1am Sun-Thu, to 3am Fri & Sat; ☎; ☒1/2/4/5/9/13/16/17/24 Centraal Station) Asian takes on classic cocktails at this designer spot include a Tom Yam Collins, green-tea mojito, Tokyo Sling, five-spice whisky sour and black-sesame martini. Drinks are served in its main skylit room and in a secret bar out back (ask the staff to show you through). Food-truck caterers HotMamaHot collaborate in the kitchen, serving four kinds of dumplings.

★BROUWERIJ DE PRAEL   BREWERY
Map p290 (www.deprael.nl; Oudezijds Armsteeg 26; ☺noon-midnight Mon-Wed, to 1am Thu-Sat, to 11pm Sun; ☒1/2/4/5/9/13/16/17/24 Centraal Station) Sample organic beers (Scotch ale,

IPA, barley wine and many more varieties) at the socially minded De Prael brewery (p72), known for employing people with a history of mental illness. Its multilevel tasting room has comfy couches and big wooden tables strewn about. There's often live music. A four-beer tasting flight costs €10.

BIERFABRIEK
MICROBREWERY

Map p294 (☑020-528 99 10; www.bierfabriek. com; Nes 67; ⊘3pm-1am Mon-Thu, to 2am Fri, 1pm-2am Sat, to 1am Sun; ☐4/9/14/16/24 Rokin) Bierfabriek's Pure pilsner, Nero porter and Rosso ruby ale (plus a seasonally changing variety) are brewed in these raw-concrete surrounds and best accompanied by its signature grilled chicken served with a hefty portion of fries and mayonnaise (or just help yourself to the in-shell peanuts that abound on the tables). Reserve to guarantee a table at busy times.

'T MANDJE
GAY

Map p290 (www.cafetmandje.amsterdam; Zeedijk 63; ⊘4pm-1am Tue-Thu, 3pm-3am Fri & Sat, to 1am Sun; ☐1/2/4/5/9/13/16/17/24 Centraal Station) Amsterdam's oldest gay bar opened in 1927, then shut in 1982 when the Zeedijk grew too seedy. But its trinket-covered interior was lovingly dusted every week until it reopened in 2008. The devoted bartenders can tell you stories about the bar's brassy lesbian founder Bet van Beeren. It's one of the most *gezellig* places in the centre, gay or straight.

GREENHOUSE
COFFEESHOP

Map p294 (www.greenhouse.org; Oudezijds Voorburgwal 191; ⊘10am-1am; ☎; ☐4/9/16/24 Dam) This is one of the most popular coffeeshops in town, with a mostly young, backpacking crowd partaking of the wares. Smokers love the funky music, multicoloured mosaics and high-quality weed and hash. It also serves breakfast, lunch and dinner to suit all levels of the munchies.

TONTON CLUB
BAR

Map p290 (www.tontonclub.nl; St Annendwarsstraat 6; ⊘4pm-midnight Mon & Tue, noon-midnight Wed-Sun; ☐4/9/16/24 Dam) It's a simple concept: craft beers plus arcade games in a neon-bathed room in the Red Light District. You can play retro games such as pinball (machines include Walking Dead, Addams Family and Avatar), Street Fighter 2, Sega Rally and Galaga. Deep-fried Dutch snacks provide sustenance.

WINSTON KINGDOM
CLUB

Map p290 (www.winston.nl; St Christopher's at the Winston, Warmoesstraat 127; ⊘9pm-4am Sun-Thu, to 5am Fri & Sat; ☐4/9/16/24 Dam) Even nonclubbers will love Winston Kingdom for its indie-alternative music beats, great DJs and live bands. No matter what's on – from 'dubstep mayhem' to Thailand-style full-moon parties – the scene can get pretty wild in this good-time little space inside St Christopher's at the Winston (p214). Check its agenda for events.

DE ROODE LAARS
BROWN CAFE

Map p290 (Zeedijk 17; ⊘noon-1am Sun-Thu, to 2am Fri & Sat; ☐1/2/4/5/9/13/16/17/24 Centraal Station) A *roode laars* (red boot) on the facade above the stained-glass windows of this lamp-lit little brown cafe remains from its earlier incarnation as a shoemaker's shop. *Jenevers* (Dutch gins) and liqueurs are served alongside local beers. Its tiny size helps create a classic *gezellig* atmosphere, day or night.

MOLLY MALONE'S
IRISH PUB

Map p290 (www.mollyinamsterdam.com; Oudezijds Kolk 9; ⊘noon-1am Mon-Thu, to 3am Fri, 11am-3am Sat, to 1am Sun; ☐1/2/4/5/9/13/16/17/24 Centraal Station) Dark, woody Molly's holds spontaneous trad-music sessions (bring your own instrument and let loose) as well as various blues, rock and indie gigs. Irish beverages include ciders and fabulous

---

LOW-KEY COFFEESHOPS

If loud music, trippy decor and big crowds aren't your thing, consider one of these smaller, more relaxed establishments:

Tweede Kamer (Map p294; Heisteeg 6; ⊘10am-1am; ☐1/2/5 Spui)

Dutch Flowers (Map p294; Singel 387; ⊘10am-11pm Sun-Thu, to 1am Fri & Sat; ☐1/2/5 Spui)

Coffeeshop Rusland (Map p294; www. coffeeshop rusland amsterdam.com; Rusland 16; ⊘8am-12.30am; ☐4/9/14/16/24 Rokin)

Galway Hooker craft beers in addition to stout and whiskeys. Live sports screen on big HD TVs; pub grub ranges from burgers to ribs and roasts.

EAGLE GAY

Map p290 (www.theeagleamsterdam.com; Warmoesstraat 90; ⌚11pm-4am Sun-Thu, to 5am Fri & Sat; 🚋1/2/4/5/9/13/16/17/24 Centraal Station) Around since 1979, the Eagle is a classic. This men-only, leather-denim bar offers three levels of action, including basement darkrooms and a house-music-thumping, laser-light-swirling dance floor. Queues can be lengthy at weekends. Regular events range from DJs to naked nights and bondage play parties.

KAPITEIN ZEPPO'S BAR

Map p294 (www.zeppos.nl; Gebed Zonder End 5; ⌚11am-1am Mon-Thu, to 3am Fri & Sat, noon-1am Sun; 🚋4/9/14/16/24 Rokin) Tucked down an alleyway off Grimburgwal, this site has assumed many guises throughout the centuries: a cloister during the 14th, a horse-carriage storehouse in the 17th and a cigar factory in the 19th. The soulful little *café* has a timeless bohemian feel, whether you're at the tile-top, candlelit tables or in the garden with its twinkling lights.

GETTO GAY & LESBIAN

Map p290 (www.getto.nl; Warmoesstraat 51; ⌚4.30pm-1am Tue-Thu, to 2am Fri & Sat, to midnight Sun; 🚋1/2/4/5/9/13/16/17/24 Centraal Station) This groovy, long restaurant-bar is loved for its open, welcoming attitude, great people-watching from the front, and rear lounge where you can chill. It's a haven for the gay and lesbian crowd and anyone who wants a little bohemian subculture in the Red Light District's midst. Food includes 'diva burgers'; happy hour is from 5pm to 7pm.

☆ ENTERTAINMENT

BITTERZOET LIVE MUSIC

Map p290 (☎020-421 23 18; www.bitterzoet.com; Spuistraat 2; ⌚8pm-late; 🚋1/2/5/13/17 Nieuwezijds Kolk) Always full, always changing, this venue with a capacity of just 350 people is one of the friendliest places in town, with a diverse crowd. Music (sometimes live, sometimes courtesy of a DJ) can be funk, roots, drum 'n' bass, Latin, Afro-beat, old-school jazz or hip-hop groove.

FRASCATI THEATRE

Map p294 (☎020-626 68 66; www.frascatitheater.nl; Nes 63; ⌚closed Aug; 🚋4/9/14/16/24 Rokin) This experimental theatre is a draw for young Dutch directors, choreographers and producers. Expect multicultural dance and music performances, as well as hip hop, rap and break-dancing. Check the website for upcoming events.

DE BRAKKE GROND THEATRE

Map p294 (☎020-622 90 14; www.brakkegrond.nl; Flemish Cultural Centre, Nes 43; 📶; 🚋4/9/14/16/24 Rokin) De Brakke Grond sponsors a fantastic array of music, experimental video, modern dance and exciting young theatre at its nifty performance hall in the Flemish Cultural Centre. Upcoming events are listed on its website.

CASA ROSSO LIVE PERFORMANCE

Map p294 (www.casarosso.nl; Oudezijds Achterburgwal 106-108; admission with/without drinks €55/45; ⌚7pm-2am Sun-Thu, to 3am Fri & Sat; 🚋4/9/16/24 Dam) It might be stretching it to describe a live sex show as 'classy', but this theatre is clean and comfortable and always packed with couples and hen's-night parties. Acts can be male, female, both or lesbian (although not gay...sorry, boys!). Performers demonstrate everything from positions of the Kama Sutra to pole dances and incredible tricks with lit candles.

Tickets are €3 cheaper online.

SHOPPING

Kalverstraat and its surrounds are filled with high-street chains and get crammed with shoppers, while Damrak is awash with souvenir shops. More unique shops, selling everything from Dutch-designed homewares, fashion and art to reconditioned retro computer games, can be found in the backstreets. The Red Light District is home to a wild assortment of adult and fetish shops, as well as 'smart shops' selling magic truffles.

🏛 Medieval Centre

⭐X BANK   DESIGN
Map p294 (www.xbank.amsterdam; Spuistraat 172; ◷10am-6pm Mon-Wed, to 9pm Thu-Sat, noon-8pm Sun; 🚊1/2/5/13/14/17 Dam) More than just a concept store showcasing Dutch-designed haute couture and ready-to-wear fashion, furniture, art, gadgets and homewares, the 700-sq-metre X Bank – in a former bank that's now part of the striking W Amsterdam (p214) hotel – also hosts exhibitions, workshops, launches and lectures. Interior displays change every month; check the website for upcoming events.

LOCALS   FASHION & ACCESSORIES
Map p294 (www.localsamsterdam.com; Spuistraat 272; ◷1-6pm Mon, 11.30am-6pm Tue-Sat, noon-6pm Sun; 🚊1/2/5 Spui) Jeweller Suzanne Hof set up this boutique to showcase designs from her own label, Sugarz, but also to provide a platform for small-scale designers from the Netherlands and especially from Amsterdam. Along with men's and women's fashion (T-shirts, jeans, dresses), you'll find scarves, hats, gloves, handbags and homewares (vases, cushions, crockery, paintings and contemporary twists on hand-painted Delftware tiles).

MARK RAVEN GRAFIEK   GIFTS & SOUVENIRS
Map p290 (www.markraven.nl; Nieuwezijds Voorburgwal 174; ◷10.30am-6pm; 🚊1/2/5/13/14/17 Dam/Raadhuisstraat) Artist Mark Raven's distinctive vision of Amsterdam is available on posters, coasters and stylish T-shirts that make great souvenirs. Prices are impressively reasonable, and there's often a sale rack out front.

BY AMFI   FASHION & ACCESSORIES
Map p294 (www.amfi.nl/byamfi; Spui 23; ◷1-6pm Mon-Fri, hours vary Sat; 🚊1/2/5 Spui) Students, teachers and alumni of the Amsterdam Fashion Institute show and sell their wares at this small boutique. It's mostly clothing and decor wildly inventive in style but sure to be one of a kind.

ANDRIES DE JONG BV   GIFTS & SOUVENIRS
Map p291 (www.andriesdejong.nl; Muntplein 8; ◷10am-6pm Mon-Sat; 🚊4/9/14/16 Muntplein) Since 1787, when seafarers have needed ship fittings, rope or brass lamps, they've come to Andries de Jong. Traditional clocks, bells, boats in bottles and other quaint maritime gifts weigh down the crowded shelves among the workers' items, along with strong, brightly coloured flags.

OUDEMANHUISPOORT
BOOK MARKET   BOOKS
Map p294 (Oudemanhuispoort; ◷11am-4pm Mon-Sat; 🚊4/9/14/16/24 Spui/Rokin) Secondhand books weigh down the tables in the atmospheric covered alleyway between Oudezijds Achterburgwal and Kloveniersburgwal, where you'll rub tweed-patched elbows with University of Amsterdam professors thumbing through volumes of Marx, Aristotle et al. Old posters, maps and sheet music are for sale too. Most tomes are in Dutch, though you'll find a few in English mixed in. Cash only.

PGC HAJENIUS   GIFTS & SOUVENIRS
Map p294 (www.hajenius.com; Rokin 96; ◷noon-6pm Mon, 9.30am-6pm Tue-Sat, noon-5pm Sun; 🚊4/9/14/16/24 Spui/Rokin) With its century-old stained glass, gilt trim, Italian marble and soaring leather ceilings, this tobacco emporium is worth checking out even if you're not a cigar connoisseur. Regular customers, including members of the Dutch royal family, have private humidors here. You can sample Cuban and other exotic cigars in the handsome smoking lounge.

DE BIJENKORF   DEPARTMENT STORE
Map p294 (www.debijenkorf.nl; Dam 1; ◷11am-8pm Sun & Mon, 10am-8pm Tue & Wed, 10am-9pm Thu & Fri, 9.30am-8pm Sat; 🚊4/9/16/24 Dam) Amsterdam's most fashionable department store has a grander exterior than interior, but it occupies the city's highest-profile location, facing the Royal Palace (p66). Shoppers will enjoy the well-chosen clothing, cosmetics, accessories, toys, homewares and books. The snazzy cafe on the 5th floor has a terrace with steeple views.

GASTRONOMIE NOSTALGIE   HOMEWARES
Map p294 (www.gastronomienostalgie.nl; Nieuwezijds Voorburgwal 304; ◷11am-5pm; 🚊1/2/5 Spui) The owner scours international auctions for the gorgeous china plates, crystal goblets, silver candlesticks and other antique homewares spilling out of this jam-packed shop. Ring the brass bell to get in, then prepare to browse for a good long while.

LAUNDRY INDUSTRY CLOTHING

Map p294 (www.laundryindustry.com; St Lucien-steeg 18; ◷noon-6.30pm Sun & Mon, 10am-6.30pm Tue-Sat; 🚊4/9/14/16/24 Spui/Rokin) Hip, urban shoppers head here for well-cut, well-designed women's and men's clothes by this Dutch design house. Shoes, jewellery and designer knick-knacks are also for sale. A coffee bar provides a caffeine fix.

POSTZEGELMARKT MARKET

Map p294 (Stamp & Coin Market; Nieuwezijds Voorburgwal 280; ◷10am-4pm Wed & Sat; 🚊1/2/5 Spui) This little street-side market sells stamps, coins and medals.

RUSH HOUR RECORDS MUSIC

Map p290 (www.rushhour.nl; Spuistraat 116; ◷1-7pm Mon, 11am-7pm Tue, Wed, Fri & Sat, 11am-9pm Thu, 1-6pm Sun; 🚊4/9/16/24 Dam) House and techno are the main genres on offer in this vast space, but funk, jazz, dubstep, electronica and disco fill the bins too. A favourite with DJs and multimedia artists, it's an excellent spot to find out what's going on in the underground dance-music scene.

ART MARKET MARKET

Map p294 (www.artplein-spui.com; Spui; ◷11am-6.30pm Sun Mar-Dec; 🚊1/2/5 Spui) Save on gallery fees by buying direct from the artists at Amsterdam's art market. Some 60 Dutch and contemporary artists set up on the square every week.

3-D HOLOGRAMMEN/ PRINTED IN SPACE GIFTS & SOUVENIRS

Map p294 (www.printedinspace.nl; Grimburgwal 2; ◷1-5.30pm Sun & Mon, noon-6pm Tue-Fri, noon-5.30pm Sat; 🚊4/9/14/16 Spui/Rokin) This fascinating (and trippy) collection of holographic pictures, jewellery and stickers will delight all ages. You can even get a hologram of yourself custom-made. The shop also offers 3D printed bracelets, vases, lamps and other items.

AMERICAN BOOK CENTER BOOKS

Map p294 (ABC; www.abc.nl; Spui 12; ◷noon-8pm Mon, 10am-8pm Tue-Sat, 11am-6.30pm Sun; 🚊1/2/5 Spui) Rambling over three storeys, this excellent bookshop is the biggest source of English-language books in Amsterdam. Its greatest strengths are in the artsy ground-floor department, but on the upper floors there's fiction and oodles of special-interest titles, plus a good travel section. It also stocks foreign periodicals such as the *New York Times* and top-notch postcards.

🔒 Red Light District

CONDOMERIE HET GULDEN VLIES ADULT

Map p290 (https://condomerie.com; Warmoesstraat 141; ◷11am-9pm Mon & Wed-Sat, to 6pm Tue, 1-6pm Sun; 🚊4/9/14/16/24 Dam) In the heart of the Red Light District, this brightly lit boutique sells condoms in every imaginable size, colour, flavour and design (horned devils, marijuana leaves, Delftware tiles...), along with lubricants and saucy gifts. Photos aren't allowed inside the shop.

HEMPSTORY COSMETICS, HOMEWARES

Map p294 (www.hempstory.nl; Oudezijds Achterburgwal 142; ◷10am-6pm Sun-Wed, to 9pm Thu-Sat; 🚊4/9/14/16 Dam) Everything at this light-filled, contemporary boutique is made from hemp: skincare ranges (soaps, moisturisers, and body washes such as hemp and ginseng), insect repellent, homewares (blankets, throws, cushions, botanical prints on hemp paper), men's and women's clothing (shirts, jackets, scarves, hats), and hemp-cord jewellery. Its tiny cafe serves (non-active) hemp tea, hemp-seed cakes and hemp-seed smoothies.

RED LIGHT RECORDS MUSIC

Map p290 (Oudekerksplein 26; ◷noon-6pm Mon & Sat, noon-7pm Tue-Fri; 🚊4/9/16/24 Dam) Tucked in a courtyard off the street, this shop sits in a former Red Light window. Ring the doorbell to get buzzed in and join the DJs flicking through stacks of spacey Euro-disco, house and funk music. Headphone stations let you listen before you buy. The underground Red Light Radio station (www.redlightradio.net) operates from a window across the way.

KOKOPELLI ADULT

Map p290 (www.kokopelli.nl; Warmoesstraat 12; ◷11am-10pm; 🚊4/9/16/24 Centraal Station) Were it not for its trade in 'magic truffles' (similar to the now-outlawed psilocybin mushrooms, aka 'magic mushrooms'), you might swear this large, beautiful space was a fashionable clothing or homewares store. There's a coffee and juice bar and a chill-out lounge area overlooking Damrak.

Nieuwmarkt, Plantage & the Eastern Islands

Neighbourhood Top Five

❶ **Museum het Rembrandthuis** (p87) Viewing Rembrandt's studio, where you can see his brushes, sketches and cabinet stuffed with seashells and Roman busts.

❷ **Het Scheepvaartmuseum** (p92) Fathoming the history of Dutch seafaring through the extensive maritime collection.

❸ **Muziekgebouw aan 't IJ** (p98) Catching live classical music or jazz at this acoustically and visually stunning venue.

❹ **Amsterdam Roest** (p98) Swinging on hammocks above an artificial beach or taking in a cultural happening at one of Amsterdam's quirk-tastic counter-culture venues.

❺ **Rederji Lampedusa** (p101) Taking a tour with storytelling, theatre or music co-run by migrants, on a former refugee boat.

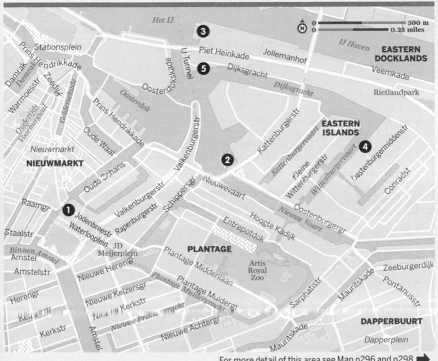

For more detail of this area see Map p296 and p298 ➡

Lonely Planet's Top Tip

Nieuwmarkt and the Eastern Islands have an eclectic mix of architecture, from the imposing Scheepvaarthuis (a classic example of the Amsterdam School) to Renzo Piano's green-tinged NEMO Science Museum building. Several unique buildings cluster near where Kloveniersburgwal and Oude Hoogstraat intersect, while on the Eastern Islands there are some seminal modern buildings, including the 'Whale'.

✕ Best Places to Eat

➡ Greetje (p96)

➡ Sterk Staaltje (p93)

➡ Tokoman (p93)

➡ Frenzi (p94)

➡ De Plantage (p95)

For reviews, see p93.➡

🍷 Best Places to Drink

➡ Amsterdam Roest (p98)

➡ Brouwerij 't IJ (p97)

➡ SkyLounge (p97)

➡ Hannekes Boom (p98)

➡ KHL (p98)

➡ HPS (p98)

For reviews, see p96.➡

🔒 Best Places to Shop

➡ A Boeken (p100)

➡ Hôtel Droog (p99)

➡ Waterlooplein Flea Market (p100)

➡ Knuffels (p100)

➡ Frank's Smokehouse (p101)

For reviews, see p99.➡

Explore Nieuwmarkt, Plantage & the Eastern Islands

Centred on its namesake square, busy Nieuwmarkt (New Market) bursts with historic reminders of its glorious past, even if it's more about nightlife and shopping these days. Rembrandt painted canalscapes here, and Jewish merchants built up thriving businesses until the community's decimation during WWII.

The neighbourhood's most entrancing sight is Museum het Rembrandthuis, the master's impressive home and studio. In the old Jewish quarter is an excellent collection of museums housed in historic synagogues. You can also take a free tour around the fascinating Gassan Diamond factory here.

East of Nieuwmarkt, you enter the city's leafiest neighbourhood. Plantage (Plantation) was developed from a former swamp area in the 17th century, but economic crisis led to many plots of land remaining unsold. The authorities decided to develop these into parks rather than more housing. It's a lovely place to stroll and laze. Beside its splendid 19th-century architecture there is the historic Artis Royal Zoo, and close by is the verdantly exotic Hortus Botanicus.

Further east, there's another completely contrasting area of the city, the former shipyard and warehouse district of the Eastern Islands (Oostelijke Eilanden) and their Eastern Docklands (Oostelijk Havengebied).

Local Life

➡**Waterside life** Head to the houseboats and riverside cafes off the beaten track on the Eastern Islands to enjoy a laid-back drink local style.

➡**Snack life** Join the queues to fit in a fiery bite of Suriname at Tokoman (p93), famed for its *broodje pom* (chicken-and-tuber-mash sandwich).

➡**Brewery life** You can't get more classically Dutch than sitting in the shadow of a windmill, sampling the fragrant beers of organic Brouwerij 't IJ (p97).

Getting There & Away

➡**Tram** Trams 9 and 14 go to Waterlooplein and the Jewish sights, as well as Plantage. Tram 10 goes to the Eastern Islands and Eastern Docklands. Tram 26 travels along the IJ river waterfront.

➡**Metro** There are stops at Waterlooplein and Nieuwmarkt.

➡**Bus** Buses 22 and 48 are useful for areas of the Eastern Islands and Eastern Docklands that the tram doesn't reach.

TOP SIGHT
MUSEUM HET REMBRANDTHUIS

This evocative museum provides an unparalleled insight into one of the Netherlands' greatest artistic geniuses, Rembrandt van Rijn. The museum is set in the three-storey canal house where the artist lived at the height of his success, and the interiors have been reconstructed according to a detailed inventory made when he had to leave the house when his fortunes took a dive.

The house dates from 1606. Rembrandt ran the Netherlands' largest painting studio here between 1639 and 1658. However, the house was ultimately Rembrandt's financial undoing. As his work fell out of fashion, he was unable to pay off the mortgage, and in 1656 the house and its effects were sold to compensate his creditors. It's thanks to the debt collector's itemised list that the museum has been able to reproduce the interior so authentically. Rembrandt lived the rest of his years in cheaper digs in the Jordaan.

On the ground floor you'll see Rembrandt's living room and bedroom, furnished with the type of box bed fashionable at the time; it was believed that to sleep sitting up prevented death during the night. An anteroom where he received clients is covered in paintings: wares for sale. The house gives an insight into art as a trade, with the showroom downstairs and, upstairs, the cubicles for Rembrandt's pupils.

Climb the narrow staircase and you'll come to the master's light-filled studio, laid out as though he's just nipped down to the kitchen for an inspirational snack. Facing north, offering ideal light, this is where he painted masterpieces such as *The Night Watch*. The room is recognisable from an etching on display, and artists give demonstrations here on how Rembrandt sourced and mixed paints. Across the hall is Rembrandt's 'Cabinet', a mind-blowing room crammed with curiosities like those he collected: seashells, glassware, Roman busts and stuffed alligators.

A small room on the same floor is devoted to Rembrandt's famous etchings. The museum has a near-complete collection of them (about 250), although they're not all on display at once. Demonstrators crank up an oak press to show etching techniques several times daily.

DON'T MISS

➡ The paint-filled studio
➡ The seated box beds
➡ Etching demos
➡ Rembrandt's re-created collection 'Cabinet'
➡ The audio tour

PRACTICALITIES

➡ Rembrandt House Museum
➡ Map p296, C5
➡ 020-520 04 00
➡ www.rembrandthuis.nl
➡ Jodenbreestraat 4
➡ adult/child €13/4
➡ 10am-6pm
➡ 9/14 Waterlooplein

SIGHTS

⊙ Nieuwmarkt

MUSEUM HET REMBRANDTHUIS   MUSEUM
See p87.

SCHEEPVAARTHUIS   ARCHITECTURE
Map p296 (Shipping House; Prins Hendrikkade 108; ☑4/9/16/24 Centraal Station) Now the five-star Grand Hotel Amrath, the grand 1916-built Scheepvaarthuis is a neo-Gothic art-deco beauty, the first and finest example of the expressionist Amsterdam School of architecture. The exterior resembles a ship's bow, awash with nautical detailing; look for figures of Neptune, his wife and four females that represent the compass points. Staff are happy for tourists to have a nose around: head up to the 3rd floor to see the Great Hall with its leaded glass designed by Willem Bogtman.

MONTELBAANSTOREN   HISTORIC BUILDING
Map p296 (Montelbaan Tower; Oude Schans 2; ☑4/9/16/24 Centraal Station) This graceful tower looks monumental rather than functional, but it was originally built to strengthen Amsterdam's eastern defences in 1512. Positioned on the old city wall, it gave sentries a good view of suspicious characters on the wharves along Oude Schans. The decorative topping, octagonal base and open wooden steeple were added in 1606 to dampen the bells on the clock after neighbours complained. A few years later, it began to list under the weight, but residents attached cables and pulled it upright.

The elegant tower has two sets of bellworks, four clock faces and a nautical vane like the one on top of the Oude Kerk.

WAAG   HISTORIC BUILDING
Map p296 (www.indewaag.nl; Nieuwmarkt 4; Ⓜ Nieuwmarkt) The multi-turreted Waag was built as a gate in the city walls in 1488. In 1601 the walls were destroyed so that the city could expand, and the building was turned into Amsterdam's main weigh house, and later a spot for public executions. A bar-restaurant (open 9am to 1am) occupies it today. Out the front, Nieuwmarkt square hosts a variety of events, including a Saturday farmers' market and a Sunday antiques market.

In its early days the Waag looked more like a castle, fronted by a moatlike canal. By the 17th century it was home to various guilds. The surgeons' guild, which occupied the upper floor, commissioned Rembrandt's famous *The Anatomy Lesson of Dr Tulp* (displayed in the Mauritshuis museum in Den Haag). The masons' guild was based in the tower facing the Zeedijk; note the superfine brickwork.

OOSTINDISCH HUIS   ARCHITECTURE
Map p296 (East Indies House; Oude Hoogstraat 24; Ⓜ Nieuwmarkt) The mighty Dutch East India Company (Verenigde Oost-Indische Compagnie; VOC) was founded in 1602 and was one of the earliest multi-national companies, trading spices, opium and more with Asia. This imposing red-and-white edifice is the company's former office. It was built between 1551 and 1643 and attributed in part to Hendrick de Keyser, the busy city architect. The VOC sailed into rough waters and was dissolved in 1798. The building is now owned by the University of Amsterdam.

ZUIDERKERK   CHURCH
Map p296 (www.zuiderkerkamsterdam.nl; Zuiderkerkhof 72; Ⓜ Nieuwmarkt) Famed Dutch Renaissance architect Hendrick de Keyser built the 'Southern Church' in 1611. This was

the first custom-built Protestant church in Amsterdam – still Catholic in design but with no choir. The final church service was held here in 1929. During the 'Hunger Winter' of WWII it served as a morgue.

The interior is now used for private events, but you can climb the recently renovated tower for a sky-high city view.

PINTOHUIS
ARCHITECTURE

Map p296 (Openbare Bibliotheek; www.huis depinto.nl; St Antoniesbreestraat 69; ⊙10.30-5.30pm Tue-Fri, 1-5pm Sat; MNieuwmarkt) St Antoniesbreestraat was once a busy street, but it lost many of its old buildings during the metro's construction. The Pintohuis remains, however. It was once owned by wealthy Sephardic Jew Isaac de Pinto, who had it remodelled with Italianate pilasters in the 1680s. It's now a *bibliotheek* (library) – pop inside to admire the beautiful ceiling frescoes, featuring lots of gold and soaring birds.

GASSAN DIAMONDS
FACTORY

Map p296 (www.gassan.com; Nieuwe Uilenburgerstraat 173-175; ⊙9am-5pm; 🚊9/14 Waterlooplein) **FREE** See diamond cutters and polishers in action at this workshop. You'll have a one-hour guided tour (no charge), which will prime you on assessing diamonds, then land you up in the shop with a chance to own your own sparklers, at a price.

The factory sits on Uilenburg, one of the rectangular islands reclaimed in the 1580s during a sudden influx of Sephardic Jews from Spain and Portugal. In the 1880s Gassan became the first diamond factory to use steam power.

PORTUGUESE-ISRAELITE SYNAGOGUE
SYNAGOGUE

Map p296 (www.portugesesynagoge.nl; Mr Visserplein 3; adult/child €15/7.50; ⊙10am-5pm Sun-Thu, to 4pm Fri, closed Sat Mar-Oct, reduced hours Nov-Feb; 🚊9/14 Mr Visserplein) With dizzying wooden barrel-vaulted ceilings, this was the largest synagogue in Europe when it was completed in 1675. It's still in use today, and has no electric light – after dark the candles in the vast chandeliers are lit for services. The large library belonging to the Ets Haim seminary is one of the oldest and most important Jewish book collections in Europe. Outside (near the entrance) stairs lead underground to the treasure chambers to see 16th-century manuscripts and gold-threaded tapestries.

Admission also provides entry to the Joods Historisch Museum and the Holocaust Museum.

TOP SIGHT
JOODS HISTORISCH MUSEUM

In an impressive complex of four beautiful Ashkenazic synagogues dating from the 17th and 18th centuries, the Jewish Historical Museum is full of fascinating insights into Amsterdam's Jewish past. The enormous Great Synagogue is home to displays showing the rise of Jewish enterprise and its role in the Dutch economy, and the history of Jews in the Netherlands, from when they first fled here in the 1600s, to the horror of their treatment during the German occupation of WWII through interviews with those who lived through it. The exhibition also covers how 25,000 Dutch Jews went into hiding (18,000 survived) and what life was like after the war as they tried to repatriate.

The complex has a Children's Museum set up as the Jewish home of a family, the Hollanders. There are regular activities, whereby kids can bake challah bread in the kitchen and play tunes in the music room.

The free, English-language audio tour that guides you through the collection is excellent, as is the bright cafe serving kosher dishes.

DON'T MISS
➡ Beautiful early illustrated books
➡ WWII interviews
➡ Children's Museum
➡ Free audio tour

PRACTICALITIES
➡ Jewish Historical Museum
➡ Map p296, D7
➡ 🕿020-531 03 80
➡ www.jhm.nl
➡ Nieuwe Amstelstraat 1
➡ adult/child €15/7.50
➡ ⊙11am-5pm
➡ 🚊9/14 Mr Visserplein

LOCAL KNOWLEDGE

GROENBURGWAL
••••••••••••••••••••••••••••••••••••

Step out onto the white drawbridge that crosses the Groenburgwal and look north towards the Zuiderkerk for one of Amsterdam's prettiest canal views (see p5). Impressionist Claude Monet certainly took a shining to it, and painted it in 1874 as *The Zuiderkerk (South Church) at Amsterdam: Looking up the Groenburgwal*.

The synagogue's architect, Elias Bouman, was inspired by the Temple of Solomon but the building's classical lines are typical of the Dutch capital. It was restored after WWII.

DOCKWORKER STATUE   STATUE
Map p296 (Ⓜ Waterlooplein) Mari Andriessen's *Dockworker* statue (1952) is a monumental, aghast-looking figure beside the Portuguese-Israelite Synagogue, in triangular JD Meijerplein. It was commissioned to commemorate the general strike that began among dockworkers on 25 February 1941 to protest against the treatment of Jews. The first deportation round-up had occurred here a few days earlier.

The anniversary of the strike is still an occasion for wreath-laying, but has become a low-key affair with the demise of the Dutch Communist Party.

STOPERA   NOTABLE BUILDING
Map p296 (☑020-625 54 55; www.operaballet. nl; Waterlooplein 22; ☐9/14 Waterlooplein) This curved waterside building is called 'Stopera' because it houses both the *stadhuis* (town hall) and the opera hall, aka Muziektheater (p99). It opened in 1986. For a peek behind the scenes, take a guided tour (adult/child €6/5) on Saturdays at 12.15pm.

Free lunchtime concerts usually take place from 12.30pm to 1pm on Tuesdays from September to June; doors open at 12.15pm.

◉ Plantage

HORTUS BOTANICUS   GARDENS
Map p298 (Botanical Garden; www.dehortus. nl; Plantage Middenlaan 2a; adult/child €9/5; ⊙10am-5pm daily, to 7pm Jul & Aug; ☐9/14 Mr Visserplein) A botanical garden since 1638, it bloomed as tropical seeds and plants were brought in (read: smuggled out of other countries) by Dutch trading ships. From here, coffee, pineapple, cinnamon and palm-oil plants were distributed throughout the world. The 4000-plus species are kept in wonderful structures, including the colonial-era seed house and a three-climate glasshouse.

The butterfly house is a hit with kids in particular. Free one-hour guided tours take place at fixed times or on request; pick up a ticket from the entrance and give it to the guide.

WERTHEIMPARK   PARK
Map p298 (Plantage Parklaan; ⊙7am-9pm; ☐9/14 Mr Visserplein) Adding to the lush greeness of the Plantage area, this park is a brilliant, willow-shaded spot for lazing by the Nieuwe Herengracht. It contains the **Auschwitz Memorial**, designed by Dutch writer Jan Wolkers: a panel of broken mirrors installed in the ground reflects the sky, and an inscription reads Nooit Meer (Never Again).

HOLLANDSCHE SCHOUWBURG   MEMORIAL
Map p298 (National Holocaust Museum; Holland Theatre; ☑020-531 03 10; www.hollandsche schouwburg.nl; Plantage Middenlaan 24; ⊙11am-5pm; ☐9/14 Plantage Kerklaan) Few theatres have had a history of such highs and lows. It was opened as the Artis Theatre in 1892 and became a hub of cultural life in Amsterdam, staging major dramas and operettas. In WWII the occupying Germans turned it into a Jew-only theatre, and later, horrifyingly, a detention centre for Jews held for deportation.

The occupiers processed up to 80,000 Jews here on their way to the death camps. Glass panels are engraved with the names of all Jewish families deported, and upstairs is a modest exhibit hall with photos and artefacts of Jewish life before and during the war.

MUIDERPOORT   GATE
Map p298 (Alexanderplein; ☐9 Alexanderplein) A dome tops this neoclassical arch, which was built in 1770 as a gateway to the city. On the south side you'll see the Amsterdam emblem of three St Andreas' crosses, while on the other side there's a cog ship emblem, which appeared on Amsterdam's coat of arms in medieval times.

TOP SIGHT
VERZETSMUSEUM

The museum of the Dutch Resistance illuminates the reality of German occupation in WWII, using personal stories, films, letters and photographs. To see the museum properly will take at least a couple of hours.

Beginning with the build-up to WWII in the 1930s, the chronologically-arranged exhibits give a powerful insight into the difficulties of this most painful period of Dutch history. Details about attempts to resist the Nazis – such as regular strikes, which resulted in harsh punishments and murders – have particular resonance. There is also unflinching evidence about the minority of locals who fell in with the Nazis. The museum uncovers the kind of active and passive resistance that took place, how the illegal Resistance press operated, how 300,000 people were kept in hiding and how all this could be funded. Beneath the mezzanine an exhibit covers the Dutch role in the Pacific War, particularly in relation to Indonesian independence from the Netherlands. Labels are in Dutch and English.

Included in admission, the new Verzetsmuseum Junior relates the stories of four Dutch children with engaging hands-on exhibits.

DON'T MISS

→ The Resistance press exhibits

→ The Pacific War exhibit

→ Letters and personal stories

PRACTICALITIES

→ Map p298, B4

→ ☎020-620 25 35

→ www.verzets museum.org

→ Plantage Kerklaan 61

→ adult/child €10/5

→ ⊙10am-5pm Tue-Fri, from 11am Sat-Mon

→ ▣9/14 Plantage Kerklaan

In 1811 Napoleon rode triumphantly through the gate with his royal entourage, and promptly demanded food for his ragged troops.

DE GOOYER WINDMILL   WINDMILL
Map p298 (Funenkade 5; ▣10 Hoogte Kadijk) This 18th-century grain mill is the sole survivor of five windmills that once stood in this part of town. It was moved to its current spot in 1814. The mill was fully renovated in 1925 and is now a private home. The public baths alongside the windmill were converted into Brouwerij 't IJ (p97) in 1985.

WERFMUSEUM 'T KROMHOUT   MUSEUM
Map p298 (☎020-627 67 77; www.kromhout museum.nl; Hoogte Kadijk 147; adult/child €5/ free; ⊙10am-3pm Tue; ▣10 Hoogte Kadijk) Boats are still repaired at the 18th-century wharf on the outer side of the dyke, and this is a 'working' museum in the eastern hall, devoted to shipbuilding and to the indestructible marine engines that were designed and built here. If the thought of seeing the first 12HP petrol engine from 1904 gets you going, you'll love it. Signage is primarily in Dutch only.

ENTREPOTDOK   ARCHITECTURE
Map p298 (▣9/14 Plantage Kerklaan) In an area northeast of the Plantage, there is a 500m row of warehouses that once belonged to the Dutch East India Company (VOC). This powerful organisation, the Amazon of its day, grew rich on sea trade in the 17th century. This was the largest storage depot in Europe at the time – located in a customs-free zone.

Some of the original facades have been preserved, and the warehouses are now used as hip offices, apartments and dockside cafes, with tables perfect for lazing away an afternoon at the water's edge.

KADIJKSPLEIN   SQUARE
Map p298 (Kadijksplein; ▣22/48 Kadijksplein) With several laid-back *cafés* (pubs-bars), with perfectly positioned terraces for when the rays are worth catching, this tranquil square sits on the edge of 17th-century canals at the point before they widen out to the docklands.

NIEUWMARKT, PLANTAGE & THE EASTERN ISLANDS SIGHTS

⊙ Eastern Islands

★**NEMO SCIENCE MUSEUM** MUSEUM
Map p298 (✍020-531 32 33; www.nemoscience
museum.nl; Oosterdok 2; €16.50, roof terrace
free; ⊙10am-5.30pm, closed Mon Sep-Mar, roof
terrace to 9pm Jul & Aug; ☒22/48 IJ-Tunnel)
Perched atop the entrance to the IJ Tunnel
is the unmissable slanted-roof green-copper building, designed by Italian architect Renzo Piano, almost surrounded by
water. Its rooftop square has great views
and water- and wind-operated hands-on
exhibits. Inside, everything is interactive,
with three floors of investigative mayhem.
Experiment lifting yourself up via a pulley,
making bubbles, building structures, divid-
ing light into colours, racing your shadow
and discovering the teenage mind.

Piano conceived the design as the inverse
of the IJ Tunnel below. Inside, Piano's
design reflects a 'noble factory', with
exposed wiring and pipes.

ARCAM ARCHITECTURE
Map p298 (Stichting Architectuurcentrum
Amsterdam; ✍020-620 48 78; www.arcam.
nl; Prins Hendrikkade 600; ⊙1-5pm Tue-Sat;
☎; ☒22/48 Kadijksplein) FREE The sharply
curved Amsterdam Architecture Foundation is a striking waterside building hosting
changing architectural exhibitions.

★**HET SCHEEPVAARTMUSEUM** MUSEUM
Map p298 (Maritime Museum; ✍020-523 22 22;
www.hetscheepvaartmuseum.nl; Kattenburgerplein 1; adult/child €15/7.50; ⊙9am-5pm; ⧉;
☒22/48 Kattenburgerplein) A waterfront 17th-
century admiralty building houses this
renovated, state-of-the-art presentation of

maritime memorabilia. Highlights include
exquisite and imaginatively presented
Golden Age maps, fascinating 19th-cen-
tury photo albums of early voyages and an
audiovisual immersive journey evoking a
voyage by ship. Outside, you can clamber
over the full-scale replica of the Dutch East
India Company's 700-tonne *Amsterdam* –
one of the largest ships of the fleet – with
its tiny bunks and sailors' hammocks, and
the chance to mock-fire its cannons.

**OBA: CENTRALE
BIBLIOTHEEK AMSTERDAM** LIBRARY
Map p298 (Amsterdam Central Library; ✍020-
523 09 00; www.oba.nl; Oosterdokskade 143;
⊙10am-10pm; ☎; ☒4/9/16/24/26 Centraal)
FREE This being Amsterdam, it has the
funkiest library you can imagine, built in
2007, and spread over multiple light, bright
floors. The basement is devoted to kids, and
has a wigwam, a huge polar bear and the
magical, marvelous Mouse Mansion, with
100 incredibly beautifully detailed rooms,
the work of artist Karina Content. On the
7th floor is the reasonably priced cafe, with
an outdoor terrace from where thrilling
panoramic views roll across the water to
Amsterdam's old town.

MUZIEKGEBOUW AAN 'T IJ ARCHITECTURE
Map p298 (www.muziekgebouw.nl; Piet Heinkade
1; ☒26 Muziekgebouw) Even if you don't catch
a performance (p98) here, the cool contemporary architecture makes the magnificent
'Music Building on the IJ' worth swinging by
for a visit. Work on it began in 1995, spanning 20 years until the opening in 2005. It
comprises a large concert hall and the more
intimate Bimhuis (p98) for jazz, and was
designed by the Danish firm 3xNielsen.

NAP: AMSTERDAM'S SEA LEVEL MEASUREMENT

It is widely known that Amsterdam (and indeed more than half of the Netherlands)
lies a couple of metres below sea level, but when's the last time you heard anyone ask
'which sea level'? In fact, sea levels vary around the globe and even around the Netherlands. The average level of the former Zuiderzee, in the lee of Friesland, was slightly
lower than that of the North Sea along the Netherlands' exposed west coast.

The Normaal Amsterdams Peil (NAP; Normal Amsterdam Level) was established in
the 17th century as the average high-water mark of the Zuiderzee and it still forms the
zero reference for elevation countrywide. It is now used throughout the EU as the European Vertical Reference System (EVRS). The **NAP Visitors Centre** (www.normaal
amsterdamspeil.nl) shows the ins and outs of the NAP. Water columns here represent
different sea levels, as well as disastrous flood levels in 1953 (4.55m above NAP).
Information sheets and a touch-screen explain the details.

TOP SIGHT
ARTIS ROYAL ZOO

Rambling, leafy and full of interesting historic architecture, this is mainland Europe's oldest zoo. The diverse wildlife occupies extensive habitats, including African savannah and tropical rainforest, and there are 900 different animal species, 200 species of tree, an aquarium with coral reefs, as well as a planetarium and kids' petting zoo. There are also lots of opportunities to see the feeding times of various animals: check the daily schedule.

Next door is the marvellous **Micropia** (www.micropia.nl; ⊙9am-6pm Sun-Wed, to 8pm Thu-Sat; ⊞9/14 Artis), which will leave you feeling uncomfortably aware of the invisible world of the microbe. Hands-on exhibits and microscopes enable you to peer through and witness fascinating, if unsettling, facts about how many living organisms there are on everyday objects. There are also glass models of and information on viruses from ebola to smallpox. It's aimed at those aged eight and over, but younger kids will enjoy collecting the stamps as you go around the exhibits.

Locals as well as tourists visit to stroll the paths laid out through the former Plantage gardens. The grounds are packed with heritage-listed 19th-century buildings and monuments, and there are several cafes on-site.

DON'T MISS
➜ Micropia museum
➜ The aquarium
➜ The lion habitat
➜ African savannah

PRACTICALITIES
➜ Map p298, B4
➜ ☑020-523 34 00
➜ www.artis.nl
➜ Plantage Kerklaan 38-40
➜ adult/child €20.50/17, incl Micropia €27.50/23.50
➜ ⊙9am-6pm Mar-Oct, to 5pm Nov-Feb
➜ ⊞9/14 Plantage Kerklaan

NIEUWMARKT, PLANTAGE & THE EASTERN ISLANDS EATING

You can visit the concert hall during box-office opening hours (noon to 6pm Monday to Saturday) or during performances.

With huge windows overlooking the IJ, the venue's wow-factor Zouthaven (p96) restaurant specialises in seafood.

✖ EATING

You've got lots of eating-out choices in Nieuwmarkt, with some gems amid this central Amsterdam hub. Plantage is only a short bike ride away, but a different world in atmosphere. Head to this leafy district for laid-back neighbourhood restaurants. You can expect the spectacular on the Eastern Islands and Eastern Docklands, with many of the best places to dine having fantastic river views.

✖ Nieuwmarkt

Map p296 (www.sterkstaaltje.com; Staalstraat 12; dishes €4-8; ⊙8am-7pm Mon-Fri, to 6pm Sat, 11am-5pm Sun; ⊞4/9/14/16/24 Muntplein) With pristine fruit and veg stacked up outside, Sterk Staaltje is worth entering just to breathe in the scent of the foodstuffs, with a fine range of ready-to-eat treats: teriyaki meatballs, feta and sundried tomato quiche, pumpkin-stuffed wraps, a soup of the day and particularly fantastic sandwiches – roast beef, horseradish and rucola (arugula/rocket) or marinated chicken with guacamole and sour cream.

★TOKOMAN   SOUTH AMERICAN €
Map p296 (Waterlooplein 327, sandwiches €3-4.50, dishes €6-14; ⊙11am-8pm Mon-Sat; ⊞9/14 Waterlooplein) Queue with the folks getting their Surinamese spice on at Tokoman. It makes a sensational *broodje pom* (a sandwich filled with a tasty mash of chicken and a starchy Surinamese tuber). You'll want the *zuur* (pickled-cabbage relish) and *peper* (chilli) on it, plus a cold can of coconut water to wash it down.

There's another **branch** (Map p296; Zeedijk 136; sandwiches €3-4.50, dishes €6-13; ⊙noon-9pm; ⊞9/14 Waterlooplein) close by.

TISFRIS
CAFE €

Map p296 (www.tisfris.nl; St Antoniebreestraat 142; dishes €5-15; ☺9am-7pm; 🚊9/14 Waterlooplein) High-ceilinged TisFris floods with light through huge plate-glass windows, has outdoor seating for sunny days, and is handily located almost next door to Rembrandthuis. It's ideal for a light lunch, such as avocado, beetroot hummus and olives, or courgette (zucchini) and goat's cheese salad.

TOKO JOYCE
INDONESIAN €

Map p296 (www.tokojoyce.nl; Nieuwmarkt 38; dishes €8-11; ☺1-8pm Sun & Mon, from 11am Tue-Sat; Ⓜ Nieuwmarkt) With a few bar-stool seats, this cheap and cheerful choice is great for a quick bite. You choose from a selection of Indonesian-Surinamese food, with the 'lunch box' (you choose noodles or rice, plus two spicy, coconutty toppings) particularly good value. To finish, there's *spekkoek* (layered gingerbread). If you don't fancy eating in, canal-side benches beckon a few steps from the door.

SOUP EN ZO
SOUP €

Map p296 (www.soupenzo.nl; Jodenbreestraat 94; soup €5-7; ☺11am-8pm Mon-Fri, noon-7pm Sat & Sun; Ⓜ Waterlooplein) Great when you need your cockles warmed, this is one of a chain that serves delicious fresh soups of the day, which may include a creamy fish soup or the Dutch classic pea, as well as imaginative salad combinations (*en zo* means 'and so on' in Dutch). There are some outside tables as well as bar stools inside.

FRENZI
MEDITERRANEAN €€

Map p296 (📞020-423 51 12; www.frenzi-restaurant.nl; Zwanenburgwal 232; mains lunch €7-15, dinner €18-22, tapas €5-7; ☺10am-10pm; 🚊4/9/14/16/24 Muntplein) Frenzi has lots of atmosphere (scrubbed wood tables, lit with candles) and serves delicious Italian tapas – Manchego cheese and fig compote; marinated sardines; portobello mushrooms with melted Gorgonzola – but save room for mains like pan-fried cod with fennel mash, pumpkin gnocchi with wilted spinach, and leg of lamb with roast asparagus.

It stocks 110 types of grappa, and live jazz plays on Saturdays at 3pm.

HEMELSE MODDER
DUTCH €€

Map p296 (📞020-624 32 03; www.hemelse modder.nl; Oude Waal 11; 3-/4-/5-course menu €36/43/49; ☺6-11pm daily, plus noon-2.30pm Sat & Sun; Ⓜ Nieuwmarkt) 'Heavenly Mud', named after its signature dark and white chocolate mousse, has blonde-wood tables and a Dutch-meets-global menu that emphasises North Sea fish and farm-fresh produce, with dishes like pan-fried fillet of North Sea plaice with capers, cream, mashed potatoes, samphire and sea aster. There's a lovely terrace for when the sun comes out.

NAM KEE
CHINESE €€

Map p296 (📞020-638 28 48; www.namkee.net; Geldersekade 117; mains €7-20; ☺noon-10.30pm; 🍴; Ⓜ Nieuwmarkt) A long-running favourite, this is the stylish branch of Amsterdam's Chinese icon; the best-known Nam Kee (p76) is in the Medieval Centre. You may have to queue.

POCO LOCO
CAFE €€

Map p296 (www.diningcity.net/pocoloco; Nieuwmarkt 24; mains lunch €4-12, dinner €12-18; ☺9am-1am Mon-Thu, to 3am Fri, 10am-3am Sat, to 1am Sun; 🍴🍴; Ⓜ Nieuwmarkt) Poco Loco is a good spot for people-watching on Nieuwmarkt square, while tucking into funked-up salads and sandwiches for lunch, or pan-European tapas with a Dutch twist for dinner, such as prawn skewers. Grab a terrace seat or there's room in the 1970s-styled interior.

LATEI
CAFE €€

Map p296 (www.latei.net; Zeedijk 143; lunch dishes €4-7, dinner mains €7-18; ☺8am-6pm Mon-Wed, to 10pm Thu & Fri, 9am-10pm Sat, 11am-6pm Sun; 🍴; Ⓜ Nieuwmarkt) If you like any of the vintage furnishings at Latei, you can take them home: they're for sale. This is one of the hipper cafes around Nieuwmarkt, a laid-back split-level cafe. It serves dinner from Thursday through Saturday, often an Ethiopian, Indian or Indonesian dish by the local 'cooking collective'. Otherwise, it's sandwiches, apple pie and *koffie verkeerd* (milky coffee).

NYONYA
ASIAN €€

Map p296 (www.nyonya-malaysia-restaurant. com; Kloveniersburgwal 38; mains €10-19; ☺1-9pm; Ⓜ Nieuwmarkt) This little place, a simple cafe with a black and white tiled floor, makes a mean bowl of laksa (spicy noodle soup), a complex rendang curry (spicy and coconutty) with beef, chicken or prawns, and several other Malaysian specialities, including nasi goreng (fried rice). There's no alcohol, but you can sip milky tea or Sarsae (a Chinese root beer).

LASTAGE
FRENCH €€€

Map p296 (☑020-737 08 11; www.restaurant lastage.nl; Geldersekade 29; 3-/4-/5-/6-course menus from €43/53/63/73; ☺6.30-10pm Tue-Sun Sep-Jul; ☐4/9/16/24 Centraal Station) Classy Lastage is a gastronomic oasis at the edge of the Red Light District. Step inside and you're a world away from the sleaze nearby. Food is equally sophisticated, with creative cooking: smoked eel, black pudding, green peas, sea lavender and smoked-eel foam may be followed by lamb with marrow-fat peas, broad beans, purple-sweet-potato gnocchi and cinnamon sauce.

✗ Plantage

IJSCUYPJE
ICE CREAM €

Map p298 (www.ijscuypje.nl; Plantage Kerklaan 33; ☺noon-10pm; ☐Plantage Kerklaan) Great ice-cream shop with locations across Amsterdam, including this one close to the zoo. Scoops of dairy-free sorbets or creamy treats, such as salted caramel and strawberry, are satisfyingly large.

IJSMOLEN
ICE CREAM €

Map p298 (Zeeburgerstraat 2; 1/2/4 scoops €1.50/2.75/4.75; ☺noon-9pm; ☐10 Hoogte Kadijk) Homemade ice cream at this spot near De Gooyer Windmill comes in Dutch flavours like *stroopwafel* (classic caramel-syrup-filled wafers) and *speculaas* (spicy Christmas biscuits); plus *stracciatella* (vanilla with shredded chocolate) and lemon cheesecake; and pure fruity flavours including mango, mint and watermelon. On hot days it stays open to 10pm.

CAFÉ SMITH EN VOOGT
CAFE €€

Map p298 (www.cafesmitenvoogt.nl; Plantage Parklaan 10; mains lunch €4-8, dinner €10-19; ☺kitchen 10am-9.30pm; ☎; ☐9/14 Plantage Kerklaan) On a leafy corner, with high ceilings and a relaxed vibe, this cool and laid-back cafe is ideal for a salad or sandwich for lunch, or a coffee or slice of apple pie when visiting Museum het Rembrandt Huis (p87) or the adjacent Wertheimpark (p90). There's also a more substantial dinner menu.

CAFÉ KADIJK
INDONESIAN €€

Map p298 (☑06 1774 4441; www.cafekadijk.nl; Kadijksplein 5; mains €15-20; ☺4pm-1am, to 3am Fri & Sat, kitchen 4-10pm; ☐22/48 Kadijksplein) This snug split-level cafe has a big terrace with views across the water in summer, and is popular for its excellent, good-value Indonesian food, including a mini version of the normally gigantic rijsttafel (Indonesian banquet). No credit cards.

GARE DE L'EST
INTERNATIONAL €€

Map p298 (☑020-463 06 20; www.garedelest.nl; Cruquiusweg 9; 4-course menu €33; ☺6-10pm; ☐22 Het Funen) Off the beaten track, this popular local haunt has the novelty of a surprise menu: four courses chosen by the chef will arrive (dietary requirements, including vegetarianism can be accommodated). Deep colours and lanterns decorate the exotic-looking interior of the 1901 building, but in warm weather the best seats are in the courtyard.

✗ Eastern Islands

★GEBR HARTERING
DUTCH €€

Map p298 (☑020-421 06 99; www.gebr-hartering. nl; Peperstraat 10; 5-/7-course menu €55/80, mains around €28; ☺6-10.30pm Tue-Sun; ☐32/33 Prins Hendrikkade) Lined in pale rustic wood, this gem was founded by two food-loving brothers, who offer either à la carte or a multi-course menu that changes daily according to the best seasonal produce available. A meal here is always a delight to linger over, so settle in and enjoy the accompanying wines and canal-side location.

DE PLANTAGE
MODERN EUROPEAN €€

Map p298 (☑020-760 68 00; www.caferestau rantdeplantage.nl; Plantage Kerklaan 36; mains lunch €7-22, dinner €17-22; ☺9am-1am Mon-Fri, 10am-1am Sat & Sun, kitchen closes 10pm; ☐9/14 Plantage Kerklaan) Huge and graceful, this is an impressive space in a 1870s-built, 1900-expanded former greenhouse decked with blonde wood and black chairs, with hothouse views of strutting geese in the grounds of the Artis Royal Zoo (p93). Food is creative and tasty, if not outstanding, with dishes like salad with roasted octopus, gild fried and naked cod), mussels and saffron mayo.

Tables scatter beneath trees strung with fairy lights in summer.

INSTOCK
INTERNATIONAL €€

Map p298 (www.instock.nl; Czaar Peterstraat 21; dishes €4-14, 3-/4-course dinner menu €24/29; ☺8.30am-10pm Sun-Wed, to 11pm Thu-Sat; ☑; ☐10 Eerste Coehoornstraat) ✦ Instock's food is extremely tasty, with some surprising combinations – like a talented chef has conjured up a great meal from leftovers! This is precisely the raison d'être of Instock, reducing food waste, using products that are still in date but would otherwise be thrown out. It also offers the fine Pieper beer, made from some of the Netherlands' 340 million annually discarded potatoes.

There's a terrace on the quiet street, the interior is light and bright, and there's live music on Saturday afternoons. Cards only – no cash.

ÉÉNVISTWÉÉVIS
SEAFOOD €€

Map p298 (☑020-623 28 94; www.eenvistweevis. nl; Schippersgracht 6; mains €19-29; ☺6-10pm Tue-Sat; ☐22/48 Kadijksplein) This unassuming yet classy local favourite is the type of place locals put on their best shirt to go to, with a shell-and-chandelier interior, and a short menu that revels in simplicity and utilises whatever is in season, like oysters, prawns with garlic, or prime beefsteak.

DE KLEINE KAART
INTERNATIONAL €€

Map p298 (☑020-354 78 38; www.dekleinekaart. nl; Piraeusplein 59; mains €15-19; ☺noon-9pm Tue-Sun; ☐10 Azartplein) The 'Small Menu' is a charming little neighbourhood restaurant with an idyllic view of boats bobbing on the water. At its small, flower-adorned tables you can tuck into fresh, simple pleasures, such as steak, hamburgers and salad bowls.

ZOUTHAVEN
SEAFOOD €€

Map p298 (☑020-788 20 90; www.zouthaven.nl; Muziekgebouw aan 't IJ, Piet Heinkade 1; mains lunch €8-15, dinner €17-27; ☺11.30am-11.30pm; ☐26 Muziekgebouw) ✦ IJ waterfront music venue Muziekgebouw aan 't IJ has triple-height plate-glass windows for wow-factor river views, a prime spot for boat-watching. It all feels expense-account fabulous, with food that is suitably fancy, with an emphasis on sustainable seafood.

SEA PALACE
CHINESE €€

Map p298 (☑020-626 47 77; www.seapalace. nl; Oosterdokskade 8; mains €10-19, dim sum €4.50-7; ☺noon-11pm; ☐4/9/16/24/26 Centraal Station) Palatial floating on the Chinese restaurant Sea Palace has three floors busy with locals and visitors who aren't only here for the great views of the city from across the IJ, but also for the lip-smacking Chinese fare, from duck with pancakes to notably good dim sum. Reservations recommended, especially if you want a window seat. Service can be slow.

KOMPASZAAL
CAFE €€

Map p298 (☑020-419 95 96; www.kompaszaal.nl; KNSM-laan 311; mains lunch €6-14, dinner €15-21, high tea €18; ☺kitchen 10am-6pm Wed, to 1am Thu, to 2am Fri 11am-2am Sat, 11am-1am Sun; ☎; ☐10 Azartplein) Set in the century-old Royal Dutch Steamboat Company (KNSM in Dutch) arrivals hall, this huge, airy cafe has kept some vintage fittings and there's a long balcony overlooking the river. Snacky lunches include croque-monsieurs and smoked salmon and scrambled eggs, while for dinner you can tuck into substantial dishes, like risotto, or have a drink with some *bitterballen* (croquettes).

Regular 1950s swing, jazz, tango and salsa events take place on Friday nights.

★GREETJE
DUTCH €€€

Map p298 (☑020-779 74 50; www.restaurant greetje.nl; Peperstraat 23-25; mains €23-29; ☺kitchen 6-10pm Sun-Thu, to 11pm Fri & Sat; ☐22/34/35/48 Prins Hendrikkade) ✦ Greetje is Amsterdam's most creative Dutch restaurant, using the best seasonal produce to resurrect and re-create traditional Dutch recipes, like pickled beef, braised veal with apricots and leek *stamppot* (traditional mashed potatoes and vegetables), and pork belly with Dutch mustard sauce. Kick off with the Big Beginning (€18), with a sampling of hot and cold starters.

If you can't decide on dessert, which includes dishes like lemon buttermilk pie with crushed candy-cookie crust, and ice-cream soufflé of apricots, curd with soaked prunes and marinated grapes, there's the Dutch cheese selection with apple syrup, soaked prunes and dark rye bread.

🍷 DRINKING & NIGHTLIFE

There are plenty of bars and coffeeshops around Nieuwmarkt, whose pavement cafes are perfect for watching the world go by. For something a bit more

quirky, head to the Brouwerij 't IJ (p97) microbrewery adjacent to De Gooyer Windmill. Want something even cooler? Go to one of the Eastern Islands' fabulous shack-like hang-outs, including Amsterdam Roest (p98), with its canal-side beach, or Hannekes Boom (p98), a hipster beer garden with a waterfront location.

🍴 Nieuwmarkt

★DE SLUYSWACHT   BROWN CAFE

Map p296 (www.sluyswacht.nl; Jodenbreestraat 1; ⊙noon-1am Sun-Thu, to 3am Fri & Sat; 🚊9/14 Waterlooplein) Built in 1695 and listing like a ship in a high wind, this tiny black building, out on a limb by the canal, was once a lock-keeper's house on the Oude Schans. Today the canal-side terrace with gorgeous views of the Montelbaanstoren is a charming spot to relax with a Dutch or Belgian beer, and rib-sticking bar snacks like *bitterballen,* chips and toasties.

BLUEBIRD   COFFEESHOP

Map p296 (Sint Antoniesbreestraat 71; ⊙9.30am-1am; 🛜; MNieuwmarkt) Away from Nieuwmarkt's main cluster of coffeeshops, Bluebird has a less touristy, more local vibe. The multiroom space has beautiful murals and local artists' paintings, a lounge with leather chairs, a nonalcoholic bar and a kitchen serving superior snacks, such as freshly made pancakes. It's especially well known for its hash, including varieties not available elsewhere in Amsterdam.

CAFE CUBA   COCKTAIL BAR

Map p296 (www.cafecuba.nl; Nieuwmarkt 3; ⊙1pm-1am Mon-Thu, 11am-3am Fri & Sat, 11am-1am Sun; MNieuwmarkt) This is where the classic Dutch brown cafe meets the Caribbean: there's a background of faded decadence and photos of Hemingway. It's an ideal Nieuwmarkt spot for slouching behind a table with names etched into it, preparing for the night ahead with cocktails, such as mai tais, planter's punch and mojitos.

LOKAAL 'T LOOSJE   BROWN CAFE

Map p296 (www.loosje.nl; Nieuwmarkt 32-34; ⊙8.30am-1am Sun-Thu, to 3am Fri & Sat; MNieuwmarkt) A colourful mix of locals and tourists throng the tables to sip drinks – including beers from niche breweries, such

as Oedipus Brewery (p199) or 2 Chefs – at this venerable cafe on Nieuwmarkt square. Inside has fine pictorial tiling and stencilled glass, and wicker chairs spill onto the herringbone pavement terrace out the front in fine weather.

GREEN PLACE   COFFEESHOP

Map p296 (www.thegreenplace.nl; Kloveniersburgwal 4; ⊙10am-1am; MNieuwmarkt) Small, but with a reputation for a good selection, good-quality product and fair prices, so much so that there may be queues. Cash only.

CAFE DE ENGELBEWAARDER   BROWN CAFE

Map p296 (www.cafe-de-engelbewaarder.nl; Kloveniersburgwal 59; ⊙10am-1am Mon-Fri, to 3am Fri & Sat, noon-1am Sun; MNieuwmarkt) A cafe for literature and music lovers, with regular photographic exhibitions, this is a peaceful canal-side haven, renowned for its in-house live jazz band on Sunday afternoon from 4.30pm to 7pm September to June. It specialises in Belgian brews from the Palm brewery, and there are 15 beers on tap.

🍴 Plantage

★BROUWERIJ 'T IJ   BREWERY

Map p298 (www.brouwerijhetij.nl; Funenkade 7; ⊙brewery 2-8pm; 🚊10 Hoogte Kadijk) 🌿 Can you get more Dutch than drinking an organic beer beneath the creaking sails of the 1725-built De Gooyer Windmill? This is Amsterdam's leading organic microbrewery, with delicious standard, seasonal and limited-edition brews; try the fragrant, hoppy house brew, Plzeň. There's the tiled tasting room, lined by an amazing bottle collection, or the plane-tree-shaded terrace.

A beer is included in the 30-minute brewery tour (€5.50; 3.30pm Friday to Sunday).

★SKYLOUNGE   COCKTAIL BAR

Map p298 (www.skyloungeamsterdam. com; Oosterdoksstraat 4; ⊙11am-1am Sun-Tue, to 2am Wed & Thu, to 3am Fri & Sat; 🚊1/2/4/5/9/14/16/24 Centraal Station) With wow-factor views whatever the weather, this bar offers a 360-degree panorama of Amsterdam from atop the 11th floor of the DoubleTree Amsterdam Centraal Station hotel – and just gets better when you head out to its vast, sofa-strewn SkyTerrace, with an outdoor bar. To toast the view: a choice of 500 different cocktails. DJs regularly hit the decks.

DE GROENE OLIFANT
BROWN CAFE

Map p298 (www.degroeneolifant.nl; Sarphatistraat 510; 11am-1am Sun-Thu, to 2am Fri & Sat; ⊜9 Alexanderplein) A local favourite for generations, inside the Green Elephant is all 19th-century opulence with wrought-iron chandeliers, intricate woodwork and dim lighting, a setting for a drink back in time. Sit at the circa-1880 bar and admire the art-deco glass, retreat to the lofted dining room for dinner like previous elegant Plantage residents or catch some rays at the outside tables.

🍸 Eastern Islands

★AMSTERDAM ROEST
BEER GARDEN

Map p298 (www.amsterdamroest.nl; Jacob Bontiusplaats 1; ⊙noon-1am Sun-Thu, to 3pm Fri & Sat; ⊜22 Wittenburgergracht) This is one of those 'only in Amsterdam' places, and well worth the trip. Once-derelict shipyards now host an epically cool artist collective–bar–restaurant, Amsterdam Roest (Dutch for 'Rust'), with a canal-side terrace, mammoth playground of ropes and tyres, hammocks, street art, a sandy beach in summer and bonfires in winter.

The bar interior is a crazy warehouse of sofas and industrial-art confections. Regular events are hosted, including films, live music, festivals, fashion shows and markets. It's slightly tricky to find; the most direct approach is to go along Oostenburgervoorstraat and cross the bridge at the northern end – it's 150m ahead on your left.

★HANNEKES BOOM
BEER GARDEN

Map p298 (www.hannekesboom.nl; Dijksgracht 4; ⊙10am-1am Sun-Thu, to 3am Fri & Sat; ⊜26 Muziekgebouw) Reachable via a couple of pedestrian/bike bridges from the NEMO Science Museum, this nonchalantly cool, laid-back waterside *café* built from recycled materials has a beer garden that really feels like a garden, with timber benches, picnic tables under the trees and a hipster, arty crowd enjoying sitting out in the sunshine (it comes into its own in summer).

The site dates back to 1662, when it was a guard post monitoring maritime traffic into the city.

KHL
BAR

Map p298 (www.khl.nl; Oostelijke Handelskade 44; ⊙3pm-midnight Tue-Sun, from noon Sat; ⊜26 Rietlandpark) Set in a historic 1917 brick building with stunning tilework and painted a retro colour scheme of pale green and pink, KHL's bar opens to a vine-shaded terrace that makes a superb spot for a glass of wine sourced from small vineyards. Regular live music ranges from Portuguese fado to pop and *klezmer* (traditional Jewish music).

KHL stands for Koninklijke Hollandsche Lloyd shipping company, and this was formerly the canteen for captains and maritime staff.

HPS
COCKTAIL BAR

Map p298 (☏06 2528 3620; www.hps amsterdam.com; Rapenburg 18; ⊙6pm-1am Sun-Thu, to 3am Fri & Sat; ⊜32/33 Prins Hendrikkade) With art-deco lights and waistcoated mixologists-as-alchemists behind the bar, cool speakeasy-style HPS (short for Hiding in Plain Sight) is tiny so it's worth booking ahead on weekends. Maestro mixers produce concoctions like La Vie en Rose (tequila, lemon and rose petals) and Beetlejuice (tequila, jalapeno-infused Cointreau, fresh beetroot juice and balsamic vinegar). There's European folk dancing with a live band every third Thursday.

MEZRAB
CLUB

Map p298 (☏020-419 33 68; www.mezrab.nl; Veemkade 576; ⊙8pm-1am Sun-Thu, to 3am Fri & Sat; ⊜26 Kattenburgerstraat) This wonderfully eclectic harbourside cultural centre hosts storytelling sessions in English and Dutch, Iranian rock bands, hip-swinging Brazilian samba nights, comedy nights and much more. Hours can vary. Cash only.

☆ ENTERTAINMENT

MUZIEKGEBOUW AAN 'T IJ
CONCERT VENUE

Map p298 (☏tickets 020-788 20 00; www.muziek gebouw.nl; Piet Heinkade 1; tickets free-€40; ⊙box office noon-6pm; ⊜26 Muziekgebouw) A dramatic glass-and-steel box on the IJ waterfront, this multidisciplinary performing-arts venue has a state-of-the-art main hall with flexible stage layout and great acoustics. Its jazz stage, **Bimhuis** (Map p298; ☏020-788 21 88; www.bimhuis.nl; Piet Heinkade 3; tickets free-€32; ⊜26 Muziekgebouw), is

> **LOCAL KNOWLEDGE**
>
> ## AMSTERDAM, CITY OF DIAMONDS
> ....
>
> Why is Amsterdam such a diamond centre? It was the Sephardic Jews who introduced the cutting industry, shortly after their arrival here, in the 1580s. The trade lived on, and two historic diamond factories offer free guided tours. Gassan Diamonds (p89) offers the slicker version. Coster Diamonds (p170) has a convenient location at the Museumplein. You'll see lots of sparklers, and workers shining them, at both places.
>
> For those in the market to buy, note that diamonds aren't necessarily cheaper in Amsterdam than elsewhere, but between the tours and extensive descriptions and factory offers, you'll know what you're buying.
>
> A bit of diamond folklore: Cullinan, the largest diamond ever found (3106 carats), was split into more than 100 stones here in 1908, after which the master cutter spent three months recovering from stress.

more intimate. Try the Last Minute Ticket Shop (www.lastminuteticketshop.nl) for discounts.

MUZIEKTHEATER　　　　CLASSICAL MUSIC
Map p296 (☎020-625 54 55; www.operaballet.nl; Waterlooplein 22; ◎box office noon-6pm Mon-Fri, to 3pm Sat & Sun or until performance Sep-Jul; ⓖ9/14 Waterlooplein) The Muziektheater is home to the Netherlands Opera and the National Ballet, with some spectacular performances. Big-name performers and international dance troupes also take the stage here. Free classical concerts (12.30pm to 1pm) are held most Tuesdays from September to May in its Boekmanzaal.

**AMSTERDAMS
MARIONETTEN THEATER**　　　　THEATRE
Map p296 (☎020-620 80 27; www.marionetten theater.nl; Nieuwe Jonkerstraat 8; adult/child €15/7.50, 90min tour €15; ⓜNieuwmarkt) An enchanting enterprise that seems to exist in another era, this marionette theatre (in a former blacksmith's shop) presents fairy tales or Mozart operas, such as *The Magic Flute,* but kids and adults alike are just as enthralled by the magical stage sets, period costumes and beautiful singing voices that bring the diminutive cast to life.

It's possible to arrange a tour backstage; check the website for details.

KRITERION　　　　CINEMA
Map p298 (☎020-623 17 08; www.kriterion.nl; Roetersstraat 170; tickets from €5; ⓖ7/10 Wees-perplein) Kriterion was originally a student organisation involved in hiding and protecting Jews from the Nazis during WWII. In 1945 the group opened this cinema to provide employment for students unable to complete their studies. Today it's still

going strong, with a great array of art-house premieres, themed parties, classics, kids' flicks and more, plus there's a cafe.

BETHANIËNKLOOSTER　　　　CLASSICAL MUSIC
Map p296 (☎020-625 00 78; Barndesteeg 6b; ◎Sep-Jul; ⓜNieuwmarkt) This former monastery near Nieuwmarkt has a glorious ballroom, and is a superb place to take in exceptional chamber music. Jazz fills the vaulted basement cellar.

**CONSERVATORIUM
VAN AMSTERDAM**　　　　CLASSICAL MUSIC
Map p298 (☎020-527 78 37; www.ahk.nl/ conservatorium; Oosterdokskade 151; ⓖ4/9/16/24 Centraal Station) Catch a classical recital by students at the Netherlands' largest conservatory of music. There are regular festivals in this snazzy contemporary building with state-of-the-art acoustics.

🛍 SHOPPING

Nieuwmarkt has lots of small boutiques and interesting independent shops, selling everything from fetishwear to haberdashery, while there is one of Amsterdam's best flea markets on Waterlooplein, and a cluster of Amsterdam's chicest homeware shops on the Eastern Islands.

🛍 Nieuwmarkt

⭐**HÔTEL DROOG**　　　　DESIGN, HOMEWARES
Map p296 (www.droog.com; Staalstraat 7; ◎9am-7pm; ⓖ4/9/14/16/24 Muntplein) Not a hotel, but a local design house. Droog

means 'dry' in Dutch, and these products are full of dry wit. You'll find all kinds of stylish versions of useful things – a chic dish sponge or streamlined hot water bottle – as well as the kind of clothing that should probably by law be worn by a designer or an architect.

Also here is a gallery space and a high-beamed all-white cafe, overlooked by a tapestry of Rembrant's *The Night Watch*. To live the life, rent the top-floor apartment (double €290).

★WATERLOOPLEIN

FLEA MARKET MARKET
Map p296 (www.waterlooplein.amsterdam; Waterlooplein; ☺9.30am-6pm Mon-Sat; 🚊9/14 Waterlooplein) Covering the square once known as Vlooienburg (Flea Town), the Waterlooplein Flea Market draws bargain hunters seeking everything from antique knick-knacks to vintage leather coats. The street market started in 1880 when Jewish traders living in the neighbourhood began selling their wares here. During the Nazi occupation Jews were rounded up here before being sent away to camps.

KNUFFELS

TOYS, SHOES
Map p296 (www.knuffels.com; St Antonies-breestraat 39-51; ☺10am-6pm Mon-Sat, from 11am Sun; 🚼; Ⓜ Nieuwmarkt) Bobbing mobiles and suspended toys have a motor and strings keeping them in fascinating constant motion in the window of this busy toyshop. There are plenty of *knuffels* (soft cuddly toys), puppets, teddies and jigsaw puzzles.

A BOEKEN

ARTS & CRAFTS
Map p296 (✆020-626 72 05; Niewe Hoogstraat 31; ☺noon-6pm Mon, 10am-6pm Tue, Wed & Fri, 10am-8pm Thu, 10am-5pm Sat; Ⓜ Nieuwmarkt) A marvellous trove of ribbons, feathers and fabric, and some of the best iron-on patches we've ever seen (Mexican skulls, Chinese dragons and Russian dolls). You'll start to imagine you'll sew (or iron on) one day, even if you can't, and if you can, you'll be in heaven.

PUCCINI BOMBONI

FOOD
Map p296 (www.puccinibomboni.com; Staal-straat 17; ☺noon-6pm Sun, 11am-6pm Mon, 9am-6pm Tue-Sat; 🚊4/9/14/16/24 Muntplein) Piled up with pyramids of chocolate bon-bons that are works of art and full of rich

and distinctive flavours like anise, tama-rind or calvados. Note: these shops have been known to close in warm weather – for the sake of the chocolates, of course.

JACOB HOOY & CO

COSMETICS
Map p296 (www.jacobhooy.nl; Kloveniers-burgwal 12; ☺1-6pm Mon, 10am-6pm Tue-Fri, 10am-5pm Sat; Ⓜ Nieuwmarkt) A proper apothecary shop, lined by wooden draw-ers and rounded barrels, their contents inscribed in flowing font, Jacob Hooy & Co has been selling medicinal herbs, homeopathic remedies and natural cos-metics since 1743.

WEBERS

ADULT
Map p296 (www.webersholland.nl; Kloveniers-burgwal 26; ☺1-7pm; Ⓜ Nieuwmarkt) This is where to get your kinky boots, and all other forms of top-end sauce, with every kind of fetish-wear imaginable (and unimaginable).

MARBLES VINTAGE

CLOTHING
Map p296 (Staalstraat 30; ☺11am-7pm; 🚊4/9/14/16/24 Muntplein) Marbles has sev-eral branches around town and is just one of the vintage shops in this area, selling funky treasures from hats to jeans.

ANTIQUES MARKET

MARKET
Map p296 (Nieuwmarkt; ☺9am-5pm Sun May-Sep; Ⓜ Nieuwmarkt) Treasure hunters will find lots of old books and bric-a-brac to peruse.

BOERENMARKT

MARKET
Map p296 (Farmers Market; Nieuwmarkt; ☺9am-4pm Sat; Ⓜ Nieuwmarkt) 🍃 Stalls selling organic foods and produce draw crowds on Saturdays.

JOE'S VLIEGERWINKEL

TOYS
Map p296 (www.joesvliegerwinkel.nl; Nieuwe Hoogstraat 19; ☺noon-6pm Tue-Fri, to 5pm Sat; 🚼; Ⓜ Nieuwmarkt) Kids and grown-ups will appreciate this specialised kite shop, which also sells lots of other ran-dom quirk, from solar-power hula dancers to lantern fairy-lights. You can also buy build-it-yourself kits.

HENXS

CLOTHING
Map p296 (www.henxs.com; St Antonies-breestraat 136-138; ☺11am-6pm Mon-Sat, noon-4pm Sun; Ⓜ Nieuwmarkt) This indie

clothes store is skater and graffiti-artist heaven, with labels including Hardcore, Bombers Best, Evisu and G-Star, plus graffiti supplies and edgy accessories.

JUGGLE
TOYS

Map p296 (www.juggle-store.com; Staalstraat 3; ⊘noon-5.30pm Tue-Sat; 🚋4/9/14/16/24 Muntplein) Wee Juggle puts more than mere balls in the air: it also sells circus supplies, from unicycles to fire hoops to magic tricks.

🔒 Plantage

FRANK'S SMOKEHOUSE
FOOD & DRINKS

Map p298 (www.smokehouse.nl; Wittenburgergracht 303; ⊘9am-4pm Mon, to 6pm Tue-Fri, to 5pm Sat; 🚋22 Wittenburgergracht) Frank is a prime supplier to Amsterdam's restaurants, and his excellent Alaskan salmon, halibut and yellowfin tuna can be vacuum-packed for travelling (customs regulations permitting). You can also have a delicious sandwich (smoked halibut with pumpkin relish; king crab; wild boar and cranberry chutney), with some bar seating in the shop interior.

🔒 Eastern Islands

LOODS 6
SHOPPING CENTRE

Map p298 (www.loods6.nl; KNSM-laan 143; 🚋10 Azartplein) This isn't a shopping centre of the mall variety, but rather a string of shops in a 1900-built former Royal Dutch Steam Company (KNSM) customs warehouse and passenger terminal. Noteworthy shops include children's-wear designer **Imps & Elfs** (Map p298; www.imps-elfs.com; Loods 6, KNSM-laan 297; ⊘10am-6pm Mon-Sat; 🚋10 Azartplein) 🌿, and Dutch-designed pottery and homewares at **Pols Potten** (Map p298; 📞020-419 35 41; www.polspotten. nl; Loods 6, KNSM-laan 39; ⊘10am-6pm Tue-Sat, noon-5pm Sun; 🚋10 Azartplein), as well as art galleries and fashion.

🏃 SPORTS & ACTIVITIES

⭐ REDERJI LAMPEDUSA
BOATING

Map p298 (www.rederjilampedusa.nl; canal tour 1-2hr €17, VIP tours by donation; ⊘canal tours Sat & Sun, VIP tours Fri fortnightly May-Sep; 🚋26 Muziekgebouw) Take a canal-boat tour or a sunset trip around Amsterdam harbour in former refugee boats, brought from Lampedusa by Dutch founder Tuen. The tours are full of heart and offer a fascinating insight, not only into stories of contemporary migration, but of how immigration shaped Amsterdam's history – especially the canal tour. Both leave from next to Mediamatic.

TUNFUN
PLAYGROUND

Map p296 (www.tunfun.nl; Mr Visserplein 7; adult/child free/€8.50; ⊘10am-6pm, last entry 5pm; 👶; 🚋9/14 Mr Visserplein) A great way to entertain kids on a rainy day (but this is when it's busiest), this ace indoor playground is located in a former traffic underpass. Kids can clamber over soft play equipment, jump on trampolines, try to escape the 'black box' and play on a soccer pitch. There's a cafe serving kiddie favourites, such as *poffertjes* (small pancakes) and nutella sandwiches.

Kids must be accompanied by an adult. The entrance is located opposite the Portuguese-Israelite Synagogue; look for the green arches and stairs leading down.

GLOWGOLF
MINIGOLF

Map p298 (📞020-737 18 09; https://glowgolf.i-reserve.nl; Prins Hendrikkade 194, Noah's Arq; adult/child €9.75/8.75, 3D glasses €1.25; ⊘11am-9pm Sun-Wed, to 11pm Thu, to 3am Fri & Sat; 🚋22 Kadijksplein) From the street Noah's Arq looks like a normal pub but down in the basement it harbours this trippy-and-then-some minigolf course. The 15 psychedelically coloured holes are played under black light, making them glow luridly in the dark (and making you feel like you're inside a giant pinball machine). Definitely get the 3D glasses to max out the surreal experience.

Western Canal Ring

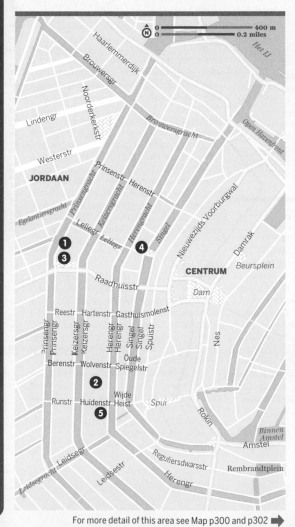

Neighbourhood Top Five

1 **Anne Frank Huis** (p104) Contemplating the amazing life and tragic death of the most famous Dutch girl in history in the poignant 'secret annexe' of the house where she and her family hid from the Nazis.

2 **Negen Straatjes** (p113) Browsing the speciality shops along these compact and captivating 'nine streets' criss-crossed by picturesque canals.

3 **Westerkerk** (p106) Scaling the bell tower, seeing the Netherlands' largest nave and catching a carillon recital.

4 **Reypenaer Cheese Tasting** (p111) Learning to distinguish an aged Gouda from a young *boerenkaas* (farmer's cheese).

5 **Bijbels Museum** (p107) Viewing rare bibles, a scale model of the Jewish Tabernacle and biblical plants in the garden of this canal-house-turned-museum.

For more detail of this area see Map p300 and p302 ➡

Explore Western Canal Ring

This whole area is a Unesco World Heritage site and although the neighbourhood is loaded with high-profile sights, half the charm here is simply soaking up the atmosphere: from the street, from a boat, from a backyard garden, from a rooftop balcony or from the terrace of a canal-side cafe.

From the neighbourhood's northern end around the hip Haarlemmerbuurt shopping district, work your way towards the south, weaving in and out of the lanes and canals to visit the Multatuli Museum (p107), admire the architecture of the Huis Met de Hoofden (p108) and pay homage to the Homomonument (p106) and the Westerkerk (p106) until you wind up at Anne Frank Huis (p104) in the early evening, when it's least crowded.

On your second day, start with some of Amsterdam's most enjoyable shopping along the Negen Straatjes (p113) in the neighbourhood's south. This chessboard of *straatjes* (small streets) is full of one-off speciality shops and quirky little boutiques stocking antiques, vintage fashions and homewares. The area is peppered with informal drinking and dining venues, and their patrons clientele spill out into the streets in warmer weather.

Tear yourself away to check out the Bijbels Museum (p107), the canal-house museum Het Grachtenhuis (p106) and the Huis Marseille (p106) photography museum, before finishing up at the Prinsengracht's bars, cafes and restaurants.

Local Life

➡ **Borrel** Brown cafes (pubs) such as Café de Vergulde Gaper (p112) are especially popular for the time-honoured Dutch tradition of *borrel* (drinks).

➡ **Snacks** Join locals queuing for fries slathered in mayonnaise or spicier sauces at Wil Graanstra Friteshuis (p110).

➡ **Canals** The Prinsengracht (p110) is a perennial favourite, whatever the weather.

➡ **Food and fashion** The Haarlemmerbuurt (p112), incorporating Haarlemmerstraat, is a hot spot for restaurants, gourmet provisions and kitchen shops, interspersed with edgy fashion boutiques.

Getting There & Away

➡ **Trams** Trams 13, 14 and 17 have stops near the main attractions, and any tram or bus that stops near the Dam is just a short walk away.

➡ **Boat** The Canal Bus stop (Map p399) near Westermarkt is handy for the Anne Frank Huis.

Lonely Planet's Top Tip

Thursday is an ideal time to discover this neighbourhood, when many businesses – including numerous shops in the jewel-box-like Negen Straatjes (Nine Streets) – are open extended hours.

✕ Best Places to Eat

➡ De Belhamel (p110)

➡ Bistro Bij ons (p110)

➡ De Luwte (p110)

➡ Petit Gâteau (p108)

➡ Vinnies Deli (p108)

For reviews, see p108 ➡

☗ Best Places to Drink

➡ 't Arendsnest (p112)

➡ Café Tabac (p112)

➡ Café de Vergulde Gaper (p112)

➡ Café Het Molenpad (p112)

➡ De Doffer (p112)

For reviews, see p111 ➡

⌂ Best Places to Shop

➡ Frozen Fountain (p114)

➡ 360 Volt (p114)

➡ Arnatør (p114)

➡ De Kaaskamer (p114)

➡ Denham the Jeanmaker (p114)

For reviews, see p113 ➡

TOP SIGHT
ANNE FRANK HUIS

Background

Stepping through the bookcase that swings open to reveal the 'Secret Annexe' and going up the steep stairs into the living quarters – where the family lived for more than two years – is to step back into a time that seems both distant and tragically real.

It took the German army just five days to occupy all of the Netherlands, along with Belgium and much of France. And once Hitler's forces had swept across the country, many Jews – like Anne Frank and her family – eventually went into hiding. Anne's diary describes how restrictions were gradually imposed on Dutch Jews: from being forbidden to ride streetcars to being forced to turn in their bicycles and not being allowed to visit Christian friends.

The Franks moved into the upper floors of the specially prepared rear of the building, along with another couple, the Van Pels (called the Van Daans in Anne's diary), and their son, Peter. Four months later Fritz Pfeffer (called Mr Dussel in the diary) joined the household. Here they survived until they were betrayed to the Gestapo in August 1944.

Ground Floor

The house itself is contained within a modern, square shell that retains the original feel of the building (it was used during WWII as offices and a warehouse). It will remain open throughout renovations that will include a new Westermarkt entrance and extensions to the museum, which shows multilingual news reels of WWII footage narrated using

DON'T MISS

➡ Anne's red-plaid diary
➡ Anne's bedroom
➡ WWII newsreels
➡ Peter van Pels' room
➡ Video of Anne's schoolmate Hanneli Goslar

PRACTICALITIES

➡ Map p300, A6
➡ ☏020-556 71 05
➡ www.annefrank.org
➡ Prinsengracht 263-267
➡ adult/child €9/4.50
➡ ⏰9am-10pm Apr-Oct, 9am-7pm Sun-Fri, to 9pm Sat Nov-Mar
➡ 🚊13/14/17 Westermarkt

segments of Anne's diary: it inextricably links the rise of Hitler with the Frank family's personal saga.

Offices

View the former offices of Victor Kugler, Otto Frank's business partner; his identity card and the film magazines he bought for Anne are on display. The other office area belonged to Miep Gies, Bep Voskuijl and Johannes Kleiman, two women and a man who worked in the office by day and provided food, clothing, school supplies and other goods – often purchased on the black market or with ration cards – for the eight members of the Secret Annexe. You can see some of their personal documents here.

Secret Annexe

While the lower levels present history with interactive modern technology, the former living quarters of the Frank family in the *Achterhuis* (rear house) retain their stark, haunting austerity. It's as if visitors are stepping back into 1942. Notice how windows of the annexe were blacked out to avoid arousing suspicion among people who might see it from surrounding houses (blackouts were common practice to disorient bombers at night).

Take a moment to observe the ingenious set-up of the Secret Annexe as you walk through. You then enter two floors of the dark and airless space where the Franks and their friends observed complete silence during the daytime until they were betrayed, arrested by the Nazis and sent to concentration camps. Otto Frank, Anne's father, was the only survivor.

Anne's Bedroom

As you enter Anne's small, simple bedroom, which she shared with Fritz Pfeffer, you can still sense the remnants of a young girl's dreams: the physical evidence of her interests and longings is on the wall with her photos of Hollywood stars and postcards of the Dutch royal family.

The Diary

More haunting exhibits and videos await after you return to the front house – including Anne's red plaid diary itself, sitting alone in its glass case. Watch the video of Anne's old schoolmate Hanneli Goslar, who describes encountering Anne at Bergen-Belsen.

AFTER THE WAR

The Franks were among the last Jews to be deported and Anne died in the Bergen-Belsen concentration camp in March 1945, only weeks before it was liberated. After the war, Otto published Anne's diary, which was found among the litter in the annexe (the furniture had been carted away by the Nazis).

TICKETS

At the time of research the only way to visit was with a ticket purchased online, although this may change so check the website (www.anne frank.org). Tickets are released in phases, from two months in advance until the day itself (subject to availability; be warned that the demand is often greater than the supply). You can print them or show them on your phone. You'll receive a set time for entry on a specific date.

⊙ SIGHTS

ANNE FRANK HUIS   MUSEUM
See p104.

WESTERKERK   CHURCH
Map p300 (Western Church; ☎020-624 77 66; www.westerkerk.nl; Prinsengracht 281; ⊘11am-4pm Mon-Sat May-Sep, Mon-Fri Oct-Apr; 🚊13/14/17 Westermarkt) The main gathering place for Amsterdam's Dutch Reformed community, this church was built for rich Protestants to a 1620 design by Hendrick de Keyser. The nave is the largest in the Netherlands and is covered by a wooden barrel vault. The huge main organ dates from 1686, with panels decorated with instruments and biblical scenes. Rembrandt (1606–69), who died bankrupt at nearby Rozengracht, was buried in a pauper's grave somewhere in the church. Its bell tower can be climbed.

Free 30-minute lunchtime concerts take place at 1pm Friday from May to September. Year-round, carillon recitals are held from noon to 1pm on Tuesday; the best place to listen is from the nearby Bloemgracht. The bells also chime mechanically every 15 minutes.

WESTERKERK BELL TOWER   TOWER
Map p300 (www.westertorenamsterdam.nl; Prinsengracht 281; tours €7; ⊘10am-7.30pm Mon-Sat Jun-Sep; 🚊13/14/17 Westermarkt) The bell tower of the Westerkerk is famously topped by the blue imperial crown that Habsburg emperor Maximilian I bestowed on the city for its coat of arms in 1489. The climb up the stairs of the 85m tower can be strenuous and claustrophobic, but the guide takes breaks on the landings while describing the bells, and the panoramic views are worth it. Tours depart every half-hour. Children under six aren't permitted.

HOMOMONUMENT   MONUMENT
Map p300 (www.homomonument.nl; cnr Keizersgracht & Raadhuisstraat; 🚊13/14/17 Westermarkt) Behind the Westerkerk (p106), this 1987-installed cluster of three 10m by 10m by 10m granite triangles recalls persecution by the Nazis, who forced gay men to wear a pink triangle patch. One of the triangles steps down into the Keizersgracht and is said to represent a jetty from which gay men were sent to the concentration camps. Others interpret the step-up from the canal as a symbol of rising hope.

BARTOLOTTI HOUSE   HISTORIC BUILDING
Map p300 (Herengracht 170-172; 🚊13/14/17 Westermarkt) Built in 1617, this ornate neck-gabled building was designed by famed architect Hendrick de Keyser, and has two bends in the facade to follow the course of the canal.

HET GRACHTENHUIS   MUSEUM
Map p302 (Canal House; ☎020-421 16 56; www.hetgrachtenhuis.nl; Herengracht 386; adult/child €12/6; ⊘10am-5pm Tue-Sun; 🚊1/2/5 Koningsplein) Learn about the remarkable feat of engineering behind the Canal Ring through this museum's holograms, videos, models, cartoons, scale model of Amsterdam and other innovative exhibits, which explain how the canals and the houses that line them were built. Unlike at most Amsterdam museums, you can't simply wander through: small groups go in together to experience the multimedia exhibits. It takes about 45 minutes, and you'll come out knowing why Amsterdam's houses tilt. Online tickets are up to €2 cheaper.

HUIS MARSEILLE   MUSEUM
Map p302 (☎020-531 89 89; www.huismarseille.nl; Keizersgracht 401; adult/child €8/free; ⊘11am-6pm Tue-Sun; 🚊1/2/5 Keizersgracht) Large-scale temporary exhibitions from its own collection are staged at this well-curated photography museum, which also hosts travelling shows. Themes might include portraiture, nature or regional

---

HERENGRACHT

Dug out during the 17th-century Golden Age, the Herengracht (Gentlemen's Canal) takes its name from the wealthy landowners who built properties here. Some buildings lean forward and have hoists in the gables: given the narrowness of the interior staircases, people used these hoists to haul large goods to upper floors.

Just north of the Herengracht, near its intersection with the Brouwersgracht, you'll find the Herenmarkt, a small square that's home to the historic 17th-century West-Indisch Huis (p107), the former headquarters of the Dutch West India Company.

The Herengracht is at its grandest along the Golden Bend (p119) in the Southern Canal Ring.

photography, and exhibitions are spread out over several floors and in a summer house behind the main house.

French merchant Isaac Focquier built Huis Marseille in 1665, installing a map of the French port Marseille on the facade, and the original structure has remained largely intact.

Look out for the 18th-century fountain in the library, and a painting of Apollo, Minerva and the muses in the garden room.

BIJBELS MUSEUM   MUSEUM

Map p302 (Bible Museum; www.bijbelsmuseum.nl; Herengracht 366-368; adult/child €8.50/4.25; ⊙11am-5pm Tue-Sun; ⊜1/2/5 Spui) A scale model of the Jewish Tabernacle described in Exodus – built by dedicated minister Leendert Schouten and drawing thousands of visitors even before it was completed in 1851 – is the star attraction at this bible museum. Inside a 1622 canal house, the museum has an extraordinary collection of bibles, including the Netherlands' oldest, a 1477-printed Delft Bible, and a 1st edition of the 1637 Dutch authorised version. Trees and plants mentioned in the Good Book feature in the garden.

The crossing of the Red Sea is referenced by stepping stones in the garden's ponds. Exhibits on the lower floors show paintings, furniture and other objects from wealthy merchant family the Cromhouts, who built the canal house and lived in it for nearly two centuries.

POEZENBOOT   ANIMAL SANCTUARY

Map p300 (Cat Boat; ☑020-625 87 94; www.depoezenboot.nl; Singel 38; by donation; ⊙1-3pm Mon, Tue & Thu-Sat; ⊜1/2/5/13/17 Nieuwezijds Kolk) Cat-lovers may want to check out this quirky boat on the Singel. It was founded in 1966 by an eccentric woman who became legendary for looking after several hundred stray cats at a time. The boat has since been taken over by a foundation and can hold some 50 kitties in proper pens. Some are permanent residents, and the rest are ready to be adopted (after being neutered and implanted with an identifying computer chip, as per Dutch law).

MULTATULI MUSEUM   MUSEUM

Map p300 (www.multatuli-museum.nl; Korsjespoortsteeg 20; ⊙10am-5pm Tue, noon-5pm Wed-Sun; ⊜1/2/5/13/17 Nieuwezijds Kolk) FREE Better known by the pen name Multatuli (Latin for 'I have suffered greatly') novelist

Eduard Douwes Dekker is most recognised for *Max Havelaar* (1860), his novel about corrupt colonialists in the Dutch East Indies. This small but fascinating museum-home chronicles his life and work, and shows furniture and artefacts from his period in Indonesia.

Dekker himself worked in colonial administration in Batavia (now Jakarta), and the book made him something of a social conscience for the Netherlands.

WEST-INDISCH HUIS   HISTORIC BUILDING

Map p300 (West Indies House; Herenmarkt 97; ☑18/21/22 Buiten Brouwersstraat) Built in 1617 as a meat market and militia barracks, this historic building was rented by the Dutch West India Company (Geoctroyeerde Westindische Compagnie; GWC) as its headquarters in 1623. It was here that the GWC's governors signed off on the construction of a fort on the island of Manhattan in 1625, establishing New Amsterdam (now New York City).

The booty of naval hero Admiral Piet Heyn was stored here in 1628 after his men captured the Spanish silver fleet off the coast of Cuba.

Today this landmark on the Herenmarkt is used as a conference venue and houses offices including the John Adams Institute, which fosters cultural ties between the USA and the Netherlands. You can enter the courtyard to see the statue of Peter Stuyvesant (c 1612–1672), the final Dutch director-general of the colony of New Netherland until its British acquisition.

The Oostindisch Huis (p88), the headquarters of the Dutch East India Company (Vereenigde Oostindische Compagnie; VOC) is in Nieuwmarkt.

DE RODE HOED   CULTURAL CENTRE

Map p300 (The Red Hat; www.rodehoed.nl; Keizersgracht 102; tickets free-€12.50; ⊜13/14/17 Westermarkt) FREE Occupying three glorious 17th-century canal houses – which once sheltered the Vrijburg, the largest clandestine church in the Netherlands – this cultural centre offers lectures, sometimes in English, by world-renowned authors and debates on the topics of the day, as well as concerts; check the agenda online. The centre was named for the former milliner located here (spot the identifying tile on the facade).

HUIS MET DE HOOFDEN
HISTORIC BUILDING

Map p300 (House with the Heads; www.huismetdehoofden.nl; Keizersgracht 123; 13/14/17 Westermarkt) **FREE** A whimsical example of Dutch Renaissance style, this 1622 canal house has a beautiful step gable with six heads at door level representing the classical muses: Apollo, Diana, Ceres, Bacchus, Minerva and Mercury. Renowned architect Hendrick de Keyser and his son Pieter designed the building. At the time of research it was being renovated to house the Ritman Library (Bibliotheca Philosophica Hermetica; www.ritmanlibrary.com).

GREENLAND WAREHOUSES
HISTORIC BUILDING

Map p300 (Keizersgracht 40-44; 18/21/22 Buiten Brouwersstraat) The distinctive red-shuttered Greenland Warehouses were built in 1620. Whale oil was a sought-after ingredient for soap, lamp oil and paint, and wells here could hold 100,000L. Nowadays the warehouses contain chic apartments, but the facade is well maintained (despite the difficulties in painting it due to the saturation of whale oil that still remains).

# EATING

The Western Canal Ring may not have the multicultural dining diversity of other parts of town, but bear in mind that the Jordaan neighbourhood is only a hop, skip and jump away. The Negen Straatjes (p113) are filled with cute cafes and small restaurants to match their lovely boutiques.

PETIT GÂTEAU
PASTRIES €

Map p300 (020-737 15 85; www.petitgateau.nl; Haarlemmerstraat 80; pastries €2.50-5.50; 10am 6pm; 18/21/22 Buiten Brouwersstraat) Paris-trained pastry chef Meike Scaling and her team create exquisite French pastries on site: intricate 'mini-minis' (tiny tarts topped with jewel-like fruits), glazed éclairs, *macarons* made from ground almond flour, shell-shaped madeleine cakes, and 15 savoury quiches. Regular two-hour pastry-making classes (in English and Dutch) cost €45; check the online agenda for dates.

VINNIES DELI
CAFE €

Map p300 (www.vinnieshomepage.com; Haarlemmerstraat 46; mains €7-13; 8am-5pm;

1/2/4/5/9/13/16/17/24 Centraal Station) Only organic, locally sourced produce is used in Vinnes' extensive breakfasts, gourmet sandwiches, lush salads, hot specials such as kale-and-mushroom frittata or roasted miso-marinated aubergine, and creative cakes, while the coffee is from Amsterdam roastery Bocca. Vegan options abound. If you're imagining the designer furniture in your lounge room, you're in luck: all the pieces are for sale.

STUBBE'S HARING
SEAFOOD €

Map p300 (Singel Haarlingersluis; dishes €2.50-4; noon-7pm Tue-Sat; 1/2/4/5/9/13/16/17/24 Centraal Station) Overlooking the Singel, footsteps from Centraal Station, Stubbe's open-air fish stall has been providing pickled herring to Amsterdammers for over a century. You can eat it straight up or on a sandwich roll; just be sure to sprinkle it with diced onion first. Hours can vary.

LETTING
DUTCH €

Map p300 (www.letting.nl; Prinsenstraat 3; mains €7-12; 8.30am-5pm Mon & Wed-Sat, 9am-5pm Sun; 13/14/17 Westermarkt) Start your day in traditional Dutch style with authentic breakfast dishes such as *wentelteefjes* (sugar bread dipped in egg and cinnamon), *uitsmijter rosbief* (eggs served sunny side up, with cheese and roast beef) and scrambled eggs with smoked halibut. At lunch, choose from soups and sandwiches. Or book for royal high tea (€25), accompanied by champagne.

SINGEL 404
CAFE €

Map p302 (Singel 404; dishes €3.50-9; 10.30am-6pm; 1/2/5 Spui) It's easy to miss this tucked-away spot, despite its location near the bustling Spui (look for the cobalt-blue awning). The menu is as simple as can be – smoked-salmon sandwiches, pumpkin soup, honey-mint lemonade – but the prices are rock bottom, the portions are generous and the quality is superb. There's a handful of tables inside and out.

PANCAKE BAKERY
DUTCH €

Map p300 (020-625 13 33; www.pancake.nl; Prinsengracht 191; mains €9-15.50; 9am-9.30pm; 13/14/17 Westermarkt) In a restored 17th-century warehouse that once belonged to the Dutch East India Company, this basement restaurant offers a dizzying 77 varieties of pancake, from sweet (like chocolate, banana or peach) to savoury

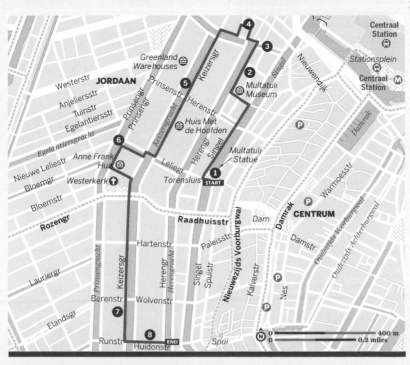

Neighbourhood Walk
Western Canal Ring

START SINGEL, TORENSLUIS
END NEGEN STRAATJES
LENGTH 3KM; 1¼ HOURS

Get to know the Western Canal Ring's 17th-century waterways during this walk.

Originally a moat that defended Amsterdam's outer limits, the ❶ **Singel** is the first canal west of the centre. Torensluis, Amsterdam's oldest bridge, crosses it. Before you do too, stop to admire the statue of novelist Eduard Douwes Dekker; the Dutch literary giant's museum is a few blocks north.

Next up is the ❷ **Herengracht** (p106), named for the rich merchants and powerful regents who clustered here to build their manors. Nearly 400 years later, it's still some of Amsterdam's choicest real estate.

The Herengracht soon intersects with the pretty ❸ **Brouwersgracht** (Brewer's Canal), which took its name from the many suds makers located here in the 16th and 17th centuries. To the north is Herenmarkt, home to the 17th-century ❹ **West-Indisch Huis**

(p107), where the Dutch West India Company's governors authorised the settlement of New Amsterdam (now New York City).

Turning south, cross the Brouwersgracht into the ❺ **Keizersgracht** (Emperor's Canal). You'll soon spot the imposing, red-shuttered Greenland Warehouses, which used to store whale oil. Further on is the Dutch Renaissance Huis Met de Hoofden, with its carvings of Apollo, Ceres and Diana.

Turn west at peaceful Leliegracht and then south onto ❻ **Prinsengracht** (p110). You'll pass the Anne Frank Huis and the soaring towers of the Westerkerk. Back on Keizersgracht, head south a few blocks, past Berenstraat; you won't be able to miss the quirky ❼ **Felix Meritis** (p113), a one-time Enlightenment society venue that's now an alternative theatre; the building's colonnaded facade served as a model for Amsterdam's renowned Concertgebouw.

Since you're probably hungry (thirsty or both by this point, head to one of the fetching little cafes lining the nearby ❽ **Negen Straatjes** (p113).

PRINSENGRACHT

The Herengracht and Keizersgracht might be grander, but locals love to hang out on the Prinsengracht, the liveliest of Amsterdam's inner canals. In summertime you could spend a whole weekend just enjoying its warm-weather charms – exploring the shops and kicking back on its cafe terraces – as boats glide by and houseboats bob against the quays in the breeze. During the chillier months, it's a winter wonderland where (conditions permitting) you might see skaters take to the iced-over canal.

(eg Canadian, topped with bacon, cheese and barbecue sauce, or Norwegian, with smoked salmon, cream cheese and sour cream). Kids' varieties include Pirate, Fireman and Princess pancakes.

WIL GRAANSTRA FRITESHUIS   FAST FOOD €
Map p300 (Westermarkt 11; frites €2.50-4, sauce €0.50; ⊙noon-7pm Mon-Sat; 🚊13/14/17 Westermarkt) Legions of Amsterdammers swear by the crispy spuds at Wil Graanstra Friteshuis. The family-run business has been frying on the square by the Westerkerk since 1956. Most locals top their cones with mayonnaise, though *oorlog* (a peanut sauce–mayo combo), curry sauce and piccalilli (relish) rock the taste buds too.

PANCAKES!   DUTCH €
Map p302 (🕿020-528 97 97; www.pancakes. amsterdam; Berenstraat 38; mains €6-11; ⊙9am-6pm; 🗷🗷🗷; 🚊13/14/17 Westermarkt) The blue-tile tables at snug little Pancakes! are always packed with diners tucking into the signature dish, whether sweet (apple, nuts and cinnamon) or savoury (ham, chicory and camembert cheese). Gluten-free pancakes are also available. Smiley-face pancakes are a favourite with kids.

⭐DE BELHAMEL   EUROPEAN €€
Map p300 (🕿020-622 10 95; www.belhamel.nl; Brouwersgracht 60; mains €23-27, 3-/4-course menus €35/45; ⊙noon-4pm & 6-10pm Sun-Thu, to 10.30pm Fri & Sat; 🚊18/21/22 Buiten Brouwersstraat) In warm weather the canal-side tables here at the head of the Herengracht are an aphrodisiac, and the richly wallpapered art-nouveau interior set over two levels provides the perfect backdrop for exquisitely presented dishes such as poached sole with wild-spinach bisque, veal sweetbreads with crispy bacon, onion confit and deep-fried sage, or a half lobster with velvety salmon mayonnaise.

BISTRO BIJ ONS   DUTCH €€
Map p300 (🕿020-627 90 16; www.bistrobijons. nl; Prinsengracht 287; mains €14-20; ⊙10am-10pm Tue-Sun; 🗷; 🚊13/14/17 Westermarkt) If you're not in town visiting your Dutch *oma* (grandma), try the honest-to-goodness cooking at this charming retro bistro instead. Classics include *stamppot* (potatoes mashed with another vegetable) with sausage, *raasdonders* (split peas with bacon, onion and pickles) and *poffertjes* (small pancakes with butter and powdered sugar). House-made liqueurs include plum and *drop* (liquorice) varieties.

Kids are warmly welcomed.

DE LUWTE   MEDITERRANEAN €€
Map p300 (🕿020-625 85 48; www.restaurant deluwte.nl; Leliegracht 26-28; mains €19-25; ⊙6-10pm Sun-Thu, to 10.30pm Fri & Sat; 🚊13/14/17 Westermarkt) Fabulously designed with recycled timbers, De Luwte also has artfully presented cooking. Baked cod with pickled beetroot, puffed rice and tiger-prawn foam, and a 'surf and turf' with roast salmon, Pata Negra ham and lemon gel are among the highlights, alongside the house-speciality Black Angus tomahawk steak for two. Great cocktails as well.

BISTROT NEUF   FRENCH €€
Map p300 (🕿020-400 32 10; www.bistrotneuf. nl; Haarlemmerstraat 9; mains lunch €11-23, dinner €20-24, 3-course lunch/dinner menu €25/34; ⊙noon-11pm; 🚊1/2/4/5/9/13/16/17/24 Centraal Station) The cooking at this wine-cork-adorned bistro covers all the classics – bouillabaisse (traditional Provençal fish stew), steak tartar with *frites* (fries), snails with garlic and parsley butter, cassoulet (slow-cooked casserole with pork and white beans), lemon-thyme-stuffed quail and *côte de bœuf* (rib steak) for two or three people – and is accompanied by a wine list spanning 60 French choices.

BLACK & BLUE   STEAK €€
Map p300 (🕿020-625 08 07; www.steakrestaurantamsterdam.nl; Leliegracht 46; mains lunch €8-16, dinner €16-30; ⊙11am-10pm; 🚊13/14/17 Westermarkt) Black & Blue's Josper

(super-hot Spanish charcoal oven) char-grills succulent Black Angus steaks, accompanied by Béarnaise sauce, herb butter or pepper relish, and generous sides of *frites* (fries) and salads. The split-level, parquet-floored space opens to a canal-side terrace overlooking the picturesque Leliegracht. Caramelised pineapple, also cooked on the Josper, is the pick of the desserts.

VAN HARTE
INTERNATIONAL €€

Map p300 (☑020-625 85 00; www.vanharte.com; Hartenstraat 24; mains lunch €7-15, dinner €17-24, 3-course menu €33; ☉10am-6pm Sun & Mon, to 10pm Tue-Sat; ☐13/14/17 Westermarkt) Behind floor-to-ceiling glass windows, a glistening mosaic-tiled bar and framed black-and-white photos of old Amsterdam make Van Harte look like an ultrachic drinking spot, but it's an even better place to dine on evening mains like braised lamb shanks with pearl barley, or a surf and turf of rib-eye and a half lobster. Generous salads and sandwiches feature at lunch.

CAFÉ RESTAURANT VAN PUFFELEN
CAFE €€

Map p302 (☑020-624 62 70; www.restaurant vanpuffelen.com; Prinsengracht 375-377; mains €19, 2-/3-course menus €26/32; ☉4-9.30pm Mon-Thu, noon-10pm Fri-Sun; ☐13/14/17 Westermarkt) Changing dishes are made from local organic produce at this large cafe-restaurant in a canal house beautifully decorated with ruby-coloured light fittings and dark timber furniture. Its nooks and crannies are enticing for a cosy drink. There's a landing stage out front, where you can be served meals on board your boat.

STOUT
INTERNATIONAL €€

Map p300 (☑020-616 36 64; www.restaurant stout.nl; Haarlemmerstraat 73; mains lunch €7-15, dinner €20-23, platters per person €29.50; ☉11am-9.30pm Mon-Thu, to 10pm Fri & Sun, 10am-10pm Sat; ☐18/21/22 Buiten Brouwersstraat) Rack of lamb with truffles and porcini jus, and mackerel and smoked eel with beetroot mousse are among the choices at this contemporary restaurant, but if you can't decide, it also offers tasting platters with 10 mini versions of its menu's daily dishes. In warm weather, sit at the outdoor tables to watch the world go by.

DE STRUISVOGEL
BISTRO €€

Map p302 (☑020-423 38 17; www.restaurant destruisvogel.nl; Keizersgracht 312; 3-course

---

CHEESE TASTING

Take your chance to become a *kaas* (cheese) connoisseur with. **Reypenaer Cheese Tasting** (Map p300; ☑020-320 63 33; www.reypenaer cheese.com; Singel 182; from €16.50; ☉tastings by reservation; ☐1/2/5/13/14/17 Dam). Century-old Dutch cheesemaker Reypenaer offers tastings in a rustic classroom beneath its shop. The hour-long session includes six cheeses – two goat's milk, four cow's milk – from young to old, with wine and port pairings. Expert staff members guide you through them, helping you appreciate the cheeses' look, aroma and taste.

Other options include an hour-long cheese tasting paired with *corenwyn* and *jenever* (Dutch gins; €25 per person).

---

menu €26.50; ☉5.30-10pm Sun-Fri, 5-10pm Sat; ☐13/14/17 Westermarkt) This former basement kitchen to some large canal houses offers great value. The bird (*struisvogel* means 'ostrich'), served with butter-poached pear and port, stars on the menu, alongside a nightly rotating menu of local, mostly organic produce, including caramelised Schiphol goose with sauerkraut, and desserts such as warm apple crumble with cinnamon and vanilla ice cream.

CASA PERÚ
PERUVIAN €€

Map p302 (☑020-620 37 49; www.casaperu.nl; Leidsegracht 68; mains €16-21; ☉noon-11pm Apr-Sep, 5.30-11pm Oct-Mar; ☎; ☐1/2/5 Prinsengracht) There's nothing quite like enjoying a *chupe de camarones* (fisherman's soup) or *lomo saltado* (beef with onion, tomato and rice) while looking out over the Leidsegracht and the Prinsengracht from this bright, busy spot.

🍷 DRINKING & NIGHTLIFE

Cafés (pubs) in this refined district tend to have swish interiors and elaborate drinking (and dining) menus. There are a few down-to-earth brown cafes, and more in the nearby Jordaan.

HAARLEMMERBUURT
....

Amsterdam's coolest neighbourhood-within-a-neighbourhood (or two – it straddles the Western Canal Ring and the Jordaan), the Haarlemmerbuurt (www.haarlemmerbuurt-amsterdam.nl) is exploding with restaurants, food shops, designer workshops and boutiques. Its website (in Dutch, but easy to navigate) has an interactive map of Haarlemmerstraat and its western extension, Haarlemmerdijk, and details of one-off events.

★ 'T ARENDSNEST   BROWN CAFE
Map p300 (www.arendsnest.nl; Herengracht 90; ⊙noon-midnight Sun-Thu, to 2am Fri & Sat; 📶1/2/5/13/17 Nieuwezijds Kolk) This gorgeous restyled brown cafe, with its glowing copper *jenever* (Dutch gin) boilers behind the bar, only serves Dutch beer – but with over 100 varieties (many from small breweries, including 52 rotating on tap, you'll need to move here to try them all. It also has more than 40 gins, ciders, whiskies and liqueurs, all of which are Dutch too.

CAFÉ TABAC   BAR
Map p300 (www.cafetabac.eu; Brouwersgracht 101; ⊙noon-1am Mon-Thu, to 3am Fri, 11am-3am Sat, to 1am Sun; 📶; 📶18/21/22 Buiten Brouwersstraat) Is Café Tabac a brown cafe, a designer bar, a fantastic place for Indonesian dishes or simply an idyllic place to while away a few blissful hours at the intersection of two of Amsterdam's most stunning canals? The regulars don't seem concerned about definitions but simply enjoy the views and kicking back beneath the beamed ceilings.

CAFÉ DE VERGULDE GAPER   BROWN CAFE
Map p300 (www.deverguldegaper.nl; Prinsenstraat 30; ⊙10am-1am Mon, 11am-1am Tue-Thu & Sun, 11am-3am Fri, 10am-3am Sat; 📶; 📶13/14/17 Westermarkt) Decorated with old chemists' bottles and vintage posters, this former pharmacy has a canal-side terrace with afternoon sun and occasional live jazz. It's popular with locals, especially for after-work drinks. The name translates to the 'Golden Gaper', for the open-mouthed bust of a Moor traditionally posted at Dutch apothecaries.

CAFÉ HET MOLENPAD   BAR
Map p302 (www.cafehetmolenpad.nl; Prinsengracht 653; ⊙noon-1am Sun-Thu, to 3am Fri & Sat; 📶; 📶1/2/5 Prinsengracht) By day, this updated brown cafe is full of people catching the afternoon sun on the terrace. By night the atmosphere turns quietly romantic, with low lamps and candlelight illuminating little tables beneath pressed-tin ceilings. The meat-filled *bitterballen* and cheese croquettes are outstanding and justify a stop in their own right.

DE DOFFER   BROWN CAFE
Map p302 (www.cafededoffer.nl; Runstraat 12-14; ⊙11am-3am; 📶1/2/5 Spui) Writers, students and artists frequent this popular brown cafe for affordable food and good conversation. The dining room, with its old Heineken posters, large wooden tables and, occasionally, fresh flowers, is particularly atmospheric at night.

JAY'S JUICES   JUICE BAR
Map p300 (www.jaysjuices.nl; Haarlemmerstraat 14; ⊙9am-6pm Mon-Fri, 10am-6pm Sat & Sun; 📶1/2/5/13/17 Centraal Station) Set yourself up for a day of sightseeing (and/or detox from the night before) at Jay's. There's a huge range of fruit and vegetable juices, and combinations thereof, as well as wheatgrass shots, ginger shots and almond milk.

KOFFIEHUIS DE HOEK   COFFEE
Map p302 (📞020-625 38 72; Prinsengracht 341; ⊙9am-6pm Mon & Sat, 8.30am-6pm Tue-Fri, 10am-6pm Sun; 📶13/14/17 Westermarkt) This *koffiehuis* (espresso bar; not to be confused with a coffeeshop selling cannabis) is one of the best places in the city to get an old-fashioned coffee-house experience in Amsterdam. Come for a coffee and a slice of its famous apple pie (baked throughout the day) in a charming, chequered-tablecloth atmosphere.

GREY AREA   COFFEESHOP
Map p300 (www.greyarea.nl; Oude Leliestraat 2; ⊙noon-8pm; 📶1/2/5/13/14/17 Dam) Owned by a couple of laid-back American guys, this tiny shop – plastered with stickers inside and out – introduced the extra-sticky, potent 'Double Bubble Gum' weed to the city's smokers. Its volcano vaporiser is free for patrons to use.

PÂTISSERIE POMPADOUR
TEAHOUSE

Map p302 (www.pompadour.amsterdam/en; Huidenstraat 12; ⊘10am-6pm Mon-Fri, 9am-6pm Sat, noon-6pm Sun; 🚊1/2/5 Spui) Sip top-notch tea and Spanish-roasted coffee and nibble homemade Valrhona-chocolate pralines and pastries at this beautiful little Negen Straatjes tearoom with wood panelling dating from 1795.

VYNE
WINE BAR

Map p302 (www.vyne.nl; Prinsengracht 411; ⊘6pm-midnight Mon-Thu, 5pm-1am Fri & Sat, 6-11pm Sun; 🚊13/14/17 Westermarkt) With blond timber floors, walls and ceiling, the slickest wine bar in town looks like a stylish sauna (wine bottles notwithstanding). Over 70 wines are available by the glass; knowledgeable staff guide you in the right direction, no matter your price point. The only tables are outside on the pavement; inside there are bar stools only.

BARNEY'S
COFFEESHOP

Map p300 (www.barneysamsterdam.com; Haarlemmerstraat 102; ⊘9am-1am; 🚊18/21/22 Buiten Brouwersstraat) Decades ago, Barney's became famous for its bargain all-day breakfasts, along with marijuana. In recent years the weed has vastly improved, but breakfasts are now across the street in the smoke-friendly, somewhat-slick Barney's Uptown. A vaporiser dots each table at the coffeeshop, and milkshakes quiet hunger pangs until you're ready to dig in at Uptown.

SIBERIË
COFFEESHOP

Map p300 (Brouwersgracht 11; ⊘11am-11pm Sun-Thu, to midnight Fri & Sat; 🚊; 🚊1/2/5/13/17 Nieuwezijds Kolk) Popular among locals, Siberië has offerings beyond marijuana – its owners regularly schedule cultural events such as art exhibits, poetry slams, acoustic concerts, DJ nights and even horoscope readings. It's one of the better places for an actual coffee too.

BRIX FOOD 'N' DRINX
BAR

Map p302 (📞020-639 03 51; www.cafebrix.nl; Wolvenstraat 16; ⊘9am-1am Sun-Thu, to 3am Fri & Sat; 🚊1/2/5 Spui) The loungey setting makes this a great place to chill over cocktails (including three different Bloody Marys) or sample the astutely chosen wines. There's live soul, blues and jazz on Mondays from about 7pm.

DE ADMIRAAL
DISTILLERY

Map p302 (www.proeflokaaldeadmiraal.nl; Herengracht 319; ⊘noon-midnight Sun-Wed, to 1am Thu, to 2am Fri & Sat; 🚊1/2/5 Spui) The grandest and largest of Amsterdam's tasting houses, De Admiraal only pours its Jordaan-produced house brands: 17 *jenevers* (Dutch gins) and 60 liqueurs.

☆ ENTERTAINMENT

FELIX MERITIS
THEATRE

Map p302 (📞020-627 94 77; www.felix.meritis.nl; Keizersgracht 324; 🚊; 🚊1/2/5 Spui) Amsterdam's centre for arts, culture and science is renowned for staging innovative modern theatre, music and dance, as well as talks on politics, diversity, art, technology and literature. It was closed for renovations when we last visited, and was due to reopen in autumn 2018.

🛍 SHOPPING

You could easily spend all of your shopping time in the Negen Straatjes, with its abundance of small, specialist boutiques, but be sure to check out the hip shops in the Haarlemmerbuurt too.

★ NEGEN STRAATJES
AREA

Map p302 (Nine Streets; www.de9straatjes.nl; 🚊1/2/5 Spui) In a city packed with countless shopping opportunities, each seemingly more alluring than the last, the Negen Straatjes represent the very densest concentration of consumer pleasures. These nine little streets are indeed small, each just a block long. The shops are tiny too, and many are highly specialised. Eyeglasses? Cheese? Single-edition art books? Each has its own dedicated boutique.

The streets – from west to east, and north to south: Reestraat, Hartenstraat, Gasthuismolensteeg, Berenstraat, Wolvenstraat, Oude Spiegelstraat, Runstraat, Huidenstraat, Wijde Heisteeg – form a grid bounded by Prinsengracht to the west and Singel to the east.

To help navigate the welter of shops here, pick up a copy of *The Nine Streets* shopping guide, available at many tourist offices and in many of the shops themselves, as well as online at www.theninestreets.com.

★FROZEN FOUNTAIN   HOMEWARES

Map p302 (www.frozenfountain.nl; Prinsengracht 645; ◷1-6pm Mon, 10am-6pm Tue-Sat, noon-5pm Sun; ▣1/2/5 Prinsengracht) Frozen Fountain is Amsterdam's best-known showcase of furniture and interior design. Prices are not cheap, but the daring designs are offbeat and very memorable (designer penknives, kitchen gadgets and that birthday gift for the impossible-to-wow friend). Best of all, it's an unpretentious place where you can browse at length without feeling uncomfortable.

LOVE STORIES   FASHION & ACCESSORIES

Map p302 (www.lovestoriesintimates.com; Herengracht 296; ◷11am-6pm Tue-Sat, noon-6pm Sun & Mon; ▣1/2/5 Spui) On the Herengracht, this boutique is the flagship store of lingerie brand Love Stories, which was set up by Amsterdam interior designer and stylist turned fashion designer Marloes Hoedeman. Her comfortable, affordable lingerie comes in a range of playful, unexpected colour combinations and prints, and is designed to work with outerwear; there's also a great line of swimwear.

360 VOLT   HOMEWARES

Map p302 (☎020-810 01 01; www.360volt. com; Prinsengracht 397; ◷11am-6pm Thu-Sat, by appointment Tue & Wed; ▣13/14/17 Westermarkt) One of the keys to creating a quintessentially *gezellig* (cosy, convivial) atmosphere is ambient lighting, making this shop stocking vintage industrial lighting (restored to meet energy-efficient international standards) a real find. Its lights grace some of the world's hottest bars, restaurants, hotels and film sets, such as the James Bond instalment *Spectre*. Worldwide shipping can be arranged.

MARIE-STELLA-MARIS   COSMETICS

Map p302 (www.marie-stella-maris.com; Keizersgracht 357; ◷10am-6pm Tue-Sat, noon-6pm Sun & Mon; ▣1/2/5 Keizersgracht) ✍ Marie-Stella-Maris was set up as a social enterprise to provide clean drinking water worldwide. It donates a percentage from every purchase of its locally bottled mineral waters and its aromatic plant-based skincare products (body lotions, hand soaps, shea butter) and home fragrances (from travel pillow sprays to scented candles) to support its cause. Its basement cafe–water bar opens at weekends.

AMATØR   FASHION & ACCESSORIES

Map p302 (www.amatorcollection.com; Runstraat 26; ◷10am-6pm Tue, Wed, Fri & Sat, to 7pm Thu, noon-6pm Sun & Mon; ▣1/2/5 Spui) Suits, dresses, separates and accessories from Amsterdam label Amatør are designed by its Dutch-born founder Eline Starink, who identified a gap in the market for young, ambitious businesswomen seeking sophisticated, powerful and individual clothes that can adapt from the office to social events as well as the Dutch cycling lifestyle. Seasonal collections incorporate strong accent colours and bold prints.

DENHAM THE JEANMAKER
MEN'S STORE   CLOTHING

Map p302 (www.denhamthejeanmaker.com; Prinsengracht 495; ◷noon-6pm Sun & Mon, 10am-6pm Tue, Wed, Fri & Sat, 10am-8pm Thu; ▣1/2/5 Spui) Next door to its studio, where jeans are produced, this flagship, 'zoned' boutique carries the cutting-edge jeanmaker's menswear lines. Jeans aside, you'll find jackets, knitwear and accessories. Cool vintage touches in-store include an antique haberdashery display case and a vintage scissor collection.

Other nearby boutiques include its **women's store** (Map p302; Runstraat 17) around the corner.

DE KAASKAMER   FOOD

Map p302 (www.kaaskamer.nl; Runstraat 7; ◷noon-6pm Mon, 9am-6pm Tue-Fri, 9am-5pm Sat, noon-5pm Sun; ▣1/2/5 Spui) The name means 'the cheese room' and De Kaaskamer is indeed stacked to the rafters with Dutch and organic varieties, as well as olives, tapenades, salads and other picnic ingredients. You can try before you buy or pick up a cheese-filled baguette. Vacuum-packing is available to take cheeses home.

TENUE DE NÎMES   CLOTHING

Map p300 (www.tenuedenimes.com; Haarlemmerstraat 92-94; ◷noon-7pm Mon, 11am-7pm Tue-Fri, 10am-6pm Sat, noon-6pm Sun; ▣18/21/22 Buiten Brouwersstraat) Denim clothing by legendary brands such as Levi's, Rogue Territory, Pure Blue Japan, Edwin, Naked & Famous, Acne and Rag & Bone are the speciality of this hip boutique.

MARLIES DEKKERS   CLOTHING

Map p302 (www.marliesdekkers.com; Berenstraat 18; ◷1-6pm Mon, 11am-6pm Tue-Sat, noon-5pm Sun; ▣13/14/17 Westermarkt) Pre-eminent

WESTERN CANAL RING SHOPPING

Dutch lingerie designer Marlies Dekkers is known for her subtle hints of bondage, detailed on exquisite undergarments. Summer sees an equally seductive range of swimwear. The shop itself has a sultry air of decadence, with hand-painted wallpaper and a titillating lounge area with a fireplace.

NUKUHIVA · CLOTHING
Map p300 (www.nukuhiva.nl; Haarlemmerstraat 36; ☻noon-7pm Mon, 10.30am-7pm Tue-Fri, 10am-6pm Sat, noon-6pm Sun; ☐18/21/22 Buiten Brouwersstraat) 🍃 This eco-friendly boutique stocks only ethical and fair-trade clothing and accessories, by brands such as Veja (vegan shoes) and Dutch designer Kuyishi (organic denim).

GAMEKEEPER · TOYS
Map p300 (www.gamekeeper.nl; Hartenstraat 14; ☻10am-6pm Mon & Sat, to 6.30pm Tue, Wed & Fri, to 8.30pm Thu, 11am-6pm Sun; ☐13/14/17 Westermarkt) The selection of board games here is dizzying, as is the imagination that went into making them. Start with checkers, chess and mah-jong, and move on to Cathedral (build a city in the style of the Great Wall of China or the souk in Marrakesh) or Rush Hour (help a car get out of traffic).
'Cooperative' games encourage players to play with, not against, each other.

AMSTERDAM WATCH COMPANY · FASHION & ACCESSORIES
Map p300 (www.awco.nl; Reestraat 3; ☻11am-6pm Tue-Fri, to 5pm Sat; ☐13/14/17 Westermarkt) A small, passionate and highly skilled team here restores old watches (postwar to mid-1970s). The company is also the exclusive Amsterdam dealer of Dutch watchmakers including Van der Gang, Roland Oostwegel, and Christiaan van der Klaauw, who makes fewer than 200 watches a year.

BRILMUSEUM · FASHION & ACCESSORIES
Map p300 (☎020-421 24 14; www.brilmuseum amsterdam.nl; Gasthuismolensteeg 7; ☻11.30am-5.30pm Wed-Fri, to 5pm Sat; ☐13/14/17 Westermarkt) This spectacles shop is an institution, both for its wares and for its presentation. You can take in the 700-year history of eyeglasses as well as a very 21st-century collection, some of which is pretty outlandish.

LAURA DOLS · VINTAGE
Map p302 (☎020-624 90 66; www.lauradols. nl; Wolvenstraat 7; ☻11am-6pm Mon-Sat, noon-6pm Sun; ☐1/2/5 Spui) Compulsive style-watchers head to this vintage-clothing store for fur coats, 1920s beaded dresses, lace blouses and '40s movie-star accessories such as hand-stitched leather gloves. Vintage wedding dresses are available to view by appointment.

VAN RAVENSTEIN · CLOTHING
Map p302 (www.van-ravenstein.nl; Keizersgracht 359; ☻1-6pm Mon, 11am-6pm Tue-Fri, 10.30am-5.30pm Sat; ☐1/2/5 Spui) Style-conscious men and women shop here for clothing by upmarket designers, including many from Belgium's famed 'Antwerp Six': Dries Van Noten, Ann Demeulemeester, Walter Van Beirendonck and Dirk Van Saene.

ZIPPER · VINTAGE
Map p302 (www.zipperstore.nl; Huidenstraat 7; ☻noon-6.30pm Mon, 11am-6.30pm Tue, Wed, Fri & Sat, 11am-8pm Thu, 1-6.30pm Sun; ☐1/2/5 Spui) Hip Amsterdammers head here for seriously nostalgic, retro secondhand gear: wacky printed shirts, stovepipe jeans, '40s zoot suits, pork-pie hats and the like.

MENDO · BOOKS
Map p302 (www.mendo.nl; Berenstraat 11; ☻10.30am-6pm Mon-Sat, noon-5pm Sun; ☐13/14/17 Westermarkt) Graphic-design agency Mendo runs this smart, black-walled bookshop specialising in books in the creative realm: art, design, architecture, fashion and photography.

Southern Canal Ring

Neighbourhood Top Five

❶ Hermitage Amsterdam (p118) Goggling at blockbuster exhibitions drawn from the treasures at the original St Petersburg museum, housed here in a former retirement home.

❷ Golden Bend (p119) Ambling along the stretch of canal-side property that practically purrs with Golden Age elegance, and imagining which house you would choose if you could.

❸ Reguliersgracht (p121) Enjoying romantic ahhs on the so-called 'canal of seven bridges', and seeing how many of them you can spot at once.

❹ Museum Van Loon (p119) Getting an insight into the lavish lifestyle of Amsterdam's top rung from the Golden Age up to the 19th century in this gracious canal-side abode.

❺ Museum Willet-Holthuysen (p120) Exploring the lavishness of patrician canal-house life in this historic former family home.

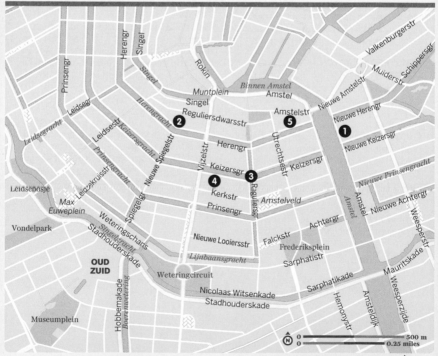

For more detail of this area see Map p304 ➡

Explore Southern Canal Ring

The graceful arc of the Southern Canal Ring spans the area from the radial Leidsegracht in the west to the Amstel in the east. Packed with museums, restaurants, cafes, shops and miles of gorgeous canals, the district deserves at least a day to explore. Anchored by the night-life centres of Leidseplein (p118) and Rembrandtplein (p121) (including the gay hub of Reguliersdwarsstraat), the neighbourhood offers plenty to occupy you after dark.

Highlights include the cacophonous, touristy and flower-filled Bloemenmarkt (p119), the grand and exquisite houses of the Golden Bend (p119), and the splendid interior decoration of Museum Van Loon (p119).

Check out the big-name exhibitions at the Hermitage Amsterdam (p118), then stroll past the Amstelsluizen (p122) and the Gijsbert Dommer Huis (p122) ('House with the Blood Stains'!). Around the corner, canal house Museum Willet-Holthuysen (p120) offers a look at the lifestyle of the 19th-century A-list.

There are tons of eating options around Utrechtsestraat; to feed your soul, take in the view of the seven bridges along Reguliersgracht (p121). End your night on lively Rembrandtplein.

Local Life

→**Cakes** Feast like the Dutch royals on beautiful baked goods from Patisserie Holtkamp (p126), given the seal of approval with the royal coat of arms.

→**Cafes** Off Prinsengracht, tiny Weteringstraat feels like a secret passage; look out for local *bruin café* (brown cafe; traditional Dutch pub), Café de Wetering (p127).

→**Cocktails** The door's unmarked and you'll need to reserve ahead to get in, but the cocktails at speakeasy Door 74 (p126) are worth it.

→**Music** Locals scan the manifold riches of Concerto (p132), a rambling vinyl shop with regular live gigs and a cafe for hanging out with musos all day.

Getting There & Away

→**Tram** This area is well-served by trams. For the Leidseplein area, take tram 1, 2, 5, 7 or 10. To reach Rembrandtplein, take tram 4, which travels down Utrechtsestraat, or tram 9. Trams 16 and 24 cut through the centre of the neighbourhood down busy Vijzelstraat.

Lonely Planet's Top Tip

At first glance, Leidseplein and Rembrandtplein may look like nothing more than tourist traps for the stag and hen or travel-in-pack brigades. But they're serious (or not-so-serious) fun, with plenty of authentic bars and cafes just waiting to be discovered. To escape the hullabaloo and hang out with the locals, head to happening Utrechtsestraat.

✖ Best Places to Eat

→ Van Dobben (p122)
→ Pantry (p124)
→ Buffet van Odette (p123)
→ La Cacerola (p123)
→ Ron Gastrobar Oriental (p124)

For reviews, see p122 ➡

☕ Best Places to Drink

→ Bar Moustache (p126)
→ Eijlders (p127)
→ The Otherside (p127)
→ Door 74 (p126)

For reviews, see p126 ➡

◉ Best Places for Entertainment

→ Melkweg (p131)
→ Paradiso (p131)
→ Sugar Factory (p131)
→ Koninklijk Theater Carré (p131)
→ Pathé Tuschinskitheater (p130)

For reviews, see p130 ➡

TOP SIGHT
HERMITAGE AMSTERDAM

On the Amstel riverbank, this grand 17th-century almshouse contains the Amsterdam branch of the State Hermitage Museum of St Petersburg. Why is this bastion of Russian culture here? It's all down to long-standing ties between Russia and the Netherlands: Tsar Peter the Great learned shipbuilding here in 1697, eventually leading to the establishment of this Hermitage outpost.

The Portrait Gallery of the Golden Age displays 30 group portraits that are contemporaries of Rembrandt's famous *The Night Watch*. The works are startlingly large, showing the importance of the associations they depict and holding up a mirror to a section of 17th-century society; paintings include Rembrandt's *The Anatomy Lesson of Dr Deijman*. Temporary exhibitions, often drawing from the Russian museum's amazing cache of more than three million art objects, change about twice a year.

Outside the main museum is the Outsider Art Museum, a collaboration between the Hermitage, the Dolhuys Museum of the Mind in Haarlem and Dutch healthcare facility Cordaan. It features changing exhibitions of work produced by artists whilst in psychiatric institutions. Admission is usually free; enter from the garden.

DON'T MISS

➡ Portrait Gallery of the Golden Age
➡ Outsider Art Museum

PRACTICALITIES

➡ Map p304, G3
➡ ☎020-530 74 88
➡ www.hermitage.nl
➡ Amstel 51
➡ single exhibitions adult/child €17.50/free, all exhibitions adult/child €25/free
➡ ◷10am-5pm
➡ Ⓜ Waterlooplein, ☷9/14 Waterlooplein

◉ SIGHTS

LEIDSEPLEIN SQUARE
Map p304 (☷1/2/5/7/10 Leidseplein) Historic architecture, beer, clubs and steakhouses – welcome to Leidseplein. The square is always busy, but after dark it gets thronged by a mainstream crowd of party lovers (more tourists than locals). A major hub for nightlife and trams, it has countless pubs and clubs, masses of restaurants and an aroma of roasted meat. Pavement cafes at the northern end are perfect for people-watching. Entertainment venues line the streets around the square; nearby Kerkstraat has a cluster of gay venues.

On the square's eastern side, farmers would once leave their horses and carts at the Leidsepoort (Leiden Gate) before entering town; it was demolished in 1870. The strip of greenery with large chestnut trees on the other side of the Singelgracht is called Leidsebosje (Leiden Wood).

BLAUW JAN PUBLIC ART
Map p304 (Kleine Gartmanplantsoen; ☷1/2/5/7/10 Leidseplein) There's a surprise waiting in Kleine Gartmanplantsoen park:

40 huge, lifelike lizards nestled in the grass and sunning themselves on the brickwork. It's a surreal sight. Cast in bronze, the life-sized reptiles were created by Dutch artist Hans van Houwelingen in 1994. They're collectively known as Blauw Jan, after an old Amsterdam inn of the same name which, in the 17th and 18th centuries, had a menagerie of exotic animals brought to the port city from faraway lands.

MAX EUWE CENTRUM NOTABLE BUILDING
Map p304 (☎020-625 70 17; www.maxeuwe.nl; Max Euweplein 30a-1; ◷noon-4pm Tue-Fri, limited hours Jul & Aug; ☷1/2/5/7/10 Leidseplein) FREE There's a small exhibition on the history of chess at this centre, named after Max Euwe (1901–81), who, in the 1930s, became the Netherlands' only World Chess Champion. Visitors can play against live or digital opponents. Outside, the oversized chessboard is usually in use, watched by rapt spectators; there will also be a few games in progress on the surrounding benches.

AMSTERDAM PIPE MUSEUM MUSEUM
Map p304 (www.pipemuseum.nl; Prinsengracht 488; adult/child €8/4; ◷noon-6pm Wed-Sat;

⊟1/2/5 Prinsengracht) This museum is located in the grand 17th-century canal house of the marvellously single-minded pipe collector who gathered this unexpectedly fascinating collection from around 60 different countries over 40 years. Knowledgeable guides take you through the exhibits, from the earliest South American pipes, dating from 500 BC, to 15th-century Dutch pipes, Chinese opium pipes, African ceremonial pipes and much more. A peek into the house is worth the price of admission alone.

KRIJTBERG   CHURCH

Map p304 (☑020-623 19 23; www.krijtberg.nl; Singel 446; ⊘1-5pm Tue-Thu, Sat & Sun; ⊟1/2/5 Koningsplein) The spiky spires of this neo-Gothic church are an unmissable landmark amid rows of handsome Singel homes. Officially known as the St Franciscus Xaveriuskerk, Krijtberg (Chalk Hill) replaced a clandestine Jesuit chapel on the same site in 1883; it's remained Jesuit to this day. If you get the chance, have a peek inside: the interior is typically, lavishly Jesuit, covered with paintings and statuary.

BLOEMENMARKT   MARKET

Map p304 (Flower Market; Singel, btwn Muntplein & Koningsplein; ⊘8.30am-7pm Mon-Sat, to 7.30pm Sun Apr-Oct, 9am-5.30pm Mon-Sat, 11am-5.30pm Sun Nov-Mar; ⊟1/2/5 Koningsplein) Flowers are not treats, but essentials in Amsterdam. Ever since 1860, this famous flower market has been located at the spot where nurserymen and women, having sailed up the Amstel from their smallholdings, would moor their barges to sell their wares directly to customers. No longer floating (it's now perched on piles), the market has plenty of high-kitsch miniature clogs, fridge magnets and wooden tulips; it's also a good place to buy (real) tulips in season and bulbs year-round.

GOLDEN BEND   ARCHITECTURE

Map p304 (Gouden Bocht; Herengracht, btwn Leidsestraat & Vijzelstraat; ⊟1/2/5 Koningsplein) The Golden Bend is Amsterdam's swankiest stretch of property. Its handsome mansions are a monument to the Golden Age, when precious goods swelled in the cellars of homes already stuffed with valuables. The richest Amsterdammers

SOUTHERN CANAL RING SIGHTS

TOP SIGHT
MUSEUM VAN LOON

This beautiful house-turned-museum plunges you into the lavish lifestyle of the wealthy, time-travelling you to 19th-century Amsterdam. Built in 1672, it was first home to painter Ferdinand Bol. By the late 1800s, the Van Loons, a prominent family, had moved in and have lived here ever since; they still occupy the upper floors.

The house is filled with opulent furniture and family portraits that seem to whisper secrets as you pass from room to gorgeous room. Among the 150 portraits of the Van Loon family, you'll see important paintings such as *The Marriage of Willem van Loon and Margaretha Bas* by Jan Miense Molenaer. But the main exhibit is the house itself. It's full of set-piece interior decoration, with intricate wedding-cake stucco on the ceilings, a garden room overlooking the formal hedges of the garden, and the glorious – but surely nightmare-inducing – decoration of the guest bedroom. It's the only such mansion where you can still see a rear coach house, which once housed horse-drawn carriages.

The powerhouse below is the old-fashioned basement kitchen. Over the next few years, the family intends to open the wine cellar and the pantry to visitors.

DON'T MISS

➡ The interior details
➡ The 19th-century basement kitchen
➡ The dramatic bedrooms

PRACTICALITIES

➡ Map p304, E4
➡ ☑020-624 52 55
➡ www.museum vanloon.nl
➡ Keizersgracht 672
➡ adult/child €9/5, free with Museum & I Amsterdam cards
➡ ⊘10am-5pm
➡ ⊟16/24 Keizersgracht

TOP SIGHT
MUSEUM WILLET-HOLTHUYSEN

Built in 1687 for Amsterdam mayor Jacob Hop and redesigned in 1739, this house-turned-museum offers insight into the 19th-century lives of the merchant class' superrich. Now managed by the Amsterdam Museum, it's named after Louisa Willet-Holthuysen, who lived a lavish, bohemian life here with her husband Abraham from 1861. She bequeathed the property to the city in 1895.

As you stroll through the patrician house, you'll find plenty of information illustrating the lifestyle and interests of Abraham and Louisa. They were keen art collectors, and the rich selection of furniture and art includes notable paintings by Jacob de Wit. Also look for the *place de milieu* (centrepiece) that was part of the family's 275-piece Meissen table service. Downstairs, the preserved kitchen and scullery provide a glimpse of the work required to keep the house running, with simple decoration and lovely original tiling on the walls.

The intimate garden with sundial is a reconstruction dating from 1972, created in the French Classical style as was fashionable in the 19th century. You can also peek at the garden through the iron fence at the Amstelstraat end.

DON'T MISS

→ de Wit paintings
→ The French garden
→ The Louis XVI–style ground floor

PRACTICALITIES

→ Map p304, F3
→ ☑020-523 18 22
→ www.willet holthuysen.nl
→ Herengracht 605
→ adult/child €9/4.50, audio guide €1
→ ◷10am-5pm Mon-Fri, from 11am Sat & Sun
→ Ⓜ Waterlooplein, ⓖ4/9/14 Rembrandt-plein

---

lived and ruled their affairs from here. The earliest mansions date from the 1660s, when the Canal Ring was expanded south. Thanks to some city-hall lobbying, the gables here were built twice as wide as the standard Amsterdam model, and the rear gardens deeper.

Apart from the Kattenkabinet museum, the homes are only open to the public on Open Monument Day (Open Monumentendag; second weekend in September).

KATTENKABINET
MUSEUM

Map p304 (Cat Cabinet; ☑020-626 90 40; www.kattenkabinet.nl; Herengracht 497; adult/child €7/free; ◷10am-5pm Mon-Fri, from noon Sat & Sun; ⓖ1/2/5 Koningsplein) When kitties go to the great sofa in the sky, most doting owners comfort themselves with a photo on the mantel; wealthy financier Bob Meijer founded an entire museum in memory of his red tomcat John Pierpont Morgan III. The collection includes artworks by Tsuguharu Foujita, Théophile Alexandre Steinlen and Amsterdam's chief sculptor, Hildo Krop. A visit here also gives you the opportunity to explore one of the Golden

Bend's grand houses; it's the only one open to the public.

You may get the chance to admire the cats that live in the building along with the art collection.

STADSARCHIEF
MUSEUM

Map p304 (Municipal Archives; ☑tour reservations 020-251 15 10; www.amsterdam.nl/stadsarchief; Vijzelstraat 32; ◷10am-5pm Tue-Fri, from noon Sat & Sun; ⓖ16/24 Keizersgracht) FREE A distinctive striped building dating from 1923, this former bank now houses 23km of shelving storing Amsterdam archives. Fascinating displays of archive gems, such as the 1942 police report on the theft of Anne Frank's bike and a letter from Charles Darwin to Artis Royal Zoo in 1868, can be viewed in the enormous tiled basement vault.

Tours (adult/child €6/free, 1¼ hours) run at 2pm on Saturdays and Sundays, and must be booked in advance.

Upstairs, a **gallery space** mounts temporary exhibits (admission €3). Its excellent bookshop, the **Stadsboekwinkel** (www.stadsboekwinkel.nl), sells city-oriented tomes.

★FOAM GALLERY

Map p304 (Fotografiemuseum Amsterdam; www. foam.org; Keizersgracht 609; adult/child €11/ free; ⏰10am-6pm Sat-Wed, to 9pm Thu & Fri; 🚊16/24 Keizersgracht) From the outside it looks like a grand canal house, but this is the city's most important photography gallery. Its simple, spacious galleries, some with skylights or large windows for natural light, host four major exhibitions annually, featuring world-renowned photographers such as William Eggleston and Helmut Newton. There's a cafe in the basement.

REGULIERSGRACHT CANAL

Map p304 (🚊4/9/14 Rembrandtplein) Crossing Herengracht, Keizersgracht & Prinsengracht canals, this, the prettiest of Amsterdam's waterways, was dug in 1658 to link the Herengracht with the canals further south. The canal is famous for its seven bridges, though if you stand where it crosses Herengracht, you can count 15 bridges in all directions. The houses lining the canal are a decorative feast of gables and adornments. Reguliersgracht was named after an order of monks whose monastery was located nearby.

Where Prinsengracht crosses Reguliersgracht, there is a house with a statue of a stork outside – the dwelling once belonged to a midwife.

TASSENMUSEUM HENDRIKJE MUSEUM

Map p304 (Museum of Bags & Purses; 📞020-524 64 52; www.tassenmuseum.nl; Herengracht 573; adult/child €12.50/3.50; ⏰10am-5pm; 🚊4/9/14 Rembrandtplein) This grand 17th-century canal house museum has a covetable collection of arm candy. More than 5000 bags can be found here, including a medieval pouch, Perspex 1960s containers, design classics by Chanel, Gucci and Versace, an '80s touchtone phone bag and Madonna's ivy-strewn 'Evita' bag from the film's premiere. The cafe has pricey-but-nice high teas and cakes.

REMBRANDTPLEIN SQUARE

Map p304 (🚊4/9/14 Rembrandtplein) First called Reguliersplein, then Botermarkt for the butter markets held here until the mid-19th century, this somewhat-brash square now takes its name from the statue of the painter erected in 1876. Beneath Rembrandt is a photo-op favourite: imposing life-sized bronze sculptures re-creating his famous painting, *The Night Watch* (see the original in the Rijksmuseum).

Rembrandtplein evolved into a nightlife hub as cafes, restaurants and clubs opened their doors, and remains a cornerstone of Amsterdam nightlife.

BLAUWBRUG BRIDGE

Map p304 (Blue Bridge; btwn Waterlooplein & Amstelstraat; Ⓜ️Waterlooplein) Built in 1884, this highly decorated stone bridge replaced an old, blue (hence the name) wooden crossing that had connected these shores of the Amstel since the 17th century. The current version was modelled on the Alexander III bridge in Paris, and features tall, ornate street lamps topped by the imperial crown of Amsterdam, fish sculptures and foundations shaped like the prow of a medieval ship.

MAGERE BRUG BRIDGE

Map p304 (Skinny Bridge; btwn Kerkstraat & Nieuwe Kerkstraat; 🚊4 Prinsengracht) Dating from the 1670s, the nine-arched 'Skinny

---

AMSTERDAM AMERICAN HOTEL

This **hotel** (Map p304; 📞020-556 30 00; www.hampshirehotelamsterdamamerican.com; Leidsekade 97; d from €140; 🚊1/2/5/7/10 Leidseplein) is a magnificent art nouveau beast. The founder of the original hotel, Cornelis Alidus Anne (CAA) Steinigeweg had helped establish a Dutch settlement on Grand Island, New York, hence the 'American' in the name. Designed by architect Willem Kromhout, today's hotel is an expansion of the original 1880s Viennese Renaissance–style building, which was covered in symbols of Americana. Life-sized statues on the facade represent the five continents.

You can, of course, stay at the luxury hotel. Its **Café Americain** (📞020-556 30 10; www.cafeamericain.nl; ⏰5.30am-midnight) is a heritage-listed showpiece with a beautifully restored art nouveau interior featuring stained glass, exquisite light fittings and murals; it's long been affectionately dubbed 'Amsterdam's living room', and is open to non-guests.

Bridge' has had several incarnations, first in timber and later in concrete. It has a hand-operated central section that can be raised to let boats through. The bridge is especially pretty at night, when it glows with 1200 tiny lights. It's appeared in several films, including the 1971 James Bond thriller *Diamonds are Forever*. Stand in the middle and feel it sway under the passing traffic.

AMSTELSLUIZEN   ARCHITECTURE

Map p304 (Amstel Locks; Amstel river, near Koninklijk Theater Carré; ⊞4 Prinsengracht) These impressive sluices (locks) date from 1674 and are still in use to refresh the city's canals. They allow the canals to be flushed with fresh water from lakes north of the city, rather than saltwater from the IJ river, an innovation that made the city more liveable. The locks are shut while fresh water flows in, while the sluices on the western side of the city are left open as the stagnant water is pumped out to sea.

AMSTELKERK   CHURCH

Map p304 (☑020-520 00 70; www.amstelkerk.net; Amstelveld 10; ⊘9am-5pm Mon-Fri; ⊞4 Prinsengracht) Looking more like a country house than a church, the pinewood Amstelkerk was erected in 1668 as a *noodkerk* (makeshift church) under the direction of the city architect, Daniël Stalpaert, who also designed the town hall on the Dam. The idea was that a permanent church would be built next to it, but plans for this were abandoned in the 1840s.

During the French occupation, Napoleon used the building to keep his horses. Later, in 1840, the square-shaped interior was updated with a neo-Gothic look and the addition of a pipe organ. Van Gogh heard his uncle's sermon here in 1877.

DE DUIF   CHURCH

Map p304 (The Dove; ☑020-520 00 90; www.deduif.net; Prinsengracht 756; ⊘hours vary; ⊞4 Prinsengracht) In 1796, following the French-installed government's proclamation of religious freedom, De Duif became the Netherlands' first Catholic church to be built with a public entrance in more than two centuries. The original church was demolished due to unstable construction; its replacement was built in 1857. Today, De Duif is an ecumenical church, and is also used as a venue for concerts, opera and private events.

If you're able to peek inside, check out the clay friezes of the Stations of the Cross on the right wall, the pulpit carvings of St Willibrordus of Utrecht, and the organ reaching up to the vaulted ceiling, a sight in its own right.

GIJSBERT DOMMER HUIS   HISTORIC BUILDING

Map p304 (Amstel 216; ⊞4 Keizersgracht) This handsome greystone house is known dramatically as the 'House with the Blood Stains'. Six-time mayor and diplomat Coenraad van Beuningen lost his fortune, then his mind, and scribbled graffiti on the facade, allegedly in his own blood. His mysterious 17th-century writing – which includes Hebrew letters and obscure Kabbalah symbols – is still faintly visible.

Wealthy businessman Gijsbert Dommer commissioned the house in 1671, hence the name.

✗ EATING

Leidseplein has steakhouses cheek-by-jowl, though there are more interesting gems to be found that are not just about slabs of beef. For more scenic and singular eateries, your best bet is on the nearby side streets or canals. Rembrandtplein has a somewhat brash feel; for a better meal, walk a few steps to Utrechtsestraat, one of the finest restaurant rows in town.

★ VAN DOBBEN   DUTCH €

Map p304 (☑020-624 42 00; www.eetsalonvandobben.nl; Korte Reguliersdwarsstraat 5-9; dishes €3-8; ⊘10am-9pm Mon-Wed, to 1am Thu, to 2am Fri & Sat, 10.30am-8pm Sun; ⊞4/9/14 Rembrandtplein) Open since the 1940s, Van Dobben has a cool diner feel, with white tiles and siren-red walls. Traditional meaty Dutch fare is its forte: low-priced, finely sliced roast beef sandwiches with mustard are an old-fashioned joy, or try the *pekelvlees* (akin to corned beef) or *halfom* (if you're keen on *pekelvlees* mixed with liver).

The meat *kroketten* (croquettes) are up there with the best in town and are almost compulsory after a late-night Rembrandtplein booze-up. White-coated staff who've worked here for decades specialise in snappy banter.

There's a second branch in De Pijp.

VISHUISJE HERENGRACHT
STREET FOOD €

Map p304 (Utrechtsestraat 1017; snacks €2-5; ⊙9am-6pm Mon-Wed & Fri, to 9pm Thu, to 5pm Sat; 🚋4, 9 Rembrandtplein) Not everyone digs raw herring, but if you do, you're in luck: of the many herring stalls in the city, this is lauded as one of the best. You can also choose from other tasty seafood, such as smoked eel, whitefish or prawns.

POKÉ PERFECT
HAWAIIAN €

Map p304 (www.pokeperfect.com; Prinsengracht 502; mains around €10; ⊙11.30am-9pm Sun-Thu, to 10pm Fri & Sat; 🚋Leidseplein) Exercise lovers on the run flock to this pale, gleaming place, which offers fast food that is as healthy as takeaway gets. The poké (pronounced *poh*-kay) consists of sushi rice, raw fish, tofu, smoked chicken or lobster, and several different toppings served in a bowl: it's fresh, light and tasty. There's counter service and just a couple of tables.

SOUP EN ZO
SOUP €

Map p304 (www.soupenzo.nl; Nieuwe Spiegelstraat 54; soup €5-7; ⊙11am-8pm Mon-Fri, noon-7pm Sat & Sun; 🖋; 🚋7/10 Spiegelgracht) On a chilly Amsterdam day, you can't beat a steaming cup of soup from this little specialist restaurant. Daily choices might include potato with Roquefort; lentil and minced beef, prunes and pumpkin; or spicy spinach and coconut.

LITE/DARK
CAFE €

Map p304 (www.litedark.nl; Utrechtsestraat 22; dishes €4-6; ⊙8am-7pm Mon-Fri, 10am-6pm Sat, 10am-7pm Sun; 🚋4 Keizersgracht) Friendly and cool, this monochromatic cafe manages to make a convincing case for the health benefits of chocolate (or at least the dark variety), serving chocolate shots and chocolate fondue alongside a huge range of 'lite' smoothies, energy shakes and wheatgrass shots. The short menu includes salads, bagels and sandwiches, as well as choc-dipped fruit.

LOEKIE
SANDWICHES €

Map p304 (www.loekie.net; Utrechtsestraat 57; sandwiches €5-8; ⊙9.30am-5.30pm Mon-Sat; 🚋4 Keizersgracht) A great place to nip into for fresh, piled-high deli sandwiches to take out and eat by a nearby canal. Try fillings such as smoked beef with egg and salt, or extra-mature cheese, rocket, Parma ham, pine nuts and truffle sauce.

BAR HUF
AMERICAN €

Map p304 (www.barhuf.nl; Reguliersdwarsstraat 43; mains €8-15; ⊙kitchen 5pm-midnight Sun-Thu, to 1am Fri & Sat; 🛜; 🚋1/2/5 Koningsplein) It can be hard to find good late-night dining in Amsterdam, but this place is a boon for nightbird burger lovers. Dig into the Mango Jerry (crab, coleslaw and wasabi mayo) or Rocky Balboa (chicken, jalapenos and cheddar) burgers, or try rum- and apple-glazed ribs or macaroni and cheese (made with five different cheeses). Finish with lemon meringue pie.

★ BUFFET VAN ODETTE
CAFE €€

Map p304 (☎020-423 60 34; www.buffetvanodette.nl; Prinsengracht 598; mains €13-19; ⊙kitchen 10am-10pm; 🚋7/10 Spiegelgracht) Chow down at Odette's, a white-tiled cafe with an enchanting canal-side spot, where delicious dishes are made with great ingredients and a dash of creativity. Try the splendid platter of cured meats and dips, or mains such as ravioli with mature cheese, watercress and tomato, or smoked salmon, lentils and poached egg.

★ LA CACEROLA
SPANISH €€

Map p304 (☎020-627 93 97; www.restaurant lacacerola.nl; Weteringstraat 41; mains €18.50-25; ⊙6-10.30pm Tue-Sat; 🚋7/10 Spiegelgracht) Open since 1958, this romantic gem serves up gourmet meals prepared according to Slow Food principles. Try the chef's surprise four-course menu, or, if you like to know what you're going to eat, go a la carte, with hearty dishes such as rack of lamb with Mediterranean vegetables and potato ratatouille.

DIGNITA HOFTUIN
CAFE €€

Map p304 (www.eatwelldogood.nl; Nieuwe Herengracht 18a; dishes €9-14; ⊙9am-7pm; 🖋🍴; 🚋Weesperstraat) Set in the garden behind the Hermitage (p118), this cafe serves a brunchy menu of Ottolenghi-style salads, sandwiches and light snacks. Its walls are glass, and the place is flooded with light; there are also chairs and tables outside. It's a dreamy spot on a sunny summer's day.

This is a good choice for families: children can play on the enclosed grass area and there are toys inside. The cafe is part of the Not for Sale social-enterprise model, providing training and employment for vulnerable people.

RON GASTROBAR ORIENTAL ASIAN €€

Map p304 (☎020-223 53 52; www.rongastro
baroriental.nl; Kerkstraat 23; dim sum €2-10,
mains €15; ☺5.30-11pm; ☏; ☐1/2/5 Prinsengracht) Michelin-starred chef Ron Blaauw
began his food revolution at Ron Gastrobar (p163) near Vondelpark, introducing
a one-price menu of tapas-style dishes so
diners could eat fine cuisine without set-
tling down for a long formal meal. This is
his Asian version. The menu includes delicacies such as dim sum of steamed scallop
with glass noodles, and crispy sweet and
sour prawns.

PANTRY DUTCH €€

Map p304 (☎020-620 09 22; www.thepantry.
nl; Leidsekruisstraat 21; mains €13-18, 3-course
menus €21-30; ☺11am-10.30pm; ☐1/2/5 Leidseplein) With wood-panelled walls and sepia
lighting, this little restaurant is *gezellig*
(cosy, convivial) indeed. Tuck into classic
Dutch dishes such as *zuurkool stamppot*
(sauerkraut and potato mash served with
a smoked sausage or meatball) or *hutspot*
('hotchpotch', with stewed beef, carrots and
onions).

ROSE'S CANTINA MEXICAN €€

Map p304 (☎020-625 97 97; www.rosescantina.
com; Reguliersdwarsstraat 38-48; mains €16-
24; ☺5.30-10.30pm; ☏; ☐1/2/5 Koningsplein)
Rose's has a grass-green interior topped
by massive glitter balls, and a greenery-
fringed courtyard. Both are great settings
for enjoying starters such as ceviche (raw
fish cured in lime juice) and Mexican
mains with a twist, such as pulled pork
or crab tacos, black-bean-filled enchiladas
with sour cream, and spicy sweet-potato
empanadas with chipotle mayo and salsa.

IN DE BUURT INTERNATIONAL €€

Map p304 (www.indebuurt-amsterdam.nl; Lijnbaansgracht 246; mains €12-20; ☺noon-3.30pm
& 5-10.30pm; ☐1/2/5 Leidseplein) It may be
in the Leidseplein, but In de Buurt keeps
it classy, dishing up fantastic mini-burgers
with truffle mayo and roasted cherry tomatoes, and serving delicious gin and tonics. It
has a canal-side summer terrace and a cosy
interior with exposed-brick walls, beams
and bottles.

CAFÉ VAN LEEUWEN BRASSERIE €€

Map p304 (www.cafevanleeuwen.nl; Keizersgracht 711; mains €7-20; ☺kitchen 9am-10pm
Mon-Fri, 10am-10pm Sat, 11am-9pm Sun; ☐4

Keizersgracht) Brown cafe in style, with lots
of dark-wooded charm, dangling light bulbs
and an exposed brick wall, this spot offers
fine brasserie-style dishes such as succulent hamburgers and open sandwiches. It's
a great place for breakfast or brunch, and
the canal-side setting is fabulous.

DE BLAUWE HOLLANDER DUTCH €€

Map p304 (☎020-627 05 21; www.deblauwe
hollander.nl; Leidsekruisstraat 28; mains €14-20;
☺noon-11pm; ☐1/2/5 Leidseplein) It's all cosiness and comfort food at this red-lamp-lit
place, with a menu including Dutch staples
such as pea soup with bacon, and *stamppot*
(veggie mash) with pork sausage. Look for
the Dutch flag flying out front.

BOUCHON DU CENTRE FRENCH €€

Map p304 (☎020-330 11 28; www.bouchon
ducentre.nl; Falckstraat 3; mains €15-20; ☺noon-
3pm & 5-8pm Wed-Sat; ☐4/7/10 Frederiksplein)
Classic red-and-white gingham tablecloths
set the scene at this authentic-feeling Lyon-
nais *bouchon* (informal rustic bistro). The
menu changes daily, but revolves around
bouchon staples such as *andouillette* (offal
sausage) and *quenelles de brochet* (pike
dumplings). Don't miss a round of wonderfully gooey St Marcellin cheese and Rhône
Valley wines such as Beaujolais.

LO STIVALE D'ORO ITALIAN €€

Map p304 (☎020-638 73 07; www.lostivaledoro.
nl; Amstelstraat 49; pizzas €7-13, mains €8-22;
☺5-10.30pm Wed-Mon; ☐4/9/14 Rembrandtplein) Conviviality is the name of the game
at the 'Golden Boot', which offers a textbook
gregarious Italian welcome, plus awesome
pizzas and pastas. Italian owner Mario
occasionally pulls out his guitar and strums
for the crowd.

PIET DE LEEUW STEAK €€

Map p304 (☎020 623 71 81; www.pietdeleeuw.nl;
Noorderstraat 11; mains €13-23; ☺noon-10.30pm
Mon-Fri, from 5pm Sat & Sun; ☐16/24 Keizersgracht) With its dark wood furniture and
wood-panelled walls hung with pictures,
this feels like an old-school pub. The building dates from 1900, but it's been a steak-
house and a hang-out since the 1940s. Sit
down at individual or communal tables and
tuck into good-value steaks topped with a
choice of sauces and served with salad and
piping-hot *frites* (French fries).

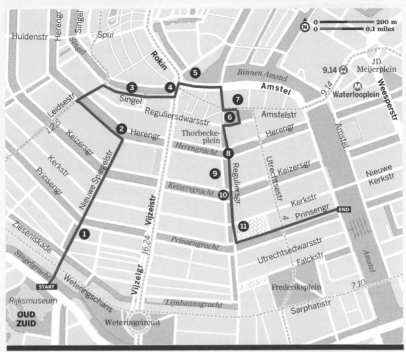

Neighbourhood Walk
Southern Canal Ring

START SINGELGRACHT
END AMSTEL RIVER
LENGTH 4KM; TWO HOURS

Set off at the Singelgracht and head north into the nexus of art and antique shops of the ❶ **Spiegel Quarter**, the heart of which is Nieuwe Spiegelstraat. On Herengracht, Amsterdam's swankiest patch of real estate – the appropriately named ❷ **Golden Bend** (p119) – has a row of double-fronted houses awash with classical French flourishes.

Stop by the bustling ❸ **Bloemenmarkt** (p119); from the eastern end, you'll be striking ❹ **Munttoren (Mint Tower)**. From the tower, head east along the Amstel river to take in the grand ❺ **Hotel de l'Europe** (p215), where polished skiffs moor at the terrace restaurant. At the bridge, turn south into tiny Halvemaansteeg and the beating heart of the entertainment district around ❻ **Rembrandtplein** (p121). As you cross the square, you'll pass the life-sized figures re-creating Rembrandt's *The Night Watch*,

before stopping at ❼ **De Kroon** (p129), one of the square's most stylish cafés.

Pass through shady Thorbeckeplein to the Herengracht, lean on the bridge and do your Insta-thing on ❽ **Reguliersgracht** (p121), aka the 'canal of seven bridges'. The ❾ **house** at Reguliersgracht 34 has an unusual twin entrance and an eagle gable for the original owner, Arent van den Bergh (*arend* is a Dutch word for 'eagle').

Where Herengracht and Reguliersgracht join up, you can count a whopping ❿ **15 bridges** as you peer east–west and north–south. Take a few steps further south and you'll come to the ⓫ **Amstelkerk** (p122), a curious wooden church with a belfry that looks makeshift despite being built more than 300 years ago.

Head east down a quiet section of the Prinsengracht until you reach the shores of the Amstel river. From this vantage point, you can admire the petite Magere Brug (p121) and, beyond the *sluizen* (locks), the neon-lit roof of the Koninklijk Theater Carré (p131).

ROYAL PASTRIES

The Dutch royals stock up on baked goods at **Patisserie Holtkamp** (Map p304; www.patisserieholtkamp.nl; Vijzelgracht 15; dishes €3-7; ☺8.30am-6pm Mon-Fri, to 5pm Sat; ☐4/7/10/16/24 Weteringcircuit). It was founded in 1886; the gorgeous art-deco interior was added in 1928 by architect Piet Kramer. There's a lavish fit-for-a-queen spread inside, with delicacies including creamy cakes and its famous *kroketten* (croquettes) with fillings such as lobster and veal. Its prawn versions are reputably Amsterdam's finest.

The *kroketten* are on the menus of some of the city's top restaurants.

Check out the gilded royal coat of arms, topped by a crown, on the building's facade.

BOJO INDONESIAN €€

Map p304 (☎020-622 74 34; www.bojo.nl; Lange Leidsedwarsstraat 49-51; mains €11-18; ☺4pm-midnight; ☐1/2/5 Prinsengracht) Bojo was started by two cousins who'd worked on a cruise ship together more than 40 years ago, and is a good choice for some late-night, stomach-lining Indonesian food. It's surprisingly peaceful, given the location. Clubbers come for sizzling satay, filling fried rice and steaming bowls of noodle soup.

SAIGON CÁPHÊ VIETNAMESE €€

Map p304 (Leidsestraat 95; dishes €9-21; ☺noon-11pm; ☐1, 2, 5 Leidsestr) Look past the somewhat-drab brown decor of this 1st-floor Vietnamese restaurant, and focus instead on its spicy, fresh dishes, including good *pho* (Vietnamese noodle soup), the ideal food for a chilly Dutch day. Grab a window seat.

TEMPO DOELOE INDONESIAN €€€

Map p304 (☎020-625 67 18; www.tempodoeloerestaurant.nl; Utrechtsestraat 75; mains around €35, rijsttafel & set menus €30-50; ☺6-11.30pm Mon-Sat; ☐; ☐4 Prinsengracht) Cosy Tempo Doeloe, with white tablecloths, chandeliers and draped curtains, is among Amsterdam's best, if *pittig* (spicy), Indonesian choices. It's recommended for a rijsttafel (Indonesian banquet) comprising

20-plus different concoctions. Warning: dishes marked 'very hot' are indeed like napalm. The wine list is excellent.

☕ DRINKING & NIGHTLIFE

There's something for everyone in this nightlife zone. Choose from the more laid-back, if often heaving, theatre *cafés* (bars) and brown cafes (pubs), frenetic gay bars, smoky coffeeshops and pumping house clubs. The bars and clubs of Leidseplein feel more full of tourists than locals, but there is a mix here, and they're always fun if you're up for it. If you're looking for more serious club action, Rembrandtplein's the ticket. Utrechtsestraat is great for more sophisticated local haunts, while rainbow flags abound on Reguliersdwarsstraat, Amsterdam's major gay street.

★DOOR 74 COCKTAIL BAR

Map p304 (☎06 3404 5122; www.door-74.nl; Reguliersdwarsstraat 74; ☺8pm-3am Sun-Thu, to 4am Fri & Sat; ☐9/14 Rembrandtplein) You'll need to leave a voice message or, better yet, send a text for a reservation to gain entry to this speakeasy behind an unmarked door. Some of Amsterdam's most amazing cocktails are served in a classy, dark-timbered, Prohibition-era atmosphere beneath pressed-tin ceilings. Themed cocktail lists change regularly. Very cool.

★BAR MOUSTACHE BAR

Map p304 (www.barmoustache.nl; Utrechtsestraat 141; ☺8am-1am Mon-Thu, 9am-3am Fri & Sat, 9am-1am Sun; ☐4 Prinsengracht) Designed by lifestyle magazine editor Stella Willing, this loft-style, exposed brick, New York-esque bar mixes up communal and private tables. It's a hotspot for hip locals, who make a beeline for the bar's window seats. Keeping everyone happily sated is the pared-down Italian menu and a great drink selection that includes Italian wines by the glass.

★AIR CLUB

Map p304 (www.air.nl; Amstelstraat 16; ☺usually 11pm-4am Fri-Sun; ☐4/9/14 Rembrandtplein) Big names like Pete Tong cut loose on the awesome sound system at it-club Air, which has interiors – including a tiered dance floor – by Dutch designer Marcel Wanders. Thoughtful touches include lockers and refillable cards that preclude fussing with change at the five bars.

THE OTHERSIDE COFFEESHOP

Map p304 (www.theotherside.nl; Reguliersdwarsstraat 6; ☉10am-midnight; ⌐1/2/5 Koningsplein) This buzzing choice has designer chandeliers and a lively, laid-back vibe. It's on the neighbourhood's main gay street and is favoured by a mixed crowd.

EIJLDERS BROWN CAFE

Map p304 (www.cafeeijlders.com; Korte Leidsedwarsstraat 47; ☉4.30pm-1am Mon-Wed, from noon Thu, noon-2am Fri & Sat, noon-midnight Sun; ⌐1/2/5/7/10 Leidseplein) During WWII, this stained-glass-trimmed brown cafe was a meeting place for artists who refused to toe the cultural line imposed by the Nazis, and the spirit lingers on. It's still an artists' cafe, with waistcoated waiters and a low-key feel by day, but getting noisier at night, fitting with its Leidseplein surrounds.

Events range from musical bingo to poetry slams.

LION NOIR COCKTAIL BAR

Map p304 (www.lionnoir.nl; Reguliersdwarsstraat 28; ☉noon-1am Mon-Thu, to 3am Fri, 6pm-3am Sat, 6pm-1am Sun; ⌐1/2/5 Koningsplein) Lion Noir hosts a glamorous crowd, here for excellent cocktails as well as superlative dining on creative French-inspired dishes with an Asian twist. Interior artist Thijs Murré designed the eclectic, satisfyingly out-there interior of green walls, plants, birdcages and taxidermied birds; the greenery-shaded terrace is equally lovely.

CAFE MANKIND BAR

Map p304 (www.mankind.nl; Weteringstraat 60; ☉noon-midnight Mon-Sat; ⌐24 Vijzelgracht) This tucked-away gay-friendly cafe-bar is convenient for the museums and has an appealing narrow terrace right alongside the canal.

BETTY BOOP COFFEESHOP

Map p304 (Reguliersdwarsstraat 29; ☉9am-1am; ☎; ⌐Rembrandtplein) The 2nd floor of this cool gay-friendly coffeeshop is a great vantage point over the Reguliersdwarsstraat nightlife strip, and a popular place to hang out and sample some quality smokes. Its now-closed sister branch was where Quentin Tarantino wrote some of *Pulp Fiction*.

It's uncertain whether the brand's infamous space cakes contributed to his creative flow.

VAN DYCK BAR CLUB

Map p304 (www.vandyckbar.com; Korte Leidsedwarsstraat 28-32; ☉10pm-4am Wed, Thu & Sun, to 5am Fri & Sat; ⌐1/2/5/7/10 Leidseplein) Van Dyck brings Ibiza-style clubbing to Amsterdam, with a heavyweight mix of international and local DJs who know how to work the 20-something up-for-it crowd. There's usually no cover before midnight; dress up to get past the door.

CLUB UP CLUB

Map p304 (☎020-623 69 85; www.clubup.nl; Korte Leliedwarsstraat 26; ☉11pm-4am Thu, to 5am Fri & Sat; ⌐1/2/5/7/10 Leidseplein) Garage, house, funk, soul, hip hop, techno, live bands and performance art keep the punters happy at this small, quirky club. Entrance is occasionally through social club De Kring, at Kleine Gartmanplantsoen 7–9; check the Club Up website for details.

NJOY COCKTAIL BAR

Map p304 (www.njoycocktails.com; Korte Leidsedwarsstraat 93; ☉5pm-3am Sun-Thu, to 4am Fri & Sat; ⌐1/2/5/7/10 Leidseplein) Creative cocktails at this decidedly foxy bar are grouped by personality. 'Seductive' drinks are extremely creamy, with chocolate and mascarpone, 'sparkling star' drinks are champagne-based, 'dreamer' drinks are fruity, 'skinny bitch' drinks are low-cal, and so on. Its chilled-out vibe is a refreshing break from the madness of the street outside. Under-23s aren't admitted. Cocktailmaking courses are available (€35).

CAFÉ LANGEREIS CAFE

Map p304 (www.cafelangereis.nl; Amstel 202; ☉11am-3am Sun-Thu, to 4am Fri & Sat; ☎; ⌐4/9/14 Rembrandtplein) By the Amstel, Café Langereis is a re-creation of a brown cafe, a look the friendly young owner so admires that she scoured the city for antique fixtures and furniture to evoke the lived-in vintage feel. Freshly ground coffee, fresh flowers on the tables, an upright piano and a classic rock soundtrack keep things vibrant.

CAFÉ DE WETERING BROWN CAFE

Map p304 (Weteringstraat 37; ☉4pm-1am Mon-Thu, to 3am Fri, 3pm-3am Sat, 3pm-1am Sun; ⌐7/10 Spiegelgracht) With a cascade of greenery draped over the outside, Café de

Wetering is a cosy charmer for a drink or a snack, with a large fireplace and gloriously faded interior that wouldn't look out of place in a Vermeer painting. It's always packed with locals, and is not far from the antiques corridor of Nieuwe Spiegelstraat.

CAFÉ BRECHT   BAR
Map p304 (www.cafebrecht.nl; Weteringschans 157; noon-1am Sun-Thu, to 3am Fri & Sat; 🚊4/7/10/16/24 Weteringcircuit) Café Brecht is one of Amsterdam's loveliest bars, with mismatched armchairs, vintage furniture, books and board games; all are a hit with a young and gorgeously boho crowd – it gets absolutely crammed in here. It's named after seminal German dramatist and poet Bertolt Brecht, hence the German poetry inscribed on the walls.

PATA NEGRA   BAR
Map p304 (www.pata-negra.nl; Utrechtsestraat 124; ⊘noon-1am Sun-Thu, to 3am Fri & Sat; 🚊4 Prinsengracht) Ablaze with tiling the colour of sunshine, this Spanish tapas bar has an agreeably battered interior and its margaritas are the business. It gets busy with a lively crowd downing sangria with garlic-fried shrimps and grilled sardines (tapas €6 to €12.50).

FREDERIX   CAFE
Map p304 (Fredericksplein 29; ⊘8am-6pm Mon-Fri, from 8.30am Sat, from 9am Sun; 🚊4 Prinsengracht) This tucked-away, skylit place on lush Fredericksplein specialises in roasting beans from international coffee specialists; as you'd expect, the coffee is damn fine. It offers exceedingly good poached eggs and other brunch staples.

COFFEESHOP FREE   COFFEESHOP
Map p304 (Reguliersdwarsstraat 70; ⊘10am-1am; 🚊4/9/16/24 Muntplein) Pocket-sized Coffeeshop Free has sported its bamboo-heavy tiki bar vibe for decades. The South Seas mural provides a nicely faded, balmy days setting, though there's a TV screen showing sport too.

JIMMY WOO   CLUB
Map p304 (📞020-626 31 50; www.jimmywoo.com; Korte Leidsedwarsstraat 18; ⊘11pm-3am Thu & Sun, to 4am Fri & Sat; 🚊1/2/5/7/10 Leidseplein) It's been around a while, but super-luxe Jimmy Woo is still the go-to place for a crowd of beautiful young things. Its sultry look is by designer Thijs Murré, and the lower floor has a ceiling covered in tiny lights that pulsate to the music. Queues are extremely long, and the door policy strict – you have to look the part.

Arrive early or call ahead to try to get on the list.

BULLDOG PALACE   COFFEESHOP
Map p304 (www.thebulldog.com; Leidseplein 13-17; ⊘coffeeshop 8am-1am, bar 9am-1am Mon-Thu, to 3am Fri & Sat, to 2am Sun; 🛜; 🚊1/2/5/7/10 Leidseplein) Bulldog's as corporate as a coffeeshop gets, with a chain of outlets, a hotel and merchandise, but it's one of the oldest and most famous in Amsterdam. Housed in a former police station, it has two sides: one for smoking, one for drinking. Both crowds are pretty much the same: stags and hens, backpackers and corporate travellers blowing off steam.

ESCAPE   CLUB
Map p304 (www.escape.nl; Rembrandtplein 11; ⊘11pm-4am Thu & Sun, to 5am Fri & Sat; 🚊4/9/14 Rembrandtplein) Running since the '90s, this huge club gets busy with a happy crowd of 20-somethings, here for the cream of local and international DJs, who rock several dance floors with a soundtrack of house, electro, techno and pop. Escape regularly hosts theme nights such as House Rules and Brainwash. There's a video-screen-filled studio and an adjoining cafe.

Dress up to get past the door police.

NEL   BAR
Map p304 (www.nelamstelveld.nl; Amstelveld 12; ⊘10am-1am Sun-Thu, to 3am Fri & Sat; 🚊4 Prinsengracht) NeL, a stately white house on a hidden-away square, is a contender for having the best terrace in Amsterdam. Outside, mature trees provide a canopy that dapples the sunshine on a good day – it's hard to believe it's so close to Rembrandtplein. Inside, there's a mellow brasserie on one side and a stylish bar on the other.

CAFÉ SCHILLER   CAFE
Map p304 (www.cafeschiller.nl; Rembrandtplein 24a; ⊘7am-7pm; 🚊4/9/14 Rembrandtplein) Schiller has fabulous original art-deco fittings. It's presently the long-term location for the evening filming of TV chat show *RTL*, which explains the early closing time and the purple lighting additions hung around the interior. The walls are lined with portraits of Dutch actors and cabaret artists from the 1920s and '30s.

SOUTHERN CANAL RING GAY & LESBIAN NIGHTLIFE VENUES

Taboo Bar (Map p304; www.taboobar.nl; Reguliersdwarsstraat 45; ☺5pm-3am Mon-Thu, to 4am Fri, 4pm-4am Sat, 4pm-3am Sun; 🛜; 🚊1/2/5 Koningsplein) Gay favourite Taboo has plentiful two-for-one happy hours (6pm to 7pm – to 8pm on Sunday – and 1am to 2am). It's snug inside, though on warmer days everyone spills out onto the street. On Wednesdays, cocktails cost €6 and a drag show and competitions like 'pin the tail on the sailor' take place.

Church (Map p304; www.clubchurch.nl; Kerkstraat 52; ☺8pm-1am Tue & Wed, 10pm-4am Thu, 10pm-5am Fri & Sat, 4-8pm Sun; 🚊1/2/5 Keizersgracht) There are no sermons or psalms at this church: this is a hardcore gay cruise club that holds themed events. Unless you come dressed appropriately (check the website for details) or with super-hot boys (or are one yourself), you probably won't get in.

Montmartre (Map p304; www.cafemontmartre.nl; Halvemaansteeg 17; ☺5pm-1am Sun-Thu, to 4am Fri & Sat; 🚊4/9/14 Rembrandtplein) A crammed gay bar that's long been a local favourite. It's known for its Dutch music, and patrons sing (or scream) along to recordings of Dutch ballads and old top-40 hits. There's also a lively programme of karaoke, drag, and '80s and '90s hits.

Lellebel (Map p304; www.lellebel.nl; Utrechtsestraat 4; ☺9pm-3am Mon-Wed, from 1pm Thu, 8pm-4am Fri & Sat, 3pm-3am Sun; 🛜; 🚊4/9/14 Rembrandtplein) This diddy place just off Rembrandtplein specialises in drag queen fabulousness, with lots of themed nights including karaoke, singing drag queens, shows and bingo.

DE KROON
BAR

Map p304 (www.dekroon.nl; Rembrandtplein 17; ☺4pm-1am Mon-Thu & Sun, to 3am Fri & Sat; 🚊4/9/14 Rembrandtplein) Rembrandtplein's renovated *grand café* De Kroon dates from 1898. It has dizzyingly high ceilings, armchairs to sink into and glittering chandeliers. There's a a long list of cocktails, wine and beers, plus a barbecue-oriented menu of grilled fish and meat. It converts into a club on Friday and Saturday nights.

OOSTERLING
BROWN CAFE

Map p304 (Utrechtsestraat 140; ☺3pm-midnight Mon-Wed, noon-1am Thu-Sat, 1-8pm Sun; 🚊4 Prinsengracht) Opened in the 1700s as a tea and coffee outlet for the Dutch East India Company, Oosterling is now run by friendly brothers Oscar and Marcel, the fourth generation of Oosterlings at the helm since 1877. It's one of the very few *cafés* with an off-licence bottle shop permit.

SUZY WONG
BAR

Map p304 (www.suzy-wong.nl; Korte Leidsedwarsstraat 45; ☺10am-1am Sun-Thu, to 3am Fri & Sat; 🚊1/2/5/7/10 Leidseplein) A knowingly fabulous crowd frequents Suzy Wong, a celeb magnet for its exclusive feel and louche drawing room interior featuring red-velveteen wallpaper and a bamboo garden. Fresh fruit mojitos are the tipple of choice; on Thursday's Mojito Night, they cost just €5.

BOCCA COFFEE
COFFEE

Map p304 (📞321 314 667; www.bocca.nl; Kerkstraat 96; ☺8am-6pm Mon-Fri, from 9am Sat & Sun; 🚊Prinsengracht) The team behind Bocca Coffee knows its stuff, having sourced beans from Ethiopia to sell to cafes across the city for more than 15 years. They're now serving some seriously good caffeine hits in this light, spacious coffee house. Take a seat at the large wooden bar or get comfy in a vintage armchair.

SWEET CUP
COFFEE

Map p304 (www.sweetcupcafe.com; Lange Leidsedwarsstraat 101; ☺8am-6pm Wed-Fri, from 10am Sat & Sun; 🚊1/2/5 Leidseplein) Much loved by caffeine heads, this microroastery supplies coffee to many local cafes, but you can drink it here at the source or pick up a cup to take away. There's a choice of five espresso styles and five slow brews. It also sells roasted beans.

DOLPHINS COFFEESHOP
COFFEESHOP

Map p304 (Kerkstraat 39; ☺10am-1am; 🛜; 🚊1/2/5 Prinsengracht) Painted with blue fishtank-style murals and decorated with fake rocks and other underwater ephemera, this trippy space feels like you're smoking

LOCAL KNOWLEDGE

PHOTOGRAPHING THE SEVEN BRIDGES

It's easy to get swept away in the raucous local nightlife and forget that one of Amsterdam's most romantic canals flows through this neighbourhood. The Reguliersgracht (p121), aka the 'canal of seven bridges', is especially enchanting by night, when its humpbacked arches glow with tiny gold lights.

Though the best views are from aboard a boat, you can still get great vistas from land. Stand with your back to the Thorbeckeplein and with the Herengracht flowing directly in front of you to the left and right. Lean over the bridge and look straight ahead down the Reguliersgracht. Ahhh. Now kiss your sweetie.

underwater (if you squint). Upstairs, there's table football and a pool table; you can also get toasties, pastries, tea and juices.

CHICAGO SOCIAL CLUB BAR

Map p304 (☎020-760 11 71; www.chicago socialclub.nl; Leidseplein 12; ⊙bar 8pm-4am Sun-Thu, to 5am Fri & Sat, club from 11pm Thu-Sat; ☐1/2/5/7/10 Leidseplein) Founded in 1923, this intimate bar and club on Leidseplein is still going strong, though the music policy has somewhat changed: these days, the sonic menu is filled with house and techno. Nights here attract a laid-back, cool crowd. The minimum age is 21.

WHISKEY CAFÉ L&B BAR

Map p304 (Korte Leidsedwarsstraat 92; ⊙8pm-3am Mon-Thu, to 4am Fri & Sat, 5pm-3am Sun; ☐1/2/5/7/10 Leidseplein) If amber spirits are your thing, you're in luck: this friendly, busy bar has 1350 (yes, 1350!) different varieties from Scotland, Ireland, America and Japan. The knowledgeable bar staff will help you navigate the list.

CAFÉ DE SPUYT BROWN CAFE

Map p304 (www.cafedespuyt.nl; Korte Leidsedwarsstraat 86; ⊙4pm-3am Mon-Thu, 3pm-4am Fri & Sat, 3pm-3am Sun; ☐1/2/5/7/10 Leidseplein) Amid the hubbub off busy Leidseplein, this is a mellow, friendly brown cafe filled with – for reasons that remain obscure – chicken-themed decorations. The other attraction here is the massive chalkboard menu of

more than 100 Dutch and Belgian speciality beers, including abbey and Trappist brews and seasonal tipples.

MULLIGANS IRISH PUB

Map p304 (www.mulligans.nl; Amstel 100; ⊙4pm-1am Mon-Thu, to 3am Fri, 2pm-3am Sat, to 1am Sun; ☎; ☐4/9/14 Rembrandtplein) Foremost among Amsterdam's Irish pubs, Mulligans has properly-poured Guinness and Magners cider on tap. It's great fun, with live Irish trad music most nights from around 9pm (no cover charge). Bring your own instrument to take part in the Sunday sessions (from 7pm); on Wednesdays, sing along to Irish tunes in the back room.

☆ ENTERTAINMENT

On either side of the Southern Canal Ring, the nightlife centres of Leidseplein and Rembrandtplein throng with people and buzz with a party atmosphere. You'll be spoilt for choice with live music venues and nightclubs featuring big-name DJs. On Leidseplein, the grand Stadsschouwburg theatre stages major plays and festivals; smaller theatres and cinemas are scattered throughout the neighbourhood.

★PATHÉ TUSCHINSKITHEATER CINEMA

Map p304 (www.pathe.nl; Reguliersbreestraat 26-34; ⊙11.30am-12.30am; ☐4/9/14 Rembrandtplein) This fantastical cinema, with a facade that's a prime example of the Amsterdam School of architecture, is worth visiting for its sumptuous art deco interior alone. The *grote zaal* (main auditorium) is the most stunning; it generally screens blockbusters, while the smaller theatres play arthouse and indie films. Visit the interior on an audio tour (€10) when films aren't playing.

Interiors were returned to their former glory at the turn of the century; the Wurlitzer organ has also been restored. An orchestra once accompanied film screenings, and Marlene Dietrich and Judy Garland have performed live here.

The cinema was built by Abraham Tuschinski, a Polish Jewish immigrant. He and most of his family were murdered in Nazi concentration camps, and the cinema renamed 'Tivoli'. After the war it returned to its original name.

**KONINKLIJK THEATER
CARRÉ** PERFORMING ARTS

Map p304 (☑0900 25 25 255; www.carre.nl; Amstel 115-125; tour adult/child €9.50/6.50; ⊙box office 4-6pm; Ⓜ Weesperplein) The Carré family started their career with a horse act at the annual fair, progressing to this circus theatre in 1887. The classical facade is richly decorated with faces of jesters, dancers and theatre folk. It hosts a great programme of quality music and theatre; its Christmas circus is a seasonal highlight. one-hour Saturday-morning tours (at 11am) are in English and Dutch.

The first structure was of wood, but it was eventually rebuilt in concrete due to fire hazards (early performances for 2000 spectators were lit by gas lamps).

Comic essayist David Sedaris, the Pet Shop Boys and the National Theatre London's *Curious Incident of the Dog in the Night-time* have all appeared on stage here in recent years.

STADSSCHOUWBURG THEATRE

Map p304 (☑020-624 23 11; www.stadsschouw burgamsterdam.nl; Leidseplein 26; ⊙box office noon-6pm Mon-Sat; ☐1/2/5/7/10 Leidseplein) When this theatre with the grand balcony arcade was completed in 1894, public criticism of the design was so fierce that the exterior decorations were never completed; architect Jan Springer was so upset, he retired. The horseshoe auditorium seats 1200 spectators and is used for large-scale plays, operettas and festivals. Don't miss the chandeliered splendour of its **Stanislavski** (⊙10am-1am Sun-Thu, to 3am Fri & Sat; ☎) theatre *café*.

Be sure to check out the its **International Theatre & Film Books** (www. theatreandfilmbooks.com; ⊙noon-6pm Mon, from 11am Tue-Sat, noon-5pm Sun) shop.

PARADISO LIVE MUSIC

Map p304 (☑020-622 45 21; www.paradiso.nl; Weteringschans 6; ⊙hours vary; ☐1/2/5/7/10 Leidseplein) In 1968, a beautiful old church turned into the 'Cosmic Relaxation Center Paradiso'. Today, the vibe is less hippy than funked-up odyssey, with big all-nighters, themed events and indie nights. The smaller hall hosts up-and-coming bands, but there's something special about the Main Hall where its arching church-window windows might shatter under the force of the fat beats.

**BOURBON STREET JAZZ
& BLUES CLUB** JAZZ, BLUES

Map p304 (www.bourbonstreet.nl; Leidsekruisstraat 6-8; admission varies; ⊙10pm-4am Sun-Thu, to 5am Fri & Sat; ☐1/2/5 Prinsengracht) This intimate venue has a full and eclectic weekly music programme. Take part in open jam sessions on Mondays, or come by on Tuesdays for soul and reggae. It's blues and rock on Wednesdays; soul and funk on Thursdays; rock, pop and Latin on Fridays; pre-rock on Saturdays; and world, folk and samba on Sundays.

Entry is free before 11pm (10.30pm on Friday and Saturday), when most concerts start.

MELKWEG LIVE MUSIC

Map p304 (Milky Way; www.melkweg.nl; Lijnbaansgracht 234a; ⊙6pm-1am; ☐1/2/5/7/10 Leidseplein) In a former dairy, the nonprofit 'Milky Way' offers a dazzling galaxy of diverse gigs, featuring both DJs and live bands. One night it's electronica, the next reggae or punk, and the next heavy metal. Roots, rock and mellow singer-songwriters all get stage time too. Check out the website for information on its cutting-edge cinema, theatre and multimedia offerings.

SUGAR FACTORY LIVE MUSIC

Map p304 (www.sugarfactory.nl; Lijnbaansgracht 238; ⊙6pm-5am; ☐1/2/5/7/10 Leidseplein) With a creative vibe and many eclectic events, this is not your average club. Most nights start with music (from indie rock to techno), cinema, dance or a spoken-word performance, followed by late-night DJs and dancing. Sunday's Wicked Jazz Sounds party is a sweet one, bringing DJs, musicians, singers and actors together to improvise.

JAZZ CAFÉ ALTO JAZZ

Map p304 (www.jazz-cafe-alto.nl; Korte Leidsedwarsstraat 115; ⊙9pm-3am Sun-Thu, to 4am Fri & Sat; ☐1/2/5/7/10 Leidseplein) This is an intimate, atmospheric brown cafe-style venue for serious jazz and (occasionally) blues. There are live gigs nightly: doors open at 9pm but music starts around 10pm – get here early if you want to snag a seat.

CAVE LIVE MUSIC

Map p304 (☑020-620 64 38; www.thecave.nl; Prinsengracht 472; live music tickets from €5; ⊙8pm-3am Sun-Thu, to 4am Fri & Sat; ☐1/2/5 Prinsengracht) This grunge-fest is buried in a basement. Metalheads rejoice: there are live hard rock and metal gigs Thursday to Saturday, and DJs spin the same the rest of the week. For those about to rock, we salute you.

DE UITKIJK   CINEMA

Map p304 (www.uitkijk.nl; Prinsengracht 452; €10; ⊙hours vary; 🚊1/2/5 Prinsengracht) Located in a 1913 canal house, this fun art-house stalwart is the city's second-oldest surviving cinema, and has a great pro-gramme that mixes classic oldies with more recent offerings.

DE HEEREN VAN AEMSTEL   LIVE MUSIC

Map p304 (www.deheerenvanaemstel.nl; Thor-beckeplein 5; ⊙noon-3am Mon-Thu, to 4am Fri & Sat; 🚊4/9/14 Rembrandtplein) A student favourite, this is a *grand café*-style club, with a roster of live bands and themed nights, all oiled by cheap drinks, especially mid-week.

🛍 SHOPPING

Whether you're after tulip bulbs, quirky Dutch fashion and design or rare *jenever*, you'll find it on the Southern Canal Ring. The Nieuwe Spiegelstraat (the spine of the Spiegel Quarter) is renowned for its antique stores, bric-a-brac, collectables, tribal and oriental art, and commercial art galleries.

★CONCERTO   MUSIC

Map p304 (www.concerto.amsterdam/en; Utre-chtsestraat 52-60; ⊙10am-6pm Mon, Wed & Sat, to 7pm Thu & Fri, noon-6pm Sun; 🚊4 Prinsen-gracht) This rambling shop is muso heaven, with a fabulous selection of new and sec-ond-hand vinyl and CDs encompassing every imaginable genre, from rockabilly to classical and beyond. It's good value and has listening facilities, plus a sofa-strewn living-room-style cafe and regular live ses-sions (see the website for details).

★VLIEGER   STATIONERY

Map p304 (www.vliegerpapier.nl; Amstel 34; ⊙noon-6pm Mon, from 9am Tue-Fri, 11am-5.30pm Sat; 🚊4/9/14 Rembrandtplein) Love stationery and paper? Make a beeline for Vlieger. Since 1869, this two-storey shop has been supplying it all: Egyptian papy-rus, beautiful handmade papers from Asia

and Central America, papers inlaid with flower petals or bamboo, and paper tex-tured like snakeskin.

YOUNG DESIGNERS UNITED   CLOTHING

Map p304 (YDU; www.ydu.nl; Keizersgracht 447; ⊙1-6pm Mon, from 10am Tue-Sat; 🚊1/2/5 Keiz-ersgracht) This sleek boutique has a stylish array of affordable items by young design-ers working in the Netherlands. You might spot durable basics by Agna K, handmade leggings by Leg-Inc and geometric dresses by Fenny Faber. Accessorise with YDU's select range of jewellery and bags.

SKATEBOARDS
AMSTERDAM   SPORTS & OUTDOORS

Map p304 (www.skateboardsamsterdam.nl; Vijzelstraat 77; ⊙1-6pm Sun & Mon, from 11am Tue, Wed, Fri & Sat, 11am-8pm Thu; 🚊16/24 Keizersgracht) Skater-dude heaven, with everything required for the freewheeling lifestyle: cruisers, longboards, shoes, laces, caps, beanies, bags, backpacks, and cloth-ing including Spitfire and Skate Mental T-shirts and a fantastic selection of band tees.

MAISONNL   HOMEWARES, CLOTHING

Map p304 (www.maisonnl.com; Utrechtsestraat 118; ⊙10am-6pm Tue-Sat, 1-5pm Sun; 🚊4 Prin-sengracht) This little concept store sells all sorts of beautiful things you didn't real-ise you needed, such as Christian Lacroix crockery and cute-as-a-button mouse toys in matchboxes by Maileg. There's a clothing rack down the back.

EICHHOLTZ DELICATESSEN   FOOD & DRINKS

Map p304 (www.eichholtzdeli.nl; Leidsestraat 48; ⊙10am-6.30pm Mon, from 9am Tue, Wed, Fri & Sat, 9am-9pm Thu, noon-6.30pm Sun; 🚊1/2/5 Keizersgracht) Being in this store, with brightly coloured wrappers blazing from the shelves, feels like walking into a piece of pop art. Americans missing Hershey's, Brits wanting Hobnobs and Aussies crav-ing Vegemite will find them all – and much, much more – at this import-specialist gro-cer that's been in business for more than a century.

SHIRT SHOP   CLOTHING

Map p304 (www.shirtshopamsterdam.com; Reg-uliersdwarsstraat 64; ⊙1-7pm; 🚊4/9/16/24 Muntplein) On Amsterdam's main gay street, this shop has a kaleidoscopic array of the go-to going-out garb for many local males:

nicely patterned smart shirts, as well as some funky T-shirts featuring Mexican skulls and more.

EDUARD KRAMER ANTIQUES

Map p304 (www.antique-tileshop.nl; Prinsengracht 807; ⊘11am-6pm Mon, from 10am Tue-Sat, from 1pm Sun; ⊠7/10 Spiegelgracht) Specialising in antique blue-and-white Dutch tiles, this engrossing, crammed-to-the-rafters shop is chock-a-block with fascinating antiques, silver candlesticks, crystal decanters, jewellery and pocket watches.

MARK RAVEN AMSTERDAM ART ART

Map p304 (www.markraven.nl; Leidsestraat 42; ⊘10.30am-6pm; ⊠1/2/5 Keizersgracht) Dutch artist Mark Raven's calligraphic paintings, drawings and sketches depict Amsterdam's cityscapes. They're sold here as affordable artworks and printed on T-shirts, hoodies, posters and coffee mugs, all of which make good gifts or souvenirs.

WALLS GALLERY ART

Map p304 (⊅020-616 95 97; Prinsengracht 737; ⊘noon-6pm Thu-Sun; ⊠1/2/5 Prinsengracht) A former garage houses this edgy art gallery, which hosts six to eight exhibitions a year. Also representing young, up-and-coming art students, it's a place to spot the next big thing and buy their works at reasonable prices.

MOBILIA HOMEWARES

Map p304 (www.mobilia.nl; Utrechtsestraat 62; ⊘9.30am-6pm Mon-Sat; ⊠4 Prinsengracht) Dutch and international design is stunningly showcased at this three-storey 'lifestyle studio', with sofas, workstations, bookshelves, lighting, cushions, rugs and much more.

HART'S WIJNHANDEL ALCOHOL

Map p304 (www.hartswijn.nl; Vijzelgracht 27; ⊘9.30am-6pm Mon-Fri, 10am-5pm Sat; ⊠4/7/10/16/24 Weteringcircuit) Browsing for *jenever* and French and Italian wines at this genteel, galleried shop is an absolute pleasure, with classical music playing, knowledgeable staff on hand and a pedigree stretching back to 1880.

JASKI ART

Map p304 (www.jaski.nl; Nieuwe Spiegelstraat 27-29; ⊘noon-6pm; ⊠16/24 Keizersgracht) A large commercial gallery selling paintings, prints, ceramics and sculptures by some of the most famous members of the CoBrA (Copenhagen, Brussels, Amsterdam) movement.

REFLEX MODERN ART GALLERY ART

Map p304 (www.reflexamsterdam.com; Weteringschans 79a; ⊘11am-6pm Tue-Sun; ⊠7/10 Spiegelgracht) This stylish and prominent gallery shows and sells contemporary art, prints and photography, including occasional works by members of the CoBrA and Nouveau Réalisme movements.

LIEVE HEMEL ART

Map p304 (www.lievehemel.nl; Nieuwe Spiegelstraat 3; ⊘noon-6pm Tue, Wed, Fri & Sat, to 9pm Thu, 2-6pm Sun; ⊠16/24 Keizersgracht) This small, fine gallery specialises in magnificent contemporary Dutch realist paintings and sculptures.

TINKERBELL TOYS

Map p304 (www.tinkerbelltoys.nl; Spiegelgracht 10; ⊘1-6pm Mon, from 10am Tue-Sat, noon-5pm Sun; ⊠7/10 Spiegelgracht) The mechanical bear blowing bubbles outside this shop fascinates kids, as do the intriguing technical and scientific toys inside. You'll also find historical costumes, plush toys and a section for babies.

Jordaan & the West

Neighbourhood Top Five

❶ De Twee Zwaantjes (p144) Losing yourself in the labyrinth of narrow streets and charming canals before spending the evening in the neighbourhood's *bruin cafés* (brown cafes; traditional Dutch pubs) such as De Twee Zwaantjes – nothing is more quintessentially Amsterdam.

❷ Amsterdam Tulip Museum (p136) Learning about the fascinating history and production of the country's favourite bloom.

❸ Pianola Museum (p136) Listening to rare jazz and classical tunes play on vintage pianolas.

❹ Houseboat Museum (p137) Discovering what life is like on the city's waterways aboard this barge dating from 1914.

❺ Westerpark (p139) Cycling around the unique mash-up of reedy wilderness and old gasworks buildings turned into design studios, cafes, restaurants and theatres.

For more detail of this area see Map p303, p308 and p310 ➡

Explore Jordaan & the West

Though gentrified today, the Jordaan was a rough, densely populated *volksbuurt* (district for the common people) until the mid-20th century, and that history still shows. You'll discover that this neighbourhood is a curiously enchanting mix of its traditional gritty, hard-drinking, leftist character and its revitalised, trend-conscious sheen.

Start the day at the northern end of the Jordaan and criss-cross towards the neighbourhood's south, catching the area's museums, architecture and, if you time it right, markets along the way. Take a coffee break at one of the many canal-side cafes along the Prinsengracht.

On day two, go west. Hop on a bike and wend through the Western Islands before a spin around verdant Westerpark. In the evening, revel in the possibilities that any night in the Westergasfabriek presents, from an arthouse film to jazz or rock 'n' roll.

Local Life

→**Markets** Morning bliss in the Jordaan means cruising the weekly outdoor markets – Noordermarkt (p148), Lindengracht Market (p148) and Westermarkt (p148) – for mouthwatering food, bargain clothes and funky flea-market treasures.

→**Cultural hang-outs** Locals flock to former gasworks and now cutting-edge cultural complex Westergasfabriek (p145) to hang out at its festivals, bars and restaurants...and more markets (p145) too.

→**Docklands dining** Two of Amsterdam's most extraordinary bar-restaurants – in a former offshore pirate radio and TV rig, and aboard a moored 1927-built ferry – are just north of the Western Islands in the Houthavens (p142) area.

Getting There & Away

→**Tram** Trams 3 and 10 along Marnixstraat skirt the neighbourhood's western edge; trams 13, 14 and 17 along Rozengracht go through its centre.

→**Bus** Buses 18, 21, 22 and 48 provide the quickest access from Centraal Station to the neighbourhood's north and west, and the Western Islands.

→**Car** Whatever you do, don't try to drive through the Jordaan's narrow streets. Seriously.

Lonely Planet's Top Tip

Be aware that trams 3 and 10 don't pass by Centraal Station but take ring routes around the centre instead. If you're heading to areas such as Westerpark and Westergasfabriek from Centraal, a bus is by far your best bet.

JORDAAN & THE WEST

Best Places to Eat

→ Wolf Atelier (p141)
→ Mossel En Gin (p142)
→ Balthazar's Keuken (p140)
→ Marius (p142)
→ REM Eiland (p142)

For reviews, see p139 →

Best Places to Drink

→ 't Smalle (p143)
→ Monks Coffee Roasters (p145)
→ Brouwerij Troost Westergas (p145)
→ Westergasterras (p146)
→ Café Papeneiland (p143)
→ Cafe Soundgarden (p143)

For reviews, see p142 →

Best Places to Shop

→ Moooi Gallery (p147)
→ Het Oud-Hollandsch Snoepwinkeltje (p147)
→ Lindengracht Market (p148)
→ Robins Hood (p147)
→ Concrete Matter (p147)

For reviews, see p147 →

◉ SIGHTS

◉ Jordaan

HAARLEMMERPOORT   GATE

Map p308 (Haarlemmerplein; 🚊3 Haarlemmer-plein) Once a defensive gateway to the city, the Haarlemmerpoort marked the start of the journey to Haarlem, which was a major trading route. The neoclassical structure, with Roman temple–styled Corinthian pillars, was finished just in time for King William II's staged entry for his 1840 investiture, hence its little-known official name of Willemspoort (see the plaque inside). Traffic stopped running through the gate when a bypass was built over the Westerkanaal.

BROUWERSGRACHT   CANAL

Map p308 (Brewers Canal; 🚊3 Haarlemmerplein) Pretty as a Golden Age painting, the Brewers Canal took its name from the many breweries located here in the 16th and 17th centuries. Goods such as leather, coffee, whale oil and spices were also stored and processed here in giant warehouses, such as those with the row of spout gables that still stand at Brouwersgracht 188–194. The newspaper *Het Parool* dubbed the Brouwersgracht the most beautiful street in Amsterdam.

It's a great place to stroll and to see the waterborne action on King's Day (p23).

NOORDERKERK   CHURCH

Map p308 (Northern Church; www.noorderkerk. org; Noordermarkt 48; ⊘10.30am-12.30pm Mon, 11am-1pm Sat; 🚊3/10 Marnixplein) Near the Prinsengracht's northern end, this imposing Calvinist church was completed in 1623 for the 'common' people in the Jordaan. (The upper classes attended the Westerkerk further south.) It was built in the shape of a broad Greek cross (four arms of equal length) around a central pulpit, giving the entire congregation unimpeded access. Hendrick de Keyser's design, unusual at the time, would become common for Protestant churches throughout the country. It hosts the well-regarded Saturday-afternoon Nooderkerkconcerten (p146) concert series.

Sunday services take place at 10am and 6.30pm.

PIANOLA MUSEUM   MUSEUM

Map p308 (📞020-627 96 24; www.pianola.nl; Westerstraat 106; museum adult/child €5/3, concert tickets from €7.50; ⊘2-5pm Sun; 🚊3/10 Marnixplein) This is a very special place, crammed with pianolas from the early 1900s. The museum has around 50, although only a dozen are on display at any given time, as well as some 30,000 music rolls and a player pipe organ. The curator gives an hour-long guided tour and music demonstrations with great zest. Regular concerts are held on the player pianos, featuring anything from Mozart to Fats Waller and rare classical or jazz tunes composed especially for the instrument.

More eclectic musical offerings include a popular tango series.

KOCHXBOS   GALLERY

Map p308 (📞06 2224 0808; www.kochxbos.nl; 1e Anjeliersdwarsstraat 36; ⊘1-6pm Wed-Sat; 🚊3/10 Marnixplein) FREE The art here goes by many names: North European low-brow, pop surrealism, contemporary underground. Whatever the label, the paintings, photos and digital prints are awesomely bright, weird and polychromatic. The welcoming space sits in the converted living room of an apartment.

AMSTERDAM TULIP MUSEUM   MUSEUM

Map p308 (📞020-421 00 95; www.amsterdam tulipmuseum.com; Prinsengracht 116; adult/child €5/3; ⊘10am-6pm; 🚊13/14/17 Westermarkt) Allow around half an hour at the diminutive Amsterdam Tulip Museum, which offers a nifty overview of the history of the country's favourite bloom. Through exhibits, timelines and two short films (in English), you'll learn how Ottoman merchants encountered the flowers in the Himalayan steppes and began commercial production in Turkey, how fortunes were made and lost during Dutch 'Tulipmania' in the 17th century, and how bulbs were used as food during WWII. You'll also discover present-day growing and harvesting techniques.

There's a great collection of tulip vases designed to accommodate separate stems, and a gift shop overflowing with floral souvenirs.

AMSTERDAM CHEESE MUSEUM   MUSEUM

Map p308 (📞020-331 66 05; www.cheese museumamsterdam.com; Prinsengracht 112; ⊘9am-7pm; 🚊13/14/17 Westermarkt) FREE

WESTERN ISLANDS

In the early 17th century, the wharves and warehouses of the Western Islands, north of the Jordaan, were abuzz with activity. The Golden Age was taking off, the Dutch still dominated the sea trade and money flowed into this old harbour like beer from a barrel. The wealthy Bicker brothers, both mayors of Amsterdam, even built their own Bickerseiland here to cater for their ships.

Few tourists visit here today, partly because the district is shielded from view by the railway line. Yet it's roughly a 10-minute walk (or five-minute bike ride) from Centraal Station and a wonderful area to wander, with cute drawbridges and handsome old warehouses nestled in quiet lanes. Many addresses have been converted to charming homes as well a few artists' studios. Most are closed to the public, but the **Ravestijn Gallery** (Map p303; 020-530 60 05; www.theravestijngallery.com; Westerdoksdijk 603; 9am-5pm Mon-Fri, noon-5pm Sat; 48 Westerdoksdijk) FREE hosts photography exhibitions.

The Prinseneiland (named in honour of the first three Princes of Orange) and Realeneiland (named after the 17th-century merchant Reynier Reael) are the two prettiest isles. The narrow bridge linking them, the **Drieharingenbrug** (Three Herrings Bridge; Map p303; Realengracht; 48 Barentszplein), is a quaint replacement for the pontoon that used to be pulled aside to let ships through.

Now a modern yacht harbour, the **Zandhoek** (Map p303; Realeneiland; 48 Barentszplein), on Realeneiland's eastern shore, is a picturesque stretch of waterfront. In the 17th century this area was a 'sand market', where ships purchased sand by the bagful for ballast. Galgenstraat (Gallows St), the street south of the Zandhoek, is so named as it was once possible to see the executions in Amsterdam Noord from here.

What the islands lack in quantity of drinking and dining options they make up for with quality: outstanding establishments here include gastronomic star Wolf Atelier (p141), tapas specialist and wine bar Worst Wijncafe (p141), upmarket Marius (p142), and contemporary Apostrof (p142).

It's a tourist ploy, but a good-humoured one. The main floor is a cheese shop with abundant free samples. The basement floor contains a small 'museum' with a handful of exhibits, clothes you can don to look like a Dutch cheesemaker and snap a photo, and the world's most expensive cheese slicer (encrusted with diamonds).

EGELANTIERSGRACHT   CANAL

Map p308 (13/14/17 Westermarkt) Many parts of the Jordaan are named after trees and flowers, and this canal, lined by lovely houses built for artisans and skilled traders, takes its name from the eglantine rose (sweet briar).

ELECTRIC LADYLAND   MUSEUM

Map p308 (www.electric-lady-land.com; 2e Leliedwarsstraat 5; adult/child €5/free; 2-6pm Wed-Sat; 13/14/17 Westermarkt) The world's first museum of fluorescent art features owner Nick Padalino's psychedelic sculpture work on one side and cases of naturally luminescent rocks and manufactured glowing objects (money, government ID cards etc) on the other. Jimi Hendrix, the Beatles and other trippy artists play on the stereo while Nick lovingly describes each item in the collection. His art gallery–shop is upstairs.

BLOEMGRACHT   CANAL

Map p308 (Flower Canal; 13/14/17 Westermarkt) In the 17th century the 'Herengracht of the Jordaan', as the Bloemgracht was called, was home to paint and sugar factories, and a large number of fine gabled houses, such as the Renaissance-style **De Drie Hendricken** (Map p308; Bloemgracht 87-91). Many artists also lived on Bloemgracht, including Jurriaen Andriessen, whose work is displayed in the Rijksmuseum.

HOUSEBOAT MUSEUM   MUSEUM

Map p310 (020-427 07 50; www.houseboatmuseum.nl; Prinsengracht 296k; adult/child €4.50/3.50; 10am-5pm daily Jul & Aug, Tue-Sun Sep-Dec & Jan-Jun; 13/14/17 Westermarkt)

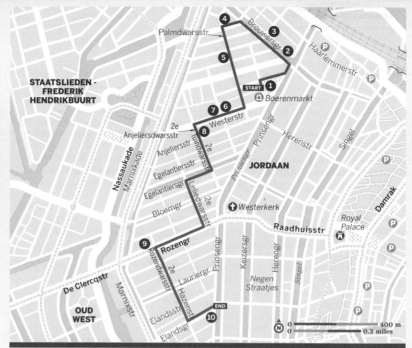

Neighbourhood Walk
Lost in the Jordaan

START NOORDERKERK
END JOHNNY JORDAANPLEIN
LENGTH 2.7KM; ONE HOUR

Begin at the ❶ **Noorderkerk** (p136). This impressive cross-shaped church was revolutionary at the time, providing the working-class congregation of the Jordaan with altar views from four transepts. Out front is the Noordermarkt, site of Amsterdam's most attractive *boerenmarkt* (farmers' market), and a flea market.

Head north to ❷ **Brouwersgracht** (p136). As you move west along this 'Brewers' Canal', you'll see the old warehouses ❸ **Groene & Grauwe Valk**. At the second drawbridge, turn left into Palmgracht and look out for the red door to the ❹ **Rapenhofje** (at 28–38). This little courtyard was home to one of Amsterdam's oldest almshouses (1648).

South along Palmdwarsstraat you'll pass tiny shops frequented by locals. Note the stone tablet of the ❺ **white fat pig** over the butcher-deli at 2e Goudsbloemdwarsstraat 26. Soon you'll reach Westerstraat, with the ❻ **Pianola Museum** (p136), a weekly clothing market and alluring eating places, such as ❼ **Café 't Monumentje** (p144). At 2e Anjeliersdwarsstraat, turn left to enter what locals call the ❽ **garden quarter** of ivy-clad lanes and diminutive squares.

Zigzag your way down to Leliedwarsstraat and continue along until you hit busy Rozengracht. ❾ **Rembrandt's sterfhuis** (death house) is at 184; the master painter died here in 1669. The part of the Jordaan on 2e Rozendwarsstraat and around is a mad jumble of styles, and though the winch beams may appear decorative they still see plenty of active duty.

Cross over the Lauriergracht, turning left into Elandsgracht. You will find ❿ **Johnny Jordaanplein** (p139), a square dedicated to the local hero and singer of schmaltzy tunes such as 'Bij ons in de Jordaan' There are bronze busts of Johnny and his band, but the real star here is the colourful utility hut splashed with nostalgic lyrics.

This quirky museum, a 23m-long sailing barge from 1914, offers a good sense of how *gezellig* (cosy, convivial) life can be on the water. The actual displays are minimal, but you can watch a presentation on houseboats (some pretty and some ghastly) and inspect the sleeping, living, cooking and dining quarters with all the mod cons. Cash only.

JOHNNY JORDAANPLEIN SQUARE
Map p310 (cnr Prinsengracht & Elandsgracht; 🚋13/14/17 Westermarkt) This shady little square is named for Johnny Jordaan (the pseudonym of Johannes Hendricus van Musscher), a popular musician in the mid-1900s who sang the romantic music known as *levenslied* (tears-in-your-beer-style ballads). The colourfully painted hut – a municipal transformer station – proudly displays one of his song lyrics: '*Amsterdam, wat bent je mooi*' (Amsterdam, how beautiful you are). Behind the hut you'll find Johnny, and members of the Jordaan musical hall of fame, cast in bronze.

On King's Day, this is where many Jordaanians head to rock out to live music.

⊙ The West

WESTERPARK PARK
Map p303 (Spaarndammerstraat; 🚋3 Haarlemmerplein) Eco-urban Westerpark – with grassy expanses of lawns (packed in summer with picnickers and sun worshippers), tree-shaded walkways and cycleways, ponds, fountains and abundant bird life – adjoins the post-industrial Westergasfabriek (p145) cultural centre.

MUSEUM HET SCHIP MUSEUM
Map p303 (☎020-686 85 95; www.hetschip.nl; Oostzaanstraat 45; tour adult/child €12.50/free; ☺11am-5pm Tue-Sun, English tour 3pm; 🚋22 Oostzaanstraat) Just north of Westerpark over the train tracks, this remarkable 1921-completed housing project is a flagship of the Amsterdam School of architecture. Designed by Michel de Klerk for railway employees and loosely resembling a ship, the triangular block has a rocket-like tower linking the wings of the complex. Admission includes a 45-minute guided tour; English tours run at 3pm but may also be available at other times.

✗ EATING

Restaurants in the Jordaan exude the conviviality that is a hallmark of the neighbourhood. Many people gravitate to the eateries along Westerstraat, while the Haarlemmerbuurt offers increasingly trendy options. Or simply wander the narrow backstreets where the next hot spot may be opening up. Self-caterers shouldn't miss the neighbourhood's markets (p148). Those looking for nouveau scenester eats will strike it rich in the West, particularly in and around Westergasfabriek (p145). For amazing fare in an even more amazing setting, head to the Houthavens (p142) district.

✗ Jordaan

WINKEL CAFE €
Map p308 (www.winkel43.nl; Noordermarkt 43; dishes €3-7, mains €8-17; ☺kitchen 7am-10pm Mon & Sat, 8am-10pm Tue-Fri, 10am-10pm Sun, bar to 1am Sun-Thu, to 3am Fri & Sat; 🚋3/10 Marnixplein) This sprawling, indoor-outdoor space is great for people-watching, popular for coffees and small meals (such as wild-boar stew with sauerkraut and cranberry sauce), and out-of-the-park for its tall, cakey apple pie, served with clouds of whipped cream. On market days (Monday and Saturday) there's almost always a queue out the door.

PAZZI PIZZA €
Map p310 (☎020-320 28 00; www.pazziamsterdam.nl; 1e Looiersdwarsstraat 4; pizzas €8-15; ☺5-10pm; 🚋7/10/17 Elandsgracht) At this parquet-floored place with marble-topped tables, wood oven–fired pizzas are made with serious care. Perfectly charred crusts come topped with fresh buffalo mozzarella, Parma ham, spicy salami, black truffles and other quality ingredients. Italian beers are the ideal accompaniment. It doesn't take reservations, so arrive early or late.

MONTE PELMO ICE CREAM €
Map p308 (www.montepelmo.nl; 2e Anjeliersdwarsstraat 17; 1/2/3/4/5 scoops €1.50/2.70/3.80/4.80/5.80; ☺1-10pm; 🚋3/10 Marnixplein) Apple pie, *stroopwafel* (traditional caramel-filled waffle), cinnamon,

and white chocolate with hazelnut are just some of the inventive flavours concocted by this 1957-founded ice-cream maker. Queues twist out the door in the evening.

JORDINO
SWEETS €

Map p308 (www.jordino.nl; Haarlemmerdijk 25a; ice cream €3.50; ☺1-6.30pm Sun & Mon, 10am-6.30pm Tue-Sat; ☐18/21/22 Buiten Oranjestraat) It's the best of both worlds: Jordino makes rich chocolates and velvety ice cream and combines the two by scooping the ice cream atop cones dipped in chocolate or caramel. Of its 100-plus flavours, 24 (including fruit-based sorbets) are available at any one time. Other creations include chocolate tulips.

★BALTHAZAR'S KEUKEN
MEDITERRANEAN €€

Map p310 (☎020-420 21 14; www.balthazars keuken.nl; Elandsgracht 108; 3-course menu €34; ☺6-10.30pm Tue-Sun; ☐7/10/17 Elandsgracht) In a former blacksmith's forge, with a modern-rustic look and an open kitchen, this is consistently one of Amsterdam's top-rated restaurants. Don't expect a wide-ranging menu: the philosophy is basically 'whatever we have on hand', which might mean wild sea bass with mushroom risotto or confit of rabbit, but it's invariably delectable. Reservations recommended.

MANTOE
AFGHANI €€

Map p308 (☎020-421 63 74; www.restaurant mantoe.nl; 2e Leliedwarsstraat 13; mains €19, 2-/3-course menus €24/29; ☺5-10pm Wed-Sun; ☐13/14/17 Westermarkt) An Afghan family runs this small restaurant, which is so snug and friendly it feels like you're dining in someone's home. There's no menu: it's just whatever they cook that day, perhaps steamed dumplings stuffed with minced meat and herbs, or a spicy lamb and rice dish. A good wine list tops it off.

Don't be in a hurry, as the multiple courses take a while.

YAM YAM
ITALIAN €€

Map p310 (☎020-681 50 97; www.yamyam.nl; Frederik Hendrikstraat 88-90; pizzas €8-14, mains €13-16; ☺5.30-10pm; ☐3 Hugo de Grootplein) Ask Amsterdammers to name the city's best pizza and many will name-check this hip, contemporary trattoria. The wood-fired oven turns out thin-crust varieties such as salami and fennel seed, and the signature Yam Yam (organic smoked ham, mascarpone and truffle sauce). There are

also great pastas and creative desserts such as salted-pecan-caramel tart.

Reservations are recommended.

SEMHAR
ETHIOPIAN €€

Map p308 (☎020-638 16 34; www.semhar.nl; Marnixstraat 259-261; mains €16-20; ☺4-10pm Tue-Sun; ☑; ☐10 Bloemgracht) Owner Yohannes gives his customers a warm welcome (as do the heavenly aromas wafting from the kitchen) and is passionate about the quality of his *injera* (slightly sour, spongy pancakes), used to scoop up richly spiced stews and vegetable combos. The most romantic tables are the handful at the back overlooking the canal.

MOEDERS
DUTCH €€

Map p310 (☎020-626 79 57; www.moeders.com; Rozengracht 251; mains €15-19, 3-course menus €27-31; ☺5-10.30pm Mon-Fri, noon-10.30pm Sat & Sun; ☐13/14/17 Marnixstraat) Mum's the word at 'Mothers'. When this welcoming place opened in 1990 customers were asked to bring their own plates and photos of their mums as donations and the decor remains a delightful hotchpotch. So does the food, from traditional pumpkin *stamppot* (potato mash) to calf's liver with bacon and onion, stews and fish dishes. Book ahead.

TRATTORIA DI DONNA SOFIA
ITALIAN €€

Map p308 (☎020-623 41 04; www.trattoriadi donnasofia.com; Anjeliersstraat 300; mains €14-28; ☺5-11pm Mon-Sat; ☐3/10 Marnixplein) With rustic decor and white-clothed tables, Donna Sofia – named for the owner's grandmother – has a daily-changing blackboard menu of Neapolitan dishes chalked in Italian. Pastas are made in-house and risottos are a speciality; fresh herbs enhance the flavours of the fish, meat and vegetarian dishes. All-Italian vintages feature on the small but well-chosen wine list.

TOSCANINI
ITALIAN €€

Map p308 (☎020-623 28 13; www.restaurant toscanini.nl; Lindengracht 75; mains €14-24, 6-course tasting menu €53; ☺6-10.30pm Mon-Sat; ☐3/10 Marnixplein) Classy Toscanini bakes its own bread, rolls its own pasta and pours Italian wines. The weekly-changing dishes that grace the white tablecloths might include crêpes stuffed with ricotta and nettle or veal with sweetbread and mushroom sauce. Desserts such as layered Palermo chocolate cake promise to weaken even the fiercest of dietary resolves. Book ahead, even on weeknights.

DE PRINS CAFE €€

Map p308 (☑020-624 93 82; www.deprins. nl; Prinsengracht 124; mains €8-18; ⊘kitchen 10am-8pm, bar to 1am Sun-Thu, to 2am Fri & Sat; ⬚13/14/17 Westermarkt) On a picturesque stretch of the Prinsengracht, this brown cafe is an idyllic spot for a drink on the canal-side terrace or in the cosy bar. But it's best known for its excellent kitchen. Lunch specialities include prawn or meat *bitterballen* (croquettes), while the pick of the dinner menu is a divine four-cheese fondue.

KOEVOET ITALIAN €€

Map p308 (☑020-624 08 46; www.koevoet amsterdam.com; Lindenstraat 17; mains €12-25; ⊘6-10pm Tue-Sat; ⬚3/10 Marnixplein) The congenial Italian owners of Koevoet took over a former cafe on a quiet side street, left the *gezellig* decor untouched and started cooking up their home-country staples such as handmade ravioli using ingredients imported from Italy's south. Don't miss the signature, drinkable dessert, *sgroppino limone:* sorbet, vodka and Prosecco whisked at your table and poured into a champagne flute.

BORDEWIJK FRENCH €€€

Map p308 (☑020-624 38 99; www.bordewijk.nl; Noordermarkt 7; mains €20-32, 3-/4-/5-course menus €40/50/60; ⊘6.30-10.30pm Tue-Sat; ⬚3/10 Marnixplein) The interior at Bordewijk is so minimal that there's little to do but appreciate the spectacular modern French cooking. The chefs aren't afraid to take risks, resulting in dishes such as crispy calf's brains with raw mackerel and salted lemon, roast turbot with stewed sea oysters and samphire, quail with foie gras or sea-salt-roasted ribs. Book ahead at weekends.

✗ The West

WORST WIJNCAFE TAPAS €

Map p303 (☑020-625 61 67; www.deworst.nl; Barentszstraat 171; tapas €7-17, brunch mains €9-12; ⊘noon-midnight Tue-Sat, 10am-10pm Sun; ⬚3 Zoutkeetsgracht) Named for its sausage-skewed tapas dishes (veal-tongue white sausage, chorizo kebab morsels with spinach and asparagus), this chequerboard-tiled wine bar is the more casual sibling of esteemed restaurant Marius (p142)

JORDAAN FESTIVAL

Practitioners of the nostalgic, tears-in-your-beer folk music called *levenslied* – a speciality of the tight-knit Jordaan – take to the stage around mid-September for this weekend-long festival (www.jordaanfestival.nl).

next door. Other dishes include pigs' trotters. There's a fantastic range of mostly French wines by the glass. Sunday brunch is a local event.

DE BAKKERSWINKEL CAFE €

Map p303 (☑020-688 06 32; www.debakkers winkel.nl; Polonceaukade 1, Westergasfabriek; snacks €4-6, dishes €8-16; ⊘8.30am-5pm Mon-Thu, 8.30am-6pm Fri, 10am-6pm Sat & Sun; ⬚10 Van Limburg Stirumstraat) The wonderful 'Bakery' has numerous branches throughout the city (and country), but this one is uniquely situated by the drawbridge in the old regulator's house at the former gasworks, with mezzanine seating, comfy sofas and a great terrace. Quiches, fish terrines, soups and sourdough sandwiches are all good choices, and the carrot cake is unmissable.

SEOUL FOOD KOREAN €

Map p310 (☑020-331 88 43; www.seoulfood amsterdam.nl; Kinkerstraat 73a; mains €3-9; ⊘noon-9pm Tue-Sun; ⛾; ⬚7/17 Bilderdijkstraat) Reasonably priced Korean specialities at this sleek little spot include *bibimbap* (rice bowls with red-pepper paste and a fried egg) and *kogi bbang* (a flatbread sandwich with spicy beef and pickled veggies). It primarily offers takeaway dishes, but there's in-store seating at a long communal table close to the shelves stacked with products imported from South Korea.

Tots have an indoor play area.

★WOLF ATELIER GASTRONOMY €€

Map p303 (☑020-344 64 28; www.wolfatelier.nl; Westerdoksplein 20; mains €24, 4-/5-/15-course menus €42/48/75; ⊘noon-5pm & 6-10pm Mon-Sat; ⬚48 Westerdoksdijk) Atop a 1920 railway swing bridge, a glass box with pivoting windows is the showcase for experimental Austrian chef Michael Wolf's 'Tartar-ia' (varying but styled of tartar, including steak, tuna and salmon, each in three sizes) and 'Atelier', where he creates wild flavour combinations. The 360-degree views are

DESTINATION DINING IN HOUTHAVENS

Just north of the Western Islands, Amsterdam's rapidly emerging Houthavens district – long-time docklands now being turned into a residential neighbourhood – is home to two incredible restaurants: **REM Eiland** (☑020-688 55 01; www.remeiland.com; Haparandadam 45; mains lunch €7.50-15, dinner €18.50-29.50; ☺noon-4pm & 5.30-10pm; ☒48 Koivistokade), in a former sea rig that previously housed a pirate radio station, and **Pont 13** (☑020-770 27 22; www.pont13.nl; Haparandadam 50; mains lunch €6.50-9.50, dinner €17-22.50; ☺noon-10pm; ☎; ☒48 Koivistokade), on a 1927-built former car ferry. From Centraal Station, take a bus or a taxi (around €10 to €15), or hop on a bike (15 minutes).

magical at night; you can linger for a drink until 1am.

Mains might feature sweetbreads with truffle foam, flambéed sea bass with champagne-steamed Zeeland mussels, and deconstructed tonka-bean, chocolate and caramel crumble.

★MOSSEL EN GIN   SEAFOOD €€

Map p303 (☑020-486 58 69; www.mosselengin.nl; Gosschalklaan 12, Westergasfabriek; mains €12-16; ☺4-10pm Tue-Fri, 1-10pm Sat & Sun, bar to 1am Tue-Thu & Sun, to 3am Fri & Sat; ☎; ☒21 Van Hallstraat) *Mosselen* (mussels) and gin are the twin specialities of this spectacular double-height mezzanine space within Westergasfabriek (p145), which opens onto two sun-soaked beer gardens. Mussels-and-fries come in four styles, including with crème fraîche and gin; it also serves inspired gin-and-tonic-battered fish and chips, and lobster or shrimp croquettes with gin mayo. Alongside seven gins, six house infusions include beetroot and basil.

APOSTROF   EUROPEAN €€

Map p303 (☑06 2491 8611; www.apostrofamsterdam.nl; Planciusstraat 49; 3-/4-/5-/6-course menus €35/43/50/56; ☺6-10pm Wed-Sun; ☒3 Zoutkeetsgracht) Well-priced European wines pair perfectly with chef Sjoerd Visser's mix-and-match multicourse menus (no à la carte) of monthly changing dishes. Choices might include shiitake-stuffed

quail, plaice with smoked eel, and rhubarb with white chocolate and star anise. Inside a curved corner building, the contemporary dining room is dominated by a vivid forest mural along one wall.

MASTINO V   VEGAN, PIZZA €€

Map p310 (Bilderdijkstraat 192; pizza €13-20; ☺5-10pm Tue-Sun; ☎☒; ☒7/17 Bilderdijkstraat) Pizzas are 100% vegan and gluten free at Mastino V, which recently opened behind a timber facade in a split-level, bare-brick space on up-and-coming Bilderdijkstraat. Rice, almond and corn are used to create the bases; toppings include several vegan cheeses (mozzarella, parmesan, brie and smoked cheese among them). Desserts, such as blueberry-and-orange cake or chocolate brownies, are gluten free and vegan too.

RAÏNARAÏ   ALGERIAN €€

Map p303 (☑020-486 71 09; www.rainarai.nl; Polonceaukade 40, Westergasfabriek; mains €19, 2-/3-course menu €32/36; ☺6-10pm Tue-Sun, lunch by reservation; ☒21 Van Hallstraat) Arabian-style cushions and copper fixtures now adorn this old industrial building in the Westergasfabriek. The Algerian menu changes constantly but might offer seared salmon on chickpea-pumpkin couscous or grilled sardines with asparagus, broad beans and tomatoes. There's usually a vegetarian dish of the day.

★MARIUS   EUROPEAN €€€

Map p303 (☑020-422 78 80; www.restaurantmarius.nl; Barentszstraat 173; 4-course menu €48; ☺6.30-10pm Tue-Sat; ☒3 Zoutkeetsgracht) Foodies swoon over pocket-sized Marius, tucked amid artists' studios in the Western Islands. Chef Kees Elfring shops at local markets, then creates his daily four-course, no-choice menu from what he finds. The result might be grilled prawns with fava-bean purée or beef rib with polenta and ratatouille. Marius also runs the fabulous wine and tapas bar Worst Wijncafe (p141) next door.

🍷 DRINKING & NIGHTLIFE

Anyone who seeks an authentic *café* (pub) experience 'with the locals' will love the Jordaan. Off the tourist radar, the West attracts an artsy crowd.

🍷 Jordaan

★ 'T SMALLE
BROWN CAFE

Map p308 (www.t-smalle.nl; Egelantiersgracht 12; ⊙10am-1am Sun-Thu, to 2am Fri & Sat; 🚊13/14/17 Westermarkt) Dating back to 1786 as a *jenever* (Dutch gin) distillery and tasting house, and restored during the 1970s with antique porcelain beer pumps and lead-framed windows, locals' favourite 't Smalle is one of Amsterdam's most charming *bruin cafés*. Dock your boat right by the pretty stone terrace, which is wonderfully convivial by day and impossibly romantic at night.

CAFÉ PAPENEILAND
BROWN CAFE

Map p308 (www.papeneiland.nl; Prinsengracht 2; ⊙10am-1am Sun-Thu, to 3am Fri & Sat; 🚊3/10 Marnixplein) With Delft-blue tiles and a central stove, this *bruin café* is a 1642 gem. The name, 'Papists' Island', goes back to the Reformation, when there was a clandestine Catholic church on the canal's northern side. Papeneiland was reached via a secret tunnel from the top of the stairs – ask the bar staff to show you the entrance.

CAFE SOUNDGARDEN
BAR

Map p310 (www.cafesoundgarden.nl; Marnixstraat 164-166; ⊙1pm-1am Mon-Thu, to 3am Fri, 3pm-3am Sat, to 1am Sun; 🚊13/14/17 Marnixstraat) In this grungy, all-ages dive bar, the 'Old Masters' are the Ramones and Black Sabbath. Somehow a handful of pool tables, 1980s pinball machines, unkempt DJs and lovably surly bartenders add up to an ineffable magic. Bands occasionally make an appearance, and the waterfront terrace scene is more like an impromptu party in someone's backyard.

All walks of life congregate here; the common denominator isn't fashion, age or politics but a diehard love of rock and roll.

CAFÉ PIEPER
BROWN CAFE

Map p310 (www.cafepieper.com; Prinsengracht 424; ⊙noon-1am Mon, Wed & Thu, 4pm-midnight Tue, noon-2am Fri & Sat, 2-10pm Sun; 🚊1/2/5 Prinsengracht) Small, unassuming and unmistakably old (1665), Café Pieper features stained-glass windows, antique beer mugs hanging from the bar and a working Dutch barrel-top pump (1875). Sip an Amsterdam-brewed Brouwerij 't IJ beer or a terrific cappuccino as you marvel at the claustrophobia of the low-ceilinged bar

(people were shorter back in the 17th century – even the Dutch, it seems).

VESPER BAR
COCKTAIL BAR

Map p308 (📞020-420 45 92; www.vesperbar.nl; Vinkenstraat 57; ⊙8pm-1am Tue-Thu, 5pm-3am Fri & Sat; 🚊18/21/22 Buiten Oranjestraat) This luxe bar's location on a low-key stretch of Jordaanian shops and businesses gives it a certain mystique. Its martinis will coax out your inner James Bond – or Vesper Lynd (the main female character in *Casino Royale*). Spice things up with the Victoria's Secret: ginger liqueur, pear brandy and elderflower with fresh lemon juice and a dash of chilli pepper.

DE KAT IN DE WIJNGAERT
BROWN CAFE

Map p308 (www.dekatindewijngaert.nl; Lindengracht 160; ⊙10am-1am Sun-Thu, to 3am Fri, 9am-3am Sat; 🚊3/10 Marnixplein) With overwhelming *gezelligheid* (cosiness, conviviality), this gorgeous bar is the kind of place where one beer soon turns to several – maybe it's the influence of the arty old-guard locals who hang out here. At least you can soak it all up with what many people vote as the best *tosti* (toasted sandwich) in town.

CAFÉ P 96
BROWN CAFE

Map p308 (www.p96.nl; Prinsengracht 96; ⊙11am-3am Sun-Thu, to 4am Fri & Sat; 📶; 🚊13/14/17 Westermarkt) If you don't want the night to end, P 96 is an amiable hang-out. When most other *cafés* in the Jordaan shut down for the night, this is where everyone ends up, rehashing their evening and striking up conversations with strangers. In summertime head to the terrace across the street aboard a houseboat.

WATERKANT
BAR

Map p310 (www.waterkantamsterdam.nl; Marnixstraat 246; ⊙11am-1am Sun-Thu, to 3am Fri & Sat; 📶; 🚊7/10/17 Elandsgracht) Tucked under an oddball circular parking garage on the Jordaan's outskirts, this rollicking canal-side pub serves good brews (many local) along with global fare from pumpkin rotis to sticky wings, nachos and duck spring rolls. For something different, try a watermelon gin and tonic. The terrace is heated in chilly weather.

TWO FOR JOY
COFFEE

Map p308 (Haarlemmerdijk 182; ⊙9am-6pm; 🚊3 Haarlemmerplein) Two for Joy roasts its

DRINK LIKE A JORDAANIAN

There's a certain hard-drinking, hard-living spirit left over from the Jordaan's working-class days, when the neighbourhood burst with 80,000 residents (compared to today's 20,000) and brown cafes functioned as a refuge from the slings and arrows of workaday life.

Local bastions that are still going strong include the following:

Café 't Monumentje

Café de Jordaan

De Twee Zwaantjes

own Mokum blend and other single-origin beans and then brews them into some of Amsterdam's best espresso. Hang out on the vintage couches and lounge chairs, check out the art on the exposed-brick walls, and enjoy the caffeine buzz.

DE TWEE ZWAANTJES   BROWN CAFE

Map p308 (☑020-625 27 29; www.cafedetwee zwaantjes.nl; Prinsengracht 114; ⊘3pm-1am Sun-Thu, to 3am Fri & Sat; ☒13/14/17 Westermarkt) The small, authentic 'Two Swans' is at its hilarious best on weekend nights, when you can join patrons belting out classics and traditional Dutch tunes in a rollicking, unforgettable cabaret-meets-karaoke evening. The fact that singers are often fuelled by the liquid courage of the Trappist beers on tap only adds to the spirited fun. Don't be afraid to join in.

CAFÉ DE KOE   BAR

Map p310 (www.cafedekoe.nl; Marnixstraat 381; ⊘4pm-1am Sun-Thu, to 3am Fri & Sat; ☒1/2/5 Leidseplein) With a shimmering bovine mosaic on its facade, 'the Cow' is loved for its homey *gezellig* atmosphere, with board games, movie nights and free gigs by local DJs and rock bands. A down-to-earth neighbourhood crowd swills beers upstairs while diners below gather around worn wooden tables and order hearty, inexpensive comfort food.

DIVINO WIJNBAR   WINE BAR

Map p308 (www.wijnbardivino.nl; Boomstraat 41a; ⊘5pm-midnight Mon-Thu, to 2am Fri, 4pm-2am Sat, to midnight Sun; ☒3/10 Marnixplein)

Only quality Italian wines by the glass and bottle are served at this wine bar, alongside charcuterie and cheese plates. The polished-wood bar, flickering candles and lofty corner windows draw you in – though the blankets strewn about the tables and chairs outside are equally inviting. Tastings of five wines and antipasti cost €50 per person.

LA TERTULIA   COFFEESHOP

Map p310 (www.coffeeshoptertulia.com; Prinsengracht 312; ⊘11am-7pm Tue-Sat; ☒7/10/17 Elandsgracht) A long-standing favourite, this mother-and-daughter-run coffeeshop has a greenhouse feel. You can sit outside by the Van Gogh–inspired murals, play some board games or contemplate the Jurassic-sized crystals by the counter. Bonus: Tertulia actually has good coffee, along with *stroopwafels* (caramel-filled Dutch waffles).

CAFÉ DE LAURIERBOOM   BROWN CAFE

Map p310 (www.laurierboom.cafe; Laurierstraat 76; ⊘2.30pm-1am Mon-Thu, to 3am Fri, 1pm-3am Sat, to 1am Sun; ☎; ☒13/14/17 Marnixstraat) The hub of the Jordaan chess circuit is one of the neighbourhood's oldest *cafés*. Local masters test their wits over a drink; you can also battle it out in international games of chess online here at one of two computers, or play card or board games.

CAFÉ DE JORDAAN   BROWN CAFE

Map p310 (☑020-627 58 63; Elandsgracht 45; ⊘10am-1am Mon-Thu, to 3am Fri, noon-3am Sat, 1pm-1am Sun; ☒7/10/17 Elandsgracht) A relaxed spot for a *biertje* (glass of beer), this old-style Jordaan *café* comes into its own at 5pm on Sunday, when crooners link arms and sing along to classic Dutch tunes.

SPIRIT   COFFEESHOP

Map p308 (Westerstraat 121; ⊘noon-1am; ☒3/10 Marnixplein) Setting this coffeeshop apart from the pack are its half a dozen or so state-of-the-art pinball machines, including the Walking Dead, Metallica and AC/DC, to play between puffs. You can also shoot pool here. Cash only.

CAFÉ 'T MONUMENTJE   BROWN CAFE

Map p308 (www.monumentje.nl; Westerstraat 120; ⊘8.30am-1am Mon-Thu, to 3am Fri, 9am-3am Sat, 11am-1am Sun; ☒3/10 Marnixplein)

LOCAL KNOWLEDGE

WESTERGASFABRIEK

A stone's throw northwest of the Jordaan, the late-19th-century Dutch Renaissance **Westergasfabriek** (Map p303; ☏020-586 07 10; www.westergasfabriek.nl; Pazzanistraat; ⊠10 Van Limburg Stirumstraat/Van Hallstraat) complex adjacent to the Westerpark (p139) was the city's western gasworks until gas production ceased in 1967. The site was heavily polluted and underwent a major clean-up before it re-emerged as a cultural and recreational park, with lush lawns, a long wading pool, cycleways and sports facilities.

The post-industrial buildings now house creative spaces such as advertising agencies and TV production studios, as well as regular festivals and events – including the **Sunday Market** (www.sundaymarket.nl; ⊗noon-6pm 1st & 3rd Sun of month), a quality craft and gourmet food event.

Westergasfabriek's slew of dining, drinking and entertainment options includes the following:

Mossel En Gin (p142) Gins are used in creative cooking and cocktails.

De Bakkerswinkel (p141) Split-level cafe inside the gasworks' former regulator's house.

Raïnaraï (p142) Algerian cuisine amid exotic decor.

Westergasterras (p146) Bar opening to one of Amsterdam's best terraces.

Brouwerij Troost Westergas Brewery for hop heads and cool cats.

Pacific Parc (p146) Indie gigs and DJ sets.

Westerunie (p146) Pumpin' post-industrial club.

This slightly scruffy yet lovable *café* is always heaving with local barflies. It's a fun spot for a beer and a snack after shopping at the Westermarkt (p148). Singalongs take place on the first Monday of the month; it also hosts occasional live music.

SAAREIN
GAY & LESBIAN

Map p310 (www.saarein2.nl; Elandsstraat 119; ⊗4pm-1am Tue-Thu & Sun, to 2am Fri, 1pm-2am Sat; ⊠7/10/17 Elandsgracht) A rainbow flag flies above this canal house dating from the 1600s. A one-time feminist stronghold, it's still a meeting place for lesbians, although these days gay men are welcome too. There's a small menu with tapas, soups and specials, as well as a pool table with purple baize.

DE TRUT
GAY & LESBIAN

Map p310 (www.trutfonds.nl; Bilderdijkstraat 165e; ⊗10pm-4am Sun; ⊠7/17 Bilderdijkstraat) In the basement of a former squat, this Sunday-night club is a gay and lesbian institution. It's run by volunteers and comes with an attitude; arrive well before 11pm (the space is fairly small). No cameras or mobile phones are allowed inside.

ⓣ The West

★MONKS COFFEE ROASTERS
COFFEE

Map p310 (Bilderdijkstraat 46; ⊗8am-5pm Tue-Sun; ⊠13/14 Bilderdijkstraat) Monks' phenomenal house blend, prepared with a variety of brewing methods, is hands down Amsterdam's best, but the cafe also serves superb coffee from small-scale specialists such as Amsterdam's Lot Sixty One and White Label Coffee, and Paris' Café Lomi. Its cavernous space is brilliant for brunch (try avocado toast with feta, chilli and lime, or banana bread with mascarpone and caramelised pineapple).

★BROUWERIJ TROOST WESTERGAS
BREWERY

Map p303 (☏020-737 10 28; www.brouwerij troostwestergas.nl; Pazzanistraat 27, Westergasfabriek; ⊗4pm-1am Mon-Thu, to 3am Fri, noon-3am Sat, to midnight Sun; ☏; ⊠10 Van Limburg Stirumstraat) De Pijp's brewery (p181) proved so popular it opened a larger outpost in this cavernous industrial Westergasfabriek space punctuated by big silver tanks cooking up saison, blond ale and smoked porter varieties; the brewery also uses the tanks to distil its own gin. Live jazz plays on Wednesday; brewery tours (€6) run at 4pm Saturday. Credit cards only (no cash). Takeaway beers and gin are sold at its shop.

★WESTERGASTERRAS · BAR

Map p303 (www.westergasterras.nl; Klönneplein 4-6, Westergasfabriek; ◉11am-1am Mon-Thu, to 3am Fri, 10am-3am Sat, to 1am Sun; 🛜; 🚊10 Van Limburg Stirumstraat) Overlooking reed-filled ponds and a weir, the massive decked terrace is hotly contested on sunny afternoons, but the soaring brick-and-steel post-industrial interior is also crammed every day of the week. Sophisticated pub food (the likes of beef carpaccio) is served until 10pm. Its popular dance club lets loose on Thursdays in summer.

WESTERUNIE CLUB

Map p303 (☑020-684 84 96; www.westerunie. nl; Klönneplein 6, Westergasfabriek; ◉hours vary; 🛜; 🚊10 Van Limburg Stirumstraat) House, techno and acid dominate at this club in a concrete, steel and brick building with exposed pipes and great acoustics for the state-of-the-art sound system in the post-industrial Westergasfabriek (p145) complex. Like many Amsterdam clubs, it uses a token system for drinks, which saves waiting for change at the bar. Mega events often spill over into neighbouring spaces.

☆ ENTERTAINMENT

THEATER AMSTERDAM PERFORMING ARTS

(☑020-705 50 59; www.theateramsterdam.nl; Danzigerkade 5; 🚊48 Koivistokade) Surrounded by the construction of docklands-turned-neighbourhood Houthavens, this gleaming theatre has a glass facade providing views over the IJ. Its 15,000-sq-metre auditorium means it can accommodate huge sets for large-scale theatre and music productions. A cutting-edge system translates the on-stage works into eight languages. If you're arriving by boat, you can pull up at its dock.

All-organic food and natural wines are served at its restaurant.

BOOM CHICAGO COMEDY

Map p310 (www.boomchicago.nl; Rozengracht 117; tickets from €15; 🛜; 🚊13/14/17 Marnixstraat) Boom Chicago stages seriously funny improv-style comedy shows in English that make fun of Dutch culture, American culture and everything that gets in the crosshairs. Edgier shows happen in the smaller upstairs theatre. The on-site bar helps fuel the festivities with buckets of ice and beer.

PACIFIC PARC LIVE MUSIC

Map p303 (☑020-488 77 78; www.pacificparc. nl; Polonceaukade 23, Westergasfabriek; tickets €3; 🚊10 Van Limburg Stirumstraat) In a faux-tropical setting, Pacific Parc is home to live music, DJ sets and plenty of rock-and-roll spirit to go along with the potent drinks and hearty food. The sprawling, picnic-table-strewn terrace and cafe open from 11am daily; bands usually start between 11pm and midnight.

NOODERKERKCONCERTEN CLASSICAL MUSIC

Map p308 (☑020-620 44 15; www.noorderkerk concerten.nl/concerten; Noorderkerk, Noorder-markt 48; tickets from €16; ◉2pm Sat; 🚊3/10 Marnixplein) Classical concerts, especially Bach, take place in the Noorderkerk (p136) most Saturday afternoons; check the agenda online. Most last around an hour.

MALOE MELO BLUES

Map p310 (☑020-420 45 92; www.maloemelo. com; Lijnbaansgracht 163; ◉9pm-3am Sun-Thu, to 4am Fri & Sat; 🚊7/10/17 Elandsgracht) This is the free-wheeling, fun-loving altar of Amsterdam's tiny blues scene. Music ranges from funk and soul to Texas blues and rockabilly. The cover charge is usually around €5.

DE NIEUWE ANITA LIVE MUSIC

Map p310 (www.denieuweanita.nl; Frederik Hendrikstraat 111; tickets free-€5; 🚊3 Hugo de Grootplein) This living-room venue expanded for noise rockers has a great *café*. In the back, behind the bookcase-concealed door, the main room has a stage and screens cult movies (in English) on Monday. DJs and vaudeville type acts are also on the eclectic agenda.

MOVIES CINEMA

Map p308 (☑020-638 60 16; www.themovies.nl; Haarlemmerdijk 161; tickets €11; 🚊3 Haarlemmer-plein) Amsterdam's oldest cinema, dating from 1912, is a *gezellig* gem screening indie films alongside mainstream flicks. From Sunday to Thursday you can treat yourself to a meal in the restaurant (open 5.30pm to 10pm) or have a pre-film tipple at the inviting *café*-bar.

🛍 SHOPPING

Shops here have an artsy, eclectic, homemade feel. The area around Elandsgracht is the place for antiques and art, as well as speciality shops covering everything from hats to cats. Straddling the Jordaan and Western Canal Ring, the Haarlemmerbuurt (p112), incorporating hip Haarlemmerdijk in the northern Jordaan, teems with trendy food and fashion boutiques. The Jordaan also has some fabulous food and flea markets (p148).

★MOOOI GALLERY   DESIGN

Map p308 (☑020-528 77 60; www.moooi.com; Westerstraat 187; ☺10am-6pm Tue-Sat; 🚊3/10 Marnixplein) Founded by Marcel Wanders, this gallery-shop features Dutch design at its most over-the-top, from the life-size black horse lamp to the 'blow away vase' (a whimsical twist on the classic Delft vase) and the 'killing of the piggy bank' ceramic pig (with a gold hammer).

ROBINS HOOD   DESIGN

Map p308 (www.robinshood.nl; 2e Tuindwarsstraat 7; ☺11am-6pm Mon-Fri, to 5pm Sat; 🚊3/10 Marnixplein) Whitewashed walls and floorboards create a blank canvas for the upcycled vintage and Dutch-designed products here. Browse for unique items like vases, bags, scarves, jewellery, sunglasses, lamps, art, stationery and some truly only-in-the-Netherlands items like *stroopwafel* coasters.

BACK BEAT RECORDS   MUSIC

Map p308 (☑020-627 16 57; www.backbeat. nl; Egelantiersstraat 19; ☺11am-6pm Mon-Sat; 🚊13/14/17 Westermarkt) Back Beat has been selling jazz, soul and funk music since 1988. Whether you're looking for Sly and the Family Stone vinyl, a Chet Baker box set or a Charles Earland Hammond-organ CD, this little shop has it covered. The owner is a font of local jazz lore; you can find out about concerts around town and buy tickets here.

RAW MATERIALS   HOMEWARES

Map p310 (www.rawmaterials.nl; Rozengracht 229-233; ☺noon-6pm Mon, 10am-6pm Tue-Sat, noon-6pm Sun; 🚊10/11/17 Marnixplein) As its name suggests, Raw Materials stocks vintage furniture, steel cabinets and pieces made from reclaimed wood, as well as a

LIQUORICE

The Dutch love their sweets, the most famous of which is *drop*, the word for all varieties of liquorice. It may be gummy-soft or tough as leather, and shaped like coins or miniature cars, but the most important distinction is between *zoete* (sweet) and *zoute* (salty, also called *salmiak*). The latter is often an alarming surprise, even for avowed fans of the black stuff. But with such a range of textures and additional flavours – mint, honey, laurel – even liquorice sceptics might be converted. **Het Oud-Hollandsch Snoepwinkeltje** (Map p308; www.snoepwinkeltje. com; 2e Egelantiersdwarsstraat 2; ☺11am-6.30pm Tue-Sat; 🚊3/10 Marnixplein) is a good place to do a taste test.

great array of fabrics, soft furnishings, ceramics and glassware that capture the spirit of Dutch design.

PAPABUBBLE   FOOD

Map p308 (☑020-626 26 62; www.papabubble.nl; Haarlemmerdijk 70; ☺noon-6pm Mon & Wed-Fri, 10am-6pm Sat; 🚊3 Haarlemmerplein) This hip sweetshop looks more like a gallery. Pull up a cushion and perch on the stairs to watch the mesmerising process of transforming sugar into sweets with flavours like pomelo and lavender.

You can get your own custom-made sweets (minimum order 6kg).

CONCRETE MATTER   GIFTS & SOUVENIRS

Map p308 (www.concrete-matter.com; Haarlemmerdijk 127; ☺1-6pm Mon, 11am-6pm Tue-Sat, noon-5pm Sun; 🚊3 Haarlemmerplein) At this concept store with a difference, everything is specifically curated for men, from casual clothing to classic car books to shaving kits, referee whistles, aviator sunglasses, flask and shot-glass sets, pocketknives and other items that make great gifts.

CATS & THINGS   GIFTS & SOUVENIRS

Map p310 (☑020-428 30 28; www.catsand things.nl; Hazenstraat 26; ☺11.30am-6pm Tue-Fri, to 5pm Sat; 🚊7/10/17 Elandsgracht) If you're a cat lover, or shopping for someone who is, this quirky shop – with its own resident cats – is a must. It stocks every feline-themed gift imaginable (statues, artworks,

LOCAL KNOWLEDGE

JORDAAN MARKETS

Lindengracht Market (Map p308; www.jordaanmarkten.nl; Lindengracht; ⊙9am-4pm Sat; 🚊3 Nieuwe Willemsstraat) Dating from 1895, Saturday's Lindengracht Market is a wonderfully local affair, with 232 stalls selling bountiful fresh produce, including fish and a magnificent array of cheese, as well as gourmet goods, clothing and homewares. Arrive as early as possible for the best pickings and thinnest crowds.

Noordermarkt (Map p308; www.jordaanmarkten.nl; Noordermarkt; ⊙flea market 9am-1pm Mon, farmers' market 9am-4pm Sat; 🚊3/10 Marnixplein) A market square since the early 1600s, the plaza in front of the Noorderkerk hosts a couple of lively markets each week. Monday morning's **flea market** has some amazing bargains, and Saturday morning sees local shoppers flock to the lush **boerenmarkt** (farmers' market), overflowing with organic produce.There's a great selection of cafes surrounding the square, including Winkel (p139), home of some of the city's best apple pie, on the southwestern corner.

Westermarkt (Map p308; www.jordaanmarkten.nl; Westerstraat; ⊙9am-1pm Mon; 🚊3/10 Marnixplein) Bargain-priced clothing and fabrics are sold at 170 stalls at the Westermarkt (which isn't in fact on Westermarkt but on Westerstraat, just near the Noordermarkt).

cat-adorned homewares) as well as presents for kitty (baskets, food, collars and climbers).

MECHANISCH SPEELGOED TOYS
Map p308 (www.mechanisch-speelgoed.nl; Westerstraat 67; ⊙10am-6pm Mon-Fri, to 5pm Sat; 🚊3/10 Marnixplein) This adorable shop is crammed full of nostalgic toys, including snow domes, glow lamps, masks, finger puppets and wind-up toys. And who doesn't need a good rubber chicken every once in a while? Hours can vary.

GALLERIA D'ARTE
RINASCIMENTO ART, ANTIQUES
Map p308 (☑020-622 75 09; www.delft-art-gallery.com; Prinsengracht 170; ⊙9am-6pm; 🚊13/14/17 Westermarkt) Royal Delftware ceramics (both antique and new) at this pretty shop span all manner of vases, platters, brooches, Christmas ornaments and intriguing 19th-century wall tiles and plaques.

'T ZONNETJE DRINKS
Map p308 (☑020-623 00 58; www.t-zonnetje. com; Haarlemmerdijk 45; ⊙9-6pm Mon-Fri, to 5pm Sat; 🚊18/21/22 Buiten Oranjestraat) At

this charming shop ensconced in a 1642 building, you can find teas from all over the world, as well as coffees, spices and accoutrements.

ARNOLD CORNELIS FOOD
Map p310 (☑020-625 85 85; www.cornelis. nl; Elandsgracht 78; ⊙8.30am-6pm Mon-Fri, to 5pm Sat; 🚊7/10/17 Elandsgracht) Your dinner hosts will be impressed if you present them with something from this long-standing shop, such as fruitcake, cheesecake or biscuits made with Malaga wine. At lunchtime grab a flaky pastry filled with cheese, meat or vegetables.

ANTIEKCENTRUM AMSTERDAM ANTIQUES
Map p310 (Amsterdam Antique Centre; www. antiekcentrumamsterdam.nl; Elandsgracht 109; ⊙11am-6pm Mon-Fri, to 5pm Sat & Sun; 🚊7/10/17 Elandsgracht) Anyone with an affinity for odd antiques and bric-a-brac may enter this knick-knack mini mall and never come out. Spanning 1750 sq metres, there are 55 stalls and larger shops, and a market where dealers (and non-dealers) can rent a table on Wednesday, Saturday and Sunday. You're just as likely to find 1940s silk dresses as you are 1970s Swedish porn.

Vondelpark & the South

Neighbourhood Top Five

❶ Rijksmuseum (p151) Getting happily lost amid its riches: Rembrandt, Vermeer, gilded dollhouses and magic lanterns.

❷ Van Gogh Museum (p154) Seeing the world's best collection of Van Gogh's work up close, from yellow sunflowers to purple-blue irises.

❸ Amsterdamse Bos (p158) Cycling, boating or communing with goats in Amsterdam's surprisingly vast forest.

❹ Stedelijk Museum (p156) Discovering works by Mondrian, Matisse, Warhol, Appel, De Kooning and more at Amsterdam's fabulous modern art museum.

❺ Vondelpark (p157) Freewheeling through the park, packing a picnic, taking it easy and catching a gig at the park's teahouse or a play at its theatre.

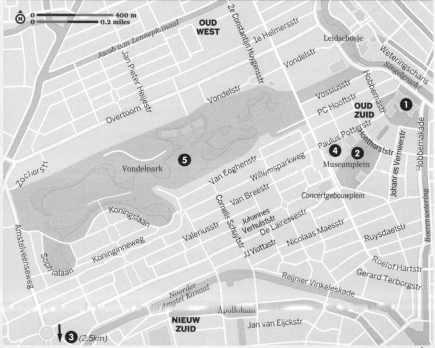

For more detail of this area see Map p312 ➡

Lonely Planet's Top Tip

Getting peckish? Amstelveenseweg, running along the western edge of the park, is a fabulous eat street, with restaurants ranging from vegan to Chinese, Japanese, Indonesian, Indian, Thai, pan-Asian, Dutch, Italian, Brazilian and American-style steaks, interspersed with stylish wine bars and cosy *cafés*. Wander along and see what you find.

✗ Best Places to Eat

➡ Ron Gastrobar (p163)

➡ Foodhallen (p161)

➡ Adam (p163)

➡ Moer (p166)

➡ Rijks (p165)

For reviews, see p161 ➡

☻ Best Places to Drink

➡ Edel (p166)

➡ 't Blauwe Theehuis (p168)

➡ Wildschut (p168)

➡ Tunes Bar (p167)

For reviews, see p166 ➡

🔒 Best Places to Shop

➡ Beer Baum (p170)

➡ Goochem Speelgoed (p170)

➡ Local Goods Store (p170)

➡ Pied à Terre (p170)

For reviews, see p170 ➡

Explore Vondelpark & the South

Amsterdam's big three museums – the Rijksmuseum, Van Gogh Museum and Stedelijk Museum – are all lined up in a walkable row on Museumplein. You could easily spend a couple of days visiting them, each a splendid treasure trove of art. In the evening, the action shifts to the Concertgebouw, the grand music hall built in conjunction with the Rijksmuseum, and genteel *cafés* (pubs) and buzzing bars spring to life in the streets around the Vondelpark.

Amsterdam's favourite green hang-out is not particularly large, but repays after some exploration, and is perfect for lingering over a drink or picnic. If you jump on a bike, bus or tram and head further south, you can explore Amsterdamse Bos, which feels almost like countryside, and is a great place to go running, biking, riding or boating. If you're in the mood for something more cultural, take the metro to the Cobra Museum, with its De Stijl masterpieces.

Local Life

➡**Cycling** If you want to gain confidence on two wheels away from the traffic-filled streets, Vondelpark is the perfect place to practise so you can whirr around like a local.

➡**Skating** Join local in-line skaters setting off from Vondelpark for a two-hour mass skate (p172) every Friday night. In winter, Museumplein's pond looks like the top of a wind-up jewellery box when it becomes a popular ice-skating rink.

➡**Street Life** Check out new openings on Overtoom or Jan Pieter Heijestraat (p168).

➡**Boating Life** Take a canoe out on the 'Amsterdam Amazon' down south in Amsterdamse Bos (p158).

Getting There & Away

➡**Tram** Trams 2 and 5 from Centraal Station stop at Museumplein and the main entrance to the Vondelpark; tram 2 travels along the southern side of the park along Willemsparkweg. Trams 3 and 12 cross the 1e Constantijn Huygensstraat bridge not far from the park's main entrance, and cross Kinkerstraat near De Hallen. Tram 1 from Centraal travels along Overtoom near the park's western edge.

➡**Bus** Bus 197 zips to Museumplein from the airport in about 30 minutes, which is handy if you're staying in the neighbourhood.

TOP SIGHT
RIJKSMUSEUM

The Rijksmuseum is a magnificent repository of art, its restaurant has a Michelin star *and* it's the only museum with a cycle lane through its centre. It was conceived to hold several national and royal collections, which occupy 1.5km of gallery space and 80 rooms.

The Layout

The museum is spread over four levels, from Floor 0 (where the main atrium is) to Floor 3. The collection is huge. You can see the highlights in a couple of hours, but you may want to allocate much longer.

Pick up a floor plan from the information desk by the entrance. Galleries are well marked; each room displays the gallery's number and theme. The 1st floor is split into two sides by the atrium, with separate access on either side.

Floor 2: 1600–1700

It's best to start your visit on the 2nd floor, which contains the highlights of the collection, with its Golden Age masterpieces, in the Gallery of Honour. It's a bit convoluted to reach, but well signposted.

Frans Hals

The first room displays several paintings by Frans Hals, who painted with broad brushstrokes and a fluidity that was unique at the time, and inspired later artists including the Impressionists. *The Merry Drinker* (1628–30) shows his seemingly loose style, which built up a personable portrait with layers of colour; the drinker is strikingly realistic and animated.

Jan Vermeer & Dutch Interiors

The next room contains beautiful works by Vermeer, with intimate domestic scenes, glimpses into private life, rendered in almost photographic detail. Check out the dreamy *Kitchen Maid* (1660). See the holes in the wall? The nail with shadow? In *Woman in Blue Reading a Letter* (1663) Vermeer shows only parts of objects, such as the tables, chairs and map, leaving the viewer to figure out the rest. Pieter de Hooch, Vermeer's contemporary, also depicts everyday life, with subjects such as the intimate quiet of *A Mother Delousing her Child* (1658), also called *A Mother's Duty*.

Jan Steen

Another Jan hangs across the hall from Vermeer. Jan Steen became renowned for painting chaotic households to convey moral teachings, such as *The Merry Family* (1668). None of the drunken adults notice the little boy sneaking a taste of wine, and an inscription translates as 'As the old sing, so shall the young twitter'. Steen's images made quite an impression: in the 18th century the expression 'a Jan Steen household' entered the local lexicon to mean a crazy state of affairs.

Rembrandt

Moving on, you'll reach several wonderful works by Rembrandt, including his resigned, unflinching self portrait as the Apostle Paul. *The Jewish Bride* (1665), showing a couple's intimate caress, impressed Van Gogh, who declared he would give up a decade of his life just to sit before the painting for a fortnight with only a crust of bread to eat. Rembrandt's gigantic *The Night Watch* (1642) is the rock star of the Rijksmuseum, with perennial crowds in front of it. The work is titled *Archers under the Command of Captain Frans Banning Cocq*,

DON'T MISS

→ *The Night Watch* by Rembrandt
→ *The Merry Drinker* by Hals
→ *Kitchen Maid* by Vermeer
→ *A Mother's Duty* by De Hooch
→ Delftware pottery
→ Dollhouses
→ Michelin-starred restaurant

PRACTICALITIES

→ National Museum
→ Map p312, H4
→ ☏020-674 70 00
→ www.rijksmuseum.nl
→ Museumstraat 1
→ adult/child €17.50/ free, audio guide €5
→ ⊙9am-5pm
→ 🚊2/5 Rijksmuseum

QUEUES & TICKETS

Entrance queues can be long. Friday, Saturday and Sunday are the busiest days. It's least crowded before 10am and after 3pm. Buy your ticket online to save time. While you still must wait in the outdoor queue, once inside you can proceed straight into the museum (otherwise you must stand in another queue to pay). Museumkaart owners get the same privilege; I Amsterdam Card holders do not (the card provides a small discount, but not free admission).

Download the museum's free app (there's free wi-fi at the museum). It either offers a guided tour, or you can select works by number. There's also a family tour available.

AIRPORT ART

The Rijksmuseum has a free mini-branch at Schiphol airport that hangs eight to 10 stellar Golden Age paintings. It's located after passport control between the E and F Piers, and is open from 7am to 8pm daily.

and *The Night Watch* name was bestowed years later, thanks to a layer of grime that gave the impression it was a scene after dark. It's since been restored to its original colours, complete with sunbeams through the windows. It was once larger than today, but had been cut down to fit a previous location.

Delftware & Dollhouses

Intriguing Golden Age swag fills the rooms on either side of the Gallery of Honour. Delftware was the Dutch attempt to reproduce Chinese porcelain in the late 1600s; Gallery 2.22 displays scads of the delicate blue-and-white pottery. Gallery 2.20 is devoted to mind-blowing dollhouses. Merchant's wife Petronella Oortman employed carpenters, glassblowers and silversmiths to make the 700 items inside her dollhouse.

Cupyers Library

There's something Escher-like about this towering book-lined space, one of the world's finest art libraries: view it from the balcony on Floor 2.

Floor 1: 1700–1900

Highlights on Floor 1 include the *Battle of Waterloo,* the Rijksmuseum's largest painting (in Gallery 1.12), taking up almost an entire wall. Three Van Gogh paintings hang in Gallery 1.18. Gallery 1.16 re-creates a gilded, 18th-century canal house room.

Floor 0: 1100–1600

This floor is packed with fascinating curiosities. The Special Collections have sections including magic lanterns, armoury and Dutch status symbols from previous eras, such as musical instruments and silver miniatures. Early gems include works by Dürer and Charles V's cutlery. The serene Asian Pavilion, a separate structure that's often devoid of crowds, holds first-rate artworks from China, Indonesia, Japan, India, Thailand and Vietnam.

Floor 3: 1900–2000

The uppermost floor has a limited, but interesting, collection. It includes avant-garde, childlike paintings by Karel Appel, Constant Nieuwenhuys and their CoBrA compadres (a post WWII movement) and cool furnishings by Dutch designers, such as Gerrit Rietveld and Michel de Klerk. There's also a Nazi chess set, and an unsettling wall of Nias islanders' facial casts, dating from 1910.

Facade & Gardens

Pierre Cuypers designed the 1885 building. Check out the exterior, which mixes neo-Gothic and Dutch Renaissance styles. The museum's gardens – aka the 'outdoor gallery' – host big-name sculpture exhibitions at least once a year. You can stroll for free amid the roses, hedges, fountains and a cool greenhouse.

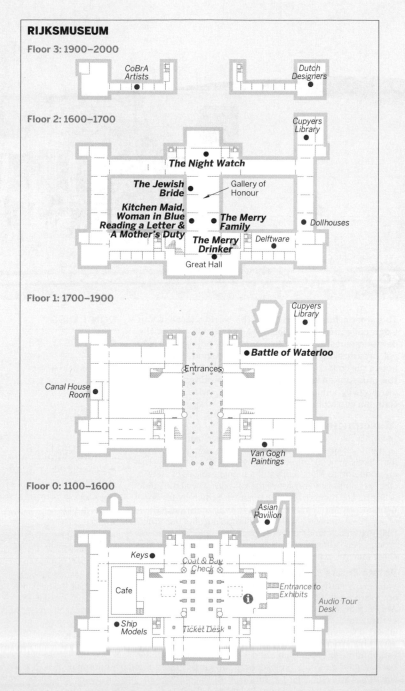

RIJKSMUSEUM

Floor 3: 1900–2000

CoBrA Artists

Dutch Designers

Floor 2: 1600–1700

Cupyers Library

The Night Watch

The Jewish Bride

Gallery of Honour

Kitchen Maid, Woman in Blue Reading a Letter & A Mother's Duty

The Merry Family

Dollhouses

The Merry Drinker

Delftware

Great Hall

Floor 1: 1700–1900

Cupyers Library

•**Battle of Waterloo**

Entrances

Canal House Room

Van Gogh Paintings

Floor 0: 1100–1600

Asian Pavilion

Keys•

Coal & Bag Check

Cafe

Entrance to Exhibits

Audio Tour Desk

•Ship Models

Ticket Desk

TOP SIGHT
VAN GOGH MUSEUM

This wonderful museum holds the world's largest Van Gogh collection. It's a poignant experience to see the perma-queues outside, then trace the painter's tragic yet breathtakingly productive life. Opened in 1973 to house the collection of Vincent's younger brother, Theo, the museum comprises some 200 paintings and 500 drawings by Vincent and his contemporaries, including Gauguin and Monet.

Museum Setup & Highlights

In 2015 a swish new extension and entrance hall added 800 sq metres of space to the museum, which now spreads over four levels, moving chronologically from Floor 0 (aka the ground floor) to Floor 3. It's still a manageable size; allow a couple of hours or so to browse the galleries. The audio guide is helpful and there's a separate version for children. It's fascinating to see Van Gogh's evolution from his early depictions of sombre countryfolk in the Netherlands to his pulsating, swirling French landscapes. The paintings tend to be moved around, depending on the current exhibition theme (say, Van Gogh's images of nature). Seminal works to look for:

Potato Eaters & Skeleton with Burning Cigarette

Van Gogh's earliest works – showing raw, if unrefined, talent – are from his time in the Dutch countryside and in Antwerp between 1883 and 1885. He painted peasant life, exalting their existence in works such as *The Potato Eaters* (1885). The symbolic *Still Life with Bible* (1885), painted after his father's death, shows a burnt-out candle, his Protestant minister father's bible and a much-thumbed smaller book, *La Joi de Vivre,* representing Van Gogh's more secular philosophy. *Skeleton with Burning Cigarette* (1886) – the print all the stoners are buying in the gift shop – was painted when Van Gogh was a student at Antwerp's Royal Academy of Fine Arts.

DON'T MISS

➜ *The Potato Eaters*
➜ *The Yellow House*
➜ *Wheatfield with Crows*
➜ *Sunflowers*
➜ *Skeleton with Burning Cigarette*

PRACTICALITIES

➜ Map p312, G5
➜ ☎020-570 52 00
➜ www.vangogh museum.com
➜ Museumplein 6
➜ adult/child €17/free, audio guide €5/3
➜ ⏰9am-7pm Sun-Thu, to 9pm Sat mid-Jul–Aug, to 6pm Sat-Thu Sep–mid-Jul, to 5pm Jan-Mar, to 10pm Fri
➜ 🚊2/3/5/12 Van Baerlestraat

Self-Portraits

In 1886 Van Gogh moved to Paris, where his brother Theo was working as an art dealer. Vincent began to paint multiple self-portraits as a way of improving his portraiture without paying for models, which he was too poor to afford. He met some of the Impressionists, and his palette began to brighten.

Sunflowers & the Yellow House

In 1888 Van Gogh left for Arles in Provence to paint its colourful landscapes and try to achieve his dream of creating an artists colony in the countryside. *Sunflowers* (1889) and other blossoms that shimmer with intense Mediterranean light are from this period. So is *The Yellow House* (1888), a rendering of the abode Van Gogh rented in Arles. The artist Paul Gauguin came to stay, but they quarrelled terribly. *The Bedroom* (1888) depicts Van Gogh's sleeping quarters at the house. In 1888 Van Gogh sliced off part of his ear during a bout of psychosis.

Wheatfield with Crows

Van Gogh had himself committed to an asylum in Saint-Rémy in 1889. While there his work became ever more extraordinary. His wildly expressive, yet tightly controlled landscapes are based on the surrounding countryside, with its cypress and olive trees. This period includes the sinuous, pulsating *Irises*. In 1890 he went north to Auvers-sur-Oise. One of his last paintings, *Wheatfield with Crows* (1890), is particularly menacing and ominous, and was finished shortly before his suicide.

Extras

The museum has multiple listening stations for diverse recordings of Van Gogh's letters, mainly to and from his closest brother Theo, who championed his work. The museum has categorised all of Van Gogh's letters online at www.vangoghletters.org. There are daily workshops (for adults and kids) where, suitably inspired, you can create your own works of art.

Other Artists

Thanks to Theo van Gogh's prescient collecting and that of the museum's curators, you'll also see works by Vincent's contemporaries, including Gauguin, Monet and Henri de Toulouse-Lautrec. In addition, paintings by Van Gogh's precursors, such as Jean-François Millet and Gustave Courbet, pepper the galleries, as do works by artists Van Gogh influenced.

Exhibition Wing

Gerrit Rietveld, the influential Dutch architect, designed the museum's main building. Behind it, reaching towards the Museumplein, is a separate wing (opened in 1999) designed by Kisho Kurokawa and commonly referred to as 'the Mussel'. It hosts temporary exhibitions by big-name artists.

QUEUES & TICKETS

Entrance queues can be long, as the number of visitors is limited. Try waiting until after 3pm. Holland Pass and I Amsterdam card holders get free entry, but have to queue with the rest. E-ticket ticket holders and Museumkaart owners fare the best, entering through the separate group entrance. E-tickets are available online or at tourist information offices, with no surcharge. Printed or digital tickets are accepted.

Van Gogh sold only one painting during his lifetime (*Red Vineyard at Arles*). It hangs at Moscow's Pushkin Museum.

FRIDAY NIGHTS

The museum stays open to 10pm on Friday, when it hosts special cultural events and opens a bar downstairs. There's usually live music or a DJ.

The museum's library (⏱10am-12.30pm & 1.30-5pm Mon-Fri) has a wealth of reference material – some 35,000 books and articles – for serious study.

 ## TOP SIGHT
STEDELIJK MUSEUM

POSTERIOR/SHUTTERSTOCK ©

This is an impressive, light, bright modern art museum, displaying artworks from its 90,000-strong collection dating from 1870 to the present day. The permanent collection rotates, but you're likely to see works by Monet, Picasso, Kandinsky, Matisse, Chagall, Warhol, Rothko, De Kooning and more. Temporary installations of the latest in contemporary art show in its newer wing.

Main Building: Matisse to Wonder Woman

AM Weissman designed the 1895 main building. On the ground floor you'll see all sorts of modern masterpieces: Henri Matisse cut-outs, Picasso abstracts, and a vivid collection of paintings by Dutch homeboys Piet Mondrian, Willem de Kooning, Charlie Toorop and Karel Appel. There's also usually an exhibition devoted to the art and design of De Stijl, with works by Mondrian and Lichtenstein.

Head upstairs, and the works become more modern, ranging from 1950 to the present. Here you might view anything from a film of the skin of a squid by Seth Price to a photography exhibition. Exhibits change regularly, so you never know what will be on hand, but count on it being offbeat and provocative.

The Bathtub: Mega Mod

The newer wing, aka 'the Bathtub' (you'll know why when you see it), opened in 2012. It houses temporary contemporary exhibitions. That smooth, white tub material, by the way, is called Twaron, a synthetic fibre that's five times as strong as steel and typically used in yacht hulls.

Families & Facilities

Kids will find inventive hands-on installations and other activities in the Family Lab.

The Stedelijk's library is a great resource, with catalogues, books, archive material, art magazines, and art and design documentaries, as well as wi-fi. Admission is free.

DON'T MISS

➡ Appel murals
➡ De Stijl exhibits
➡ Highlights tour
➡ Matisse
➡ Van Gogh

PRACTICALITIES

➡ Map p312, G5
➡ ☎020-573 29 11
➡ www.stedelijk.nl
➡ Museumplein 10
➡ adult/child €17.50/free
➡ ⏰10am-6pm Sat-Thu, to 10pm Fri
➡ 🚊2/3/5/12 Van Baerlestraat

BORISB17/SHUTTERSTOCK ©

TOP SIGHT
VONDELPARK

Amsterdam's favoured playground is the green lozenge-shaped expanse of Vondelpark, with its 47 hectares of lawns, ponds and winding paths receiving 12 million visitors a year. All of Amsterdam life is here: visitors, roller skaters, yummy mummies, kids and stoners. There's a constantly whizzing parade of bikes and on sunny day you can hardly move for picnics all around the grass.

It wasn't always so. Originally this was a private park, only open to the wealthy. Its sprawling, English-style gardens, with ponds, lawns, footbridges and footpaths, were laid out on marshland by architect Jan David Zocher and opened in 1865. Between 1875 and 1877, Zocher's son, Louis Paul Zocher, expanded the park to its current size.

It was known as Nieuwe Park (New Park), but in 1867 a statue of poet and playwright Joost van den Vondel (1587–1679) was created by sculptor Louis Royer. Amsterdammers began referring to the park as Vondelspark (Vondel's Park), which led to it being formally renamed. The rose garden, with some 70 different species, was added in 1936. Vondelpark was bought by the City Council in 1953, and finally opened to the public.

About a century after opening, the swampy location meant the park had actually sunk by 2m to 3m. After it was listed as a national monument in the mid-1990s, major renovations incorporated an extensive drainage system and refurbished walking and cycling paths, while retaining its historic appearance.

Near the eastern end, the 19th-century Italian Renaissance-style Vondelparkpaviljoen (p157) is now a cafe-bar, Vondelpark3. The park also shelters several other cafes, playgrounds and a wonderful open-air theatre, Openluchttheater (p169).

Art is strewn throughout the park, with 69 sculptures all up. Among them is Picasso's huge abstract work *Figuro degoupos l Casolla* (*The Bird*; 1965), better known locally as *The Fish*, which he donated for the park's centenary on the condition it always stayed here.

For bicycle rentals, MacBike (p29) is relatively close to the park's main entrance.

DON'T MISS

➡ Rose garden

➡ 't Blauwe Theehuis

➡ Picasso's *The Fish*

➡ Openluchttheater (Open-Air Theatre)

PRACTICALITIES

➡ Map p312, D5

➡ www.hetvondel park.net

➡ 🚊 2 Amstelveenseweg

👁 SIGHTS

VONDELPARK   PARK
See p157.

RIJKSMUSEUM   MUSEUM
See p151.

VAN GOGH MUSEUM   MUSEUM
See p154.

STEDELIJK MUSEUM   MUSEUM
See p156.

MUSEUMPLEIN   SQUARE
Map p312 (🚊2/3/5/12 Van Baerlestraat)
Amsterdam's most famous museums cluster around this public square, which has that Amsterdam essential: a skateboard ramp, as well as a playground, ice-skating pond (in winter) and 2m-high *I Amsterdam* sculpture (a favourite climbing structure/ photo op). Locals and tourists mill around, everyone picnics here when the weather warms up, and there are food and craft stalls on the third Sunday of the month. The space is also used for public concerts and special events.

Museumplein was laid out to host the World Exhibition in 1883, but gained its lasting title only when the Rijksmuseum opened two years later.

One of many facelifts raised a triangle of turf at the southern end, dubbed the 'ass's ear' for its shape; it's now a popular spot for sun worshippers. There's a large supermarket concealed below.

MOCO MUSEUM   MUSEUM
Map p312 (www.mocomuseum.com; Honthorststraat 20; adult/child under 16yr/under 6yr €12.50/7.50/free; ⊙10am-6pm; 🚊2/3/5/12 Van Baerlestraat) A private house, the 1904 Villa Alsberg has been converted into the 'Modern Contemporary' (Moco) museum by a couple who are private collectors and curators. The cramped rooms are not an ideal gallery space, but exhibitions on works by Banksy and Salvador Dalí haul in the crowds, and it's interesting to explore the building.

DIAMOND MUSEUM   MUSEUM
Map p312 (www.diamantmuseumamsterdam. nl; Paulus Potterstraat 8; adult/child €10/free; ⊙9am-5pm; 🚊2/5 Hobbemastraat) The extensive bling on display at the small, low-tech Diamond Museum is all clever re-creations.

You get a lot of background on the history of the trade and various historic sparkly crowns and jewels. Here you'll learn how Amsterdam was the globe's diamond trade epicentre for many centuries, where local Jews dominated the cutting and polishing business, and how the business moved to Antwerp after WWII following the decimation of the Jewish population here.

Those so inclined can save money by going next door to Coster Diamonds (p170) – the company owns the museum and is attached to it – and taking a free workshop tour, where you can see gem cutters and polishers doing their thing.

HOUSE OF BOLS   MUSEUM
Map p312 (www.houseofbols.com; Paulus Potterstraat 14; admission incl 1 cocktail €16.50, over 18yr only; ⊙1-6.30pm Sun-Thu, to 9pm Fri & Sat; 🚊2/5 Hobbemastraat) Cheesy but fun: here you undertake an hour's self-guided tour through this *jenever* (Dutch gin) museum. In the 'Hall of Taste' you'll try to differentiate different scents and flavours, while in the 'Distillery Room' you'll learn about the process of extraction. You'll learn more about the history of gin than you would think possible, and get to try shaking your own cocktail, plus drink a Bols confection of your choice at the end.

⭐AMSTERDAMSE BOS   PARK
(Amsterdam Forest; www.amsterdamsebos. nl; Bosbaanweg 5; ⊙park 24hr, visitors centre noon-5pm; 👶; 🚊170, 172) Amsterdam's forest is a vast swathe (roughly 1000 hectares) of almost countryside, 20 minutes by bike south of Vondelpark. It was planted in 1934 in order to provide employment during the Great Depression. Its lakes, woods and meadows are crisscrossed by paths and dotted with cafes. You can rent bicycles, feed baby goats in spring, take a horse-riding lesson, boat the rural-feeling waterways, see a play at the open-air theatre and ascend to the treetops in the climbing park.

It's a glorious place to go with kids, though best if you explore by bike due to its size. In the densest thickets you forget you're near a city at all (though you're right by Schiphol airport). A lot of locals use the park, but it rarely feels crowded. By bus from Centraal Station/Vondelpark takes about 40/25 minutes.

See the next page for a walking tour of Amsterdamse Bos.

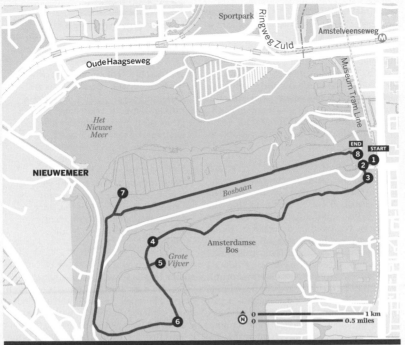

Neighbourhood Walk
Amsterdamse Bos

START VISITORS CENTRE
END DE BOSBAAN CAFE
LENGTH 3.5KM; TWO HOURS

Easy to escape to from the city, Amsterdamse Bos is a huge swathe of countryside, combining thick trees, meadows and waterways.

A good place to start is the ❶ **visitors centre** (p158) by the main entrance. It has some information on the park, and more importantly, you can buy a map (€2.50) to get your bearings. The best way to explore the park is by bike. If you don't have your wheels already, you can hire from the ❷ **bicycle rental kiosk** (p172) by the main entrance, which also has an incredibly child-friendly cafe. Likewise by the entrance is ❸ **Fun Forest** (p172), a tree-top climbing park for kids or adults.

From here head west for 2.5km and you'll come to the ❹ ~~open air theatre~~ (p170) it stages classic plays (in Dutch) throughout summer. Nearby at ❺ **Grote Vijver** you can rent canoes and kayaks (€6 per hour)

and pedal boats (€10 per hour) to explore what the owner calls the 'Amsterdam Amazon'. It may be an exaggeration but the waterway is surrounded by greenery on all sides and you'd never imagine that you're in the city.

About 0.75km south is the park's most delightful attraction: ❻ **De Ridammerhoeve** (p160), a working farm where you can meet goats, lambs, chickens, pigs, cows and horses. The cafeteria sells goat's-milk cheeses and ice cream, and there are workshops and even goat yoga if you're there on a Saturday or Sunday morning.

There are a couple of options for a meal after your park activities. A short distance from the theatre, on the northwest side of the Bosbaan (the long lake used for sculling), is ❼ **Boerderij Meerzicht** (p162), an old farmhouse that kids will adore, with its deer and peacock enclosure, plus diggers and climbing frames in the playground. Back by the park entrance, ❽ **De Bosbaan Cafe** (p165) is a lodge-like refuge with a great terrace overlooking the lake.

DE RIDAMMERHOEVE   FARM

(www.geitenboerderij.nl; Nieuwe Meerlaan 4; ⊙10am-5pm Wed-Mon; 🚊170, 172) FREE This organic working goat farm is a remarkable place in Amsterdamse Bos, where kids can feed bottles of milk to, well, kids (€8 for two bottles) in season; there are goat's cheese–making workshops, and you can even do goat yoga (€25) or regular Hatha yoga (€12.50). The cafeteria sells goat's milk smoothies and ice cream, as well as cheeses made on the premises.

COBRA MUSEUM   MUSEUM

(www.cobra-museum.nl; Sandbergplein 1; adult/child €9.50/6; ⊙11am-5pm Tue-Sun; 🚊170, 172, 🚊5 Binnehof) It's well worth making the effort to visit this out-of-the-way canal-side museum. The building designed by Dutch architect Wim Quist makes a light-flooded setting for work from the post-WWII CoBrA movement. Its members produced semi-abstract works known for their primitive, childlike qualities and the museum is full of boldly coloured, avant-garde paintings, ceramics and statues, including many by Karel Appel, the style's most famous practitioner. The charmingly surreal fountain outside is Appel's work.

Asger Jorn, Anton Rooskens, Corneille and Constant are among the other members. The CoBrA movement was active for just three years (1948–51). The art is less of a unified whole than a philosophy, inspired by Marxism, of using materials at hand to create paintings, sculpture and even poetry. Changing exhibits by contemporary artists are on show as well.

Buses arrive right by the museum. The tram stop puts you about a kilometre from the museum; follow the 'CoBrA' signs.

RIEKERMOLEN   WINDMILL

(www.molens.nl; Ⓜ RAI, 🚊4 RAI) Like a scene from another century, just outside Amstelpark's south edge, on the west bank of the Amstel river, stands this 1636 windmill. In a field southwest of the mill, you'll find a statue of a sitting Rembrandt, who sketched the windmill here along the riverbank.

AMSTELPARK   PARK

(Europaboulevard; ⊙8am-dusk; 🚾; Ⓜ RAI, 🚊4 RAI) Pastoral haven Amstelpark has particularly creative garden layouts and many different species of flowers – it was

LITTLE WOODCUTTER

Hidden up in the Leidsebosje parkland's closest tree to the pedestrian crossing on Stadhouderskade (where it intersects with Leidseplein) is an endearing surprise: the **Little Woodcutter** (Map p312; Leidsebosje; 🚊1/2/5 Leidseplein), a 50cm-high bronze sculpture of a little woodcutter leaning over and sawing a branch with both hands. The sculpture was installed in 1989, but the artist remains anonymous (rumours persist that it was commissioned by then-sovereign Queen Beatrix). The tree has since grown around the little woodcutter and now engulfs his shoes and saw.

originally created in 1972 for the bloombuster flower show, Floriade, which takes place all over the Netherlands every 10 years. The park has rose and rhododendron gardens that blaze with colour in season. As well as flower lovers, the park is surefire family territory, with a petting zoo, minigolf and a playground. In summer a miniature train chugs its way around the park.

Art exhibitions are held in the Glazen Huis (Glass House), the Orangerie and the Papillon Gallery.

ELECTRISCHE MUSEUMTRAMLIJN AMSTERDAM   MUSEUM

(Tram Museum Amsterdam; ☎020-673 75 38; www.museumtramlijn.org; Amstelveenseweg 264; return adult/child €5/3, tourist tram €7/4; ⊙11am-5pm Sun mid-Apr–Oct; 🚾; 🚊170, 172, 🚊16 Haarlemmermeer Station) Southwest of Vondelpark and just north of the Olympic Stadium is the former Haarlemmermeer Station. This handsome red-brick building is now the starting point for the tram museum, not a static experience but a chance to ride on a gleaming selection of historic European trams that run between here and Amstelveen. A return trip takes about 1¼ hours and skirts the large Amsterdamse Bos recreational area. There's also a tourist tram, which tours the city on Sunday July to September.

The tram departs two to three times per hour; see the website for details.

OLYMPIC STADIUM STADIUM

(☑020-305 44 00; www.olympischstadion. nl; Olympisch Stadion 21; tours per person €10; 🚊16/24 Olympisch Stadion) Built for the 1928 Olympic Games, this elegant stadium was designed by Jan Wils, a protégé of famous architect HP Berlage, and is functionalist in style. It has a soaring tower from which the Olympic flame burned for the first time during competition. Guided one-hour tours are available, but must be arranged in advance. It hosts occasional big-name gigs as well as sporting events.

Athletics Phanos organises a free long-distance run practice on the second Friday of the month.

✘ EATING

International options abound around Amstelveenseweg and inside De Hallen's Foodhallen. Head to Vondelpark's squats (p169) for organic vegan fare, and to the diverse restaurants along Overtoom and Jan Pieter Heijestraat. Treat yourself at Michelin-starred Rijks (p165).

★FOODHALLEN FOOD HALL €

Map p312 (www.foodhallen.nl; De Hallen, Hannie Dankbaar Passage 3; dishes €3-20; ⊙11am-11.30pm Sun-Thu, to 1am Fri & Sat; 🚾; 🚊17 Ten Katestraat) This glorious international food hall in soaring ex-tram sheds has food stands surrounding an airy open-plan eating area. Some are offshoots of popular Amsterdam eateries and breweries. Look out for Viet View Vietnamese street food and Jabugo Iberico Bar ham, and the Beer Bar, serving real ale tipples from local heroes 2 Chefs and Oedipus.

There's also a sit-down restaurant, the bright and breezy Kanarie Club (☑020-218 17 76; www.kanarieclub.nl; mains €3.50-20, 3-/4-course €32/39; ⊙noon-10pm; 🚾), with a kids' soft-play area.

★BRAAI BBQ BAR BARBECUE €

Map p312 (www.braaiamsterdam.nl; Schinkelhavenkade 1; dishes €6-12; ⊙4-9.30pm; 🚊1 Overtoomsesluis) Once a *haringhuis* (herring stand), this tiny place is now a street-food-style barbecue bar, with a great canal-side setting. Braai's speciality is marinated, barbecued ribs (half or full rack) and roasted sausages, but there are

veggie options too. Cards are preferred, but it accepts cash. Tables scatter under the trees alongside the water.

KINDERKOOKKAFÉ CAFE €

Map p312 (www.kinderkookkafe.nl; Vondelpark 6b; dishes €1-4; ⊙10am-5pm; 🚾; 🚊1 Overtoom) This 'Children Cook Cafe' is a great place to go with kids, right by the Vondelpark. This is topsy-turvy heaven, where your kids can cook for you. They can assemble pizza, croissants and cookies and then the kitchen will bake them for you, and there's indoor and outside seating (in a courtyard garden brightened by sunny murals).

DIGNITA VONDELPARK CAFE €

Map p312 (☑020-020 221 4458; www.eatwelldogood.nl; Koninginneweg 218; mains €10-14; ⊙8.30am-5pm; 🚊Amstelveenseweg) On the surface, this light, airy eatery looks like many other hipster brunch spots, but Dignita has socially worthwhile credentials too, with its profits being pumped into helping vulnerable individuals. The breakfast and brunches are delicious, offering everything from healthy smoothies to hearty mixed grills, plus plenty of tempting homemade cakes.

TOKO KOK KITA INDONESIAN €

Map p312 (☑020-670 29 33; www.kokkita.nl; Amstelveenseweg 166; mains €5-9; ⊙noon-8.30pm Tue-Sat, 5-8.30pm Sun; 🚊Amstelveenseweg) A humble Indonesian *toko* (shop) attracting queues for its authentic Indonesian dishes; diners choose either rice or noodles and then select their vegetables and meat from a pick-and-mix serving counter. Locals often top their meals off with a traditional spicy boiled egg.

ARTI CHOC SWEETS €

Map p312 (www.artichoc.nl; Koninginneweg 141; chocolates €1.50-4.50, ice cream per scoop €2; ⊙9.30am-6pm Tue-Fri, to 5pm Sat; 🚊2 Valeriusplein) Chocolate is almost too beautiful to eat at this luxury choc stop, with homemade pralines and truffles ready to melt in the mouth. There are over 50 kinds, including gluten-free, cocoa-free and lactose-free varieties. If you'd like something really unique, it also designs and makes custom chocolates, including clogs, tulips in all the blue clogs. In summer, it serves Monte Pelmo ice cream.

HOLY RAVIOLI
ITALIAN €

Map p312 (www.holyravioli.nl; Jan Pieter Heijestraat 88; mains €7-12; ⊘1-9pm Sun & Mon, 11am-9pm Tue-Sat; 🚊7/17 Jan Pieter Heijestraat) Pasta-maker Holy Ravioli supplies restaurants around town, but you can get ready-to-eat takeaway meals here (or, if you're lucky, snag a seat at its two tables). Delicious ravioli varieties include veal and sage with anchovy butter and wild spinach salad, and goat's cheese with orange, rucola (arugula) and Parmesan salad; or try the confit duck, black truffle and forest-mushroom lasagne.

SCALA DELLA PASTA
DELI €

Map p312 (www.scaladellapasta.nl; Valeriusstraat 90; dishes €5-16; ⊘9am-8pm Mon-Sat, 11am-8pm Sun; 🚊Emmastraat) A busy hub for hungry local foodies, this Italian deli-cafe proffers fantastic sandwiches, or can supply delicious picnic ingredients, such as Serrano ham, pastrami, sun-dried tomatoes, marinated artichokes and Spinata Romana salami, plus pizzas and pastas, heavenly tiramisu and Segafredo coffee. You can also buy wine by the bottle, and the ice cream passes the Italian taste test too.

BREAKFAST CLUB
CAFE €

Map p312 (www.thebreakfastclub.nl; Bellamystraat 2; dishes €5-13; ⊘8am-4pm Mon-Fri, to 5pm Sat & Sun; 🚊17 Ten Katestraat) For a hankering of breakfast any time of day, the laid-back Breakfast Club is perfect: Mexican breakfasts with *huevos rancheros* (spicy eggs); English-style, with homemade baked beans, bacon, eggs, mushrooms and sausages; or New York buttermilk pancakes with red fruits and honey butter. There are other tantalising pancake options too, plus cereals, avocado toast and other such first-world essentials.

IJSBOUTIQUE
ICE CREAM €

Map p312 (www.ijsboutique.nl; Johannes Verhulststraat 105; ice cream 1/2/3/4 scoops €1.60/4/5/5.50; ⊘noon-10pm; 🚊2 Cornelis Schuytstraat) In the upmarket shopping area around Cornelis Schuytstraat and Willemsparkweg, IJsboutique has fittingly sophisticated, seasonal ice-cream flavours, such as passion-fruit sorbet.

BOERDERIJ MEERZICHT
DUTCH €

(www.boerderijmeerzicht.nl; Koenenkade 56; pancakes €6-11; ⊘10am-7pm Tue-Sun Mar-Oct, to 6pm Fri-Sun Nov-Feb; 🚊170/172 Van

Nijenrodeweg) In Amsterdamse Bos (Amsterdam Forest), on the northwest side of the Bosbaan (the long lake used for sculling), this old farmhouse is a marvellously family-friendly restaurant, with an enclosure for peacocks and Bambi-esque deer: you can buy seeds to feed them. There's also a playground, with sandpits and diggers. Pancakes on the menu complete the child-heaven vibe.

ALCHEMIST GARDEN
VEGAN €

Map p312 (📞020-334 33 35; www.alchemistgarden.nl; Overtoom 409; dishes €4-13; ⊘8am-10pm Tue-Sat; 📱; 🚊1 Rhijnvis Feithstraat) 🌿 This bright, high-ceilinged cafe's food may be gluten-, lactose- and glucose-free, but it's tasty, with a health-rich, vitamin-filled organic menu (raw vegetable pies, avocado dumplings and pesto-stuffed portobello mushrooms), plus smoothies, juices and guilt-free treats like raw chocolate cake. Many ingredients are from the owner's own garden. Ask about wild-food foraging walks in the Vondelpark.

Tarot readings and hand chakra massages are available.

RENZO'S
ITALIAN €

Map p312 (📞020-673 16 73; www.renzosdelicatessen.nl; Van Baerlestraat 67; dishes per 100g €1.80-2.50, sandwiches €6; ⊘9am-9pm Mon-Fri, to 9pm Sat & Sun; 🚊3/5/12/16/24 Museumplein) Renzo's deli resembles an Italian *tavola calda* (hot table), where you can select ready-made dishes, hot or cold, such as meatballs, pasta or salads, plus thickly cut sandwiches and omelettes, including delicious cannoli (Sicilian 'little tubes', filled with ricotta cream). There are a few tables crammed into the space, or you can take away.

DEEGROLLERS
PIZZA €

Map p312 (📞020 221 20 98; Jan Pieter Heijestraat 10; pizzas €9-14; ⊘5-10pm; 🚊1 Jan Pieter Heijestraat) Serving authentic charred-crust Italian wood-fired pizza, with toppings including '5 formaggi' (mozzarella, buffalo mozzarella, *provola*, pecorino and Gorgonzola), 'Tartufo' (black truffle, rucola, cherry tomatoes and fresh basil), 'Diavola' (salami, olives, paprika and basil) and 'Carloforte' (tuna, cherry tomatoes and homemade pesto), Deegrollers has scrubbed heavywood tables, black-and-white tiling and warm mustard-yellow walls.

SAFFRAAN   DELI €

Map p312 (www.saffraantraiteur.nl; Jan Pieter Heijestraat 128; dishes €5-9; ⊘noon-9.30pm; 🚊1 Jan Pieter Heijestraat) An inviting deli-bistro that's all rustic bare boards under glittering chandeliers, where you can pick up or tuck into good-value gourmet sandwiches, burgers, pastas and soups. The deli counter almost groans under delicious-looking concoctions, and you can wash it all down with organic wine.

MECH MAKE & TAKE   SANDWICHES €

Map p312 (www.mech.nl; Willemsparkweg 152; dishes €5-7; ⊘8am-5pm Mon-Fri, 9am-5pm Sat; 🚊2 Cornelis Schuytstraat) This hip, red-brick cafe is especially good for upmarket sandwiches and baguettes with out-of-the-ordinary fillings, such as egg salad with truffle and crispy bacon. The long bench out the front is a prime spot to watch the action along Willemsparkweg and Cornelis Schuytstraat.

TOASTY   CAFE €

Map p312 (www.toasty.nl; Overtoom 437; toasties €3-7; ⊘8am-5pm Mon-Fri, 9am-5pm Sat & Sun; 🔊; 🚊1 Rhijnvis Feithstraat) Perfectly placed for a Vondelpark snack, this little place is devoted to toasties, and does them superbly well, with fillings including pastrami and mustard; pear and honey; brie, sun-dried tomato, rucola (arugula) and cranberry compote; and a terrific tuna melt, all on a choice of bread.

★ADAM   GASTRONOMY €€

Map p312 (🖉020-233 98 52; www.restaurant adam.nl; Overtoom 515; mains €21-23, 3-/4-/5-/6-course menus €37.50/45/52.50/60; ⊘6-10.30pm Tue-Sat; 🚊1 Overtoomsesluis) This seriously gourmet, chic and intimate restaurant serves exquisitely presented fare, such as veal check with lentils and bay sauce and *côte de bœuf* (on-the-bone rib steak) for two. Dessert is either a cheese platter or a chef's surprise. Paired wines are available for €7.50 per glass.

★DIKKE GRAAF   MEDITERRANEAN €€

Map p312 (🖉020-223 77 56; www.dikkegraaf.nl; Wilhelminastraat 153; mains €13-25; ⊘kitchen 3-10pm Wed-Sun; 🚊1 Rhijnvis Feithstraat) A local favourite, hung with industrial-styled copper lamps and with oriental wood tables, and opening to an olive-tree-ringed terrace. It's a truly fabulous spot for *borrel* (drinks),

with gin cocktails, by-the-glass wines and bar snacks, like oysters, bruschetta, charcuterie and Manchego sheep's cheese, and/or heartier, nightly changing meat, fish and pasta dishes.

★RON GASTROBAR   DUTCH €€

Map p312 (🖉020-496 19 43; www.rongastrobar. nl; Sophialaan 55; dishes €15; ⊘noon-2.30pm & 5.30-10.30pm; 🔊; 🚊2 Amstelveenseweg) Ron Blaauw ran his two-Michelin-star restaurant in these pared-down, spacious designer premises before turning it into a more affordable 'gastrobar' (still Michelin-starred), whereby you get the quality without the formality or the need to settle down for five courses. He serves around 25 gourmet tapas-style dishes, marrying surprising flavours such as foie gras, raspberry and yoghurt.

DE ITALIAAN   ITALIAN €€

Map p312 (🖉020-683 68 54; www.deitaliaan. com; Bosboom Toussaintstraat 29; mains €9-22; ⊘5.30-10pm; 🚊1 1e Constantijn Huygensstraat) With outdoor seating on leafy Bosboom Toussaintstraat, and a warm pop-art-orange interior, this contemporary restaurant serves sophisticated Italian dishes, such as ricotta and lemon-stuffed ravioli with pistachio pesto, and steak with olive oil and rocket, as well as magnificent wood-fired pizzas, including the house-speciality 'De Italiaan' – Gorgonzola, mushrooms, black truffle and rucola (arugula) – plus a gluten-free option.

SEAFOOD BAR   SEAFOOD €€

Map p312 (🖉020-670 83 55; www.theseafood bar.nl; Van Baerlestraat 5; mains €14-37; ⊘noon-10pm; 🚻; 🚊2/5 Van Baerlestraat) White-tiled and exposed-brick walls give this thronged seafood specialist a fresh, urban feel, and counter as well as table seating makes it a good choice for lone(ly) diners. Oysters, crabs, lobster and lemon sole are laid out behind glass, and the kitchen turns out a mean, crispy fish and chips. No bookings required but you may have to wait for a table.

WG CAFE   CAFE €€

Map p312 (🖉020-689 56 00; Marius van Bouwdijk Bastiaansestraat 55; dishes €6-16; ⊘10am-1am Sun-Thu, to 3am Fri & Sat; 🚻; 🚊1 Overtoom) On a little square and attached to the fringe Amsterdam Theater House just off

Overtoom, this is a laid-back local favourite for a drink or a bite to eat. The quiet off-road location makes it a good choice with kids, and food is simple, such as burgers or tuna melts.

VAN 'T SPIT ROTISSERIE €€

Map p312 (www.vantspit.nl; De Clercqstraat 95; half/whole chicken €10.50/21; ⏰kitchen 5-10pm, bar to 1am; 🚊12/13/14 Willem de Zwijgerlaan) At stripped-back Van 't Spit it's all about roast chicken, with piles of wood ready to fire up the rotisserie. Choices are simple – select from a half or whole chicken (there are no other mains), and decide if you want sides (corn on the cob, fries, salad and home-made coleslaw).

CARTER BISTRO €€

Map p312 (☏020-752 68 55; www.barcarter.nl; Valeriusstraat 85; mains lunch €6-20, dinner €16-21; ⏰4-11pm Mon-Fri, 11am-11pm Sat & Sun; 🚸; 🚊16 Emmastraat) In the swanky residential neighbourhood the Old South, Carter has a split-level dining space with black banquettes, art and photography covering the walls, and a lovely street-side terrace. The kitchen is impressive, with dishes like deep-fried whitebait with wasabi mayo, lobster *bitterballen* (croquettes) with lemon tarragon sauce, a truffle Wagyu burger, rib-eye steak with rose and pepper sauce, and lemongrass crème brûlée.

Its three-course kids menu (€16) comes with vegetable chips with tomato mayo, a make-your-own hot dog and an Oreo milkshake for dessert.

ZUS & ZUS BISTRO €€

Map p312 (☏020-616 58 25; www.restaurant zusenzus.nl; Overtoom 548; lunch €5-10, mains €15-20; ⏰noon-10pm Mon-Sat, 3-10pm Sun; 🚊1 Overtoomsesluis) Low-key Zus & Zus (Sister & Sister) is a great place to pop in for a fancy sandwich or soup for lunch, while in the evening it's bistro-style dishes like steak or tagliatelle with mussels, all served in a contemporary red-, orange- and yellow-trimmed dining space. It's fantastic value given the quality; service couldn't be friendlier.

GEORGE BISTRO BISTRO BISTRO €€

Map p312 (www.cafegeorge.nl; Valeriusplein 2; mains €8-20; ⏰11.30am-11pm Mon-Fri, 10am-11pm Sat & Sun; 🚊2 Valeriusplein) So good they named it twice, this French-style bistro has large windows, wooden chairs and a

buzzy atmosphere. George's classics include whole charcoal-grilled lobster with garlic butter and lemon, and eight different burgers (including halloumi, tuna with wasabi mayo, and smoked bacon and cheese) on toasted brioche buns. Breakfast is served on weekends from 10am to 12.30pm.

L'ENTRECÔTE ET LES DAMES FRENCH €€

Map p312 (☏020-679 88 88; www.entrecote-et-les-dames.nl; Van Baerlestraat 47-49; lunch mains €13.50, 2-course dinner menu €24.50; ⏰noon-3pm & 5.30-10pm; 🚊16/24 Museumplein) With a double-height wall made from wooden drawers and a wrought-iron balcony, this restaurant has a simple menu of steak or fish: plump for the *entrecôte* (premium beef steak), and save room for scrumptious desserts: perhaps chocolate mousse, *tarte au citron* (lemon tart) or *crêpes au Grand Marnier*.

NARBONNE BISTRO €€

Map p312 (☏020-618 42 63; www.narbonne. nl; Bosboom Toussaintstraat 28; mains €7-13; ⏰5.30-11pm Tue-Sun; 🚊1 1e Constantijn Huygensstraat) Neighbourhood favourite Narbonne offers a mix of well-executed Mediterranean tapas, with dishes to share including smoked mozzarella tortellini, fried Manchego sheep's cheese, marinated artichokes, prawns in filo pastry, fresh oysters with lime and chive dressing, green-olive tapenade with crusty bread, and grilled beef skewers. Book ahead.

RESTAURANT DE KNIJP FRENCH €€

Map p312 (☏020-671 42 48; www.deknijp.nl; Van Baerlestraat 134; mains €18-27; ⏰5.30pm-12.30am; 🚊3/5/12/16/24 Museumplein) A dark-wood eatery close to Amsterdam's museum district, this evening-only French-influenced place offers meaty classics, such as snails in creamy garlic sauce, as well as more out-there choices, including deer carpaccio. The tables on two levels tend to fill up when there's a show at the nearby Concertgebouw, and it's one of the few local places to serve food late.

BRASSERIE DE JOFFERS BRASSERIE €€

Map p312 (☏020-673 03 60; www.brasseriede joffers.nl; Willemsparkweg 163; mains €15-22; ⏰8am-10pm Mon-Sat, 9am-8pm Sun; 🚸; 🚊2 Cornelis Schuytstraat) Near the Vondelpark, this restaurant has a shaded terrace that entices you to sit nursing a drink in the sunshine, a timber and curved-glass shopfront and an interior that's all uphol-stered banquettes and old-school art deco charm. The food is up to scratch too, with salads, hamburgers and a great range of sandwiches stuffed with fillings, such as spicy beef or avocado.

PASTIS
FRENCH €€

Map p312 (⌀020-616 61 66; www.pastis amsterdam.nl; 1e Constantijn Huygensstraat 15; mains €12-24; ☺kitchen 4-10.30pm Mon-Fri, 3-10.30pm Sat & Sun; ☐1 1e Constantijn Huygensstraat) The red awning, pavement tables, rustic interior, bottle-lined walls and char-cuterie: immerse yourself in a corner of France, with house-made pâté, steak tar-tare, confit of chicken or beef shoulder with Parmesan and truffle *frites* (fries) – and, of course, some of that anise-flavoured spirit.

CAFÉ TOUSSAINT
BISTRO €€

Map p312 (⌀020-685 07 37; www.cafe-toussaint. nl; Bosboom Toussaintstraat 26; lunch dishes €7-14, dinner €10-21; ☺kitchen 10am-11pm; ☐; ☐1 1e Constantijn Huygensstraat) An enchant-ingly pretty place to stop for eats, this casual neighbourhood gem feels like it's straight out of an Edith Piaf song. Come to sip cappuccino under the trees, or in the candlelit evenings for delicious creations, such as poussin with fries, aïoli and apple-apricot compote or ravioli with red beets and burrata, hazelnut butter, hazelnuts and pecorino.

FONDUE & FONDUE
SWISS €€

Map p312 (⌀020-612 91 04; www.restaurant fondue.nl; Overtoom 415; 3-course menu €26.50; ☺kitchen 6-11pm; ☐1 Rhijnvis Feithstraat) White-tiled and exposed brick, this reason-ably priced restaurant serves silky Alpine fondues, with a choice of fish (tuna, salmon and prawns), meat (veal, steak, chicken and pork) or classic cheese (with six different vegetables), all shared between two people. Desserts include a molten chocolate fondue.

ROC ELEMENTS
INTERNATIONAL €€

Map p312 (⌀020-579 17 17; www.heerlijk amsterdam.nl; Roelof Hartstraat 6-8; lunch €10, 3-course dinner menu €20; ☺11.30am-12.30pm, dinner from 6pm; ☐3/5/12/24 Roelof Hartplein) Students of hospitality and gastronomy – the same ones who run the nearby College Hotel (p221) prepare and serve up contem-porary international dishes at this mini-malist-chic mod restaurant. The result is

white-glove service at an excellent price. Reserve in advance. No credit cards.

SAMA SEBO
INDONESIAN €€

Map p312 (⌀020-662 81 46; www.samasebo. nl; PC Hooftstraat 27; lunch €18, dinner rijsttafel per person €31.50; ☺noon-3pm & 5-10pm Mon-Sat; ☐2/5 Hobbemastraat) Cosy Sama Sebo resembles a brown cafe rather than a South Sea joint, but the food is authentic enough to be a trip for your taste buds. The rijst-tafel (Indonesian banquet) is a lavish 17 dishes, but you can get individual plates if that's too much.

DE BOSBAAN CAFE
CAFE €€

(www.debosbaan.nl; Bosbaan 4; mains €7-24; ☺10am-9pm; ☐170, 172) Located in Amster-damse Bos (Amsterdam Forest) near the entrance, De Bosbaan Cafe is a grand lodge-like refuge for coffee or meals. Its terrace overlooks the lake, so it's a perfect viewpoint for watching the rowers on a sunny afternoon.

LA FALOTE
DUTCH €€

Map p312 (⌀020-662 54 54; www.lafalote.nl; Roelof Hartstraat 26; mains €15-25; ☺1.30-9pm Mon-Sat; ☐3/5/24 Roelof Hartplein) Snug little La Falote, with its chequered table-cloths, focuses on daily changing Dutch home-style dishes, such as calf liver, meat-balls with endives, or stewed fish with beets and mustard sauce. The prices are a bargain in an otherwise ritzy neighbour-hood; and wait till the owner brings out the accordion.

LALIBELA
ETHIOPIAN €€

Map p312 (⌀020-683 83 32; www.lalibela.nl; 1e Helmersstraat 249; mains €11-17; ☺5-11pm; ☐☐; ☐1 Jan Pieter Heijestraat) Named after the ancient African city, this small and colour-ful restaurant feels like you're somewhere else. It was the Netherlands' first Ethio-pian restaurant and it's still a cracker. Sip Ethiopian beer from a half-gourd and eat rich stews, egg and vegetable dishes served with *injera* (slightly sour, spongy pancakes) instead of utensils to a soundtrack of Afri-can music.

★RIJKS
INTERNATIONAL €€€

Map p312 (⌀020-674 75 55; www.rijks restaurant.nl; Rijkmuseum; 3-76 courses €37.50/67.50; ☺11.30am-3pm daily, 5-10pm Mon-Sat; ☐2/5 Rijksmuseum) In a beautiful

DE HALLEN CULTURAL CENTRE

These red-brick 1902-built tram sheds were formerly used as a squat before being turned into this breathtaking sky-lit space (Map p312; www.dehallen-amsterdam.nl; Bellamyplein 51; ☐17 Ten Katestraat). De Hallen was stunningly converted in 2014 to create a cultural complex incorporating a food hall and family-friendly brasserie (p161), library, design shops – such as Local Goods Store (p170) and the Denim City Store (p170) – a bike seller/repairer (p170), a cinema (p169) and a hotel (p224).

Regular events held inside include themed weekend markets (such as organic produce or Dutch design); check www.localgoodsmarkets.nl to find out what's happening.

A lively street market, Ten Katemarkt (p171), takes place outside every day except Sunday.

space with huge windows and high ceilings, part of the Rijksmuseum, Rijks was awarded a Michelin star in 2016. Chef Joris Bijdendijk uses locally sourced ingredients, adheres to Slow Food ethics and draws on historic Dutch influences for his creative, highly imaginative cuisine. For lunch or dinner you can choose a set menu or à la carte.

Dishes include scallops with oyster cream or braised beef cheek with roasted onion.

MOER   INTERNATIONAL €€€

Map p312 (☑020-820 33 30; Amstelveenseweg 7; dishes €9-20; ◎noon-10pm; ☑; ☐Overtoom) Attached to the Tire Station hotel, Moer has a plate-glass wall onto the street, artful moss and green credentials – the ceiling is insulated by plants and heating is channelled from the kitchen. Chefs Dirk Mooren and Cas van de Pol cook up a storm in the open kitchen, serving largely organic and sustainable food with lots of vegetarian choices.

The lunch menu includes open sandwiches, while there is a chef's menu at dinner.

BLUE PEPPER   INDONESIAN €€€

Map p312 (☑020-489 70 39; www.restaurant bluepepper.com; Nassaukade 366; rijsttafel per person €57-65; ◎6-10pm; ☑; ☐7/10 Raamplein) This is one of Amsterdam's finest gourmet Indonesian restaurants, where Chef Sonja Pereira serves beautifully presented work-of-art Indonesian cuisine in an intimate white-walled dining room. The rijsttafel (Indonesian banquet) includes specialities from across the islands, such as wild

scallops with saffron, orange, sea greens and macadamia nuts, or venison with sambal goreng of laos, ginger and sweet pepper.

Candlelit dinner cruises are also available on a vintage boat (€120).

RESTAURANT BLAUW   INDONESIAN €€€

Map p312 (☑020-675 50 00; www.restaurant blauw.nl; Amstelveenseweg 158; mains €22-29, rijsttafel per person €27-33; ◎6-10.30pm Mon-Fri, 5-10.30pm Sat & Sun; ☐2 Amstelveenseweg) Blauw is always busy – reserve ahead. The *New York Times* voted it the 'best Indonesian restaurant in the Netherlands' and legions agree. Menu standouts include *ikan pesmol* (fried fish with candlenut sauce) and *ayam singgand* (chicken in semi-spicy coconut sauce with turmeric leaf) and mouthwatering Indonesian desserts.

☻ DRINKING & NIGHTLIFE

There are plenty of cool bars and beer specialists around Vondelpark, plus club nights at former squats.

★EDEL   BAR

Map p312 (www.edelamsterdam.nl; Postjesweg 1; ◎10am-1am Sun-Thu, to 3am Fri & Sat; ☐7/17 Kinkerstraat) Edel on Het Sieraard's waterfront has lots of waterside seating as it's at the sweet spot where two canals cross. Inside and out it's draped with creative types who work in the local buildings. With hipster staff and creative food on offer, its blonde-wood interior comes into its own in summer, lit by a canopy of twinkling fairy lights after dark.

★**LOT SIXTY ONE**   COFFEE

Map p312 (www.lotsixtyonecoffee.com; Kinker-straat 112; ☺8am-5pm Mon-Fri, 9am-5pm Sat, 10am-5pm Sun; 🚊3/12 Bilderdijkstraat) 🖉
Look downstairs to the open cellar to see (and better still, smell) fresh coffee beans being roasted at this streetwise spot. Beans are sourced from individual ecofriendly farms; varieties include chocolate-orange Fivr from Brazil, citrussy Kii from Kenya and toffee stonefruit Bombora. All coffees are double shots (unless you specify other-wise); watch Kinkerstraat's passing parade from benches at the front. You can also buy bags of beans to take away.

DE VONDELTUIN   BAR

Map p312 (www.vondeltuin.nl; Vondelpark 7; ☺from 10am-closing hours vary; 🚊2 Amstelveenseweg) Inside the Vondelpark, at its western edge, is this laid-back, hippyish-feeling bar-cafe and beer garden. Drink amid greenery in this cheery corner, with beer and snacks on the menu, and space for kids to play.

BUTCHER'S TEARS   BREWERY

(www.butchers-tears.com; Karperweg 45; ☺4-9pm Wed-Sun; 🚊16 Haarlemmermeersta-tion) In-the-know hop heads like to go straight to the source of cult brewsters Butcher's Tears. The brewery's artsy tap-room is tucked down an industrial alley, and offers myriad esoteric bottled beers, as well as six brews on tap. Look for Far Out (a saison) and Misery King (a triple-hopped amber ale).

DUTCH DRAFTS   BROWN CAFE

Map p312 (www.craftanddraft.nl; Overtoom 417; ☺bar 2pm-midnight Sun-Thu, to 2am Fri & Sat, shop 2-10pm daily; 🚊1 Rhijnvis Feithstraat) Craft-beer fans are spoilt for choice, with no fewer than 40 different beers on tap and a further 100 by the bottle. There are daily draught offerings, such as Belgian 3 Floyds' Lips of Faith, American Coronado's Stupid Stout and Evil Twin's Yang, British Red Willow's Thoughtless, Swedish Sigtuna's Organic Ale and Danish Mikkeller's Peter, Pale & Mary.

You can have a drink in the bar, or take a beer by tap parkwards in a *growler* (1L).

BARREA   BAR

Map p312 (☎020-789 52 09; Jan Pieter Heijestraat 137; ☺5pm-1am Tue-Thu, to 3am Fri & Sat; 🚊1 Jan Pieter Heijestraat) *Brå* means 'good' in Swed-ish and Norwegian, and this intimate hang-out lives up to its name. The mismatched, recycled furniture and industrial light fittings makes it feel more like a party in someone's apartment, with comfy vintage sofas and armchairs, and stools around the bar. There's a mini terrace at the front, but it's so popular it's usually standing-room only out there.

TUNES BAR   COCKTAIL BAR

Map p312 (www.conservatoriumhotel.com; Conservatorium Hotel, Van Baerlestraat 27; ☺12.30pm-1am Mon-Thu, to 2am Fri & Sat, to midnight Sun; 🚊2/3/5/12/16 Van Baerlestraat) A small but exceedingly sleek bar inside the stunning Conservatorium Hotel, this has a long transparent bar and wow-factor flower displays to admire while you sample one of its speciality G&Ts, such as a Gin Mare, with orange, basil and fevertree tonic, or Monkey 47, with elderflower and blackber-ries. There's also a fine cocktail list, with all drinks around the €20 mark.

CAFÉ BÉDIER   BROWN CAFE

Map p312 (☎020-662 44 15; Sophialaan 36; ☺noon-1am Mon-Thu, to 3am Fri, 11am-3am Sat, to 1am Sun; 🚊2 Amstelveenseweg) A post-work favourite, on a sunny evening, the ter-race out the front of Café Bédier is often so crowded it looks like a street party in full swing. Inside it also gets rammed; the leather-upholstered wall panels, modular seats and hardwood floors put a 21st-cen-tury twist on classic brown cafe decor. Top-notch bar food, too.

GOLDEN BROWN BAR   BAR

Map p312 (www.goldenbrownbar.nl; Jan Pieter Heijestraat 146; ☺11am-1am Mon-Thu, to 3am Fri & Sat; 🛜; 🚊1 Jan Pieter Heijestraat) This peren-nially hip, two-level bar with painted brickwork and cool colour palette attracts a young professional crowd that spills out onto the pavement. In winter, the cream-and-brown interior with its mod woodwork and neon-pink-lit bar offers a stylish respite from the chill, especially if you snag a seat on the faux-velvet couch.

WELLING   BROWN CAFE

Map p312 (www.cafewelling.nl; Jan Willem Brou-wersstraat 32; ☺4pm-1am Mon-Fri, 9pm-1am Sat & Sun; 🚊3/5/12/16/24 Museumplein) Tucked away behind the Concertgebouw (Concert

LOCAL KNOWLEDGE

JAN PIETER HEIJESTRAAT

One of the most happening-right-now streets in the 'hood is back-street artery Jan Pieter Heijestraat, which runs south from Kinkerstraat to Overtoom. Hip bars, great local restaurants and out-of-the-box shops continue to pop up here, thanks in large part to the street's proximity to the cultural and design complex De Hallen.

Hall), this wood-panelled lovely is a relaxed spot to sip a frothy, cold *biertje* (glass of beer) and mingle with intellectuals and artists. Don't be surprised if the cafe's friendly cat hops onto your lap. There's often live music, such as by jazz musicians after their gigs at the Concertgebouw.

HET GROOT MELKHUIS   CAFE

Map p312 (📞020-612 96 74; www.grootmelkhuis.nl; Vondelpark 2; ◷10am-5.30pm Wed-Sun; 🛜; 🚊1 Jan Pieter Heijestraat) This rambling Swiss-chalet-style timber house has a gingerbread look about it, at the edge of the Vondelpark forest. It's a regular cafe with coffees, beers, wine and light snacks. It's the go-to hang-out for families with kids, as it encompasses a playground with sandpits, diggers and so on, but there's deck seating by a swan-gliding pool as well.

In summer kids can do craft activities here in the afternoon (€5).

WILDSCHUT   CAFE

Map p312 (www.cafewildschut.nl; Roelof Hartplein 1; ◷9am-1am Mon-Fri, 10am-1am Sat & Sun; 🚊3/5/12/24 Roelof Hartplein) A fabulously unreconstructed vintage bar, this is a grand cafe that is a real gathering place for the Old South. When the weather's warm, pretty much everyone heads to the terrace for views of the Amsterdam School. When the weather's not great, soak up the atmosphere in the art deco interior.

'T BLAUWE THEEHUIS   CAFE

Map p312 (www.blauwetheehuis.nl; Vondelpark 5; ◷9am-10pm; 🛜; 🚊2 Jacob Obreachstraat) No, it's not a blue and white UFO cake stand landed in the park, this is the Vondelpark's most grown-up, fabulous and laid-back cafe. It's encircled by greenery, and in summer the terrace is packed with seemingly everyone in town enjoying coffee and cake or cocktails and dinner.

COLD PRESSED JUICERY   JUICE BAR

Map p312 (www.thecoldpressedjuicery.com; Willemsparkweg 8; ◷7.30am-7pm Mon-Fri, 9am-6pm Sat, 10am-6pm Sun; 🚊2 Cornelis Schuytstraat) 🍃 You'll be bursting with health after a cold-pressed, oxidant-free, all-natural juice, such as the Pro (apple, fennel, lemon, probiotic) or Glow (pineapple, strawberry, beetroot and ginger). Smoothies include Apple Crumble (apple, buckwheat granola, allspice and almond milk) and the Sinner (banana, caramel, coconut, vanilla, cinnamon and cashew milk). Some 99% of its ingredients are organic and, where viable, locally sourced.

CAFÉ SCHINKELHAVEN   BROWN CAFE

Map p312 (www.cafeschinkelhaven.nl; Amstelveenseweg 126; ◷11am-1am Sun-Thu, to 3am Fri & Sat; 🛜; 🚊2 Amstelveenseweg) Close to the Vondelpark, Café Schinkelhaven's hugely popular candle-topped terrace tables make an irresistible pit stop before heading along Amstelveenseweg in search of dinner. Super-friendly staff make you feel like a regular from the moment you arrive.

PLAN B   BAR

Map p312 (www.planbovertoom.nl; Overtoom 209; per hour €12.50; ◷4pm-1am Mon, 2pm-1am Tue-Thu, to 3am Fri, noon-3am Sat, to 1am Sun; 🚊1 Jan Pieter Heijestraat) If your Vondelpark football game's washed out, switch to Plan B and shoot some pool at this friendly hang-out, with 13 pool tables (and two dartboards) and a bar. It also hosts pool comps (beginners 7.30pm Monday, advanced players 7.30pm Thursday) and quiz nights from 7.30pm on Wednesdays.

☆ ENTERTAINMENT

★CONCERTGEBOUW   CLASSICAL MUSIC

Map p312 (Concert Hall; 📞020-671 83 45; www.concertgebouw.nl; Concertgebouwplein 10; ◷box office 1-7pm Mon-Fri, to 7pm Sat & Sun; 🚊3/5/12/16/24 Museumplein) The Concert Hall was built in 1888 by AL van Gendt, who managed to engineer its near-perfect acoustics. Bernard Haitink, former conductor of the Royal Concertgebouw Orchestra, remarked that the world-famous hall was the orchestra's best instrument. Free

VONDELPARK SQUATS

The Vondelpark and its surrounds have strong links to the cultural revolution, when Amsterdam became the *magisch centrum* (magic centre) of Europe. Hippies flocked to Amsterdam during the 1960s and '70s, a housing shortage saw speculators leaving buildings empty and squatting became widespread. The Dutch authorities turned the park into a temporary open-air dormitory. Although the sleeping bags are long gone today, an indie spirit persists.

Buried beneath the park's 1e Constantijn Huygensstraat bridge (you could take the tram straight over it or walk right past it and never know it was there) is the **Vondelbunker** (Map p312; www.vondelbunker.nl; Vondelpark 8a; ⊘hours vary; 🚃1 1e Constantijn Huygensstraat). A fallout shelter dating from 1947, it became Amsterdam's first youth centre in 1968 and a hotbed of counterculture creativity and activism. If the unmarked black metal doors are open, you might catch an underground gig, film or 'activist salon'.

Fringing the Vondelpark are several squats that have gone legit and been turned into alternative cultural centres:

OT301 (Map p312; www.ot301.nl; Overtoom 301; 🚃1 Jan Pieter Heijestraat) In the former Netherlands Film Academy, graffiti-covered ex-squat OT301 hosts an eclectic lineup of bands and DJs. There are two bars as well as the friendly vegan restaurant **De Peper** (🖉020-412 29 54; www.depeper.org; mains €7-10; ⊘6-8.30pm, bar to 1am Tue, Thu, Fri & Sun; 🖉), serving cheap, organic meals in a lovable dive-bar atmosphere. Sit at the communal table to connect with like-minded folk. Same-day reservations are required; call between 3 and 6.30pm.

OCCII (Map p312; 🖉020-671 77 78; www.occii.org; Amstelveenseweg 134; ⊘hours vary; 🖈; 🚃2 Amstelveenseweg) This former squat maintains a thriving alternative scene, and books underground bands, many from Amsterdam. It has a collectively run, no-frills restaurant **Eetcafé MKZ** (🖉020-679 07 12; www.veganamsterdam.org/mkz; 1e Schinkelstraat 16; mains from €5; ⊘from 7pm Tue & Thu-Sat; 🖉) serving vegan food. Call between 2.30pm and 6pm to reserve your spot.

half-hour concerts take place Wednesdays at 12.30pm from September to June; arrive early. Try the Last Minute Ticket Shop (www.lastminuteticketshop.nl) for half-price seats to all other performances.

Those aged 30 or younger can queue at the box office for €15 'Sprint' tickets 45 minutes prior to shows. All tickets include a free drink in the Concert Hall lobby. Guided tours (€10, 75 minutes) show that, in spite of Van Gendt's limited musical knowledge, he gave the two-tiered Grote Zaal (Main Hall) acoustics that are the envy of sound designers worldwide, along with a baroque trim, panels inscribed with the names of classical composers, a massive pipe organ and a grand staircase via which conductors and soloists descend to the stage.

FILMHALLEN CINEMA

Map p312 (www.filmhallen.nl; De Hallen, Hannie Dankbaar Passage 12; tickets adult/child from €11/7.50; ⊘10am-midnight; 🚃17 Ten Katestraat) Art-house films and new mainstream

releases run in both Dutch and English at this cinema inside De Hallen (p170). In the polished-concrete foyer, check out the vintage film-making equipment as well as the retro caravan selling popcorn and other snacks.

OPENLUCHTTHEATER THEATRE

Map p312 (Open-Air Theatre; www.openluchttheater.nl; Vondelpark 5a; ⊘May-mid-Sep; 🖈; 🚃1 1e Constantijn Huygensstraat) The Vondelpark's marvellous open-air theatre hosts free concerts in summer, with a laid-back, festival feel, as you might expect from Amsterdam's hippiest park. The program includes world music, dance, theatre and more. You can make a reservation (€5 per seat) on the website up to 1½ hours prior to showtime.

ORGELPARK CONCERT VENUE

Map p312 (🖉020-515 81 11; www.orgelpark.nl; Gerard Brandtstraat 26; tickets €12.50-20; 🚃1 Jan Pieter Heijestraat) A unique performance space for organ music, with four big organs in a lovely restored church on the edge of the Vondelpark. More than 100 events take place each year, including concerts of classical, jazz and improvised music.

AMSTERDAMSE BOS THEATRE   THEATRE
(www.bostheater.nl; Bosbaanweg 5; ⊗Jun-early Sep; 🚍170, 172) This large, open-air amphitheatre stages plays from Shakespeare to *The Gruffalo* in Dutch, as well as regular gigs. It's close to Schipol airport, and so actors pause for planes passing overhead.

🛍 SHOPPING

★**LOCAL GOODS STORE**   ARTS & CRAFTS
Map p312 (www.localgoodsstore.nl; De Hallen, Hannie Dankbaar Passage 39; ⊗noon-7pm Tue-Fri & Sun, 11am-7pm Sat; 🚍17 Ten Katestraat) As the name implies, everything at this concept shop inside De Hallen is created by Dutch designers, from skateboards and tasteful toys to I Made Gin gin production kits and Dutch-designed casual men's and women's fashion.

★**PIED À TERRE**   BOOKS
Map p312 (☎020-627 44 55; www.piedaterre. nl; Overtoom 135-137; ⊗1-6pm Mon, 10am-6pm Tue, Wed & Fri, to 9pm Thu, to 5pm Sat; 🚍1 1e Constantijn Huygensstraat) Travel lovers will be in heaven in the galleried, sky-lit interior of Europe's largest travel bookshop. If it's travel or outdoor-related, you can dream over it here: gorgeous globes, travel guides in multiple languages (especially English) and over 600,000 maps. Order a coffee and plan your next trip.

BEER BAUM   DRINKS
Map p312 (www.thebeertree.nl; Jan Pieter Heijestraat 148, ⊗noon-10pm Mon-Fri, 11am-10pm Sat & Sun; 🚍1 Jan Pieter Heijestraat) Beer Baum offers an enticing 250-plus craft beers from over 25 different countries, which are available cold from the fridge, making them perfect to take to the Vondelpark on a hot day, as well as four rotating beers on tap that can be bottled to take away cold, too.

GOOCHEM SPEELGOED   TOYS
Map p312 (www.goochem.nl; 1e Constantijn Huygensstraat 80; ⊗1-6pm Mon, 9.30am-6pm Tue-Sat, to 5.30pm Sat; 🚍1 1e Constantijn Huygensstraat) This multistorey toy shop has

been putting grins on small faces for over three decades. Overlooked by a huge stuffed giraffe, toys are arranged by children's age groups; there's a fine range of board games, musical instruments, dolls, costumes, tea sets, puzzles and super-soft cuddly toys.

JOHNNY AT THE SPOT   FASHION & ACCESSORIES
Map p312 (www.johnnyatthespot.com; Jan Pieter Heijstraat 94; ⊗1-6pm Mon, 11am-6pm Tue, Wed & Sat, to 7pm Thu & Fri, 1-5pm Sun; 🚍7/17 Jan Pieter Heijestraat) Cool concept store Johnny at the Spot fills several interconnected buildings with uber-hip men's and women's clothing, shoes and raincoats from all over the globe. Groovy homewares include everything from plants and soaps to bowls, vases, crockery and furniture.

VAN AVEZAATH BEUNE   FOOD & DRINKS
Map p312 (www.vanavezaath-beune.nl; Johannes Verhulststraat 98; ⊗8am-6pm; 🚍2 Cornelis Schuytstraat) Counter staff in serious black aprons box up chocolate *amsterdammertjes* (the bollards along city pavements) – a great gift, assuming you can keep from eating them yourself.

COSTER DIAMONDS   JEWELLERY
Map p312 (☎020-305 55 55; www.coster diamonds.com; Paulus Potterstraat 2; ⊗9am-5pm; 🚍2/5 Hobbemastraat) Founded in 1840, Coster is Europe's oldest working diamond factory. Watch the polishers at work – more interesting than the nearby Diamond Museum (p158).

DENIM CITY STORE   CLOTHING
Map p312 (☎020-820 86 14; www.denimcity.org; De Hallen, Hannie Dankbaarpassage 22; ⊗11am-7pm Wed-Fri, 10am-6pm Sat, noon-5pm Sun; 🚍17 Ten Katestraat) A huge store devoted to the blue stuff, with jeans by Levi, Koi, Lee, Japan Blue, Indigo People and many more. It also recycles denim into original pieces, so if you hand in old jeans for recycling you'll get 20% off a new pair.

GATHERSHOP   DESIGN
Map p312 (☎020-752 06 81; www.gathershop. nl; Hannie Dankbaarpassage 19; ⊗1-6pm Mon-Wed, 11am-7pm Thu-Fri, noon-6pm Sun; 🚍17 Ten Katestraat) The beautifully curated Gathershop is a gift buyer's dream, stocking handmade and fair-trade items from clothing to homewares. Between the carefully-arranged plants and cacti, which are also for sale, you'll discover delicate jewellery,

simple glazed ceramic cups, minimalist stationery and natural skincare products. The illustrated Amsterdam cards on sale make a perfect alternative to your standard city postcard.

MASHED CONCEPT STORE GIFTS & SOUVENIRS
Map p312 (✆06 4028 7335; www.mashed-concept-store.com; Jan Pieter Heijestraat 168; ◔noon-6pm Mon, 11am-6pm Tue-Wed, 11am-6.30pm Thu, 10am-6.30pm Fri, 10am-5.30pm Sat, noon-5pm Sun; ☐Jan Pieter Heijestraat) Natty fedoras hanging from stag antlers, quirky yet tasteful T-shirts, artsy jewellery, one-off-designed clothing: funk up your life at Mashed, a cool concept store selling trinkets and gifts.

NIKKIE FASHION & ACCESSORIES
Map p312 (www.nikkie.com; Willemsparkweg 175; ◔1-6pm Mon, 10am-6pm Tue-Sat, noon-5.30pm Sun; ☐2 Cornelis Schuytstraat) Amsterdam-based Nikkie Plessen was a familiar face on Dutch TV as an actress and presenter, but she's now swapped the screen for women's fashion design, establishing two boutiques in town and several others in the Netherlands. Street-smart collections run from red-leather twinsets to hole-punch dresses.

VLVT FASHION & ACCESSORIES
Map p312 (www.vlvt.nl; Cornelis Schuytstraat 22; ◔noon-6pm Mon, 10am-6pm Tue-Sat, noon-5pm Sun; ☐2 Cornelis Schuytstraat) Up-and-coming Dutch-designed fashion for women is stocked at this chic, light-filled boutique, including Dutch and international designers, all carefully curated and including labels for those in the know, such as Elisabetta Franchi, Pinko, Pierre Balmain and Furla of Zoe Karssen.

MANWOOD SHOES
Map p312 (www.manwood.nl; Willemsparkweg 173; ◔1-6pm Mon, 10am-6pm Tue-Sat, noon-5pm Sun; ☐2 Cornelis Schuytstraat) Dutch shoemaker Manwood sells stylish men's and women's footwear (boots, lace-ups, heels, ballerina flats, sneakers and slippers), including its own designs. It also stocks other Dutch designs and selected international labels, as well as scarves, belts, hats and bags.

TEN KATEMARKT MARKET
Map p312 (www.tenkatemarkt.nl; Ten Katestraat; ◔9am-5pm Mon-Sat; ☐17 Ten Katestraat) Outside food hall and cinema De Hallen, this

small yet thronged-daily street market has fresh fish, fruit and veg, wheels of Dutch cheeses, antipasti, nuts, spices, ready-to-eat snacks like steaming-hot *frites* (fries), fashion, fabrics, homewares and bike locks: almost everything you need for Amsterdam daily life.

RECYCLE SPORTS & OUTDOORS
Map p312 (✆020-489 70 29; www.recyclefietsen.nl; De Hallen, Hannie Dankbaar Passage 27; ◔9am-6pm Mon-Wed & Fri, to 9pm Thu, 10am-5pm Sat; ☐17 Ten Katestraat) In a warehouse-like space in De Hallen, ReCycle sells both new and secondhand bikes, carries out bike repairs and restores classic two-wheelers – and because a bikeless Amsterdammer would be an oxymoron, there's a free bike-rental service while you wait.

EDHA INTERIEUR HOMEWARES
Map p312 (www.edha-interieur.nl; Willemsparkweg 5-9; ◔10am-6pm Tue-Sat; ☐2/3/5/12 Van Baerlestraat) A sofa, kitchen unit or bathroom suite will be hard to squeeze into your carry-on luggage, however tempting, but Edha has plenty of smaller pieces of cutting-edge Dutch design, including textiles, stylish lights and kitchen gadgets – you can always ship it.

BUISE FASHION & ACCESSORIES
Map p312 (www.buise.nl; Cornelis Schuytstraat 12; ◔1-6pm Mon, 10am-6pm Tue-Fri, to 5.30pm Sat; ☐2 Cornelis Schuytstraat) A chic boutique selling cool fashion-pack favourites, such as pieces by Isabel Marant, dresses by Malene Birger and other labels, including Paul & Joe.

DE WINKEL VAN NIJNTJE TOYS
(www.dewinkelvannijntje.nl; Scheldestraat 61; ◔1-6pm Mon, 10am-6pm Tue-Fri, to 5pm Sat, noon-5pm Sun; ☐; ☐12 Scheldestraat) A Miffy (Nijntje in Dutch) emporium, devoted entirely to the much-adored character of Dutch illustrator Dick Bruna. The mouthless one is celebrated in all sorts of enticing merchandise, from crocheted dolls to Royal Delftware plates.

**MUSEUM SHOP
AT THE MUSEUMPLEIN** GIFTS & SOUVENIRS
Map p312 (Hobbemastraat; ◔shop 10am-6pm, ticket window for museum entrance 8.30am-6pm; ☐2/5 Hobbemastraat) The Van Gogh Museum and Rijksmuseum jointly operate the Museum Shop at the Museumplein, so

NEOCLASSICAL RIDING SCHOOL

The neoclassical **Hollandsche Manege** (Map p312; ☎020-618 09 42; www.dehollandschemanege.nl; Vondelstraat 140; adult/child €8/4, private riding lessons per 30/60min €38/62; ☺10am-5pm; 🚊1 1e Constantijn Huygensstraat) is a surprise to discover just outside the Vondelpark. Entering is like stepping back in time, into a grandiose indoor riding school inspired by the famous Spanish Riding School in Vienna. Designed by AL van Gendt and built in 1882, it retains its charming horse-head facade and has a large riding arena and inside.

Take a riding lesson and/or watch the instructors put the horses through their paces at the elevated cafe.

you can pick up posters, cards and other art souvenirs from both institutions in one fell swoop (and avoid the museums' entrance queues). While the selection is not as vast as the in-house stores, there's still a good choice of culture-based souvenirs.

🏃 SPORTS & ACTIVITIES

ZUIDERBAD   SWIMMING

Map p312 (☎020-252 13 90; Hobbemastraat 26; €3.75; ☺7am-6pm Mon, 7-9am & noon-10pm Tue-Fri, 8am-3.15pm Sat, 10am-3.30pm Sun; 🏊; 🚊2/5 Hobbemastraat) Once the Velox cycling school, this was converted into a beguilingly splendid public pool. It's a grand 1912 edifice behind the Rijksmuseum, restored to its original glory, full of tiles, character and appreciative paddlers.

KANOSCHOOL   CANOEING

Map p312 (www.kanoschool.nl; Admiralengracht 60; rental per hour €10; ☺hours vary; 🚊7 Postjesweg) Rents one- and two-person kayaks for paddling along the canals (waterway map and tips supplied; photo ID required as a deposit). Also has stand-up paddleboards (SUPs). Located in the west, near Rembrandtpark.

FRIDAY NIGHT SKATE   SKATING

Map p312 (www.fridaynightskate.com; Vondelpark; ☺8.30pm Fri; 🚊2/5 Hobbemastraat) 𝗙𝗥𝗘𝗘 Every Friday night (except in rain and snow), the Vondelpark is the start of a 20km, two-hour-long mass skate through Amsterdam. It's open to anyone with reasonable skating proficiency (ie knowing how to brake!). Arrive at the meeting point, adjacent to the Vondelparkpaviljoen by 8pm (8.15pm in winter). Check the website for details of skate (and safety gear) rental outlets.

FUN FOREST   ADVENTURE SPORTS

(www.funforest.nl; Bosbaanweg 3; adult/child €25/20; ☺10am-6pm daily Jul, hours vary other months; 🏊; 🚊170, 172) Next to the entrance to Amsterdamse Bos is Fun Forest, a tree-top climbing park for children or adults that uses ropes, ladders and bridges. Admission provides three hours of activities. Check website for opening hours.

AMSTERDAMSE BOS BIKE RENTAL   CYCLING

(www.amsterdamsebosfietsverhuur.nl; rental per 2hr/day €6/9.50; ☺10am-6pm, closed Mon & Tue in winter; 🏊; 🚊170, 172) The park's bicycle-rental kiosk is opposite the main entrance and comprises a splendidly fun child-friendly cafe with hammocks and toys. If you plan to explore the park in depth, two wheels are vital.

De Pijp

Neighbourhood Top Five

1 **Albert Cuypmarkt** (p176) Feasting your senses on the international free-for-all of fresh produce, cheese, fish, colourful clothing, accessories and quirky Dutch souvenirs at the largest street market in Europe to open daily (except Sunday).

2 **Sarphatipark** (p175) Strolling through an urban oasis of lawns, statues, ponds and fountains in De Pijp's central park.

3 **Boca's** (p182) Bar hopping between exuberantly friendly neighbourhood watering holes, starting with *borrel* (drinks) at lively bars such as Boca's.

4 **Heineken Experience** (p175) Touring the boisterously fun brewery before boarding its canal boat for a cruise across town to A'DAM Tower.

5 **Bakers & Roasters** (p180) Delving into De Pijp's burgeoning brunch scene at specialists like Bakers & Roasters.

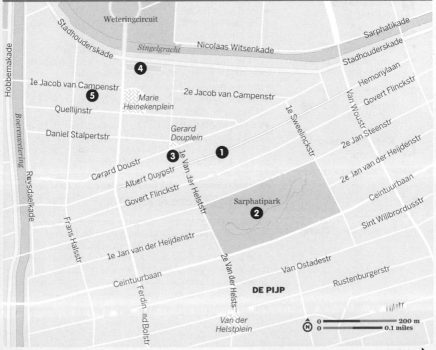

For more detail of this area see Map p316 ➡

Lonely Planet's Top Tip

Many successful Amsterdam businesses put down their first roots in De Pijp, and this innovative neighbourhood has a constant turnover of pop-ups, startups and new openings. Backstreets to watch include Frans Halsstraat, 1e Van der Helststraat, 2e Van der Helststraat, Cornelis Troostplein and Ruysdaelkade.

DE PIJP

✕ Best Places to Eat

➡ Ciel Bleu (p181)

➡ Bakers & Roasters (p180)

➡ Graham's Kitchen (p181)

➡ Avocado Show (p176)

For reviews, see p176 ➡

🍷 Best Places to Drink

➡ Brouwerij Troost (p182)

➡ Watering Hole (p182)

➡ Twenty Third Bar (p182)

➡ Glouglou (p182)

➡ Café Sarphaat (p182)

For reviews, see p181 ➡

🔒 Best Places to Shop

➡ Albert Cuypmarkt (p176)

➡ Hutspot (p183)

➡ Good Genes (p184)

➡ Tiller Galerie (p184)

For reviews, see p183 ➡

Explore De Pijp

De Pijp's village character is due in part to the fact that it's an island, connected to the rest of the city by 16 bridges. Its name, 'the Pipe', is thought to reflect its straight, narrow streets that resemble the stems of old clay pipes.

But the district's feel is more attributable to its history. The area's 1860s tenement blocks provided cheap housing for newly arrived industrial-revolution workers. In the 1960s and '70s many working-class residents left for greener pastures and the government refurbished the tenement blocks for immigrants. Inhabited today by all walks of life, with gentrification continuing apace, this arty, foodie neighbourhood retains a strong community-oriented spirit.

Start your day trawling the stalls at the Albert Cuypmarkt (p176) before strolling peaceful Sarphatipark (p175). Explore the streets' boutiques and speciality shops – and choose your dinner destination from the overwhelming options – before heading to the Heineken Experience (p175). If you time it for the late afternoon, the tasting at the end provides a built-in happy hour (though of course in fun-loving De Pijp it almost always feels like happy hour).

Local Life

➡**Local beer** Heineken might not brew in De Pijp any more, but the 'hood has a fantastic craft brewery that does, Brouwerij Troost (p182).

➡**Seafood snacks** Locals love to hit up De Pijp's herring stands (p179) on and around Albert Cuypmarkt; Volendammer Vishandel (p177) is a favourite.

➡**Hidden hangout** Tucked-away square Van der Helstplein is lined with low-key local *cafés* (pubs) such as Café Ruis (p182).

➡**Red Light District** On De Pijp's western border, along Ruysdaelkade, opposite Hobbemakade, there's a little red-light district (minus the stag parties and drunken crowds that frequent its city-centre counterpart).

Getting There & Away

➡**Tram** Trams 16 and 24 roll north–south from Centraal Station along Ferdinand Bolstraat right by De Pijp's main sights. Tram 4 travels from Rembrandtplein, while tram 3 cuts east–west across the neighbourhood. Tram 12 cuts through De Pijp en route to Vondelpark. (Beware of old transport maps; tram 25 no longer runs.)

➡**Metro** From mid-2018, the Noord/Zuidlijn (north–south metro line) will serve De Pijp.

TOP SIGHT
HEINEKEN EXPERIENCE

Heineken has been going strong since 1864 and this multisensory 'Experience' is an appropriately immodest (read: commercial) celebration of its place in Dutch brewing history.

On the site of the company's old De Pijp brewery, which closed in 1988, the 'Experience' is a rollicking self-guided tour. Allow at least 90 minutes to learn the storied history of the Heineken family, find out how the logo has evolved, and follow the brewing process from water and hops through to bottling. Along the way you can watch Heineken commercials from around the world, sniff the mash in copper tanks, visit the horse stables and make your own music video. The crowning glory is Brew You – a 4D multimedia exhibit where you 'become' a beer as you get shaken up, heated up, sprayed with water and 'bottled'. True beer connoisseurs will shudder, but it's a lot of fun.

Self-guided tours conclude with two tastings; there are also 2½-hour VIP guided tours incorporating a five-beer tasting with cheese pairings, and Rock the City tickets that include a 45-minute one-way canal cruise across town to A'DAM Tower (p196). Prebooking tickets online saves adults €2 and, crucially, allows you to skip the ticket queues.

DON'T MISS

➡ 'Becoming' a beer with Brew You

➡ Learning to pour a proper frothy pint, Dutch style

PRACTICALITIES

➡ Map p316, C1

➡ 020-523 92 22

➡ www.heineken experience.com

➡ Stadhouderskade 78

➡ adult/child self-guided tour €18/12.50, VIP guided tour €49, Rock the City ticket €25

➡ 10.30am-7.30pm Mon-Thu, to 9pm Fri-Sun

➡ 16/24 Stadhouderskade

DE PIJP SIGHTS

◉ SIGHTS

SARPHATIPARK   PARK
Map p316 (Sarphatipark; 3 2e Van der Helststraat) While the Vondelpark is bigger in size and reputation, this tranquil English-style park delivers an equally potent shot of pastoral summertime relaxation, with far fewer crowds. Named after Samuel Sarphati (1813–66), a Jewish doctor, businessman and urban innovator, the grounds incorporate ponds, gently rolling meadows and wooded fringes. In the centre is the 1886-built **Sarphati memorial**, a bombastic temple with a fountain, gargoyles and a bust of the great man himself.

HUIS MET DE KABOUTERS   ARCHITECTURE
Map p316 (House with the Goblins; Ceintuurbaan 251; 3 Van Woustraat) Look up as you pass Ceintuurbaan 251: on the elaborately carved wooden gables of the 1884 neo-Gothic mansion here you'll see two cheeky lime-green goblin sculptures dressed in red hats and shorts; one is holding a red ball and the other is reaching to catch it. The building was designed by architect AC Boerma; it's thought the sculptures symbolise his client's surname, Van Ballegooijen, which translates in part to 'throwing a ball'. It's been a listed national monument since 1984.

Local legend has it that the ball changes between the goblins' hands at midnight on February 29 every leap year.

DE DAGERAAD   ARCHITECTURE
Map p316 (Dawn Housing Project; Pieter Lodewijk Takstraat; 4 Amstelkade) Following the key Housing Act of 1901, which forced the city to rethink neighbourhood planning and condemn slums, De Dageraad housing estate was developed between 1918 and 1923 for poorer families. One of the most original architects of the expressionist Amsterdam School, Piet Kramer, drew up plans for this idiosyncratic complex in collaboration with Michel de Klerk.

✕ EATING

De Pijp's thriving foodie scene is experimental and multicultural yet also quintessentially Dutch. Choices include street-food stalls, salad bars, cheap, filling Surinamese and Asian spots, on-trend addresses like the world's first all-avocado cafe, gastronomic standouts and atmospheric brown cafes (pubs) serving food. Brunch is especially good in this neighbourhood, with many cafes specialising in exceptional mid-morning menus. Albert Cuypstraat, Ferdinand Bolstraat and Ceintuurbaan are ideal starting points.

★ AVOCADO SHOW   CAFE €

Map p316 (www.theavocadoshow.com; Daniël Stalpertstraat 61; mains €8-15; ⊙8.30am-5pm Thu-Tue, 11am-5pm Wed; 🖥📶; 🚊16/24 Marie Heinekenplein) A world first, this cafe uses avocado in *every* dish, often in ingeniously functional ways (burgers with avocado halves instead of buns, salad 'bowls' made from avocado slices...). Finish with avocado ice cream or sorbet. Avocado cocktails include a spicy Guaco Mary and an avocado daiquiri. It doesn't take reservations, so prepare to queue. Cards only; no cash.

A 'living wall' greens the interior, and staff are upbeat and efficient.

FOU FOW RAMEN   RAMEN €

Map p316 (www.foufow.nl; Van Woustraat 3; mains €10-16; ⊙noon-3pm & 5-9pm Tue-Sun; 🚊4 Stadhouderskade) Paper lanterns sway from the ceiling of this restaurant, which opens to a covered, plant-filled courtyard out back – an idyllic spot for a bowl of chilled ramen in summer. Year round you can also get steaming-hot, aromatic ramen dishes, and various sides such as spicy tofu with chilli sauce and crispy chicken wings.

MASSIMO   GELATO €

Map p316 (Van Ostadestraat 147; 1/2/3/4 scoops €1.50/3/4.50/6; ⊙noon-10pm; 🚊3 2e Van der Helststraat) Gelato is made daily on-site from family recipes using local, organic milk, butter and yoghurt, along with imported Italian ingredients such as lemons from the passionate fourth-generation gelato maker's native Liguria. Scrumptious flavours including cinnamon and fig; honey, yoghurt and cherry; coffee and hazelnut;

◉ TOP SIGHT
ALBERT CUYPMARKT

Want to experience Amsterdam at its wonderfully chaotic, multicultural best? Head to Europe's most sprawling street market that's open daily (except Sunday).

Named after landscape painter Albert Cuyp (1620–91), Albert Cuypmarkt is Amsterdam's largest and busiest market, and it's legendary for its huge variety. Scores of aromatic stalls sell Dutch cheeses – from a four-year-old Gouda to a creamy *boerenkaas* (farmer's cheese) – fish, crustaceans, olives, oils, herbs and spices, and bushels of fresh fruit and veggies. Need some Saturday-night bling or a new phone cover? How about a bike lock, a hair-curling iron or some flowers to brighten your hotel room? There's also a staggering array of (mostly funky, sometimes junky) men's and women's clothing and accessories, as well as ceramics, fabrics and a host of other homewares.

Don't miss the shops hidden behind the stalls, selling everything from kitchen gadgets to luggage, bolts of fabric, soaps, shampoos and much more.

Be sure to come hungry: classic Dutch snacks to eat as you wander range from herring to *frites* (fries), *poffertjes* (icing-sugar-dusted mini pancakes) and piping-hot *stroopwafels* (caramel-syrup-filled waffles).

DON'T MISS

➡ Cheeses galore
➡ Only-in-the-Netherlands gifts such as fluffy clog slippers
➡ On-the-go snacks

PRACTICALITIES

➡ Map p316, D3
➡ www.albertcuyp-markt.amsterdam
➡ Albert Cuypstraat, btwn Ferdinand Bolstraat & Van Woustraat
➡ ⊙9.30am-5pm Mon-Sat
➡ 🚊16/24 Albert Cuypstraat

and pear and walnut are spatula'd into hand-rolled waffle cones or tubs.

SUGO

PIZZA €

Map p316 (www.sugopizza.nl; Ferdinand Bolstraat 107; pizza slice €3-4; ⊘11am-10pm; 🖋; 🚊3/12 Ferdinand Bolstraat) 🍴 Spectacular pizza slices at this two-storey restaurant are cooked daily, displayed beneath glass and warmed in ovens. Topping combinations include caramelised onion, mascarpone, walnut and black olive or potato, mushroom and truffle cream sauce. Veggies are locally sourced, while meats and cheeses are from small farms in Italy. Takeaway packaging is made from recycled paper and energy is 100% sustainable.

FRNZY

VIETNAMESE €

Map p316 (🖉06 5063 3221; www.frnzy amsterdam.com; 1e Jacob van Campenstraat 27; mains €6-10; ⊘11am-10pm; 🚊16/24 Marie Heinekenplein) Fast, fresh, authentic Vietnamese street food at this black-painted corner restaurant includes *bánh mì* (baguettes), *bún* (noodle salad) and *gỏi cuốn* (spring rolls), filled with various combinations of ingredients such as *gà* (chicken), *bò* (beef), *heo* (pork), *nem nướng* (marinated meatballs) and *chay* (vegetables). There are tables in view of the open kitchen and out on the street.

GEFLIPT

BURGERS €

Map p316 (www.gefliptburgers.nl; Van Woustraat 15; dishes €9-11; ⊘11.30am-9.30pm Sun-Thu, to 10.30pm Fri & Sat; 🕾; 🚊4 Stadhouderskade) Competition is fierce for the best burgers in this foodie neighbourhood, but Geflipt is a serious contender. In a stripped-back, industrial-chic interior, it serves luscious combinations (like Gasconne beef, bacon, golden cheddar, red-onion compote and fried egg) on brioche buns with sauces cooked daily on the premises from locally sourced ingredients. Bonus points for its Amsterdam-brewed Brouwerij 't IJ beers.

SIR HUMMUS

MIDDLE EASTERN €

Map p316 (www.sirhummus.nl; Van der Helstplein 2; dishes €6-12; ⊘noon-8pm Tue-Fri, noon-5pm Sat & Sun; 🖋; 🚊3 2e Van der Helststraat) 🍴 Sir Hummus is the brainchild of three young Israelis whose passion for the chickpea dip led to a London street market stall and then this hummus-dedicated cafe. Creamy, all-natural, preservative- and additive-free hummus is served with pillowy pita bread

and salad; SH also makes fantastic falafels. You can eat in or take away, but arrive early before it sells out.

FAT DOG

HOT DOGS €

Map p316 (www.thefatdog.nl; Ruysdaelkade 251; dishes €4-12; ⊘noon Wed-Sun; 🚊12 Cornelis Troostplein) Super-chef Ron Blaauw, of Ron Gastrobar (p163), elevates the humble hot dog to an art form. Ultra-gourmet options include Naughty Bangkok (pickled vegetables, red-curry mayo and dry crispy rice), Vive La France (fried mushrooms, foie gras and truffle mayo), Gangs of New York (sauerkraut, bacon and smoked-onion marmalade) and Vega Gonzalez (vegetarian sausage, corn, guacamole, sour cream and jalapeño mayo).

BUTCHER

BURGERS €

Map p316 (🖉020-470 78 75; www.the-butcher. com; Albert Cuypstraat 129; burgers €7-12; ⊘11am-midnight; 🚊16/24 Albert Cuypstraat) Burgers at this sizzling spot are cooked right in front of you (behind a glass screen, so you won't get splattered). Mouthwatering choices include Silence of the Lamb (with spices and tahini), the Codfather (beer-battered blue cod and homemade tartar sauce), an Angus-beef truffle burger and a veggie version. Ask about its 'secret kitchen' cocktail bar.

VOLENDAMMER VISHANDEL

SEAFOOD €

Map p316 (1e Van der Helststraat; dishes €2-6; ⊘8am-5pm Mon-Sat; 🚊16/24 Albert Cuypstraat) Dutch flags fly from this traditional *haringhuis* ('herring house', ie takeaway fish shop), which has its own fishing fleet at the seaside resort of Volendam, 20km northeast. Along with herring served chopped with diced onion on a fluffy bread roll, classic deep-fried snacks include *kibbeling* (fried whitefish pieces), *lekkerbekje* (whole fried whitefish) and *gerookte paling* (smoked eel).

Locals flock here after shopping at the Albert Cuypmarkt just around the corner. There are a handful of benches and upturned barrels out front; otherwise the Sarphatipark is footsteps to the south.

THRILL GRILL

AMERICAN €

Map p316 (🖉020-760 67 50; www.thrillgrill.nl; Ferdinand Bolstraat 50; mains €9-13; ⊘noon-10pm Sun-Wed, to 11pm Thu-Sat; 🕾📶; 🚊16/24 Albert Cuypstraat) Burgers are the big deal at Thrill Grill (including its signature double-beef

Thrill Burger with Gouda and bacon), accompanied by truffle-parmesan fries, but it also offers lighter lunchtime dishes (open sandwiches, salads), while evening alternatives span grilled chicken, hot dogs and nachos. Milkshakes include boozy options like chocolate and bourbon. There are mini burgers and hot dogs for kids.

VENKEL
CAFE €

Map p316 (www.venkelsalades.nl; Albert Cuypstraat 22; mains €8-12; ⊙11am-9pm; 🖘🖉; 🚊16/24 Albert Cuypstraat) 🍃 Timber tables at this light-filled salad bar are made from a fallen Vondelpark tree, as are planks on which dishes such as homemade hummus, house-baked breads and vegetable chips are served. Salads come in bamboo bowls. Ingredients – red quinoa, hazelnuts, aubergine, goat's cheese, beetroot, lentils, spinach, micro herbs, edible flowers, fruits and berries – are organic; virtually everything is vegetarian.

STROOM
CAFE €

Map p316 (www.stroomindepijp.nl; Ferdinand Bolstraat 151; dishes €4-11; ⊙8.30am-6pm; 🖘🖉; 🚊12 Cornelis Troostplein) A charming timber-framed corner building with large windows houses this split-level cafe with mezzanine seating, which opens onto one of De Pijp's sunniest terraces. Breakfast options include organic yoghurt with muesli or a Dutch breakfast with ham, cheese and eggs, while lunch dishes range from elaborate open-face sandwiches, toasties and salads to burgers (including veggie varieties).

FRITES UIT ZUYD
FAST FOOD €

Map p316 (www.cafeparhasard.nl; Ceintuurbaan 113-115; dishes €2-4; ⊙2-11pm Mon-Thu, from 1pm Fri-Sun; 🚊3 Ferdinand Bolstraat) De Pijp's best *frites* (fries) by far are at takeaway shop Frites uit Zuyd, with black-and-white chequerboard tiling on the walls and floors, and at its sleek sit-down restaurant Friterie par Hasard (p181) next door. Crispy, fluffy *frites* are accompanied by traditional pickles, mustard, or sauces such as satay, mayo or chilli-spiced sambal. Wooden benches line the pavement out front.

SLA
CAFE €

Map p316 (www.ilovesla.com; Ceintuurbaan 149; dishes €8-11; ⊙11am-9pm; 🖉; 🚊3 2e Van der Helststraat) 🍃 Amsterdam's fashionistas flock to this super-stylish salad bar for its soups, its juices and especially its extensive array of fresh, healthy salads you design yourself. All of the meat, poultry and dairy products, 90% of the vegetables, and the wines are organic. This flagship branch proved so popular that there are now offshoots all over Amsterdam.

SPANG MAKANDRA
SURINAMESE, INDONESIAN €

Map p316 (🖉020-6705081; www.spangmakandra.nl; Gerard Doustraat 39; mains €6-10; ⊙11am-10pm Mon-Sat, 1-10pm Sun; 🚊16/24 Albert Cuypstraat) There are just 26 seats at this cosy restaurant, and it's a red-hot favourite with students and Surinamese and Indonesian expats, so you'll need to book for dinner. The reward is a fabulous array of dishes like fish soups and satay with spicy sauces at astonishingly cheap prices. All the food is halal; no alcohol is served.

STACH
DELI, CAFE €

Map p316 (🖉020-754 26 72; www.stach-food.nl; Van Woustraat 154; dishes €4-9; ⊙8am-10pm Mon-Sat, 9am-10pm Sun; 🚊4 Lutmastraat) 🍃 An Aladdin's cave of fresh produce, jams, preserves, teas, coffees, juices and chocolates, this food emporium also makes some of the best (and best-value) sandwiches around, loaded with gourmet ingredients. If it's not picnic weather, there's a mezzanine dining area inside.

TAART VAN M'N TANTE
BAKERY €

Map p316 (🖉020-776 46 00; www.detaart.com; Ferdinand Bolstraat 10; dishes €4-8; ⊙10am-6pm; 👪; 🚊16/24 Stadhouderskade) One of Amsterdam's best-loved cake shops operates from this ultra-kitsch parlour, turning out apple pies (Dutch, French or 'tipsy'), pecan pie and wish-you-could-bake-like-this cakes. Hot-pink walls accent cakes dressed like Barbie dolls – or are they Barbies dressed as cakes?

MISS KOREA BBQ
KOREAN, BARBECUE €€

Map p316 (🖉020-679 06 06; www.misskorea.nl; Albert Cuypstraat 66-70; adult/child €28.50/12.50; ⊙5-11pm Tue-Sun; 👪; 🚊16/24 Albert Cuypstraat) Tables at this wildly popular all-you-can-eat restaurant have inset barbecue plates to sizzle up pork belly, seasoned beef, squid, prawns and vegetables yourself. You can order an unlimited number of ingredients, but there's a penalty for uneaten food to minimise wastage. Korean spirits, rice wine and beers dominate the drinks menu; ice-cream flavours include green tea and black sesame.

HOW TO EAT A HERRING

'Hollandse Nieuwe' isn't a fashion trend – it's the fresh catch of super-tasty herring, raked in every June. The Dutch love it, and you'll see vendors selling the salty fish all over town. Although Dutch tradition calls for dangling the herring above your mouth, this isn't the way it's done in Amsterdam. Here the fish is served chopped in bite-size chunks and eaten with a toothpick, topped with *uitjes* (diced onions) and *zuur* (sweet pickles). A *broodje haring* (herring roll) is even handier, as the fluffy white roll holds on the toppings and keeps your fingers fish-fat-free – think of it as an edible napkin.

VAN 'T SPIT   ROTISSERIE €€

Map p316 (www.vantspit.nl; Frans Halsstraat 42; half/full roast chicken €11/21, sides €3-4; ⏰5pm-midnight; 🚊16/24 Marie Heinekenplein) Van 't Spit does one thing – chicken (half or full), marinated overnight and spit-roasted over a wood-burning fire, with optional sides like salad or fries – but it does it so well that it's always packed. No reservations, so get in early or head to the bar for a cock-tail such as a kickin' vodka-and-ginger-beer Dutch Mule while you wait.

SURYA   INDIAN €€

Map p316 (📞020-676 79 85; www.surya restaurant.nl; Ceintuurbaan 147; mains €14-23; ⏰5-11pm Tue-Sun; 🚊3 2e Van der Helststraat) Indian restaurants can be surprisingly hit and miss in this multicultural city, making classy Surya an invaluable address for fans of Subcontinental cuisine. Menu standouts include a feisty madras, a fire breathing vindaloo, tandoori tikka dishes and silky tomato-based *paneer makhni* with soft cottage cheese made fresh on the premises each day. Mains come with pappadams, rice and salad.

DÈSA   INDONESIAN €€

Map p316 (📞020-671 09 79; www.restaurant desa.com; Ceintuurbaan 103; mains €13-22, rijst-tafel €19-35; ⏰5-10.30pm; 📞; 🚊3 Ferdinand Bolstraat) Named for the Indonesian word for 'village' (apt for this city, but especially this 'hood), Dèsa is wildly popular for its *rijsttafel* (Indonesian banquet). À la carte

options include *serundeng* (spiced fried coconut), *ayam besengek* (chicken cooked in saffron and coconut milk), *sambal goreng telor* (stewed eggs in spicy Balinese sauce), and *pisang goreng* (fried banana) for dessert.

SPAGHETTERIA   ITALIAN €€

Map p316 (www.spaghetteria-pastabar.nl; Van Woustraat 123; pasta €9-16; ⏰5-10.15pm; 🚊4 Ceintuurbaan) Freshly made pastas at this hip Italian-run 'pasta bar' come in six daily options that might include beetroot ravioli with goat's cheese; basil fettucini with clams; squid-ink spaghetti with pesto and sun-dried tomatoes; and ham tortellini in creamy truffle sauce. The huge wooden communal table (and well-priced Italian wines) adds to the electric atmosphere.

BRASSERIE SENT   BARBECUE €€

Map p316 (📞020-676 24 95; www.restaurant sent.nl; Saenredamstraat 39; mains €17-29; ⏰6-10.30pm; 🚊16/24 Albert Cuypstraat) Smoke-infused meats at this barbecue specialist are cooked in a Big Green Egg (ceramic Japanese-*kamado*-style grill and charcoal smoker), including veal rib-eye, lamb leg, pork rib and Chateaubriand steak for two. There's also the option of sea bass with clams, or for non-carnivores choices (cooked separately) include mushroom-and-truffle ravioli. Book ahead, especially at weekends.

LOS FELIZ   MEXICAN €€

Map p316 (www.losfeliz.nl; Albert Cuypstraat 88; mains €7-17; ⏰11am-11pm Mon-Sat, 10am-4pm Sun; 🚊16/24 Albert Cuypstraat) With fresh flowers, bright murals, colourful bowls of *huevos rancheros* (Mexican eggs) and ample portions of sea-bass ceviche with grapefruit, red onion, pineapple, avocado, citrus and chilli, this Cali-Mexican res-taurant injects a dash of sunshine into De Pijp's food scene. Terrific craft cocktails include its zesty Rosarito (tequila, agave syrup, lime juice, fresh chilli and corian-der). Cards only.

MANA MANA   ISRAELI €€

Map p316 (📞06 4163 1098; 1e Jan Steenstraat 85; mains lunch €5-8, dinner €8-15; ⏰10am-midnight Tue-Sun; 🚊16/24 Albert Cuypstraat) Diners crowd around communal tables up on a mezzanine level at this small restaurant serving dishes designed for sharing. The psychedelic cauliflower (fried cauliflower served with tahini, tomato cream and grapefruit) is a firm favourite.

DE PIJP'S TOP FIVE BRUNCH SPOTS

Bakers & Roasters (Map p316; www.bakersandroasters.com; 1e Jacob van Campenstraat 54; dishes €7-16; ⏰8.30am-4pm; 🚊16/24 Stadhouderskade) Sumptuous brunch dishes served up at Brazilian-Kiwi-owned Bakers & Roasters include banana-nutbread French toast with homemade banana marmalade and crispy bacon; Navajo eggs with pulled pork, avocado, mango salsa and chipotle cream; and a smoked-salmon stack with poached eggs, potato cakes and hollandaise. Wash your choice down with a fiery Bloody Mary. Fantastic pies, cakes and slices, too.

Scandinavian Embassy (Map p316; www.scandinavianembassy.nl; Sarphatipark 34; dishes €5-12; ⏰7.30am-6pm Mon-Fri, 9am-6pm Sat & Sun; 🚊3 2e Van der Helststraat) Oat-meal porridge with blueberries, honey and coconut, served with goat's-milk yoghurt; salt-cured salmon on Danish rye with sheep's-milk yoghurt; muesli with strawberries; and freshly baked pastries (including cinnamon buns) make this blond-wood-panelled spot a perfect place to start the day – as does its phenomenal coffee, sourced from Scandinavian micro-roasteries (including a refreshing cold brew with tonic water).

Little Collins (Map p316; 📞020-673 22 93; www.littlecollins.nl; 1e Sweelinckstraat 19; tapas €4-16, brunch €9-16; ⏰9am-4pm Mon, 10.30am-10pm Wed & Thu, 9am-10pm Fri-Sun; 🚊16/24 Albert Cuypstraat) On a side street near Albert Cuypmarkt, this hip hang-out is hopping during brunch, when dishes might include toasted brioche with grilled halloumi, homemade plum jam, crème fraîche, hazelnuts, basil and mint (plus four different Bloody Marys). The evening tapas menu is equally inspired: seared calamari with green-mango salsa, for instance, or crispy duck with cucumber and chilli.

Omelegg (Map p316; www.omelegg.com; Ferdinand Bolstraat 143; dishes €6-10; ⏰7am-4pm Mon-Fri, 8am-4pm Sat & Sun; 📶; 🚊12 Cornelis Troostplein) In sparing surrounds with polished-concrete floors, wooden furniture and a mural of traditional Dutch windmills on the back wall, this omelette specialist serves a weekly changing option, plus menu regulars like Mariachi (spicy jalapeños, mushrooms and sun-dried tomatoes), Viking Fisherman (smoked salmon, dill, crème fraîche and lemon zest) and Chilli Hernandez (homemade chilli con carne and cheese). No reservations.

CT Coffee & Coconuts (Map p316; www.coffeeandcoconuts.com; Ceintuurbaan 282-284; mains €9-23; ⏰8am-11pm; 📶; 🚊3 Ceintuurbaan) A 1920s art-deco cinema has been stunningly transformed into this open-plan, triple-level, cathedral-like space (with a giant print of John Lennon at the top). Brunch dishes like coconut, almond and buck-wheat pancakes; French-toast brioche with apricots; avocado-slathered toast with dukkah (North African spice-and-nut blend) and lemon dressing; and scrambled eggs on sourdough with crumbled feta are served to 1pm.

EN AMSTERDAM
JAPANESE €€

Map p316 (📞020-470 36 66; www.en-amsterdam.nl; Dusartstraat 53; mains €14-28, sushi & sashimi plates €22-38, 3-, 5- & 7-course menu €40/60/80, with sake €59/87/102; ⏰5-10.30pm Mon-Sat; 🚊12 Cornelis Troostplein) Secluded in a leafy, residential corner of the neighbour-hood, this elegant restaurant serves equally refined Japanese fare: crispy lotus root with prawns; miso chicken with black garlic; *gyoza* dumplings; and sushi and sashimi. There are alsoover 30 types of sake.

VOLT
MEDITERRANEAN €€

Map p316 (📞020-471 55 44; www.restaurantvolt.nl; Ferdinand Bolstraat 178; mains €9-19, tapas €5-12; ⏰4-10pm Mon-Fri, 11am-10pm Sat & Sun; 🚊12 Cornelis Troostplein) Strung with coloured lightbulbs, Volt is a neighbourhood gem for light tapas-style bites (olives and marinated sardines; aioli and tapenade) and more substantial mains (artichoke ravioli with walnuts and rocket (arugula); oxtail with celeriac and potato mousseline; or steak tartare with pickled beetroot). Its bar stays open until late, or head across the street to its brown cafe sibling, Gambrinus (p183).

MASTINO
PIZZA €€

Map p316 (www.mastinopizza.nl; 1e Van der Helst-straat 78; pizzas €10-16; ⏰4.30-10pm Tue-Fri, noon-10pm Sat & Sun; 📶; 🚊3 2e Van der Helst-straat) Choose from classic flour, spelt or soya for the base, and from topping combinations like Parma (ham, rocket, tomato and buffalo mozzarella), Flower Power (courgette flowers, anchovies and mozzarella), and Veggie (vegan cheese, artichokes, black olives, cherry tomatoes and basil), then dine in the exposed-brick interior or out on the terrace, or take your pizza away.

FRITERIE PAR HASARD DUTCH €€

Map p316 (www.cafeparhasard.nl; Ceintuurbaan 113-115; mains €12-24; ◷2-10.30pm Mon-Thu, from 1pm Fri-Sun; 🚊3 Ferdinand Bolstraat) Fronted by a red-and-white chequered awning, low-lit Friterie par Hasard is fêted for its *frites* (fries), served with dishes like ribs in traditional Limburg stew with apple, elderberry and bay-leaf sauce; marinated chicken thighs with satay sauce and pickled cucumber; bavette steak; and beer-battered cod. Its adjacent Frites uit Zuyd (p178) fries up takeaway *frites*.

MAMOUCHE MOROCCAN €€

Map p316 (📞020-670 07 36; www.restaurant mamouche.nl; Quellijnstraat 104; mains €16-24; ◷5-11pm Tue-Sun; 🚊16/24 Stadhouderskade) Refined Mamouche's minimalist dining room, with mottled raw-plaster walls and slat-beam ceilings, complements its French-accented North African cuisine: *tajines* (Moroccan stews), couscous (with spicy sea bass and saffron butter, for example), and other mainstays including duck confit with sweet-potato mash and cinnamon.

PHO 91 VIETNAMESE €€

Map p316 (📞020-752 68 80; www.pho91.nl; Albert Cuypstraat 91; mains €12-14; ◷5.30-10pm Tue-Thu, noon-10pm Fri-Sun; 🚊16/24 Albert Cuypstraat) Behind a large glass frontage, this small eatery has an intimate atmosphere and authentic Vietnamese fare, including its signature *pho*. A chalkboard with hand-drawn designs dominates one wall, along with hanging plants and rustic crates. Most ingredients are sourced from the market out front. The majority of dishes are gluten, egg and dairy free, although vegetarian options are limited.

DE WAAGHALS VEGETARIAN €€

Map p316 (📞020-679 96 09; www.waaghals.nl; Frans Halsstraat 29; mains €15-20; ◷5-9.30pm; 📞; 🚊16/24 Stadhouderskade) 🌿 The popular white-walled 'Daredevil' is stylish enough for non-veggies to re-examine their dining priorities. The menu features a rotating array of inventive, seasonal, organic dishes

using locally sourced ingredients. In summer, dine on the flower-framed pavement terrace. Bookings are recommended.

★GRAHAM'S KITCHEN GASTRONOMY €€€

Map p316 (📞020-364 25 60; www. grahamskitchen.amsterdam; Hemonystraat 38; lunch mains €12-17, 3-/4-/5-/6-course menus €38/47/56/62; ◷6-10pm Tue & Wed, noon-2.30pm & 6-10pm Thu-Sat; 🚊4 Stadhouderskade) A veteran of Michelin-starred kitchens, chef Graham Mee now crafts intricate dishes at his own premises. Multicourse evening menus (no à la carte) might include a venison and crispy smoked-beetroot *macaron*, cucumber and gin-cured salmon, veal with wasabi and ghost crab, and deconstructed summer-berry crumble with wood-calamint ice cream. Mee personally explains each dish to diners.

★CIEL BLEU GASTRONOMY €€€

Map p316 (📞020-450 67 87; www.okura.nl; Hotel Okura Amsterdam, Ferdinand Bolstraat 333; mains €45-120, 6-course menu €160, with paired wines €255; ◷6.30-10.30pm Mon-Sat; 🚊12 Cornelius Troostplein) Mind-blowing, two-Michelin-star creations at this pinnacle of gastronomy change with the seasons; spring, for instance, might see scallops and oysters with vanilla sea salt and gin-and-tonic foam, king crab with salted lemon, beurre blanc ice cream and caviar, or saddle of lamb with star anise. Just as incomparable is the 23rd-floor setting with aerial views north across the city.

If your budget doesn't stretch to dining here, try the bar snacks at the adjacent Twenty Third Bar (p182).

🍷 DRINKING & NIGHTLIFE

The neighbourhood that houses the old Heineken brewery is chock-full of places to drink. The area also has a wonderful craft brewery, and some superb wine bars and cocktail bars. In particular, the streets around Gerard Douplein heave with high-spirited local crowds that spill onto *café* (pub) terraces.

★BROUWERIJ TROOST REFINERY

Map p316 (📞020-760 58 20; www.brouwerij troost.nl; Cornelis Troostplein 21; ◷4pm-1am Mon-Thu, to 3am Fri, 2pm-3am Sat, to midnight

Sun; ☎; 🚋12 Cornelis Troostplein) 🏷 Watch beer being brewed in copper vats behind a glass wall at this outstanding craft brewery. Its dozen beers include a summery blonde, a smoked porter, a strong tripel and a deep-red Imperial IPA; it also distils cucumber and juniper gin from its beer, and serves fantastic bar food, including crispy prawn tacos and humongous burgers. Book on weekend evenings.

★ WATERING HOLE   CRAFT BEER

Map p316 (www.thewateringhole.nl; 1e Van der Helststraat 72; ⊙11.30am-1am Sun-Thu, to 3am Fri & Sat; ☎; 🚋16/24 Albert Cuypstraat) At this bare-brick space, the 30 taps feature a rotating range of obscure brews such as New Zealand Yeastie Boys, Austrian Bevog, Spanish Naparbier and Amsterdam-brewed Two Chefs, alongside 45 bottled varieties, but it's also a fabulous place for gastropub fare (crab burgers, pork ribs with sage slaw). English-language pub quizzes take place on Monday.

TWENTY THIRD BAR   COCKTAIL BAR

Map p316 (www.okura.nl; Hotel Okura Amsterdam, Ferdinand Bolstraat 333; ⊙6pm-1am Sun-Thu, to 2am Fri & Sat; 🚋12 Cornelius Troostplein) High up in the skyscraping Hotel Okura Amsterdam (p222), Twenty Third Bar has sweeping views to the west and south, a stunning bar-snack menu prepared in the adjacent twin-Michelin-starred kitchen of Ciel Bleu (p181) (dishes €9 to €26; caviar €38 to €75 per 10g), champagne cocktails and Heineken on tap.

BOCA'S   BAR

Map p316 (www.bar-bocas.nl; Sarphatipark 4; ⊙10am-1am Mon-Thu, to 3am Fri & Sat, 11am-1am Sun; ☎; 🚋3 2e Van der Helststraat) Boca's (inspired by the Italian word for 'mouth') is the ultimate spot for *borrel* (drinks). Mezzanine seating overlooks the cushion-strewn interior, but in summer the best seats are on the terrace facing leafy Sarphatipark. Its pared-down wine list (seven by-the-glass choices) goes perfectly with its lavish sharing platters.

CAFÉ RUIS   BAR

Map p316 (www.cafe-ruis.nl; Van der Helstplein 9; ⊙3pm-1am Mon-Thu, to 3am Fri, noon-3am Sat, to 1am Sun; ☎; 🚋3 2e Van der Helststraat) Opening to one of the liveliest terraces on plane-tree-shaded square Van der Helstplein, Café Ruis has a lounge-room-like interior

with mismatched furniture, board games and a resident dog, Moe. Craft beers on tap include Amsterdam Brewboys' Amsterdam Pale Ale; Texelse Bierbrouwerij's Tripel, brewed on the Dutch island of Texel, is among the bottled options.

BLENDBAR   JUICE BAR

Map p316 (Ferdinand Bolstraat 21; ⊙8am-6pm Mon-Sat, noon-6pm Sun; 🚋16/24 Albert Cuypstraat) Alongside freshly squeezed juices and smoothies, this hole-in-the-wall place on busy Ferdinand Bolstraat has protein shakes such as banana, whey, chocolate and oats, or espresso, cocoa fibre and raw cocoa. Yoghurt (in smoothies or served by itself with toppings such as goji berries) comes in skimmed, goat's-milk and soy varieties.

GLOUGLOU   WINE BAR

Map p316 (www.glouglou.nl; 2e Van der Helststraat 3; ⊙5pm-midnight Mon-Thu, 4pm-1am Fri, 3pm-1am Sat, to midnight Sun; 🚋3 2e Van der Helststraat) 🏷 Natural, all-organic, additive-free wines are the stock-in-trade of this convivial neighbourhood wine bar in a rustic stained-glass-framed shop, where the party often spills out into the street. More than 40 well-priced French wines are available by the glass; it also sells bottles to drink on-site or take away.

CAFÉ SARPHAAT   BROWN CAFE

Map p316 (☎020-675 15 65; Ceintuurbaan 157; ⊙9am-1am Sun-Thu, to 3am Fri & Sat; 🚋3/4 Van Woustraat) Grab an outdoor table along Sarphatipark, order a frothy beer and see if you don't feel like a local. This is one of the neighbourhood's most genial spots, with a lovely old bar that makes sipping a *jenever* (Dutch gin) in broad daylight seem like a good idea. Free live jazz takes place most Sunday afternoons.

CAFÉ BINNEN BUITEN   BROWN CAFE

Map p316 (www.cafebinnenbuiten.nl; Ruysdaelkade 115; ⊙10am-1am Sun-Thu, to 3am Fri & Sat; 🚋16/24 Ruysdaelstraat) The minute there's a sliver of sunshine, this place gets packed. Sure, the food's good and the bar's candlelit and cosy. But what really draws the crowds is simply the best canal-side terrace in De Pijp – an idyllic spot to while away an afternoon.

GAMBRINUS   BROWN CAFE

Map p316 (www.gambrinus.nl; Ferdinand Bolstraat 180; ⊙11am-1am Sun-Thu, to 3am Fri &

Sat; ☎; 🚇12 Cornelis Troostplein) Named for legendary medieval European figure King Gambrinus, renowned for his love of beer and brewing and his joie de vivre, this congenial split-level cafe, with giant windows and a sprawling terrace, is a local favourite.

CAFÉ BERKHOUT   BROWN CAFE

Map p316 (www.cafeberkhout.nl; Stadhouderskade 77; ☺10am-1am Mon-Thu, to 3am Fri & Sat, 11am-1am Sun; ☎; 🚇16/24 Stadhouderskade) With its dark wood, mirrored-and-chandelier-rich splendour and shabby elegance, this brown cafe is a natural post–Heineken Experience (p175) wind-down spot (it's right across the street). Great food includes house-speciality burgers.

KATSU   COFFEESHOP

Map p316 (www.katsu.nl; 1e Van der Helststraat 70; ☺10am-midnight Mon-Thu, to 1am Fri & Sat, 11am-midnight Sun; 🚇16/24 Albert Cuypstraat) Like the surrounding neighbourhood, this relaxed coffeeshop brims with colourful characters of all ages and dispositions. When seating on the ground floor and terrace gets tight, head up to the 1st-floor lounge.

BARÇA   BAR

Map p316 (www.barca.nl; Marie Heinekenplein 30-31; ☺11am-midnight Sun-Thu, to 2am Fri & Sat; 🚇16/24 Stadhouderskade) One of the hottest hang-outs in the 'hood, this 'Barcelona in Amsterdam'–themed bar is the heartbeat of Marie Heinekenplein. Tapas and Catalan mains are served alongside an extensive choice of Spanish wines and sparkling *cava*. Cosy up in the plush gold and dark-timber interior or spread out on the terrace.

☆ ENTERTAINMENT

Due to its residential make-up, De Pijp doesn't have much in the way of entertainment. A few bars, such as Café Sarphaat (p182), host mellow live music, and there's a central cinema (p183) screening art-house films. Otherwise, you'll find plenty of options in the nearby Southern Canal Ring, and Vondelpark & the South neighbourhoods.

RIALTO CINEMA   CINEMA

Map p316 (☎020 676 87 00; www.rialtofilm.nl; Ceintuurbaan 338; adult/child from €10/7.50; 🚇3 2e Van der Helststraat) This great old cinema near Sarphatipark focuses on premieres,

THE NETHERLANDS' LARGEST BAROMETER

Rising 75m above low-rise Amsterdam, the landmark Hotel Okura Amsterdam (p222) building is visible from afar both day and evening. Each night the roof's perimeter is illuminated by LED lights, which change colour depending on the barometer's reading for the following day. Blue lights mean a bright, sunny day is forecast. Green lights mean bad weather is on the way. 'White' (more like a pale-pinkish colour and the most common) means the weather will be changeable.

The lights also change colour on special occasions, producing a variegated rainbow effect for Amsterdam's Gay Pride Parade (p24) and New Year's Eve, and, of course, turning orange for King's Day (p12).

and shows eclectic art-house fare from around the world (foreign films have Dutch subtitles). There are three screens and a stylish on-site cafe.

🛍 SHOPPING

After you've hit the Albert Cuypmarkt (p176), head to the surrounding streets, which are less crowded and are dotted with boutiques and galleries.

★HUTSPOT   DESIGN

Map p316 (www.hutspotamsterdam.com; Van Woustraat 4; ☺shop & cafe 10am-7pm Mon-Sat, noon-6pm Sun; ☎; 🚇4 Stadhouderskade) Named after the Dutch dish of boiled and mashed vegies, 'Hotchpotch' was founded with a mission to give young entrepreneurs the chance to sell their work. As a result, this concept store is an inspired mishmash of Dutch-designed furniture, furnishings, art, homewares and clothing plus a barber and a cool in-store cafe as well as various pop-ups.

GOOD GENES   FASHION & ACCESSORIES

Map p316 (www.thegoodgenes.com; Albert Cuypstraat 33-35; ☺noon-6pm Mon, 11am-6pm Tue-Fri, 10am-5pm Sat; 🚇16/24 Albert Cuypstraat) Premium fray-resistant selvedge denim is used by Good Genes' designers to create its seasonally themed jeans collections, such as 1930s aviators. Designs are then sent to Italy to be made up; you can also get jeans custom-made and returned to Amsterdam in around four days. The shop-studio occupies a pair of 19th-century warehouses that retain original industrial fittings.

CHARLIE + MARY FASHION & ACCESSORIES
Map p316 (☑020-662 82 81; www.charliemary. com; Gerard Doustraat 84; ◎1-6pm Mon, 10am-6pm Tue-Sat, noon-6pm Sun; ☒16/24 Albert Cuypstraat) 🖋 This thoughtfully curated concept store sells ethical and sustainable labels, without compromising on style or fashion. Its selection of guilt-free products includes knitwear by Granny's Finest, wallets from O My Bag, do-it-yourself art by Soroche and some enticing chocolates.

BRICK LANE FASHION & ACCESSORIES
Map p316 (www.bricklane-amsterdam.nl; Gerard Doustraat 78; ◎1-6pm Mon, 10.30am-6pm Tue-Sat, 12.30-5.30pm Sun; ☒16/24 Albert Cuypstraat) Individual, affordable designs arrive at this London-inspired boutique every couple of weeks, keeping the selection up-to-the-minute.

RECORD MANIA MUSIC
Map p316 (www.recordmania.nl; Ferdinand Bolstraat 30; ◎noon-6pm Mon-Sat; ☒16/24 Stadhouderskade) Fantastically old school, Record Mania stocks vinyl (singles and LPs) and CDs, including rare recordings by artists including Johnny Cash, JJ Kale, Eric Clapton, Def Leppard, the Beatles and the Wailers. The shop, with old posters, stained-glass windows, and records and CDs embedded in the floor, is a treasure in itself.

'T KAASBOERTJE FOOD & DRINKS
Map p316 (Gerard Doustraat 60; ◎1-5.30pm Mon, 9am-5.30pm Tue-Fri, to 4pm Sat; ☒16/24 Albert Cuypstraat) Enormous wheels of Gouda line the walls of this enticing cheese shop, and more cheeses fill the glass display cabinet.

Crispbreads and crackers are on hand, as well as reds, whites and rosés from the Netherlands, Belgium and Germany.

VAN BEEK ART
Map p316 (www.vanbeekart.nl; Stadhouderskade 63-65; ◎1-6pm Mon, 9am-6pm Tue-Fri, 10am-5pm Sat; ☒16/24 Stadhouderskade) If you're inspired by Amsterdam's masterpiece-filled galleries, street art and picturesque canalscapes, the De Pijp branch of this venerable Dutch art-supply shop is a great place to pick up canvases, brushes, oils, watercolours, pastels, charcoals and more.

RAAK FASHION & ACCESSORIES
Map p316 (www.raakamsterdam.nl; 1e Van der Helststraat 46; ◎noon-6pm Mon, 10am-6pm Tue-Sat; ☒16/24 Albert Cuypstraat) Unique casual clothing, bags, jewellery and homewares by Dutch and Scandinavian designers fill Raak's shelves and racks.

TILLER GALERIE ART
Map p316 (www.tillergalerie.com; 1e Jacob van Campenstraat 1; ◎noon-6pm Wed-Sat; ☒16/24 Stadhouderskade) This intimate, friendly gallery has works by George Heidweiller (check out the surreal Amsterdam skyscapes), Peter Donkersloot's portraits of animals and iconic actors like Marlon Brando, and Herman Brood prints.

STENELUX GIFTS & SOUVENIRS
Map p316 (☑020-662 14 90; 1e Jacob van Campenstraat 2; ◎11am-5pm Thu-Sat; ☒16/24 Stadhouderskade) Browse Stenelux' delightful collection of gems, minerals, stones and fossils. The fascinating collection from this world and beyond includes meteorites.

DE EMAILLEKEIZER HOMEWARES
Map p316 (☑020-664 18 47; www.emaillekeizer. nl; 1e Sweelinckstraat 15; ◎10.30am-6pm Mon-Fri, 10am-6pm Sat; ☒16/24 Albert Cuypstraat) This colourful shop brims with enamel treasures, including metal tableware. The Dutch signs, such as the unmistakable 'coffeeshop' signs, make quirky souvenirs.

Oosterpark & East of the Amstel

Neighbourhood Top Five

❶ Tropenmuseum (p188) Browsing the impressive and creatively displayed ethnographic collection, plus imaginative exhibitions and a children's museum.

❷ Dappermarkt (p187) Sniffing out the Turkish pide stall amid multi-pack sock vendors.

❸ Oosterpark (p187) Relaxing with the locals, and seeking out the political monuments and wild parrots.

❹ Park Frankendael (p187) Exploring the thousand shades of green in this romantic park, formerly the weekend escape of Amsterdam's glitterati.

❺ Distilleerderij 't Nieuwe Diep (p191) Sampling some of the 100 or so gins at this divine little lakeside distillery, tucked away in Flevopark like the gingerbread house from *Hansel and Gretel*.

For more detail of this area see Map p318 ➡

Lonely Planet's Top Tip

With more and more riverside cafes and bars, Oosterpark and the area to the east have no shortage of places to sit and ponder the age-old Dutch bond with water. On gorgeous summer evenings many patrons arrive by boat, settle at a terrace table and watch the freight barges, tugs and rowing teams ply the waters.

✕ Best Places to Eat

➡ De Kas (p190)

➡ Marits Eetkamer (p189)

➡ Wilde Zwijnen (p189)

➡ Roopram Roti (p189)

For reviews, see p188 ➡

☕ Best Places to Drink

➡ De Ysbreeker (p191)

➡ Distilleerderij 't Nieuwe Diep (p191)

➡ Canvas (p191)

➡ De Biertuin (p192)

For reviews, see p191 ➡

🛍 Best Places to Shop

➡ Dappermarkt (p187)

➡ Tropenmuseum (p188)

➡ De Pure Markt (p193)

➡ All the Luck in the World (p193)

➡ We Are Vintage (p193)

For reviews, see p193 ➡

Explore Oosterpark & East of the Amstel

Oost is gradually seeing the tendrils of gentrification winding through the neigbourhood, with cafes, boutiques, bread makers, restaurants and hip hotels popping up everywhere. However, this is still an area with lots of local life and vitality, with many different communities living side by side, a fact that's most obvious when you browse through the area's Dappermarkt: stalls of knickers flap in the breeze as women in headscarves push buggies through the throng and you can feast on kebabs, piled-high dried fruit or fried fish.

Close by you'll find the Tropenmuseum (Museum of the Tropics), another rich cultural mix, whose endlessly intriguing artefacts, displayed with imagination, offer insights into Dutch colonial activities in the East Indies, as well as a great music section and temporary exhibits displaying anything from body art to Aleppo.

The green expanse of Oosterpark makes a fine diversion, with its large pond and several monuments, and increasing numbers of fun bars with lively terraces line the park. Another buzzing area for bars and restaurants is the pretty neighbourhood around Transvaalkade. Further east you hit Park Frankendael, a romantic former country estate, and a little further on is leafy Flevopark with its enchanting waterside gin distillery.

Local Life

➡**Moroccan & Turkish Delights** On Javastraat (which 1e Van Swindenstraat turns into) old Dutch fish shops and working-class bars sit adjacent to Moroccan and Turkish grocers.

➡**Allotments** Toward the northwest side of Park Frankendael lies a whole community of allotments dotted with teeny sheds, often with net curtains and exterior decorations. The owners sit out on sunny days with wine and picnic fixings.

➡**Market Finds** If you're looking for an authentic place to shop, Dappermarkt is it. If gourmet burgers and artisanal cheeses are your (organic) jam, the monthly De Pure Markt in Park Frankendael is the place.

Getting There & Away

➡**Tram** Tram 9 goes from the city centre to the Tropenmuseum. Trams 10 and 14 swing through the Oosterpark area on their east–west routes as well.

➡**Bus** No 757 starts at Amsterdam Centraal Station and stops near Oosterpark.

➡**Metro** The Wibautstraat stop is a stone's throw from the mod bars and hotels at the Oost's southwest edge.

◉ SIGHTS

There are few major sights in the Oost area, but it is home to the fascinating ethnographical Tropenmuseum, as well as lovely nearby Oosterpark, Park Frankendael and Flevopark, sites of several interesting memorials. Further east still, you can relax on Amsterdam's city beach at IJburg or take a trip to the impressive fortications of Muiden.

OOSTERPARK
PARK

Map p318 (☺dawn-dusk; ⊞; ⊟9 1e Van Swindenstraat) The lush greenery of Oosterpark, with wild parakeets in the trees and herons stalking the large ponds, despite being laid out in English style, has an almost tropical richness in this diverse neighbourhood. It was established in 1891 as a pleasure park for the diamond traders who found their fortunes in the South African mines, and it still has an elegant, rambling feel.

Families will enjoy the playground with a wading pool on the park's north side.

Look for these monuments as you explore the park:

SLAVERY MEMORIAL
MONUMENT

Slavery was abolished in the Dutch colonies of Suriname and the Netherlands Antilles in 1863, and Surinamese sculptor Erwin de Vries was commissioned to create this monument, which depicts both the oppression of slaves and hope for the future.

DE SCHREEUW
MONUMENT

(The Scream) A wavy profile shouting into the sky, this tall silver sculpture in Oosterpark honours free speech – it's also a tribute to controversial filmmaker Theo van Gogh, who was murdered nearby in 2004 because of his provocative works.

SPREEKSTEEN
LANDMARK

Another (living) monument to Van Gogh and freedom of speech, established in 2005, Spreeksteen is a rock podium marking a 'speakers' corner' in Oosterpark, where organised debates occur and people come to voice their opinion on all sorts of topics.

DAPPERMARKT
MARKET

Map p318 (www.dappermarkt.nl; Dapperstraat, btwn Mauritskade & Wijttenbachstraat; ☺9am-5pm Mon-Sat; ⊟3/7 Dapperstraat) The busy, untouristy Dappermarkt is a swirl of life and colour, with around 250 stalls. It reflects the Oost's diverse immigrant population, and is full of people (Africans, Turks, Dutch, hipsters), foods (apricots, olives, fish, Turkish kebabs) and goods from costume jewellery to cheap clothes, all sold from stalls lining the street.

Dapperstraat is named after Olfert Dapper, a 17th-century doctor and writer; his book *Description of Africa* was a seminal text of its time, which he wrote despite never having travelled outside the Netherlands.

FLEVOPARK
PARK

(☺24hr; ⊟7/14 Flevopark) Formerly a Jewish cemetery, this area was bought by the city in 1956, when it was turned into a park. It has a wilder, more rambling feel than Amsterdam's more central green spaces. There's a large pond, the Distilleerderij 't Nieuwe Diep (p191) gin distillery and a large outdoor swimming pool.

PARK FRANKENDAEL
PARK

Map p318 (Middenweg 72; ⊟Middenweg 72) These lovely, landscaped gardens are the grounds of a former country estate; the mansion, Frankendael House, is still standing and there are walking paths, flapping storks, decorative bridges and the remains of follies.

FRANKENDAEL HOUSE
HISTORIC BUILDING

Map p318 (www.huizefrankendael.nl; Middenweg 72; ☺gardens dawn-dusk, house noon-5pm Sun; ⊟9 Hugo de Vrieslaan) **FREE** This area was rolling countryside several centuries ago. In the 18th century, wealthy Amsterdammers would pass their summers and weekends in large country retreats on a tract of drained land called Watergraafsmeer. There were once around 40 such mansions, but the last survivor is Frankendael, an elegant, restored Louis XIV–style mansion. Its formal gardens are open to the public.

Staff hold a free open house every Sunday from noon to 5pm when you can explore the building on your own, or go on a guided tour (in Dutch). It departs at

TOP SIGHT
TROPENMUSEUM

The gloriously quirky Tropenmuseum (Tropics Museum) has a whopping collection of ethnographic artefacts. Galleries surround a huge central hall across three floors and present exhibits with insight, imagination and lots of multimedia. The impressive arched building was built in 1926 to house the Royal Institute of the Tropics, and is still a leading research institute for tropical hygiene and agriculture.

The Tropenmuseum galleries covering former Dutch territory are particularly rich, with gorgeous Indonesian jewellery, shadow puppets, and waxworks and dioramas illustrating tropical life through history. Downstairs, the *World of Music* is a splendid exhibit, showing how music and instruments travel throughout the world, with hands-on displays and plenty of opportunities to listen. There are also excellent temporary exhibits, which can range from body art to photographs of Aleppo.

The museum has a small kids' section, good for hands-on fun, with a shadow puppet theatre, the chance to construct with building blocks and other interactive exhibits.

DON'T MISS

➡ Music exhibition
➡ Cafe and terrace
➡ Special exhibits

PRACTICALITIES

➡ Tropics Museum
➡ Map p318, C1
➡ ☑0880 042 800
➡ www.tropen museum.nl
➡ Linnaeusstraat 2
➡ adult/child €15/8
➡ ☺10am-5pm Tue-Sun
➡ 🚹
➡ 🚊9/10/14 Alexanderplein

---

noon). Often there's an art exhibition going on to boot. The Merkelbach cafe (p189) sits in the adjoining coach house and its patio overlooks the gardens. Be sure to view the house's forecourt with its gushing fountain and statues of Bacchus and Ceres.

DE BIJLMER   AREA
(Ⓜ Bijlmer ArenA) De Bijlmer is a high-rise housing estate that was built in a hexagonal formation in 1966. It's an area that became known for crime and deprivation, and in 1992 was partly destroyed when a 747 jet crashed into two of its blocks. After this, the larger blocks were demolished, and investment led to the area becoming newly known as a centre for entertainment, shopping and innovative architecture. It's accessible by metro, and you arrive via the dramatic Nicholas Grimshaw–designed **Bijlmer ArenA station**, opened in 2007.

To the west lies Amsterdam ArenA (p193), the Afas Live (p193) and Ziggo Dome (p193). To the east is the Amsterdamse Poort shopping complex. When you get off the train, walk towards the Amsterdamse Poort shops. As you continue east you'll pass various mod, glassy office buildings set next to chain stores and small ethnic shops. De Bijlmer holds the city's largest Surinamese population, along with immigrants from West and North Africa.

🍴 EATING

There are some great eating choices – especially ethnic eats and creative cuisine – in Oost: they may take a little more time to reach, but they are well worth the effort.

DE TROPEN   INTERNATIONAL €
Map p318 (☑020-568 20 00; Linnaeusstraat 2; dishes €6-13; ☺10am-6pm, 🚹; 🚊9 Swindenstraat) This grand cafe has a superb terrace overlooking Oosterpark, and offers a suitably (as it's in the Tropenmuseum) global menu. Food receives mixed reports, but the setting is a wonderfully laid-back place to take some time out.

COTTAGE   GASTROPUB €
Map p318 (Linnaeusstraat 88; dishes €5-15; ☺8.30am-10pm Wed, Thu & Sun, to 11pm Fri & Sat; 🛜; 🚇Muiderpoort) A superb, permanently thronged (but not overly so), friendly

neighbourhood cafe-bar, where the quirky decor features lots of foxes, stuffed or pictorial, and the menu focuses on that most underrated of cuisines: British comfort food! There are fresh and original salads, eggs Benedict and sandwiches, plus scones with jam. There are some outside tables as well.

HET IJSBOEFJE
ICE CREAM €

Map p318 (Beukenplein 5; ⊗11am-10pm; 🚊Camperstraat) A popular ice-cream stop close to Oosterpark, with benches outside and tons of delicious flavours inside. There are always happy punters around tucking into satisfyingly big portions of its fruity or creamy confections.

ROOPRAM ROTI
SOUTH AMERICAN €

Map p318 (1e Van Swindenstraat 4; mains €4-10; ⊗2-9pm Tue-Sun; 🚊9 1e Van Swindenstraat) This simple Surinamese cafe often has a queue out the door, but it moves fairly fast. Place your order at the bar – the scrumptiously punchy and flaky lamb roti 'extra' (with egg) and a *barra* (lentil doughnut) at least – and don't forget the fiery hot sauce.

It's super-delicious for takeaway or to eat at one of the half-dozen tables.

MARITS EETKAMER
VEGETARIAN €€

Map p318 (www.maritseetkamer.nl; Andreas Bonnstraat 34; 3-/4-/5-course dinner €30/36/42; ⊗6pm-midnight Fri-Sun Sep-Jul; 🚊Weesperplein) Dining at Marits is like eating in someone's extremely elegant front room, with adjoining conservatory. Marits and Gino cook up a storm with a vegetarian set menu that changes every month (vegan food also available). Everything possible is sourced locally, so beer comes from Brouwerij 't IJ (p97), chocolates from Van Velze's, and organic eau-de-vie and liqueur from Distilleerderij 't Nieuwe Diep (p191).

The organic vegetables come from local farmer Theo. Private dinners may be arranged.

WILDE ZWIJNEN
DUTCH €€

(⊘020-463 30 43; www.wildezwijnen.com; Javaplein 23; mains €20, 3-/4-course menu €31.50/37.50; ⊗6-10pm Mon-Thu, noon-4pm & 6-10pm Fri-Sun, Eetbar from 5pm; 🛜; 🚊14 Javaplein) 🌱 The name means 'wild boar' and there's usually game on the menu in season at this modern Dutch restaurant. With pale walls and wood tables, the restaurant has

a pared-down, rustic-industrial feel, and serves locally sourced, seasonal dishes with a creative twist. It's more of a meat-eater's paradise, but there's usually a vegetarian choice as well.

The chevron-floored Wilde Zwijnen Eetbar next door is more of a tapas-style eatery, with delicious small plates for €7 to €12.

It's about 1km east of Oosterpark; get here via 1e Van Swindenstraat, which turns into Javastraat, which runs into Javaplein.

LOUIE LOUIE
INTERNATIONAL €€

Map p318 (⊘020-370 29 81; www.louielouie. nl; Linnaeusstraat 11; dishes €7-15; ⊗9am-1am Sun-Thu, to 3am Fri & Sat; 🚊Muiderpoort) With rough wooden floorboards, big windows, a fur-backed bar, model stags and squashy leather sofas, plus a covered terrace, Louie Louie is a relaxed brasserie-style place that's perfect for a chilled-out meal with a buzzy vibe any time of day. Dishes run the gamut from eggs in the morning to tacos, steaks, burgers and ceviche later in the day.

JACOBZ
INTERNATIONAL €€

Map p318 (www.jacobsz.amsterdam; Ringdijk 1a; 3-course menu €32; ⊗6pm-midnight; 🚊Muiderpoort) Named after the building's 18th-century architect, Caspar Philips Jacobsz, this restaurant is housed in a grand old inn (a former courthouse, then turned into 'the courthouse inn' before its current incarnation) on the corner of a canal. It offers fine gastronomy and fresh seasonal ingredients at reasonable prices.

EETCAFE IBIS
ETHIOPIAN €€

Map p318 (⊘020-692 62 67; www.eetcafeibis. com; Weesperzijde 43; mains €14-17; ⊗5-11pm Tue-Sun; 🍴; 🚊3 Wibautstraat/Ruyschstraat) Bright with African art and brilliant-hued textiles, Ibis is a cosy and delightful spot to get your hands on (literally, using the spongy Ethiopian *injera* bread) herb-laced vegetable stews and spicy lamb and beef dishes; try the Ibis Special (meat or veg versions), which combines five dishes and bread. Ibis sells African beers to go with the authentic food.

MERKELBACH
CAFE €€

Map p318 (⊘020-665 08 80; Middenweg 72; dishes €7-14, lunch menu €32; ⊗8.30am-10.30pm Tue-Sat, to 6pm Sun & Mon; 🚊0 Hugo de Vrieslaan) The Merkelbach cafe sits in the coach house adjoining Frankendael House

WORTH A DETOUR

MUIDEN

Only 20 to 30 minutes from Amsterdam Centraal by train, or a more leisurely ferry ride from IJBurg (p192), Muiden is an unhurried historical town renowned for its fairy-tale red-brick castle, the Muiderslot. Life otherwise focuses on the busy central lock that funnels scores of pleasure boats out into the vast IJsselmeer.

Built in 1280 by Count Floris V, son of Willem II, exceptionally preserved moated fortress **Muiderslot** (Muiden Castle; www.muiderslot.nl; Herengracht 1; adult/child €13.50/9; ⏰10am-5pm Mon-Fri, from noon Sat & Sun Apr-Oct, noon-5pm Sat & Sun Nov-Mar) is equipped with round towers, a French innovation. The count was a champion of the poor and a French sympathiser, two factors that were bound to spell trouble; Floris was imprisoned in 1296 and murdered while trying to flee. Today it's the Netherlands' most visited castle. The interior can be seen only on 30-minute guided tours. The I Amsterdam Card (www.iamsterdam.com; per 24/48/72 hours €49/59/69) is valid here.

Off the coast lies a derelict fort on the island of **Pampus** (www.pampus.nl; adult/child ferry & tour €16.50/12.50; ⏰9am-5pm Tue-Sun Apr-Oct). This massive 19th-century bunker was a key member of a ring of 42 fortresses built to defend Amsterdam and is great fun to explore. The huge defences were designed to be flooded if the city came under attack. Unfortunately, airplanes came into the picture and the fortifications were never used. Rescued from disrepair by Unesco, Pampas is now a World Heritage Site. Ferries to Pampus depart from Muiderslot port on a varying schedule in season. Usually there's at least one morning departure, which allows a couple of hours to prowl the fort before a mid-afternoon return.

In warm weather the clientele of little bar **Café Ome Ko** (www.cafeomekomuiden.nl; cnr Herengracht & Naardenstraat; ⏰8am-2am Sun-Thu, to 3am Fri & Sat), with large green-striped awnings, turns the street outside into one big party. When there's no party on, it's a perfect spot to watch the comings and goings through the busy lock right outside. It serves lunchtime sandwiches and classic Dutch bar snacks (croquettes et al).

Muiden is easily reached from IJburg: it's a pleasant signposted 7km cycle route (you can also walk it in around 1½ hours). Alternatively, ferry is the best way to reach either Muiden or Pampas from IJburg. **Veerdienst** (p192) ferries depart from the marina and include admission to either site. Bicycles travel for free.

Alternatively, buses 320, 322 and 327 link Amsterdam's Amstel station (20 minutes, twice hourly) with Muiden. The castle is then a 1km walk.

(p187), and proffers dishes such as soups, salads and pastas with Slow Food credentials; its patio overlooks Frankendael's formal gardens (open to the public).

CAFF MOJO   INTERNATIONAL €€
Map p318 (☎020-233 13 67; www.mojo-amsterdam.nl; Ringdijk 3; lunch dishes €3-10, dinner €13-17; ⏰11am-1am Sun-Thu, to 3am Fri & Sat; Ⓜ Wibautstraat) A lovely open-fronted bar right by the canal, with a superb terrace that's just perfect for a summer drink. Quaff beers from Brouwerij'tij, the local brewery, while you chow down on burgers and steaks.

★ DE KAS   INTERNATIONAL €€€
Map p318 (☎020-462 45 62; www.restaurant dekas.nl; Park Frankendael, Kamerlingh

Onneslaan 3; lunch/dinner menu €39/49.50; ⏰noon-2pm & 6.30-10pm Mon-Fri, 6.30-10pm Sat; Ⓓ; ☷9 Hogeweg) In a row of stately greenhouses dating to 1926, De Kas has an organic attitude to match its chic glass greenhouse setting – try to visit during a thunderstorm! It grows most of its own herbs and produce right here and the result is incredibly pure flavours with innovative combinations. There's one set menu daily, based on whatever has been freshly harvested. Reserve in advance.

CAFE-RESTAURANT DAUPHINE   FRENCH €€€
Map p318 (☎020-462 16 46; www.cafe restaurantdauphine.nl; Prins Bernhardplein 175; dishes €15-38; ⏰9am-1am Mon-Fri, noon-1am Sat & Sun, kitchen closed 10.30pm; Ⓜ Amstel)

There's something pleasing about dining in such a ginormous space, and this stylish converted Renault car showroom serves up French-influenced dishes as well as hearty portions of hamburgers and steaks. It's named after a type of car produced by the company in the 1950s, and is fronted by a huge neon sign.

🍷 DRINKING & NIGHTLIFE

Oost has some of Amsterdam's quirkiest drinking options, from rooftop bars with stupendous views, to a gin distillery hidden in a park and a brewery beneath a windmill.

★DISTILLEERDERIJ 'T NIEUWE DIEP
DISTILLERY

(www.nwediep.nl; Flevopark 13; ⊙3-8pm Tue-Sun Apr-Oct, to 6pm Nov-Mar; 🚃7/14 Soembawastraat) Appearing out of the woods like a *Hansel and Gretel* cottage, the quaint architecture and rural setting of this old pumping station is enchanting and feels like you've escaped to a magical countryside retreat, though it's just leafy Flevopark. The little distillery makes around 100 small-batch *jenevers* (Dutch gin), herbal bitters, liqueurs and fruit distillates from organic ingredients according to age-old Dutch recipes.

The outdoor terrace is on a little lake next to an orchard. To get here by public transport, walk east from the tram stop; it's about a 10-minute walk into the park. Cash only.

★DE YSBREEKER
BROWN CAFE

Map p318 (www.deysbreeker.nl; Weesperzijde 23; ⊙8am-1am Sun-Thu, to 2am Fri & Sat; 🚃; 🚃3 Wibautstraat/Ruyschstraat) This historic but updated brown cafe first opened its doors in 1702, and is named after an ice-breaker that used to dock in front to break the ice on the river during the winter months (stained-glass windows illustrate the scene). Inside, stylish drinkers hoist beverages in the plush booths and along the marble bar.

It's great for organic and local beers (such as De Prael) and bar snacks like lamb meatballs, and there's a glorious

canal-side terrace for watching the river boats glide by.

★CANVAS
BAR

Map p318 (www.canvas7.nl; Wibautstraat 150; ⊙7am-1am Mon-Thu, to 4am Fri, 8am-4am Sat, to 1am Sun; Ⓜ Wibautstraat) Zoom up to the Volkshotel's 7th floor (located in the former *Volkskrant* newspaper office) for the hotel bar (open to non-guests) with one of the best views in town. A creative-folk and hipster magnet, there are few better places for a beer or cocktails than this slice of urban cool. On weekend nights, it morphs into a fresh-beat dance club.

Feeling wild? Sneak up to the roof for a dip in one of the hot tubs.

The Wibautstraat metro stop is a stone's throw away; follow signs saying 'Gijsbrecht van Aemstelstraat' as you exit the station.

BAR BUKOWSKI
BAR

Map p318 (🕿020-370 16 85; www.barbukowski.nl; Oosterpark 10; ⊙8am-1am Mon-Thu, to 3am Fri, 9am-3am Sat, to 1am Sun; 🚃3/7 Beukenweg) Exuding bohemian cool in an emulation of its namesake, barfly writer Charles Bukowski, this cafe is a fine spot to linger – under a cascade of greenery outside on sunny days, or in the art-deco interior when it's time to hunker down. Linger over a coffee, Heineken, banana milkshake or jasmine tea. Supplement with a baguette sandwich or *flammkuchen* (Alsatian thin-crust pizza).

COMMUNAL BAKERY

Breathe in the scent of fresh baking in the **Baking Lab** (Map p318; 🕿020-240 01 58; www.bakinglab.nl; Linnaeusstraat 99; 2hr workshop €20; ⊙9am-5pm Wed-Sat; 🚃3/7/9 Linnaeusstraat). You can make your own bread here, in the spirit of the idea of the old communal bakery, when people used to bring dough to knead and then put into the shared oven as few houses had ovens of their own.

Baking workshops are also offered for both adults and children.

You can also snack on hummus or soup of the day (dishes €7 to 99).

WORTH A DETOUR

IJBURG

From the Eastern Islands, it's less than 10 minutes by tram 26 to Amsterdam's new-est neighbourhood, IJburg, which feels like an architectural vision of a model city. Construction by the city of Amsterdam first started on these three artificial islands – Steigereiland, Haveneiland and Rieteilanden – in the IJmeer lake in 1996 to ease Am-sterdam's housing shortage. The first IJburg residents arrived in 2002.

Checking out striking modern architecture aside, at the eastern end of IJburg is Amsterdam's (artificial) beach, **Blijburg** (🚊IJburg), a lovely swathe of white imported sand. There's a laid-back **beach bar** (📞020-416 03 30; www.blijburg.nl; Pampuslaan 501; ☺from 9am-late; 🚊IJburg), and you can go windsurfing or paddle boarding here; **Sur-fcenter IJburg** (www.surfcenterijburg.nl; Berthaanstrakade; windsurfer/wetsuit rental per hour €20/5; ☺3-9pm Wed & Fri, 11am-6.30pm Sat & Sun Apr-Oct; 🚊26 IJburg) rents wind-surfers from its shipping container.

The neighbourhood is also home to some superb restaurants and bars. Organic produce is prioritised by the passionate Italian chefs at **Restaurant Bloem** (📞020-416 06 77; www.bloemopijburg.nl; IJburglaan 1289; mains €16-24; ☺5.30-10pm; 🚊26 IJburg), with a breezy beach-style decor that belies its exceptional food. The menu changes daily but might include house-made linguine with clams, chilli and parsley or fresh tuna grilled with white asparagus and served with green-bean salsa, as well as au-thentic wood-fired pizzas. Cash only.

Fittingly named for the Normaal Amsterdams Peil (NAP), Amsterdam's sea-level benchmark, harbourside restaurant **NAP** (www.napamsterdam.nl; Krijn Taconiskade 124; mains €13-22, tapas €4-14; ☺8.30am-midnight Mon-Thu, to 3am Fri, 10am-1am Sat, to midnight Sun; 🚻; 🚊26 IJburg) has a terrace overlooking IJburg's boat-filled marina and a chic semi-industrial interior. Tapas span crostini with carpaccio to spicy prawns and oysters with vinaigrette, while mains include chanterelle risotto and seared sea bass with tomato salsa.

Timber benches with funky red cushions line the pavement of **Dok 48** (www.dok48. nl; Krijn Taconiskade 328-330; ☺11am-midnight Tue-Sun; 🛜; 🚊26 IJburg), which also has a table- and chair-filled summer terrace right on the marina that's idyllic for watch-ing the boats docking and setting sail. There's a good range of specialist beers, as well as wines and bubbles by the glass, and top-notch food, too. DJs regularly spin at weekends.

There are also ferries from IJBurg to Muiden (p190), the most scenic way to visit its medieval castle, the Muiderslot, and fortress island, Pampus. The **boat** (www. amsterdamtouristferry.com; Krijn Taconiskade 124; adult/child ferry & admission to either Pampas or Muiderslot €20/15; ☺11am Tue-Sun Apr-Oct) leaves mid-morning, allowing a couple of hours' exploration before the return journey.

BAR BASQUIAT BAR
Map p318 (www.barbasquiat.nl; Javastraat; ☺9am-1am Sun-Thu, to 3am Fri & Sat; 🚊Muider-poort) Cool neighbourhood bar with out-side tables and a lively buzz on ever livelier Javastraat, serving up local beers and cocktails, as well as excellent Vietnamese street food.

DE BIERTUIN BEER GARDEN
Map p318 (www.debiertuin.nl; Linnaeusstraat 29; ☺11am-1am Sun-Thu, to 3am Fri & Sat; 🛜; 🚊9 1e Van Swindenstraat) With a covered terrace, 'the beer garden' (with heaters for chillier weather) attracts a young and beautiful crowd of locals for the lengthy beer list (around 12 on tap and 50 more Dutch and Belgian varieties in the bottle) accompanied by simple but tasty food, such as burgers.

COFFEE BRU COFFEE
Map p318 (📞020-751 99 56; www.coffeebru.nl; Beukenplein 14; ☺8am-6pm Mon-Fri, 9am-6pm Sat & Sun; 🛜; 🚊Camperstraat) Lots of light, tick; excellent coffee, tick; mismatched chairs, tick; scrubbed-wood tables, tick: all the requisites for a popular neighbourhood hang-out, including freshly made sand-wiches, plus a tempting selection of cakes, including some vegan-friendly treats.

SPARGO BAR

Map p318 (www.cafespargo.nl; Linnaeusstraat 37a; ☺10am-1am Sun-Thu, to 3am Fri & Sat; ☒9 1e Van Swindenstraat) Spargo has a buzzy little covered terrace, with heaters for cold weather, conveniently close to Oosterpark and the Tropenmuseum. It pours several local Dutch brews, including Brouwerij 't IJ (the windmill brewery a short distance away). FYI, the cafe's sign looks like 'Spar90'.

⭐ ENTERTAINMENT

STUDIO K CINEMA

Map p318 (☑020-692 04 22; www.studio-k.nu; Timorplein 62; ☺11am-1am Sun-Thu, to 3am Fri & Sat; ☎; ☒14 Zeeburgerdijk) This hip Oost arts centre always has something going on, with two cinemas, a nightclub, a stage for bands and a theatre, an eclectic restaurant (serving sandwiches for lunch, and vegetarian-friendly, international-flavoured dishes for dinner) and a huge terrace. Stop in for a coffee and you might wind up staying all night to dance.

You can also rent bicycles at the shop next door.

ZIGGO DOME CONCERT VENUE

(www.ziggodome.nl; De Passage 100; ☎; Ⓜ Bijlmer ArenA) The 17,000-seat, indoor Ziggo Dome hosts big-name concerts: Metallica, Katy Perry and Nick Cave have recently tramped these boards.

AMSTERDAM ARENA FOOTBALL

(www.amsterdamarena.nl; Arena Blvd 1; ☎; Ⓜ Bijlmer ArenA) Amsterdam ArenA is a high-tech complex with a retractable roof and seating for 52,000 spectators. Four-times European champion Ajax, the Netherlands' most famous football team, play here. Football games usually take place on Saturday evenings and Sunday afternoons from August to May. The arena is about 7km southeast of central Amsterdam, easily accessible by metro.

Fans can also take a one-hour guided tour of the stadium (adult/child €14.50/9). There are usually eight tours daily, and you can also book special kids' tours; see the website for the schedule.

AFAS LIVE CONCERT VENUE

(www.afaslive.nl; Arena Blvd 590; Ⓜ Bijlmer ArenA) Run by Live Nation, this midsized venue has excellent acoustics and lighting. Expect rock and pop acts from medium to big names.

🛍 SHOPPING

You can shop all over the tropics at the Tropenmuseum gift shop, while in the surrounding streets there is a smattering of interesting independent boutiques. Perhaps the best places to shop in Oost are the markets, with the multi-ethnic Dappermarkt for cheap clothes, toys, electronics and more, and the monthly organic and crafts De Pure Markt.

WE ARE VINTAGE VINTAGE

Map p318 (www.facebook.com/WeAreVintage. eu; 1e Van Swindenstraat 43; ☺11am-7pm Mon-Sat, noon-6pm Sun; ☒9 Swindenstraat) This packed-to-the-gills shop has a great range of good-quality second-hand threads, from '90s shirts to '70s maxi dresses.

DE PURE MARKT MARKET

Map p318 (www.puremarkt.nl; Park Frankendael; ☺11am-6pm last Sun of month Mar-Oct & Dec; ☒9 Hogeweg) On the last Sunday of the month De Pure Markt sets up in Park Frankendael with artisanal producers selling delicious foodstuffs, plus arts and crafts that make great gifts.

ALL THE LUCK IN THE WORLD HOMEWARES

Map p318 (www.alltheluckintheworld.nl; Linnaeusstraat 20; ☺10am-6pm; ☒7 Linnaeusstraat) A charming little concept store selling chic accessories, jewellery and quirky yet classy homewares and gifts. It's also a cafe.

Amsterdam Noord

Neighbourhood Top Five

❶ A'DAM Tower (p196) Taking in the view from this skyscraper of fantastical fun, complete with daredevil swing over the edge, plus revolving restaurants, a hotel and nightclubs.

❷ Nieuwendammerdijk (p196) Meandering along this enchantingly pretty narrow dyke of wooden houses, surrounded by nodding flowers, greenery and birdsong.

❸ EYE Film Institute (p196) Admiring the angular, gleaming-white architecture of the IJ-side Eye, with its exhibitions on all things cinema and a great cafe with waterside terrace.

❹ Kunststad (Art City) (p196) Exploring the hipster artist studios in this massive former warehouse, with artworks dangling from the ceiling and enough room to cycle around.

❺ Bars, Cafes & Restaurants (p199) Hanging out at one of Noord's ultra-cool bar-cafe-restaurants, such as Pllek, with its waterside location and artificial beach.

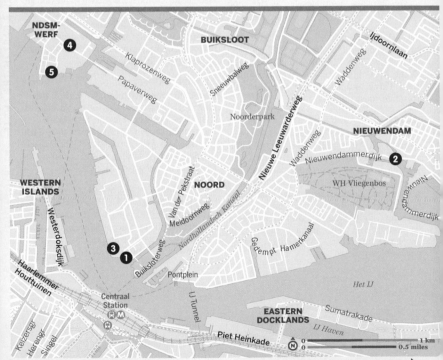

For more detail of this area see Map p319 ➡

Explore Amsterdam Noord

The NDSM former shipbuilding yard was an important industrial area that fell into disuse from the 1980s, before being taken over by squatters who filled the void. Today it has numerous cool waterside restaurants, striking modernist architecture, a hangar full of artists' studios, the huge monthly IJ Hallen flea market and an ex-USSR submarine in the harbour. From here it's a five- to 10-minute bike ride to the A'DAM Tower and the EYE Film Institute (also accessible from Centraal Station via direct ferry).

Further along the riverbank to the east are more waterside bars and restaurants, and the enchantingly pretty dike, Nieuwendammerdijk. The nearest ferry spot for this area is that to IJplein. There are plenty of cycle routes into the countryside from Amsterdam Noord, and from here you can explore the lakes and *polder* (area of drained land) that lie to the north. Pick up a free informative map at various restaurants or information points in the north, or from a tourist office before you head over the water.

Local Life

➡**Bike Rides** Take a bike ride into the countryside north of Amsterdam.

➡**Coffee with a View** Have some proper Italian coffee at the Caffè Italiano Al Ponte (p199) kiosk by the IJplein ferry stop.

➡**Treasure Hunt** Rummage for vintage furniture gems at Neef Louis Design (p199) or IJ Hallen (p199) flea market.

➡**Live Music** Spend a Saturday afternoon listening to live music on the small stage at Café Noorderlicht (p199).

Getting There & Away

➡**Boat** There are 24-hour ferries between Amsterdam Centraal Station, Buiksloterweg, NDSM-werf and IJplein.

➡**Bike** You can take bikes over on the ferry, or hire bikes locally.

➡**Metro** From mid-2018 Amsterdam's new metro line adds a link to the Noord.

Lonely Planet's Top Tip

The best way to explore Noord is via bike. Places are spread out, there isn't much traffic and there are lots of cycle routes. You can take bikes on the free ferries, or hire one on the Noord side, either through Orangebike or the Donkey Republic app.

✖ Best Places to Eat

➡ Hotel de Goudfazant (p197)
➡ Cafe-Restaurant Stork (p197)
➡ Landmarkt (p197)
➡ Cafe Modern (p197)
➡ Moon (p197)

For reviews, see p197 ➡

🍷 Best Places to Drink

➡ Café de Ceuvel (p197)
➡ Café Noorderlicht (p199)
➡ Oedipus Brewery & Tap Room (p199)
➡ Pllek (p199)
➡ Caffè Italiano Al Ponte (p199)

For reviews, see p197 ➡

🔒 Best Places to Shop

➡ IJ Hallen (p199)
➡ Neef Louis Design (p199)
➡ Blom & Blom (p199)
➡ Van Dijk and Ko (p199)

For reviews, see p199 ➡

◉ SIGHTS

★ A'DAM TOWER
NOTABLE BUILDING

Map p319 (www.adamtoren.nl; Overhoeksplein 1; Lookout adult/child €12.50/6.50, premium €15/7.50, family ticket min 3 people €10/5; ⊙Lookout 10am-10pm; 🚊Badhuiskade) The 22-storey A'DAM Tower used to be the Royal Dutch Shell oil company offices, but has been funked up to become Amsterdam's newest big attraction. Take the trippy lift to the rooftop for awe-inspiring views in all directions, with a giant four-person swing that kicks out over the edge for those who have a head for heights (you're well secured and strapped in).

Before you take the lift, you can have a green-screen photo taken that looks like you're sitting on a metal bar vastly high up; a digital download is included in the Premium ticket.

There's a swish bar for drinks and light meals and the Moon (p197) revolving restaurant on the 19th floor. There are also two nightclubs (one up high, and one in the basement) and a funky hotel. The tower has wheelchair access.

EYE FILM INSTITUTE
MUSEUM, CINEMA

Map p319 (☏020-589 14 00; www.eyefilm.nl; IJpromenade 1; ⊙10am-7pm Sat-Thu, to 9pm Fri; 🚊Buiksloterweg) At this modernist architectural triumph that seems to balance on its edge on the banks of the IJ (also pronounced 'eye') river, the institute screens movies from the 40,000-title archivein four theatres, sometimes with live music. Exhibits (€9 to €15) of costumes, digital art and other cinephile amusements run in conjunction with what's playing. A view-tastic bar-restaurant with a fabulously sunny terrace (when the sun makes an appearance) is a popular hang-out on this side of the river.

EYE does not accept cash; you must use a credit or debit card.

★ NDSM-WERF
AREA

Map p319 (www.ndsm.nl; 🚊NDSM-werf) NDSM-werf is a derelict shipyard turned edgy arts community 15 minutes upriver from the city centre. It wafts a post-apocalyptic vibe: an old submarine slumps in the harbour, abandoned trams rust by the water's edge, and graffiti splashes across almost every surface. Young creatives hang out at the smattering of cool cafes. Hip businesses like MTV and Red Bull have their European headquarters here. The area is also a centre for underground culture and events, such as the Over het IJ Festival (p24).

SUBMARINE B-80
SUBMARINE

Map p319 (NDSM Harbour; 🚊NDSM-werf) Soviet Project 611 submarine B-80 dates from 1952, and was built in Severodvinsk, Russia. It was moored previously in the Dutch Navy port of Den Helder in North Holland, but was brought to Amsterdam. It had its interior stripped as the owners hoped to rent it as a party venue, but it now lies as an empty, if visually arresting, shell in the harbour.

KUNSTSTAD
ART STUDIO

Map p319 (Art City; 🚊NDSM-werf) This former shipbuilding warehouse is filled with artists' studios, with 175 artists working in the NDSM *broedplaats* (breeding ground). It's a big enough space that you can cycle or walk around the area, with huge artworks hanging from the ceiling, and structures within the hangar.

SEXYLAND
ARTS CENTRE

Map p319 (www.sexyland.amsterdam; Ms van Riemsdijkweg 39; weekly membership €2.50, admission dependent on event; ⊙hours vary; 🚊NDSM-werf) See the neon sign and you'll be forgiven for thinking this is an outpost of the Red Light District. But Sexyland is a members' club that has 365 co-owners, each of whom puts on an annual event. This can range from ping-pong to tantric tango, with club nights at weekends; the public can attend any of the activities during that week by buying a week-long membership.

KRAANSPOOR
ARCHITECTURE

Map p319 (🚊NDSM-werf) 'Craneway' is an extraordinary piece of architecture, built above a repurposed (you've guessed it) craneway, by OTH Architecten in 2007. The glass box above the stilts of the industrial base looks almost weightless, and houses offices with amazing waterfront views.

★ NIEUWENDAMMERDIJK
AREA

Map p319 (🚊Badhuiskade) Enchanting chocolate-box prettiness characterises this long, narrow street of wooden Dutch houses, now prime real estate, with hollyhocks nodding beside every porch. Many houses date from the 1500s, and numbers 202 to 204 were where the shipbuilding family De Vries-Lentsh lived. Numbers 301 to 309 were once captains' houses.

 EATING

Noord has some spectacular places to eat, with superlative cooking, often sourcing fresh local ingredients, in striking waterfront spaces.

LANDMARKT   INTERNATIONAL €

(www.landmarkt.nl; Schellingwouderdijk 339; ⊙9am-8pm Mon-Sat, 11am-7pm Sun; ♠) This large covered food market is wonderland for Noord foodies, with fresh fruit, vegetables, an on-site bakery, special foodstuffs, and a fine selection of cheese, wine and beers. There's also an in-house eatery with well-priced snacks and dishes. It's a great place to go with kids on a sunny day as there's a field and swings, and there's outdoor seating that feels immersed in countryside.

WAARGENOEGEN   CAFE €

Map p319 (Papaverweg 46; snacks €4-6; ⊙10am-4pm Tue-Fri, to 5pm Sat, 11am-5pm Sun; ♠; ⬛NDSM-werf) This hippie-feeling cafe in a container behind two large vintage stores, Neef Louis (p199) and Van Dijk & Ko (p199), serves deliciously good toasties and a particularly fantastic apple tart.

CAFE-RESTAURANT STORK   SEAFOOD €€

Map p319 (☑020-634 40 00; Gedempt Hamerkanaal 201; lunch €9-17, dinner €14-22; ⊙11am-late, closed Mon Oct-Mar; ⬛IJplein) A sometime factory on the IJ river, this huge place has a dramatically soaring interior and a cool terrace shaded with sails on the waterfront. It feels right that Stork should specialise in fish and seafood (though there are a few veggie and meat dishes too), serving especially good crab as well as other crustaceans and fresh fish of the day.

CAFE MODERN   ITALIAN €€

Map p319 (Meidoornweg 2; 4-course menu €40, mains €12-16; ⊙from 6pm Mon-Sat; ⬛Buiksloterweg) Amid artful yet simple decor with a mid-century feel, Cafe Modern is serious about its gastronomy and is a good value option for fine cooking, with lots of veggie choices using fresh seasonal ingredients for dishes like artichoke with walnut, saffron risotto or broad beans with burrata.

HANGAR   RESTAURANT €€

Map p319 (☑020-363 86 57; Aambeeldstraat 36, snacks & mains €13-24, ⊙10am-1am Mon-Thu, to 3am Fri & Sat, to midnight Sun; ⬛IJplein) A restaurant, in a...hangar, this relaxing choice is on the water's edge, with a great deck and laid-back music, giving it a beachy vibe. Food includes dishes such as crunchy Ottolenghi salads, succulent burgers and steaks.

★HOTEL DE GOUDFAZANT   FRENCH €€€

Map p319 (☑020-636 51 70; www.hoteldegoudfazant.nl; Aambeeldstraat 10h; 3-course menu €32; ⊙6pm-1am Tue-Sun; ⬛32/33 Johan van Hasseltweg, ⬛IJplein) With a name taken from lyrics of the Jacques Brel song 'Les Bourgeois', this extraordinary gourmet hipster restaurant spreads through a cavernous former garage, still raw and industrial, and sticks to the theme by having cars parked inside. Rockstar-looking chefs cook up a French-influenced storm in the open kitchen. There is no hotel, FYI, except in name.

MOON   INTERNATIONAL €€€

Map p319 (A'DAM Tower, Overhoeksplein 1; lunch 3-/4-/5-course menu €40/50/60, dinner 5-/6-/7-course menu €60/70/80; ⊙noon-2pm Thu-Sun, 6-11pm daily; ⬛Buiksloterweg) The rather swanky revolving restaurant at the top of the A'DAM Tower (p196) is an undoubtedly cheesy but nevertheless enjoyable novelty occasion restaurant. There's one revolution an hour, and the food is fairly fussy but good quality, with Moon-themed dishes on the menu. Book ahead.

🍷 DRINKING & NIGHTLIFE

Amsterdam Noord has some of the city's most fabulous bars on the waterfront, built from shipping containers, on boats, or with their own beaches and gardens.

★CAFÉ DE CEUVEL   BAR

Map p319 (☑020-229 62 10; www.deceuvel.nl; Korte Papaverweg 4; ⊙11am-midnight Tue-Thu & Sun, to 2am Fri & Sat; ⬛34/35) The inspiring Café de Ceuvel is tucked in a former shipyard in Amsterdam Noord. Designed by architect Wouter Valkenier and built from recycled materials, this waterside spot is a surprising oasis alongside the canal and built out onto an island. Drinks include homemade ginger lemonade, plus bottled beer from local heroes Oedipus Brewery.

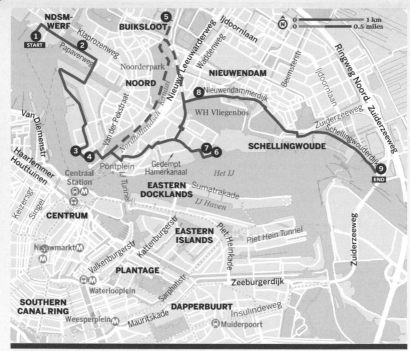

Cycling Tour
Amsterdam Noord

START NDSM-WERF
END LANDMARKT
LENGTH 12KM; 35 MINUTES TO TWO HOURS

It's great to take a bike ride around the Noord and there's a wide choice of cycleways. Tourist bike maps are available at any I Amsterdam office or various info points in the Noord, including the IJplein ferry stop.

For a bike ride that takes in some of the highlights, catch a ferry to **1 NDSM-werf** (p196), a booming shipbuilding area from 1870 until bankruptcy beckoned in 1984. Now a centre for counterculture, here you can explore the artists' studios, see the submarine and have a drink. Next stop, you can visit the vintage shops on Papaverweg, including **2 Neef Louis Design** (p199). From here, it's only around a five-minute cycle to reach the angular **3 EYE Film Institute** (p196) and the 1971 **4 A'DAM**

Tower (p196). Moving on along the riverbank, you can either cycle inland along Noordhollandsch Kanaal to see the windmill **5 Krijtmolen d'Admiraal**, or you can carry along the riverbank, in which case you'll need to take your bike along the top of a lock gate (there's a narrow path) to continue. Beyond here, it's a few minutes' cycling to **6 Hangar** (p197) and **7 Hotel de Goudfazant** (p197).

Next, the route goes a little inland, heading towards a wooded area, from where you turn right onto the top of a dyke. This leads you along the Noord's prettiest street, **8 Nieuwendammerdijk** (p196). Continue along the road that hugs the riverfront, until you reach the food emporium of **9 Landmarkt** (p197), a superb halt for a drink or a snack, before heading back or to eastern Amsterdam over Zuiderzeeweg bridge.

★CAFÉ NOORDERLICHT
BAR

Map p319 (www.noorderlichtcafe.nl; NDSM-plein 102; ☺11am-10pm, closed Mon in winter; ☻NDSM-werf) The original Café Noorderlicht was in a boat, which burned down. Safely ensconced in a soaring flag-draped greenhouse, with grassy waterside lawns outside and a mini-stage, it now has a pub-garden-meets-festival vibe. There's a big play area outside, with a tin rocket to climb on, so it's good for families. Food, craft beers and lots of other drinks are on the menu.

★PLLEK
BAR

Map p319 (www.pllek.nl; TT Neveritaweg 59; ☺9.30am-1am Sun-Thu, to 3am Fri & Sat; ☻NDSM-werf) Uber-cool Pllek is a Noord magnet, with hip things of all ages streaming over to hang out in its interior made of old shipping containers and lie out on its artificial sandy beach when the weather deems it so. It's a terrific spot for a waterfront beer or glass of wine.

OEDIPUS BREWERY & TAP ROOM
BREWERY

Map p319 (www.oedipus.com; Gedempt Hamerkanaal 85; ☺5-10pm Thu, 2-11pm Fri & Sat, 2-10pm Sun; ☻IJplein) Oedipus began with four friends trying out some experimental brewing methods, and its bright-labelled bottles are now an Amsterdam institution. This funky warehouse space is a key Noord hang-out, with outdoor seating lit by coloured fairy lights. Immerse yourself in some Oedipus history by sampling Mannenliefde 'Men Love', their first-ever beer, still going strong (not too strong, at 6%).

CAFFÈ ITALIANO AL PONTE
CAFE

Map p319 (Pontplein 1; ☺8am-5pm Mon-Fri, 10am-5pm Sat & Sun; ☻IJplein) This little kiosk next to the ferry stop serves wonderful authentic Italian coffee. The friendly Italian owners also make excellent *panino* (sandwiches), and there are a few tables so you can drink your coffee with a fabulous waterside view.

CAFÉ 'T SLUISJE
BROWN CAFE

Map p319 (Nieuwendammerdijk 297; ☺10am-1am Tue-Sun; ☻IJplein) The 'cafe of the lock' has been run by the same family for four generations, and overlooks the *sluisje* (lock) of its name in a very pretty spot. It also has a very good apple tart.

☆ ENTERTAINMENT

TOLHUISTUIN
LIVE PERFORMANCE

Map p319 (www.tolhuistuin.nl; IJpromenade 2; ☺10am-10pm; ☻Buiksloterweg) In what was the former Shell workers' canteen for 70 years from 1941, the nifty Tolhuistuin arts centre hosts African dance troupes, grime DJs and much more on its garden stage under twinkling lights, and also houses club nights in its Paradiso nightclub.

🛍 SHOPPING

Especially good for hunting down vintage or creative finds, Amsterdam Noord has increasing numbers of independent vendors hawking unusual stuff, as well as the city's best flea market. For a more local market head to Van der Pekstraat, which also has plenty of small boutiques.

BLOM & BLOM
HOMEWARES

Map p319 (www.blomandblom.com; Chrysantenstraat 20; ☺10am-6pm Tue-Fri, 11am-5pm Sat; ☻NDSM-werf) Repurposed German industrial lamps are on sale at this one-of-a-kind workshop, run by two brothers (hence, Blom & Blom). Each lamp has a description of where the fixture was found, the state it was in, its condition and its original purpose. They're costly, but glorious.

VAN DIJK & KO
VINTAGE

Map p319 (www.vandijkenko.nl; Papaverweg 46; ☺10am-6pm Mon-Sat, noon-6pm Sun; ☻NDSM-werf) Warehouse full of interesting antiques and vintage furniture, wardrobes, pictures and more for sale.

NEEF LOUIS DESIGN
VINTAGE

Map p319 (www.neeflouis.nl; Papaverweg 46; ☺10am-6pm; ☻NDSM-werf) A huge warehouse full of vintage, designer and industrial furniture, this is a treasure trove of lamps made out of books, pop-art chairs, mid-century bookcases, antique clay pipes, neon signs and much, much more. There's a cafe on-site.

IJ HALLEN
MARKET

Map p319 (www.ij-hallen.nl; Tt Neveritaweg 15; adult/child €5/2; ☺9am-4.30pm Sat & Sun monthly; ☻NDSM-werf) The whopping IJ Hallen flea market takes place once a month, with 750 stalls outside in a huge area at NDSM-werf – it goes indoors into two warehouses from October to March, when there are a mere 500 stands.

Day Trips from Amsterdam

Haarlem p201

Alleys wind among grand 17th-century buildings in this lively city, just a 15-minute hop from Amsterdam.

Leiden p204

Rembrandt's picturesque, canal-woven birthplace is home to the country's oldest and most prestigious university.

Keukenhof Gardens p204

See the world's largest, loveliest flower gardens in bloom during spring.

Delft p207

Delft's Gothic and Renaissance architecture rivals its beautiful Delftware pottery.

Zaanse Schans p210

Watch windmills twirl and meet the millers at this delightful open-air museum.

Haarlem

Explore

As you stroll from glorious art-nouveau Haarlem Centraal train station (a national monument) to the old centre along Kruisweg and Kruisstraat, past exclusive boutiques, art galleries and antiques shops, the city's wealth and elegance soon become apparent. Stop off at the Corrie ten Boom House to pay homage to one of the Netherlands' most admired Renaissance figures before heading to the lively Grote Markt. Just a few blocks south is the Frans Hals Museum. Haarlem was once more important in the art world than Amsterdam, and this incomparable museum possesses one of the country's finest assemblies of Dutch paintings.

Given Haarlem's quick and easy access to Amsterdam, you can easily stay on for sunset drinks, catch live music and enjoy the city's buzzing nightlife.

The Best...

➡ **Sight** Frans Hals Museum (p201)
➡ **Place to Eat** Brick (p203)
➡ **Place to Drink** Jopenkerk (p203)

Top Tip

Try to visit on a Saturday when Haarlem's lively market is in full swing. There's also a market on Monday, but the Frans Hals Museum is closed.

Getting There & Away

Train Services from Amsterdam Centraal Station to Haarlem Centraal are frequent (€5.40, 15 minutes, up to eight per hour); the Grote Markt is an 850m walk south of the station. When the trains stop running at night, the N30 night bus links Haarlem Centraal Station to Schiphol Airport, Amsterdam.

Car From the ring road west of Amsterdam, take the N200, which becomes the A200.

Need to Know

➡ **Area Code** ☑023
➡ **Location** 20km west of Amsterdam
➡ **Tourist Office** (VVV; ☑023-531 73 25; www. haarlemmarketing.nl; Grote Markt 2; ☺9.30am-

◉ SIGHTS

★ **GROTE KERK VAN ST BAVO** CHURCH
(www.bavo.nl; Oude Groenmarkt 22; adult/child €2.50/free; ☺10am-5pm Mon-Sat year round, plus noon-5pm Sun Jul & Aug) Topped by a towering 50m-high steeple, the Gothic Grote Kerk van St Bavo contains some fine Renaissance artworks, but the star attraction is its stunning Müller organ – one of the most magnificent in the world, standing 30m high and with about 5000 pipes. It was played by Handel and a 10-year-old Mozart. Free hour-long **organ recitals** take place at 8.15pm Tuesday and 4pm Thursday from July to October, and on occasional Sundays at 2.30pm.

★ **FRANS HALS MUSEUM** MUSEUM
(www.franshalsmuseum.nl; Groot Heiligland 62; adult/child €12.50/free; ☺11am-5pm Tue-Sat, from noon Sun; ☜) A short stroll south of the Grote Markt, the Frans Hals Museum is a must for anyone interested in the Dutch Masters. Located in the poorhouse where Hals spent his final years, the collection focuses on the 17th-century Haarlem School; its pride and joy are eight group portraits of the Civic Guard that reveal Hals' exceptional attention to mood and psychological tone. Look out for works by other greats such as Pieter Bruegel the Younger and Jacob van Ruisdael.

Among the museum's other treasures are the works of Hals' teacher, Flemish artist Karel van Mander: stunning illustrations of the human anatomy, all ceiling high with biblical and mythological references.

TOWN HALL HISTORIC BUILDING
(Grote Markt 2) At the western end of the Grote Markt is the florid 14th-century town hall, which sprouted many extensions, including a balcony where judgements from the high court were pronounced. It only opens to the public on Open Monuments Days (the second weekend of September).

LAURENS COSTER STATUE STATUE
On the square north of the Grote Kerk is the Laurens Coster statue. Haarlemmers believe that Coster has a claim, along with Gutenberg, to be called the inventor of movable type.

Haarlem

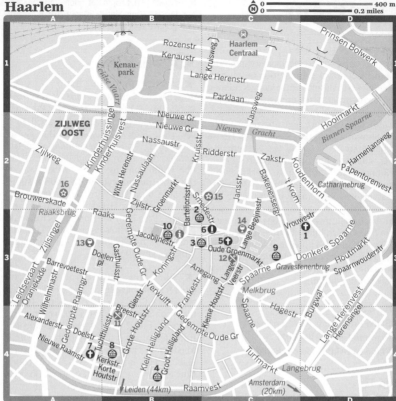

DE HALLEN GALLERY
(www.dehallen.nl; Grote Markt 16; adult/child
€12.50/free; ☺11am-5pm Tue-Sat, noon-5pm
Sun) Haarlem's modern and contemporary
art museum resides within two historic
'halls': the 17th-century Dutch Renaissance **Vleeshal**, a former meat market and
the sole place that meat was allowed to
be sold in Haarlem from the 17th through
to the 19th century, and the neoclassical
Verweyhal (fish house). Eclectic exhibits
rotate every three months and range from
Dutch impressionists and CoBrA artists
(an avant-garde group from Copenhagen,
Brussels and Amsterdam) to innovative
video, installation art and photography by
cutting-edge international artists.

PROVENIERSHUIS HISTORIC BUILDING
(☺10am-5pm Mon-Sat) **FREE** Off Grote Houtstraat southwest of the Grote Markt is
one of Haarlem's prettiest buildings, the
Proveniershuis. It started life as a *hofje*

(almshouse) and for a time became the
headquarters of St Joris Doelen (the Civic
Guard of St George).

TEYLERS MUSEUM MUSEUM
(www.teylersmuseum.nl; Spaarne 16; adult/child
€12/2; ☺10am-5pm Tue-Sat, 11am-5pm Sun)
Dating from 1778, Teylers is the country's
oldest continuously operating museum.
Its array of whiz-bang inventions includes
an 18th-century electrostatic machine
that conjures up visions of mad scientists.
The eclectic collection also has paintings
from the Dutch and French schools, and a
magnificent, sky-lighted Ovale Zaal (Oval
Room) displays natural-history specimens
in elegant glass cases on two levels. Temporary exhibitions regularly take place.

BAKENESSERKERK CHURCH
(cnr Vrouwestraat & Bakenesserstraat) The
striking Bakenesserkerk is a late-15th-
century church with a lamplit tower of

Haarlem

⊙ Sights

⊗ Eating

⊜ Drinking & Nightlife

⊛ Entertainment

sandstone. The stone was employed here when the Grote Kerk proved too weak to support a heavy steeple – hence the wooden tower. It's closed to the public.

CORRIE TEN BOOM HOUSE
HISTORIC BUILDING

(www.corrietenboom.com; Barteljorisstraat 19; admission by donation; ☉10am-3pm Apr-Oct, 11am-2.30pm Nov-Mar) Also known as 'the hiding place', the Corrie ten Boom House is named for the matriarch of a family that lived in the house during WWII. Using a secret compartment in her bedroom, she hid hundreds of Jews and Dutch resistors until they could be spirited to safety. In 1944 the family was betrayed and sent to concentration camps, where three died. Later, Corrie ten Boom toured the world espousing peace. Dutch/English-language tours alternate, with English ones every 90 minutes.

NIEUWE KERK
CHURCH

(Nieuwe Kerksplein; ☉10am-5pm Mon-Sat) FREE Walk down charming Korte Houtstraat to find the 17th-century Nieuwe Kerk; the ornate tower by Lieven de Key is supported by a rather boxy design by Jacob van Campen.

✗ EATING & DRINKING

DE HAERLEMSCHE VLAAMSE
FAST FOOD €

(Spekstraat 3; frites €2.50-4.50; ☉11am-6.30pm Mon-Wed & Fri, to 9pm Thu, to 5.30pm Sat, noon-5pm Sun) Line up at this local institution for a cone of crispy, golden fries made from fresh potatoes and one of a dozen sauces, including three kinds of mayonnaise.

★ BRICK
MODERN EUROPEAN €€

(☎023-551 18 70; www.restaurantbrick.nl; Breestraat 24-26; mains €15.50-21.50; ☉6-10pm) You can watch Brick's chefs creating risotto, steaks and gourmet burgers – not only from the street-level dining room but also from the 1st-floor space, which has a glass floor directly above the open kitchen. There are pavement tables out front, but in summer the best seats are on the roof terrace.

★ RESTAURANT MR & MRS
INTERNATIONAL €€

(☎023-531 59 35; www.restaurantmrandmrs. nl; Lange Veerstraat 4; small plates €10-13, 4-/5-/6-course menu €38/46/54; ☉5-10pm) Unexpectedly gastronomic cooking at this tiny restaurant is artfully conceived and presented. Small hot and cold plates designed for sharing might include steak tartar with black truffles, baby octopus with mango and jalapeño, mackerel with avocado dressing and caviar, hoisin-marinated steak with foie gras and portobello mushrooms, and crème brûlée with whisky meringue. Definitely book ahead.

★ JOPENKERK
BREWERY

(www.jopenkerk.nl; Gedempte Voldersgracht 2; ☉brewery & cafe 10am-1am, restaurant noon-3pm & 5.30pm-late Tue-Sat, noon-3pm Sun & Mon) Haarlem's most atmospheric place to drink is this independent brewery inside a stained-glass-windowed 1910 church. Enjoy brews such as citrusy Hopen, fruity Lente Bier and chocolatey Koyt along with Dutch bar snacks – *bitterballen* (meat-filled croquettes) and cheeses – beneath the gleaming copper vats. Or head to the mezzanine for dishes made from locally sourced, seasonal ingredients and Jopenkerk's beers, with pairings available.

PROEFLOKAAL IN DEN UIVER
BROWN CAFE

(www.indenuiver.nl; Riviervischmarkt 13; ☉4pm-1am Tue-Thu, to 2am Fri & Sat, to midnight Sun & Mon) One of many atmospheric places overlooking the Grote Markt, this

KEUKENHOF GARDENS

One of the Netherlands' top attractions, **Keukenhof Gardens** (www.keukenhof.nl; Stationsweg 166; adult/child €18/8, parking €6; ☺8am-7.30pm late-Mar–mid-May, last entry 6pm; ☏), 1km west of Lisse, is the world's largest bulb-flower garden. It attracts around 1.4 million visitors during its eight-week season, which coincides with the transient blooms on fields of multicoloured tulips, daffodils and hyacinths. Book ahead online to ensure a place.

Special buses link Keukenhof with Amsterdam's Schiphol Airport and Leiden's Centraal Station, and combination tickets covering entry and transport are available.

nautical-themed place has shipping knick-knacks and a schooner sailing right over the bar. Live jazz often plays; check the online agenda for dates.

☆ ENTERTAINMENT

CAFÉ STIELS   LIVE MUSIC
(www.stiels.nl; Smedestraat 21; ☺8pm-2am Sun-Wed, to 4am Thu-Sat) Bands play jazz and rhythm and blues on the back stage almost every night of the week from 10pm.

PATRONAAT   LIVE MUSIC
(www.patronaat.nl; Zijlsingel 2; ☺hours vary) Haarlem's top music and dance club attracts bands with banging tunes, from country to punk. Events in this cavernous venue usually start around 9pm.

Leiden

Explore

As you walk south from Leiden's striking hyper-modern Centraal Station, the city's traditional character unfolds. A five-minute stroll takes you to Leiden's historic waterways, the most notable of which are the Oude Rijn and the Nieuwe Rijn.

Leiden is renowned for being Rembrandt's birthplace; the home of the Netherlands' illustrious university (Einstein was a regular professor), with a lively nearly 27,000-strong student population; and the place where America's Pilgrims raised money to lease the leaky *Mayflower* that took them to the New World in 1620.

The city's museums, all within walking distance of each other, are a key draw, as is wandering along the pretty canals.

The Best...

➡ **Sight** Hortus Botanicus Leiden (p206)
➡ **Place to Eat** In den Doofpot (p207)
➡ **Place to Drink** Café L'Esperance (p207)

Top Tip

Explore the university precinct, where such historic sights as one of Europe's oldest botanical gardens coexist with Leiden's buzzing student life.

Getting There & Away

Train Services run from Amsterdam's Centraal Station (€8, 35 minutes, six per hour).

Car Take the A4 from the southwest point of Amsterdam's A10 ring road.

Need to Know

➡ **Area Code** ☏071
➡ **Location** 45km southwest of Amsterdam
➡ **Tourist Office** (☏071-516 60 00; www.visit leiden.nl; Stationsweg 26; ☺7am-7pm Mon-Fri, 10am-4pm Sat, 11am-3pm Sun)

◉ SIGHTS

★**RIJKSMUSEUM
VAN OUDHEDEN**   MUSEUM
(National Museum of Antiquities; www.rmo.nl; Rapenburg 28; adult/child €12.50/4; ☺11am-5pm Tue-Sun year round, plus Mon school holidays; ☏) This museum has a world-class collection of Greek, Roman and Egyptian artifacts, the pride of which is the extraordinary **Temple of Taffeh**, a gift from former Egyptian president Anwar Sadat to the Netherlands for helping to save ancient Egyptian monuments from flood.

Leiden

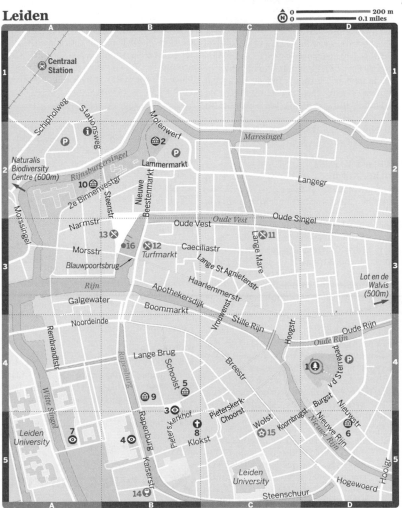

Leiden

◎ Sights

❤ Eating

☕ Drinking & Nightlife

✪ Entertainment

⚙ Sports & Activities

★HORTUS BOTANICUS LEIDEN
GARDENS

(www.hortusleiden.nl; Rapenburg 73; adult/child €7.50/3; ⊙10am-6pm daily Apr-Oct, 10am-4pm Tue-Sun Nov-Mar) The lush Hortus Botanicus is one of Europe's oldest botanical gardens (1590; the oldest was created in Padua, Italy, in 1545). It's a wonderful place to relax, with explosions of tropical colour and a fascinating (and steamy) greenhouse.

★RIJKSMUSEUM VOLKENKUNDE
MUSEUM

(National Museum of Ethnology; www.volkenkunde.nl; Steenstraat 1; adult/child €14/6; ⊙10am-5pm Tue-Sun) Cultural achievements by civilisations worldwide are on show at the Museum Volkenkunde. More than 200,000 artefacts span Asia, South America and Africa. There's a rich Indonesian collection; watch for performances by the museum's gamelan troupe. Temporary exhibitions cover subjects such as 'Cool Japan'.

PIETERSKERK
CHURCH

(www.pieterskerk.com; Pieterskerkhof 1; €3; ⊙11am-6pm) Crowned by its huge steeple, Pieterskerk is often under restoration – a good thing, as it has been prone to collapse since it was built in the 14th century.

The precinct includes the gabled **Latin School** (Lokhorststraat 16), which – before it became a commercial building – was graced by a pupil named Rembrandt from 1616 to 1620. Across the plaza, look for the **Gravensteen** (www.visitors.leiden.edu; Pieterskerkhof 6), which dates from the 13th century and was once a prison. The gallery facing the plaza was where judges watched executions.

LEIDEN AMERICAN PILGRIM MUSEUM
MUSEUM

(☑071-512 24 13; www.leidenamericanpilgrimmuseum.org/index.htm; Beschuitsteeg 9; adult/child €5/free; ⊙1-5pm Wed-Sat) The Leiden American Pilgrim Museum is a fascinating restoration of a one-room house occupied around 1610 by the soon-to-be Pilgrims. The house itself dates from 1375 (check out the original 14th-century floor tiles), but the furnishings are from the Pilgrims' period. Curator Jeremy Bangs is an author who has written extensively on the Pilgrims and has a vast knowledge of their Leiden links.

DE BURCHT
PARK

(⊙sunrise-sunset) FREE De Burcht, an 11th-century citadel on an artificial hill, lost its protective function as the city grew around it. It's now a park with lovely places to view the steeples and rooftops, with a cafe at its base.

LEIDEN UNIVERSITY
UNIVERSITY

(www.universiteitleiden.nl/en) The oldest university in the Netherlands was a gift to Leiden from Willem the Silent in 1575 for withstanding two Spanish sieges in 1573 and 1574. The campus comprises an interesting mix of modern and antique buildings that are scattered around town.

DE VALK
MUSEUM

(The Falcon; ☑071-516 53 53; www.molenmuseumdevalk.nl; 2e Binnenvestgracht 1; adult/child €4/2; ⊙10am-5pm Tue-Sat, 1-5pm Sun) Leiden's landmark windmill museum receives loving care, with constant renovation, and many consider it the best example of its kind. Its arms are free to turn 'whenever possible' – when wind conditions are right – and it can still grind grain.

NATURALIS BIODIVERSITY CENTRE
MUSEUM

(www.naturalis.nl; Darwinweg 2; €11; ⊙10am-5pm) Most of this science museum was closed for renovation at the time of writing and scheduled to reopen in late 2018. Part of the building is open if there's a temporary exhibition on. Check online or with the tourist office for details.

✖ EATING & DRINKING

OUDT LEYDEN
CRÊPES €€

(www.oudtleyden.nl; Steenstraat 49; pancakes €6.90-14.50, mains €13; ⊙11.30am-9.30pm; ☑ 🖐) The giant Dutch-style pancakes here make kids and adults alike go wide-eyed. Whether you're after something savoury (marinated salmon, sour cream and capers), sweet (apple, raisins, almond paste, sugar and cinnamon) or simply adventurous (ginger and bacon), this welcoming place hits the spot every time. Pancakes aside, choices include mushroom lasagne, sirloin with red-wine jus and salmon fillets.

BRASSERIE DE ENGELENBAK
DUTCH €€

(☑071-512 54 40; www.deengelenbak.nl; Lange Mare 38; mains lunch €8-14, dinner €17-19,

3-course chef's menu €40; ◷11am-10pm) In the shadow of the 17th-century octagonal Marekerk, this elegant bistro serves a seasonally changing menu of fresh fare that takes its cues from across the continent. Local organic produce features in many of the dishes. Tables outside enjoy views of the passing crowds. Its adjoining *café* (pub) serves snacks until midnight.

LOT EN DE WALVIS INTERNATIONAL €€
(☑071-763 03 83; www.lotendewalvis.nl; Haven 1; mains €8.50-19.50; ◷9am-10pm) Lot's sun-drenched terrace sits at the water's edge, but the reason it's a Leiden hot spot is the outstanding food, from breakfast (French toast with cinnamon sugar; eggs Benedict on sourdough) to lunch (Thai yellow-curry fish burger; smoked-mackerel pasta) and dinner (fiery harissa lamb skewers with yoghurt dip; pear-and-hazelnut cake). Book at all times.

★IN DEN DOOFPOT EUROPEAN €€€
(☑071-512 24 34; www.indendoofpot.nl; Turf-markt 9; mains €23-36, 3/4-course lunch menu €39/45, 4/5/6/8-course dinner menu €55/65/70/80; ◷noon-10pm Mon-Fri, 5-10pm Sat) Given the sky-high calibre of chef Patrick Brugman's cooking, In den Doofpot's prices are a veritable steal. Pork belly with smoked eel; grilled lobster with truffle butter and micro-herb salad; organic Dutch beef fillet with Madeira sauce; potatoes and caramelised orange, and other intense flavour combinations are all executed with artistic vision. Wines cost €8 per course.

CAFÉ L'ESPERANCE BROWN CAFE
(www.lesperance.nl; Kaiserstraat 1; ◷2.30pm-1am Mon-Wed, 10.30am-1am Thu-Sun) Decked out with wood-panelled walls lined with framed photos, this nostalgic *bruin café* (pub) overlooks an evocative bend in the canal, with tables along the pavement outside in summer.

☆ ENTERTAINMENT

CAFÉ DE WW LIVE MUSIC
(www.deww.nl; Wolsteeg 6; ◷2pm-2am Sun-Wed, to 3am Thu, to 4am Fri & Sat) On Friday and Saturday, live rock in this glossy scarlet bar  alley with crowds trailing up to the main street. On other nights DJs play. Though the emphasis is on the music, there's a great beer selection. Cash only.

🏃 SPORTS & ACTIVITIES

REDERIJ REMBRANDT BOATING
(☑071-513 49 38; www.rederij-rembrandt. nl; Blauwpoorthaven 5; adult/child €10/6.50; ◷10.30am, noon, 1pm & 3pm) Leisurely one-hour canal-boat tours taken in the channel around the old-town centre, accompanied by multilingual commentary (including English).

Delft

Explore

Compact and charming, Delft is synonymous with its blue-and-white-painted porcelain. It's very popular with visitors strolling its narrow canals, gazing at the remarkable old buildings and meditating on the career of Golden Age painter Johannes Vermeer, who was born and lived here, so getting an early start helps beat the crowds.

After touring Royal Delft's porcelain factory, Koninklijke Porceleyne Fles, pick up a walking tour brochure from the tourist office and explore the city's riches at your own pace. Be sure to allow time for shopping, eating and drinking around the Markt.

Although Delft is just an hour from Amsterdam, excellent-value hotels cater to visitors who want to linger once the day-trippers have left.

The Best

➤ **Sight** Vermeer Centrum Delft (p208)
➤ **Place to Eat** Brasserie 't Crabbetje (p209)
➤ **Place to Drink** Locus Publicus (p210)

Top Tip

It's not all Delftware and Vermeer: take time to wander the streets of one of the Netherlands' most appealing cities, a veritable treasure trove of Gothic and Renaissance architecture.

Delft

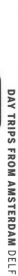

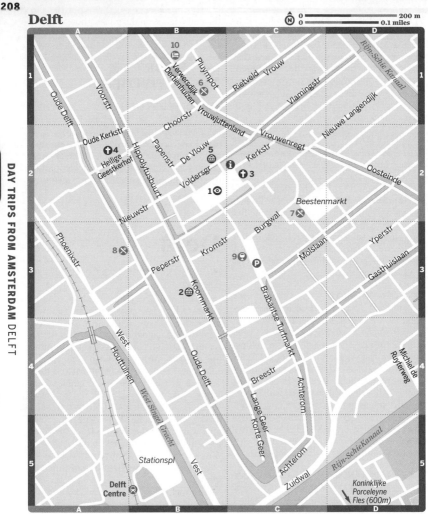

Getting There & Away

Train Services between Amsterdam Centraal Station and Delft are frequent (€14.20, one hour, four per hour).

Car From the A4 take A13/E19, which passes through Delft en route to Rotterdam.

Need to Know

→ **Area Code** ☑015

→ **Location** 55km southwest of Amsterdam

→ **Tourist Office** (☑015-215 40 51; www.delft. nl; Kerkstraat 3; ⊙10am-4pm Sun & Mon, to 5pm Tue-Sat)

◉ SIGHTS

★**VERMEER CENTRUM DELFT**   MUSEUM
(www.vermeerdelft.nl; Voldersgracht 21; adult/ child €9/free; ⊙10am-5pm) As the place where Vermeer was born, lived and worked, Delft is 'Vermeer Central' to many art-history and Dutch Masters enthusiasts. Along with viewing life-size images of Vermeer's oeuvre, you can tour a replica of his studio, which reveals the way the artist approached the use of light and colour in his craft. A 'Vermeer's World' exhibit offers insight into his environment and upbringing, while temporary exhibits show how his work continues to inspire other artists.

Delft

At 10.30am on Sunday there's a free one-hour English-language tour.

★OUDE KERK   CHURCH
(Old Church; Heilige Geestkerkhof 25; adult/child incl Nieuwe Kerk €5/1, Nieuwe Kerk tower additional €4/2, combination ticket €8/2.50; ☺9am-6pm Mon-Sat Apr-Oct, 11am-4pm Mon-Fri, 10am-5pm Sat Nov-Jan, 10am-5pm Mon-Sat Feb & Mar) The Gothic Oude Kerk, founded in 1246, is a surreal sight: its 75m-high tower leans nearly 2m from the vertical due to subsidence caused by its canal location, hence its nickname Scheve Jan ('Leaning Jan'). One of the tombs inside the church is that of painter Johannes Vermeer (p241).

★NIEUWE KERK   CHURCH
(New Church; Markt 80; adult/child incl Oude Kerk €5/1, Nieuwe Kerk tower additional €4/2, combination ticket €8/2.50; ☺9am-6pm Mon-Sat Apr-Oct, 11am-4pm Mon-Fri, 10am-5pm Sat Nov-Jan, 10am-5pm Mon-Sat Feb & Mar) Construction of Delft's Nieuwe Kerk began in 1381; the church was finally completed in 1655. Amazing views extend from the 108.75m-high tower: after climbing its 376 narrow, spiralling steps you can see as far as Rotterdam and Den Haag on a clear day. It's the resting place of William of Orange (William the Silent), in a mausoleum designed by Hendrick de Keyser. Children under five are not permitted to climb the tower.

MARKT   SQUARE
The pedestrianised city square is worth a stroll for its pleasant collection of galleries, antiques stores, clothing boutiques and quirky speciality shops.

MUSEUM PAUL TETAR VAN ELVEN   MUSEUM
(www.tetar.nl; Koornmarkt 67; adult/child €5/free; ☺1-5pm Tue-Sun) This off-the-radar museum is the former studio and home of 19th-century Dutch artist Paul Tetar van Elven, who lived and worked here from 1864 until 1894, and bequeathed it to the town. The museum features his works, including reproductions of notable paintings, along with his collection of antique furniture, oriental porcelain and Delftware. The evocative interior retains its original furnishings and lived-in feel.

KONINKLIJKE PORCELEYNE FLES   FACTORY
(Royal Delft; www.royaldelft.com; Rotterdamseweg 196; factory tour adult/child €13.50/free; ☺9am-5pm) Pottery fans will love Royal Delft, 1km southeast of the centre. Factory-tour tickets include an audio tour that leads you through a painting demonstration, the company museum and the factory production process. You can also take a workshop (€29.50 to €39.50) where you get to paint your own piece of Delft blue (tiles, plates or vases). For many, of course, the real thrill begins in the gift shop.

✕ EATING & DRINKING

STADS-KOFFYHUIS   CAFE €
(www.stads-koffyhuis.nl; Oude Delft 133; dinner mains €12.50-15, sandwiches €6.25-9, pancakes €8-13; ☺9am-8pm Mon-Fri, to 6pm Sat, 11am-6pm Sun Jun-Sep, shorter hours Oct-May) The most coveted seats at this delightful cafe are on the terrace, aboard a barge moored out front. Tuck into award-winning bread rolls, with fillings such as aged artisan Gouda with apple sauce, mustard, fresh figs and walnuts, or house-speciality pancakes, while admiring possibly the best view of the Oude Kerk, just ahead at the end of the canal.

★BRASSERIE 'T CRABBETJE   SEAFOOD €€
(☎015-213 88 50; www.crabbetjedelft.nl; Verwersdijk 14; mains €21.50-34.50, 3-/4-course tasting menus €36.50/44.50; ☺5.30-10pm Wed-Sun; ☍) Seafood is given the gourmet treatment at this cool, sophisticated restaurant, from scallops with leek and lobster reduction to skate wing with hazelnut crumb and beurre *noisette* (warm butter sauce), salmon carpaccio with smoked-eel croquette, and grilled lobster with tomato and truffle oil.

Lavish seafood platters cost €41.50. Desserts are exquisite, too.

SPIJSHUIS DE DIS   DUTCH €€

(☎015-213 17 82; www.spijshuisdedis.com; Beestenmarkt 36; mains €17-25; ⊙5-10pm Tue-Sat) Fresh fish and amazing soups served in bread bowls take centre stage at this romantic foodie haven, but meat eaters and vegetarians are well catered for, too. Creative starters include smoked, marinated mackerel on sliced apple with horseradish. Don't skip the Dutch pudding served in a wooden shoe.

LOCUS PUBLICUS   BROWN CAFE

(www.locuspublicus.nl; Brabantse Turfmarkt 67; ⊙11am-1am Mon-Thu, to 2am Fri & Sat, noon-1am Sun) Cosy little Locus Publicus is filled with cheery locals quaffing their way through the 200-strong beer list, including 13 on tap.

🛏 SLEEPING

HOTEL DE PLATAAN   BOUTIQUE HOTEL €€

(☎015-212 60 46; www.hoteldeplataan.nl; Doelenplein 10; d from €100, themed d from €155; P🛜) On a pretty canal-side square in the old town, this family-run gem has small but muralled standard rooms and wonderfully opulent theme rooms, including the 'Garden of Eden'; the Eastern-style 'Amber', with a Turkish massage shower; and the desert-island 'Tamarinde'. Modesty alert: many en suites are only partially screened from the room. Rates include breakfast and secure parking.

Zaanse Schans

. . . .

Explore

People come for an hour and stay for several at this riverside village. It's a prime place to see windmills operating, although only a few of the formerly more than 1000 windmills in the area have been restored.

Spend your time exploring the six working mills. One sells fat jars of its freshly ground mustard, while the others turn out oils, flour and sawed planks. Most are open for inspection, and it's a delight to clamber about the creaking works while the mills shake in the North Sea breeze.

The other buildings have been brought here from all over the country to recreate a 17th-century community including an early Albert Heijn market, a cheesemaker, and a popular clog factory that turns out wooden shoes as if grinding keys.

. . . .

Top Tip

Hire a bike and pedal from Amsterdam to Zaanse Schans. It only takes about 90 minutes, and the picturesque trip is a highlight of many travellers' holidays.

. . . .

Getting There & Away

Train From Amsterdam Centraal Station (€3, 16 minutes, four times hourly) take the stop train towards Alkmaar and get off at Koog Zaandijk – it's a well-signposted 1.5km walk via the Julianabrug spanning the Zaan river to Zaanse Schans.

Car Travel to the northwestern side of Amsterdam on the A10 ring road and take the A8 turn-off. Exit at Zaandijk.

. . . .

Need to Know

➡ **Area Code** ☎075

➡ **Location** 10km northwest of Amsterdam

➡ **Zaanse Schans Information Desk** (www.zaanseschans.nl; Zaans Museum; ⊙9am-5pm)

⊙ SIGHTS

ZAANSE SCHANS WINDMILLS   WINDMILLS

(www.dezaanseschans.nl; site free, per windmill adult/child €4/2; ⊙windmills 10am-5pm Apr-Nov, hours vary Dec-Mar) The working, inhabited village Zaanse Schans functions as a windmill gallery on the Zaan river. Popular with tourists, its mills are completely authentic and operated with enthusiasm and love. You can explore the windmills at your own pace, seeing the vast moving parts firsthand

The mill with paint pigments for sale will delight artists – you can see the actual materials used in producing Renaissance masterpieces turned into powders. Ask to see the storeroom where ground pigments are for sale.

The other buildings have been brought here from all over the country to recreate a 17th-century community. There's an early Albert Heijn market, a cheesemaker, a popular clog factory and an engaging pewtersmith.

🛏 Sleeping

In its typically charming way, Amsterdam has loads of hotels in wild and wonderful spaces: inspired architects have breathed new life into old buildings, from converted schools and industrial lofts to entire rows of canal houses joined at the hip. Many lodgings overlook gorgeous waterways or courtyards. But charm doesn't come cheap, and places fill fast – reserve as far ahead as possible.

Hotels

Any hotel with more than 20 rooms is considered large, and most rooms themselves are on the snug side. You'll see a 'star' plaque on the front of every hotel, indicating its rating according to the Hotelstars Union (www.hotelstars.eu). The stars (from one to five) are determined by the existence of certain facilities, rather than their quality. This means that a two-star hotel may be in better condition than a hotel of higher rank, albeit with fewer facilities.

PARTY & STONER HOTELS

A number of hotels in the budget category welcome party guests as well as pot smokers. By and large they're pretty basic affairs. If in doubt whether smoking marijuana is permitted, ask when you make your reservation. Many hotels have strict no-drugs policies.

B&Bs & Houseboats

Amsterdam has a scattering of B&Bs, but most don't have exterior signage and access is by reservation only, giving an intimate feel. A couple of particularly cool ones are on houseboats. Despite the name, many B&Bs don't serve breakfast.

Hostels

Jeugdherbergen (youth hostels) are popular in Amsterdam. The Netherlands hostel association goes by the name Stayokay (www.stayokay.com) and is affiliated with Hostelling International (HI; www.hihostels.com). Independent luxury hostels, aka 'poshtels', are starting to pop up around town too.

Amenities

Wi-fi is nearly universal across the spectrum, but air-conditioning and lifts (elevators) are not.

BUDGET

Lodgings in the lowest price bracket, other than hostels, are thin on the ground. The better options tend to be spick and span, with furnishings that are, at best, cheap and cheerful. Rates often include breakfast.

MIDRANGE

Most hotels in this category are big on comfort, low on formality and small enough to offer personal attention. Rooms usually have a toilet and shower, a TV and a phone. Not many midrange hotels of more than two storeys have lifts, and their narrow, ladder-like staircases can take some getting used to, especially with luggage. Rates often include breakfast.

TOP END

Expect lifts, minibars and room service. At the top end of top end, facilities such as air-conditioning and fitness centres are standard. Breakfast is rarely included.

NEED TO KNOW

Price Ranges

The following price ranges are for an en suite double room in high season (excluding breakfast).

€ less than €100

€€ €100–€180

€€€ more than €180

Useful Websites

➜ Lonely Planet (www.lonelyplanet.com/the-netherlands/amsterdam/hotels) Recommendations and bookings.

➜ I Amsterdam (www.iamsterdam.com) City-run portal packed with sightseeing, accommodation and event info.

Reservations

➜ It can't be overstated: book as far in advance as possible, especially for festival, summer and weekend visits.

➜ Many hotels offer discounts if you book directly via their websites.

Tipping

Tipping is not expected, though at larger hotels the porter often receives a euro or two, and the room cleaner gets a few euros for a job well done.

Tax

Properties often include the city hotel tax in quoted rates, but ask before booking; the rate is due to rise to at least 6% in 2018. If you're paying by credit card, some hotels add a surcharge of up to 5%.

Lonely Planet's Top Choices

Hoxton Amsterdam (p216) Groovy hipster style at affordable prices.

Collector (p219) Offbeat B&B near Museumplein with backyard chickens.

Sir Albert Hotel (p221) Diamond factory converted to sparkly design hotel.

ClinkNOORD (p222) Artsy, avant-garde hostel in Amsterdam Noord.

Best By Budget

€

Cocomama (p217) Red-curtained boutique hostel in a former brothel.

Generator Amsterdam (p222) Posh new hostel with bars overlooking Oosterpark.

Stayokay Amsterdam Stadsdoelen (p215) Bustling backpacker digs near Nieuwmarkt square.

€€

Hotel Fita (p220) Sweet little family-owned hotel a stone's throw from the Museumplein.

Hotel V (p217) Retro-chic hotel facing lush Frederiksplein.

Conscious Hotel Vondelpark (p220) Eco innovations include recycled materials and a living wall.

€€€

Hotel Okura Amsterdam (p222) Rare-for-Amsterdam views and four Michelin stars in the building.

Toren (p216) Blends 17th-century opulence with a sensual decadence.

College Hotel (p221) Impeccably run by hotel-school students

Best Canal Views

Canal House (p216) Gorgeous water views out front and a sofa-strewn garden out back.

Seven Bridges (p217) One of the city's most exquisite little hotels on one of its loveliest canals.

Linden Hotel (p218) A Jordaan gem.

Best Only in Amsterdam

Xaviera Hollander's Happy House (p221) B&B owned by the famed author and former madam.

Faralda Crane Hotel (p222) Inside a crane in Amsterdam Noord.

Mr Jordaan (p218) Design elements include bedheads shaped like gabled Amsterdam canal houses.

De Dageraad (p215) Boutique B&B houseboat moored in the Eastern Docklands.

Best Design Savvy

Hotel Notting Hill (p218) A lobby wall of vintage suitcases is amosng designer Wim Hoopman's touches.

Hotel Not Hotel (p219) Design academy students put together rooms that are eye-popping art installations.

Andaz Amsterdam (p216) A wonderland envisioned by iconic Dutch designer Marcel Wanders.

Sir Adam (p222) Designer rooms inside the A'DAM Tower.

Where to Stay

NEIGHBOURHOOD	FOR	AGAINST
Medieval Centre & Red Light District	In the thick of the action; close to sights, nightlife, theatres and transport.	Can be noisy, touristy and seedy; not great value for money.
Nieuwmarkt, Plantage & the Eastern Islands	Nieuwmarkt is near the action, but slightly more low-key than the Medieval Centre. Plantage hotels are amid quiet greenery.	Parts of Nieuwmarkt are close enough to the Red Light District to get rowdy spillover. Plantage and especially Eastern Islands lodgings can be a hike from the major sights, requiring a tram or bike ride.
Western Canal Ring	Tree-lined canals; charming boutiques and cafes. Within walking distance of Amsterdam's most popular sights.	Given all the positives, rooms book out early and are invariably pricey.
Southern Canal Ring	Swanky hotels, central location, handy for the restaurants of Utrechtsestraat.	Can be loud, crowded, pricey and touristy, especially around the high-traffic nightlife areas of Leidseplein and Rembrandtplein
Jordaan & the West	Cosy cafes, quirky shops and charming village character.	Sleeping options are few, due in part to the paucity of big-name sights close by.
Vondelpark & the South	Genteel, leafy streets; walking distance to Museumplein; small, gracious properties; lots of midrange options and cool design hotels.	Not much nightlife in the South; prices around Vondelpark can slide toward the high end.
De Pijp	Ongoing explosion of dining/drinking cool in the area; located near Museumplein and the Southern Canal Ring.	Easy walking distance to Museumplein, Vondelpark and Leidseplein, but a hike from the Medieval Centre; options are fairly limited.
Oosterpark & East of the Amstel	Lower prices due to remote location (albeit just a short tram/metro ride from the Medieval Centre); quiet area amid locals.	Fewer options for dining and drinking.
Amsterdam Noord	Some truly unique properties; burgeoning drinking, dining and creative scene.	Transport limited in some areas.

🛏 Medieval Centre & Red Light District

ST CHRISTOPHER'S
AT THE WINSTON
HOSTEL, HOTEL €

Map p290 (🖉020-623 13 80; www.st-chris tophers.co.uk; Warmoesstraat 129; dm/d from €52/145; @🛜; 🚊4/9/16/24 Dam) This place hops 24/7 with rock 'n' roll rooms, a busy nightclub (p81) with live bands nightly, a bar and restaurant, a beer garden and a smoking deck downstairs. En suite dorms sleep up to eight. Local artists were given free rein on the rooms, with super-edgy (entirely stainless steel) to questionably raunchy results. Rates include breakfast (and earplugs!).

FLYING PIG
DOWNTOWN HOSTEL
HOSTEL €

Map p290 (🖉020-420 68 22; www.flyingpig.nl; Nieuwendijk 100; dm €37.85-57.80, d €96.50; @🛜; 🚊1/2/4/5/9/13/16/17/24 Centraal Station) Hang out with hundreds of young, dope-smoking backpackers at this very relaxed, massive 250-bed hostel. It's a bit grungy, but no one seems to mind, especially when there's so much fun to be had in the throbbing lobby bar. There are also full kitchen facilities and a cushion-lined basement nicknamed the 'happy room'. Weekend bookings require a minimum three-night stay.

HOTEL THE EXCHANGE
DESIGN HOTEL €€

Map p290 (🖉020-523 00 80; www.hotelthe exchange.com; Damrak 50; d €162-304; @🛜; 🚊1/2/4/5/9/13/16/17/24 Centraal Station) Opposite the former stock exchange (hence the hotel's name), these 61 rooms have been dressed 'like models' in eye-popping style by students from the Amsterdam Fashion Institute. Anything goes, from oversized-button-adorned walls to a Marie Antoinette dress tented over the bed. Its one- to five-star rooms range from small and viewless to sprawling sanctums, but all have en suite bathrooms.

HOTEL BROUWER
HOTEL €€

Map p290 (🖉020-624 63 58; www.hotelbrouwer. nl; Singel 83; s/d/tr from €88/148/180; 🛜; 🚊1/2/5/13/17 Nieuwezijds Kolk) A bargain-priced (for Amsterdam) favourite, Brouwer has just eight rooms in a house dating back to 1652. Each is named for a Dutch painter and simply furnished; all have canal views. There's a mix of Delft-blue tiles and early-20th-century decor, plus a tiny lift. Reserve well in advance. Rates include a hearty breakfast. Cash only.

HOTEL RÉSIDENCE LE COIN
APARTMENT €€

Map p294 (🖉020-524 68 00; www.lecoin. nl; Nieuwe Doelenstraat 5; apt €166; 🛜; 🚊4/9/14/16/24 Muntplein) Owned by the University of Amsterdam, Hotel Résidence Le Coin offers 42 small, high-class apartments spread over seven historical buildings, all equipped with designer furniture, wood floors, fast wi-fi and kitchenettes – and all reachable by lift. It's superbly located just a five-minute stroll to pretty Nieuwmarkt.

HOTEL LUXER
HOTEL €€

Map p290 (🖉020-330 32 05; http://hotelluxer. nl; Warmoesstraat 11; d from €152; ❋🛜; 🚊1/2/4/5/9/13/16/17/24 Centraal Station) A pleasant surprise, this smart little number offers some of the best value for money in the thick of the Red Light District. Its 47 rooms are small but well equipped (air-con!), and at night the breakfast area becomes a chic little bar. Breakfast costs €8.

⭐W AMSTERDAM
DESIGN HOTEL €€€

Map p294 (🖉020-811 25 00; www.wamsterdam. com; Spuistraat 175; d/ste from €370/567; ❋@🛜🌀; 🚊1/2/5/13/14/17 Dam) Designer hotel chain W opened its Amsterdam premises in two landmark buildings, the Royal Dutch Post's former telephone exchange and a former bank (part of which now houses Dutch design mega-store X Bank (p83)). Its 238 rooms (including connecting family rooms and 28 suites) combine design and vintage elements; there's a state-of-the-art spa, a gym, an amazing rooftop lap pool, restaurants and bars.

⭐HOTEL V NESPLEIN
DESIGN HOTEL €€€

Map p294 (🖉020-662 32 33; http://hotelv nesplein.nl; Nes 49; d/ste from €250/357; ❋🛜; 🚊4/9/14/24 Rokin) Vintage and designer furniture fills the public areas and rooms of this hotel, in a fantastic location on theatre-lined Nes. Spacious rooms start at 18 sq metres and have wooden floors, exposed-brick walls and rain showers in the sleek bathrooms (some also have bathtubs). Its industrial-styled restaurant, the Lobby, serves creative modern Dutch cuisine.

INK HOTEL AMSTERDAM   DESIGN HOTEL €€€
Map p290 (☏020-627 59 00; www.sofitel. com; Nieuwezijds Voorburgwal 67; d/ste from €194/329; ✳🛜; 🚇1/2/5/13/17 Nieuwezijds Kolk) Occupying the 1904 to 1986 premises of Dutch Catholic newspaper (and later magazine) *De Tijd* (The Time), Ink honours its journalistic heritage with printing plates, old typewriters and vintage editions on the walls of its bar-restaurant, the Pressroom. Leading Amsterdam architectural firm Concrete designed its 149 rooms with features such as blackboard-style murals. The basement gym opens 24 hours.

ART'OTEL AMSTERDAM   DESIGN HOTEL €€€
Map p290 (☏020-719 72 00; www.artotels.com; Prins Hendrikkade 33; d from €299; ✳🛜🏊; 🚇1/2/4/5/9/13/16/17/24 Centraal Station) Located directly opposite Centraal Station, this stylish hotel offers 107 rooms with mod decor and original artworks on the wall. To add to the creative theme, there's an open-to-the-public gallery in the basement. The lobby is a swanky refuge with a fireplace and a library. A beyond-the-norm hot breakfast (and a sumptuous brunch on Sunday) is included in the rate.

HOTEL DE L'EUROPE   HOTEL €€€
Map p294 (☏020-531 17 77; www.leurope.nl; Nieuwe Doelenstraat 2-8; r from €479; ✳🛜🏊; 🚇4/9/14/16/24 Muntplein) Owned by the Heineken family, Amsterdam's 'other royal palace' blends classical elements (chandeliers, doorkeepers in top hats) with whimsical Dutch design. The 111 rooms are grand, with iPads, canal views, heated floors and white-marble bathtubs. Restaurants include the twin-Michelin-starred Bord'Eau; other highlights are the superb spa, on-site cigar lounge and Freddy's Bar, with brass-topped tables and leather chairs.

DIE PORT VAN CLEVE   HOTEL €€€
Map p290 (☏020-714 20 00; www.dieport vancleve.com; Nieuwezijds Voorburgwal 176-180; d from €179; ✳🛜; 🚇1/2/5/13/14/17 Dam) Opened in 1870 on the site of Heineken's first brewery, just off Dam, Die Port van Cleve is split across three monumental buildings. It takes its design cues from its beautiful blue-and-white Delft-tiled bar, De Blauwe Parade (p78), with Delftware-adorned tiled panels, troupe and painted ceiling walls of its 122 rooms. Various packages include *jenever* (gin) tastings with classic bar snacks.

🛏 Nieuwmarkt, Plantage & the Eastern Islands

CHRISTIAN YOUTH HOSTEL 'THE SHELTER CITY'   HOSTEL €
Map p296 (☏020-625 32 30; www.shelterhostel amsterdam.com; Barndesteeg 21; dm €22-45; 🛜; Ⓜ Nieuwmarkt) Extremely convenient for central Amsterdam, this rambling Christian-run hostel is just outside the Red Light District, but a world away, powered by religious zeal and operating a no-drugs-or-alcohol policy. If you can handle this, the payback is spick-and-span single-sex dorms (two to 20 beds), filling free breakfasts, a quiet cafe and a garden courtyard with bright seating. Towel/padlock rental costs €2/4.

STAYOKAY AMSTERDAM STADSDOELEN   HOSTEL €
Map p296 (☏020-624 68 32; www.stayokay. com; Kloveniersburgwal 97; dm €32.50-51, tw/d €90-150; 🛜; 🚇4/9/14/16/24 Muntplein) Efficient Stadsdoelen has friendly staff and is always full of backpackers, but slightly lacks atmosphere, and rooms are stuffy in warm weather. There are 11 single-sex and mixed rooms (each with up to 20 beds and free lockers) plus a few basic doubles. There's a big TV room, a pool table, a laundry and free continental breakfast. Towel rental costs €4.50.

★LLOYD HOTEL   BOUTIQUE HOTEL €€
Map p298 (☏020-561 36 07; www.lloydhotel.com; Oostelijke Handelskade 34; r €100-190; 🛜; 🚇26 Rietlandpark) Magnificent waterside Lloyd was a hotel for emigrants from the Netherlands back in 1921, who stayed here before setting sail. Many of the original fixtures remain, alongside contemporary-art installations and design. Rooms range from one to five stars, from budget with a bathroom down the hall to racquetball-court-sized top-end extravaganzas.

DE DAGERAAD   HOUSEBOAT €€
Map p298 (http://bedbreakfastdedageraad.nl; d €115-135; 🚇26 Rietlandpark) A two-bedroom boutique B&B houseboat, dating from 1929, moored on the easternmost tip of Zeeburg. This eco-friendly place has beautifully decorated white interior rooms (both en suite) with underfloor heating.

HOTEL REMBRANDT   HOTEL €€

Map p298 (📞020-627 27 14; www.hotel rembrandt.nl; Plantage Middenlaan 17; s/d/tr/q from €100/135/170/190; 🗗; 🚊9/14 Plantage Kerklaan) Built for a 19th-century merchant, the Rembrandt Hotel has an impressive red and white facade. Rooms are all different, but are generally light and bright, with colourful curtains or design touches, and prints on the walls. Room 8 has a nearly life-sized mural of *The Night Watch,* one room has a balcony and one a sauna.

🛏 Western Canal Ring

⭐ HOTEL IX   BOUTIQUE HOTEL €€

Map p300 (📞020-845 84 51; www.hotelix amsterdam.com; Hartenstraat 8; d from €170; 🗗; 🚊13/14/17 Westermarkt) The only hotel in the delightful Negen Straatjes (p113) shopping district, IX has super-stylish suites (sleeping up to four) named for the area's 'Nine Streets', with black-and-white murals and complimentary minibars. The pick is the Berenstraat suite, with its own roof terrace. Note there's no on-site reception (entry is via digicodes sent prior to arrival), no breakfast and no lift.

⭐ HOXTON AMSTERDAM   DESIGN HOTEL €€€

Map p300 (📞020-888 55 55; https://thehoxton. com; Herengracht 255; s/d from €169/209; ✳🗗; 🚊13/14/17 Westermarkt) Part of a Europe-based chain known for high style at affordable prices, the Hoxton has 111 rooms – in sizes from 'shoebox' to 'roomy' – splashed through five canal houses. The breakfast snack, speedy wi-fi, free international calls and low-priced canteen items are nice touches. It organises events with city artists and designers, so you get to meet creative locals. One warning though, there's a very strict cancellation policy.

⭐ 'T HOTEL   BOUTIQUE HOTEL €€€

Map p300 (📞020-422 27 41; http://thotel. nl; Leliegracht 18; d/f from €179/359; ✳🗗🃟; 🚊13/14/17 Westermarkt) Named for Amsterdam's waterways, the eight rooms in this charming 17th-century canal house are individually decorated with black-and-white sketches of old Dutch scenes, printed cushions and shower curtains, and patterned wallpapers by interior-print designer Katarina Stupavska, whose family owns the hotel. Dazzling blue-and-white Delftware

designs line the family room, which has a loft sleeping area reached by a ladder.

ANDAZ AMSTERDAM   DESIGN HOTEL €€€

Map p302 (📞020-523 12 34; www.hyatt.com; Prinsengracht 587; d/ste from €335/935; @🗗; 🚊1/2/5 Prinsengracht) Visionary Dutch designer Marcel Wanders transformed Amsterdam's former public library into a fantasy of giant gold and silver cutlery, fish murals, Delftware-inspired carpets, library-book pages writ large on the walls and other flights of imagination. The 122 guest rooms and suites have Geneva sound systems, king-size beds, and complimentary snacks and non-alcoholic drinks. Free bikes to use too.

DYLAN   BOUTIQUE HOTEL €€€

Map p302 (📞020-530 20 10; www.dylan amsterdam.com; Keizersgracht 384; d/ste from €395/629; ✳@🗗; 🚊1/2/5 Spui) Exquisite boutique hotel the Dylan occupies an 18th-century Keizersgracht canal house that is set around a herringbone-paved, topiary-filled inner courtyard. Bespoke furniture such as silver-leaf and mother-of-pearl drinks cabinets adorn its 40 individually decorated rooms and suites (some duplex). Its Michelin-starred Restaurant Vinkeles also hosts private chef's tables aboard its boat, the *Muze,* as it cruises the canals.

CANAL HOUSE   BOUTIQUE HOTEL €€€

Map p300 (📞020-622 51 82; www.canalhouse.nl; Keizersgracht 148; d from €221; ✳🗗; 🚊13/14/17 Westermarkt) A large, leafy, sofa-strewn garden is an unexpected find behind these adjoining 17th-century canal houses. Inside, the 23 rooms – in categories ranging from Good and Better to Great and Exceptional – have purple, grey and brown tones, soaring ceilings and king-size beds. There's a clubby cocktail bar; rates include a lavish buffet breakfast.

TOREN   BOUTIQUE HOTEL €€€

Map p300 (📞020-622 63 52; www.thetoren.nl; Keizersgracht 164; s/d/tr/ste from €108/189/225/342; ✳@🗗; 🚊13/14/17 Westermarkt) A title-holder for room size and personal service, the Toren has communal areas boasting a 17th-century opulence, with gilded mirrors, fireplaces and magnificent chandeliers. The 38 guestrooms are elegantly furnished and have Nespresso coffee machines. The hotel also rents historic boats (from €140 to €355 per hour) for private canal cruises.

🛏 Southern Canal Ring

⭐COCOMAMA
HOSTEL €

Map p304 (☑020-627 24 54; www.cocomama
hostel.com; Westeinde 18; d €107-212, 6-/4-bed
dm €39/44, min 2-night stay; @🖥; 🚊4/25 Stadhouderskade) Once a high-end brothel, this
boutique hostel's doubles and dorms are
light, bright and decorated with flair, with
white walls and quirky designer Delftware
or windmill themes. Amenities are way
above typical hostel standard, with en
suite bathrooms, in-room wi-fi, a relaxing
back garden, a well-equipped kitchen, a
book exchange and a super-comfy lounge
for movie nights. Breakfast is included.

HOTEL ASTERISK
HOTEL €

Map p304 (☑020-626 23 96; www.asteriskhotel.
nl; Den Texstraat 16; s/d from €74/100; @🖥;
🚊16/24 Wetering Circuit) Some of the singles
at this old-school family-owned 42-room
hotel are pretty cramped, and you're looking at function rather than atmosphere,
but the beds are comfortable and prices
cheap for central Amsterdam. Breakfast
costs €12.50 per person.

⭐HOTEL V
FREDERIKSPLEIN
BOUTIQUE HOTEL €€

Map p304 (☑020-662 32 33; www.hotelvfred
eriksplein.nl; Weteringschans 136; d €93-154; 🖥;
🚊4/7/10 Frederiksplein) With soothing, leafy
views over lush Frederiksplein, but a quick
shimmy from the bars and restaurants of
Utrechtsestraat, Hotel V exudes a style
that's well above its price bracket. Its 48
rooms have cool design cred with touches
such as funky wall stencils and mid-century leather armchairs.

HOTEL FREELAND
HOTEL €€

Map p304 (☑020-622 75 11; www.hotelfreeland.
com; Marnixstraat 386; s/d/tr from €80/130/150,
s without bathroom from €70; 🖥; 🚊1/2/5/7/10
Leidseplein) In a prime canal-side location,
the Freeland has 15 simple, nicely old-fashioned rooms with tiled walls; each has a
floral theme (tulips, roses and sunflowers).
Add in a tasty breakfast and it pretty much
kills the Leidseplein competition. The hotel
is gay-friendly and all-welcoming. Breakfast costs €6.50 per person.

CITY HOTEL
HOTEL €€

Map p304 (☑020-627 23 23; www.cityhotel
amsterdam.com; Utrechtsestraat 2; d €145-239;

@🖥; 🚊4/9/14 Rembrandtplein) Above the
Old Bell pub right near Rembrandtplein,
this friendly, family-run hotel feels more
like a hostel, and is a good midrange choice
in the centre. Rooms sleeping two to six
people have private bathrooms; larger
rooms, sleeping five to eight people, share
bathroom facilities. All come with crisp
linen. The attic annexe has a wonderful
view over the rooftops.

HOTEL ADOLESCE
HOTEL €€

Map p304 (☑020-626 39 59; http://
en.adolesce.nl; Nieuwe Keizersgracht 26; s/d
€85/140, without bathroom €80/110; @🖥;
🚊Waterlooplein) In a canal house just
across from the Hermitage Museum, this
little family-owned hotel has lots of com-
forting old-fashioned charm. Steep steps
lead to 10 spotless rooms of all shapes
and sizes; all are decorated with bright
modern prints. Breakfast is included, and
available all day.

SEVEN BRIDGES
BOUTIQUE HOTEL €€

Map p304 (☑020-623 13 29; www.sevenbridges
hotel.nl; Reguliersgracht 31; d €135-280; 🖥;
🚊4 Keizersgracht) Beautifully set on one of
Amsterdam's loveliest canals, the Seven
Bridges will immerse you in aristocratic
opulence. Rooms are sumptuously decorated with oriental rugs and polished
antiques. The urge to sightsee may fade
once breakfast (€10), served on fine china,
is delivered to your room.

AMISTAD HOTEL
BOUTIQUE HOTEL €€

Map p304 (☑020-624 80 74; www.amistad.nl;
Kerkstraat 42; s/d/tr €130/158/179, s without
bathroom from €97; @🖥; 🚊1/2/5 Keizersgracht) Red walls, white linen, Philippe
Starck chairs, sound systems and PCs in
the rooms give this small gay hotel a funky
feel, but you'll need to book well ahead.
Breakfast (included) is served until 1pm.

⭐SEVEN ONE SEVEN
BOUTIQUE HOTEL €€€

Map p304 (☑020-427 07 17; www.717hotel.nl;
Prinsengracht 717; d from €300; ✳🖥; 🚊1/2/5
Prinsengracht) Looking straight from the
pages of a style magazine, the exquisitely
decorated rooms here come with that
all-too-rare luxury: space. It'll be hard to
tear yourself away from these rooms, all
of which have soaring ceilings, vast sofas,
striking use of colour and contemporary-
meets-antique decorations.

SLEEPING SOUTHERN CANAL RING

HOTEL NOTTING HILL — DESIGN HOTEL €€€

Map p304 (📞020-523 10 35; www.hotelnotting hill.nl; Westeinde 26; d €214-499; ❋📶; 🚋4 Stadhouderskade) Decorated with flair by Dutch designer Wim Hoopman of Hoopman Interior Projects (aptly abbreviated to HIP), this office-block-turned-boutique features outsized contemporary art and 71 sleek, calm rooms with lots of feature wallpaper. Higher-priced rooms have canal views. It's in a bulls-eye location between Utrechtsestraat and De Pijp.

BANKS MANSION — HOTEL €€€

Map p304 (📞020-420 00 55; www.carlton.nl/banksmansion; Herengracht 519-525; s/d from €210/250, s/d ste €389/600; ❋@📶; 🚋16/24 Keizersgracht) This swish, renovated hotel has plush, comfortable art-deco-style rooms and a stylish Frank Lloyd Wright–inspired lobby. Bathrooms feature a huge rain shower. You'll pay around €40 more for a canal view, though rooms on the side get a glimpse for free. All drinks, minibar and breakfasts (buffet and cooked) are included in the price.

🛏 Jordaan & the West

CHRISTIAN YOUTH HOSTEL 'THE SHELTER JORDAN' — HOSTEL €

Map p310 (📞020-624 47 17; www.shelter amsterdam.com; Bloemstraat 179; dm from €30; @📶; 🚋10/13/14/17 Marnixstraat) Putting up with the 'no everything' (drinking, smoking, partying) policy at this 96-bed hostel isn't hard, because it's such a gem. Single-sex dorms are quiet and clean, there's a piano, a courtyard garden and bike rental, and the breakfasts – especially the fluffy pancakes – are great. The cafe serves cheap meals the rest of the day.

⭐ MR JORDAAN — DESIGN HOTEL €€

Map p308 (📞020-626 58 01; www.mr jordaan.nl; Bloemgracht 102; s/d/tr from €107/175.50/238.50; 📶; 🚋13/14/17 Westermarkt) Wooden bedheads shaped like a row of gabled canal houses, lighting made from plumbing pipes and bedside cacti – along with vintage fixtures in public spaces like 1960s TVs, battered suitcases and typewriters – are just some of the unexpected design elements at this super-cool, refreshingly irreverent hotel in the heart of the Jordaan.

⭐ HOUSEBOAT MS LUCTOR — B&B €€

Map p303 (📞06 2268 9506; http://boat bedandbreakfast.nl; Westerdok 103; d from €140; 📶; 🚋48 Barentszplein) 🚭 A brimming organic breakfast basket is delivered to you each morning at this metal-hulled, mahogany-panelled 1913 houseboat, moored in a quiet waterway 10 minutes' walk from Centraal Station (five from the Jordaan). Eco initiatives include solar power, two bikes to borrow and a canoe for canal explorations. Minimum stay is two nights.

Guests can take an extraordinary private tour with a local fisherman and scientist, Piet, to see waterways not usually accessible to the public (per person €75).

LINDEN HOTEL — BOUTIQUE HOTEL €€

Map p308 (📞020-622 14 60; http://lindenhotel. nl; Lindengracht 251; d from €121; 📶; 🚋3/10 Marnixplein) In a peaceful canal-side location footsteps from some of the Jordaan's best restaurants and markets, the recently renovated Linden has small but beautifully furnished rooms with jade-green feature walls, iridescent shell-pink cushions, swirl-patterned carpets and scented candles. Free tea, coffee and water infusions are available in the lobby. There's a tiny lift; staff couldn't be friendlier or more helpful.

HOTEL DE WINDKETEL — APARTMENT €€

Map p303 (www.windketel.nl; Watertorenplein 8; d from €162.50; 📶; 🚋10 Van Hallstraat) In the middle of a pedestrianised square, this diminutive octagonal water tower was constructed in 1897 as part of Amsterdam's waterworks and salvaged by local residents to share with visitors. Dutch design graces the ground-floor kitchen and dining room, 1st-floor living room, and top-floor bathroom and skylit bedroom beneath the original slatted-timber ceiling. Kids under 12 aren't permitted.

BACKSTAGE HOTEL — HOTEL €€

Map p310 (📞020-624 40 44; www.backstage hotel.com; Leidsegracht 114; s without bathroom from €85, d with/without bathroom from €155/125; 📶; 🚋1/2/5 Leidseplein) Seriously fun, this music-themed hotel is a favourite among musicians jamming at nearby Melkweg and Paradiso, as evidenced by the lobby bar's band-signature-covered piano and pool table. Gig posters (many signed) line the corridors, and rooms are done up in neo-retro black and white, with music stations and drum-kit overhead lights.

AMSTERDAM
WIECHMANN HOTEL
HOTEL €€

Map p310 (☏020-626 33 21; www.hotel
wiechmann.nl; Prinsengracht 328-332; s/d/
tr/f from €103/148/189/239; @⚟; ⊟7/10/17
Elandsgracht) Many of the 37 rooms at this
family-run hotel in three canal houses have
antique-shop-style furnishings, while the
lobby knick-knacks have been here since
the 1940s. It's in an ace location right on
the pretty Prinsengracht (it's worth paying
extra for a canal-facing room), but be aware
that there's no lift and the stairs are super
steep. Rates include breakfast.

MORGAN & MEES
BOUTIQUE HOTEL €€€

Map p310 (☏020-233 49 30; https://morgan
andmees.com; 2e Hugo de Grootstraat 2-6; d/ste
from €185/250; ✳⚟; ⊟3 Hugo de Grootplein)
It's all about comfort and cool at this stylish
little hotel at the Jordaan's edge. Nine crisp
white rooms with Coco-Mat queen- or king-
size beds, rain showers and big TVs sit on
top of Morgan & Mees' slick bar and restaurant. The easygoing staff make you feel at
home, and the off-the-beaten-path location
also lends an intimate vibe.

🛏 Vondelpark & the South

STAYOKAY AMSTERDAM
VONDELPARK
HOSTEL €

Map p312 (☏020-589 89 96; www.stayokay.com;
Zandpad 5; dm €29-59, tw from €79; ⚟📶; ⊟11e
Constantijn Huygensstraat) Practically in the
Vondelpark, this HI-affiliated 536-bed hostel, housed in former university buildings,
attracts over 75,000 guests a year, a lively
international crowd of backpackers, families and groups. It's the best Stayokay in
town, with private rooms and fresh mixed
or female-/male only rooms sleeping from
four to 10, sporting lockers, private bathrooms and well-spaced bunks. Breakfast is
a cut above most hostels.

VAN GOGH HOSTEL
& HOTEL
HOSTEL, HOTEL €

Map p312 (☏020-262 92 00; www.hotelvangogh.
nl; Van de Veldestraat 5; dm/s/d/tr/q from
€30/50/99/120/139; ✳@⚟; ⊟2/3/5/12 Van
Baerlestraat) The clue is in the name: this is a
few paces from the Van Gogh Museum, and
every room has a Van Gogh mural covering
the entire wall behind the bedhead. Next
door is the more basic hostel, with dorms
of six to eight beds, en suite bathroom and
flat-screen TV.

★HOTEL NOT HOTEL
DESIGN HOTEL €€

Map p312 (☏020-820 45 38; www.hotelnothotel.
com; Piri Reisplein 34; d with/without bathroom
from €95/125; ⊟7 Postjesweg) Stay in a work
of art at this out-there collection of installations. Sleep inside Amsterdam Tram 965 (in
a king-size bed), lounge on a private Spanish villa alfresco terrace, bed down behind
a secret bookcase, escape the daily grind in
the Crisis Free Zone framed by Transylva-
nian-inspired woodcarvings to deter evil
spirits, or climb a ladder to a crow's nest.

Students from Eindhoven's Design Academy created the rooms. Kevin Bacon (the
hotel's bar, named in homage of the actor)
mixes rockin' cocktails.

★COLLECTOR
B&B €€

Map p312 (☏020-673 67 79; www.the-collector.
nl; De Lairessestraat 46; r from €105-125; @⚟;
⊟5/16/24 Museumplein) This lovely B&B has
immaculate rooms with large windows
and leafy outlooks, plus each is furnished
with its own museum-style displays of
clocks, wooden clogs and ice skates that
the owner, Karel, collects. Each room has
balcony access and a TV. Karel stocks the
kitchen for guests to prepare breakfast at
their leisure (the eggs come from his hens
in the garden).

The kitchen is open all day if you want
to cook your own dinner. There are also a
couple of bikes Karel lends out to guests.

ALL ABOARD!
....

At **Train Lodge** (☏020-684 92 24; www.trainlodge.com; Changiweg 121, Sloterdijk; dm from
€29, 3-/6-bed private compartments from €89/179; ✳⚟; Ⓜ Sloterdijk), a laid-back hostel
on Sloterdijk Station's tracks, decommissioned Zürich–Rome sleeper carriages now
contain 123 beds in three- and six-berth compartments (some female only). Compartments have washbasins; shared showers and toilets are in the corridors. Although it's
outside the city centre, it's just a six-minute metro ride to Centraal Station. Bike rental
costs €12.50 per day; breakfast is €6.

★**PILLOWS ANNA VAN DEN VONDEL**   BOUTIQUE HOTEL **€€**

Map p312 (☑020-683 30 13; www.sandton.eu; Anna van den Vondelstraat 6; d from €190; 🐾; 🚇1 Jan Pieter Heijestraat) This grown-up hotel, housed in a row of three grand, red-and-white-striped 19th-century mansions, has rooms with views over the tranquil English garden. Beds are clothed in soft, gleaming white linen, walls are gentle dove grey, and chairs have a mid-century look and pale-blue crushed-velvet upholstery. Breakfast costs €25.

HOTEL DE HALLEN   DESIGN HOTEL **€€**

Map p312 (☑020-515 04 53; www.hoteldehallen. com; Bellamyplein 47; d €130-275; ❄️🐾; 🚇17 Ten Katestraat) Part of the De Hallen cultural centre (p166), housed in what were once tram sheds, this designer hotel has funky features, from a swing in the lobby to the industrial-chic 55 rooms, all of which have Coco-Mat mattresses, Nespresso machines and minibars. Sleek public spaces include restaurant Remise47, lounge areas, a bar and a wraparound sun-shaded terrace. Breakfast costs €20.

OWL HOTEL   HOTEL **€€**

Map p312 (☑020-618 94 84; www.owl-hotel.nl; Roemer Visscherstraat 1; s/d €140/150; 🐾; 🚇1 1e Constantijn Huygensstraat) The owl figurines in the reception of this 34-room hotel have been sent by former guests from all over the world to add to the hotel's collection. Staff are warm and welcoming, and rooms are bright and quiet. The buffet breakfast (included in the rate) is served in a bright, garden-side room.

CONSCIOUS HOTEL THE TIRE STATION   HOTEL **€€**

Map p312 (☑020-820 33 33; www.conscious hotels.com; Amstelveenseweg 5; d €100-180; P🐾; 🚇1 Rhijnvis Feithstraat) 🌱 Located in the former Michelin tyre station and doors away from its sister Conscious Hotel Vondelpark, this is the third addition to the Conscious stable. It's popular with business travellers for its sleek yet eco-friendly rooms; comfy beds are backed by cork pinboards and decorated with diving murals and quirky pictures. Small bathrooms have good showers and an encouraging 'Get Naked' sign.

CONSCIOUS HOTEL VONDELPARK   BOUTIQUE HOTEL **€€**

Map p312 (☑020-820 33 33; www.conscious hotels.com; Overtoom 519; d/tr from €90/121.50; 🐾; 🚇1 Rhijnvis Feithstraat) 🌱 The 81-room Vondelpark branch of this enviro-conscious group is a friendly place to stay, close to Overtoom restaurants and green Vondelpark. It wears its eco-heart on its sleeve, with a growing wall in the stunning lobby, plants in the rooms, huge floral murals, and recycled materials made into artful furnishings (including pressed-cardboard bathroom benchtops). The organic breakfast buffet costs €15.

CONSCIOUS HOTEL MUSEUM SQUARE   BOUTIQUE HOTEL **€€**

Map p312 (☑020-820 33 33; www.conscious hotels.com; De Lairessestraat 7; d/f from €100/167; @🐾🏠; 🚇5/16/24 Museumplein) 🌱 The most intimate of the Conscious Hotel group, and closest to the major Amsterdam museums, this location has a lush garden terrace, a living plant wall in the lobby and eco and design-conscious rooms: beds made with 100% natural materials, desks constructed from recycled yoghurt containers, and energy-saving plasma TVs. The organic breakfast costs €15 extra.

HOTEL FITA   HOTEL **€€**

Map p312 (☑020-679 09 76; www.fita.nl; Jan Luijkenstraat 37; s/d from €120/140; 🐾; 🚇2/3/5/12 Van Baerlestraat) Family-owned Fita, on a quiet street close to the museums, has 15 rooms with baroque carpeting but otherwise-plain decor, nice touches like plants in the rooms, and smart bathrooms; a bountiful free breakfast of eggs, pancakes, cheeses and breads; and a lift. The dynamic young owner keeps the property in mint condition, and service could not be more attentive.

NEIGHBOUR'S MAGNOLIA   HOTEL **€€**

Map p312 (☑020-676 93 21; www.magnolia hotelamsterdam.com; Willemsparkweg 205; s/d from €100/125; 🐾🏠; 🚇2 Emmastraat) Offering excellent value in the Old South (Amsterdam's wealthiest district, just south of Vondelpark), this is a good choice, with helpful staff, rooms with colourful touches and nice outlooks, and a peaceful location. Those at the rear have balconies overlooking a quiet, flower-filled courtyard (and, yes, there's a magnolia tree). Breakfast costs €12.50.

XAVIERA HOLLANDER'S
HAPPY HOUSE
B&B €€

(☑020-673 39 34; www.xavierahollander.com; Stadionweg 17; d from €120; 🛜; 🚋5/24 Gerrit van der Veenstraat) Xaviera Hollander was once a call girl, later a brothel owner, and wrote about her eventful life in her autobiography *The Happy Hooker*. She now welcomes guests to her home in the ritzy Beethovenstraat neighbourhood (minimum two-night stay). The two rooms, 'David' and 'Goliath' (which share a bathroom), are brightly decorated, plus furnished with books such as her *Guide to Mind-Blowing Sex*.

★HILTON AMSTERDAM
HISTORIC HOTEL €€€

Map p312 (☑020-710 60 00; www.3.hilton.com; Apollolaan 13; d from €160; 🅿🛜; 🚋2 Cornelius Schuytstraat) Famous as the place that John and Yoko staged their 'bed-in for peace' in 1969, in what may be the most laid-back demo of all time, this Hilton classic is close to Vondelpark, in the lush Old South district, and has all the five-star accoutrements, plus canal-side lawns. You can even stay in a piece of history in the 'John & Yoko' suite, with fabulous views through its huge windows, plus a balcony.

HOTEL VONDEL
BOUTIQUE HOTEL €€€

Map p312 (☑020-612 01 20; www.vondelhotels. com; Vondelstraat 26-30; d €110-230; 🛜; 🚋1 1e Constantijn Huygensstraat) Named after the famed Dutch poet Joost van den Vondel (as is the nearby park), the smart rooms at this stylish hotel have lots of designer flourishes, from Burberry-check blankets on the beds to modernist chandeliers and lots of blonde wood. Rooms come in many different shapes and sizes and thus different price points.

COLLEGE HOTEL
BOUTIQUE HOTEL €€€

Map p312 (☑020-571 15 11; www.thecollegehotel. com; Roelof Hartstraat 1; d from €169; 🅿🛜; 🚋3/5/12/24 Roelof Hartplein) Originally a 19th-century school, the impressive-looking College Hotel has 40 high-ceilinged rooms, each 25 sq metres and styled in restful shades of brown and white; you'd never think they were former classrooms. Hospitality-school students now staff the hotel to earn their stripes, and it's a celebrity favourite hosting everyone from Jamie Oliver to Faithless.

🛌 De Pijp

LITTLE AMSTEL
B&B €€

Map p316 (☑06 5021 6655; www.littleamstel. com; Amsteldijk 700; d from €110; 🛜; 🚋4 Stadhouderskade) Windows in these two cabin-style rooms aboard a houseboat look directly over the Amstel, the river that gave Amsterdam its name. The 'basic' room has one east-facing window, while the 'standard' has a double aspect. Both have private entrances, as well as en suite bathrooms, small fridges and tea- and coffee-making facilities. Breakfast isn't available, but nearby brunch cafes abound.

NINE(T)TEEN
B&B €€

Map p316 (☑020-233 32 19; www.nine-t-teen.nl; Hemonystraat 10; s/d/apt from €94/118/425; 🛜; 🚋4 Stadhouderskade) Brilliantly situated in De Pijp's northeastern corner near the Southern Canal Ring, this B&B has 16 en suite rooms across three town houses. Basement rooms have small windows; other rooms open to balconies or terraces. All come with Nespresso machines, but breakfast costs an extra €9.50. Various apartments at nearby locations sleep up to four people.

BICYCLE HOTEL AMSTERDAM
HOTEL €€

Map p316 (☑020-679 34 52; www.bicyclehotel. com; Van Ostadestraat 123; d/tr/f from €100/150/160, s/d/tr without bathroom from €30/60/120; 🏤🛜; 🚋3 Ferdinand Bolstraat) 🚲 Run by Marjolein and Clemens, this friendly, green-minded hotel has rooms that are comfy and familiar. It also rents bikes (€8 per day April to August; free between September and March) and serves a killer organic breakfast (included in the rate). Look for the bikes mounted on the brick exterior.

★SIR ALBERT HOTEL
DESIGN HOTEL €€€

Map p316 (☑020-305 30 20; www.sirhotels. com/albert; Albert Cuypstraat 2-6; d from €209; 🅿🏤🛜; 🚋16 Ruysdaelstraat) A 19th-century diamond factory houses this glitzy design hotel. Its 90 creative rooms and suites have high ceilings and large windows, with custom-made linens and Illy espresso machines; iPads are available for use in the Persian-rug-floored study. Energetic staff are genuine and professional. Of the 10 balcony rooms, west-facing 336, 337 and 338 have sunset views over the canal.

HOTEL OKURA AMSTERDAM · · · HOTEL €€€
Map p316 (☎020-678 71 11; www.okura.nl; Ferdinand Bolstraat 333; d/ste from €270/355; ❋@❋❋; 🚊12 Cornelis Troostplein) Rare-for-Amsterdam attributes that elevate this business-oriented hotel way above the competition include panoramic city views (particularly from higher-priced north-facing rooms), four Michelin stars on the premises – two at top-floor Ciel Bleu (p181), one at ground-floor Japanese restaurant Yamazato and one at ground-floor teppanyaki restaurant Sazanka – and an amazing health club with an 18m-long jet-stream swimming pool. Bountiful breakfast buffets cost €29.50.

🛏 Oosterpark & East of the Amstel

GENERATOR AMSTERDAM · · · HOSTEL €
Map p318 (☎020-708 56 00; www.generatorhostels.com; Mauritskade 57; dm €40, d €70-170, q €160-360; ❋🖐; 🚊9/10/14 Alexanderplein) Part of a reliably funky designer hostel chain, Generator occupies a century-old zoological university building with large windows overlooking lush Oosterpark, in an off-the-beaten-track area that's rapidly gentrifying. It has 566 beds spread over 168 twin and quad rooms, all with en suite bathrooms. Sociable areas include a cafe with terrace overlooking the park and a bar carved from the old lecture hall.

STAYOKAY AMSTERDAM ZEEBURG · · · HOSTEL €
Map p318 (☎020-551 31 90; www.stayokay.com; Timorplein 21; dm €18.50-45, r from €90; @❋🖐; 🚊14 Zeeburgerdijk) The sibling of Stayokay Vondelpark (p219) and Stayokay Stadsdoelen (p215), Zeeburg is efficient and impressive, with 508 beds spread over three floors in a large, handsome red-brick building; most of the spick-and-span rooms are four- or six-bed dorms, all light and bright, with en suite bathroom. Hot breakfast is included. Linens are free, but towels cost €4.50. Wi-fi is in the lobby only.

★VOLKSHOTEL · · · HOTEL €€
Map p318 (☎020-261 21 00; www.volkshotel.nl; Wibautstraat 150; r €60-100; ❋; Ⓜ Wibautstraat) The 172-room Volkshotel 'People's Hotel' has the vibe of an uber-cool media company, with glass-box meeting rooms, a shop in a caravan and lots of bright young things on laptops in the work space. There are hot tubs with fabulous views on the rooftop, and the Canvas roof-terrace bar is one of the city's coolest places for a drink with a view.

🛏 Amsterdam Noord

★CLINKNOORD · · · HOSTEL €
Map p319 (☎020-214 97 30; www.clinkhostels.com; Badhuiskade 3; dm €17-50, s/d from €90/125; ❋❋; 🚊Buiksloterweg) Clink is a designer hostel chain with other branches in London, and here occupies a 1920s laboratory on the IJ riverbank, by the ferry terminal – a free, five-minute ferry ride from Centraal Station (ferries run 24/7). Dorms are done up in minimalist-industrial style, with four to 16 beds and en suite facilities.

CAMPING VLIEGENBOS · · · CAMPGROUND €
Map p319 (☎020-636 88 55; Meeuwenlaan 138; 2-person tent or camper van €29, 4-person cabin €85; ☺Apr-Oct; ❋🖐; 🚊IJplein) Less than 2km from the IJplein ferry stop, this camp ground in woodland is small and gets busy, but it's very leafy and feels rural considering it's so close to the city. There are some basic huts with bunks available if you don't have your own tent. Staff are helpful and friendly.

★SIR ADAM · · · DESIGN HOTEL €€€
Map p319 (www.sirhotels.com; Overhoeksplein 7; d from €180; ❋@❋; 🚊Badhuiskade) Mammoth, view-framing (from the deluxe rooms) plate-glass windows: tick. Pillow menu: tick. Linen with a 300-thread count: tick. Rainfall shower: tick. Illy coffeemaker: tick. Crosley Cruiser record player: tick. Twenty-four-hour room service: tick. The rooms at Sir Adam have all a self-respecting dude who likes their comforts could want and more.

★FARALDA CRANE HOTEL · · · DESIGN HOTEL €€€
Map p319 (☎020-760 61 61; www.faralda.com; NDSM-plein 78; r €435-535; ❋❋; 🚊NDSM-werf) What's that imposing industrial crane rising up at NDSM-werf? It's a hotel. The three fantasy-world suites perched at varying heights – Free Spirit, Secret and Mystique – have looks worthy of a drug-baron's hideout, with free-standing baths, bold objets d'art and vertiginous views. On the crane's rooftop, you can soak in the heated bubbling outdoor hot tub, with astounding views across to central Amsterdam.

Understand Amsterdam

Amsterdam Today

Expansion is happening on every level in Amsterdam right now. The city's population is growing rapidly and dramatic architecture and grand urban projects continue to rise up and transform the cityscape, merging Golden Age charm with hyper-modernity. Below ground, new infrastructure and leisure facilities are being built beneath the city's streets and canals. A revolutionised nightlife scene is drawing locals and visitors away from the traditional party hubs to new 24-hour venues. And tech start-ups continue to break new ground.

Best on Film

Tulip Fever (2017) Based on the 1999 novel by Deborah Moggach, this love story takes place in 17th-century Amsterdam during the heady days of tulip mania.

The Paradise Suite (2015) A Bulgarian woman forced into prostitution, a Swedish piano prodigy, a Serbian war criminal and other troubled characters cross paths in Amsterdam.

Best in Print

The Diary of Anne Frank (Anne Frank; 1952) A moving account of a young girl's thoughts and yearnings while in hiding from the Nazis in Amsterdam. The book has been translated into 60 languages.

After the Silence (Jake Woodhouse; 2014) Noir novel in which Inspector Jap Rykel, an Amsterdam detective, hunts down a murderer in the city's tangled streets. It's book one of a four-part series.

The Miniaturist (Jessie Burton; 2014) Golden Age–set novel centred on Petronella Oortman, owner of an intricate dollhouse. The title character is an artist who helps Nella furnish it.

Spreading Out

Amsterdam's cityscape has been a work-in-progress from the get-go. During the Golden Age, 400-plus years ago, forward-thinking planners built the Canal Ring to drain and reclaim waterlogged land to accommodate the exploding population. Flash-forward to today and it's a similar story. Amsterdam is running out of room for its growing number of denizens – in 2016 alone, the city's population increased by 15,000, and it's expected to hit one million by the 2030s. Urban planners are using visionary architecture to make room for the newcomers.

The shores along the IJ have seen the most action, with swooping modern developments transforming industrial areas such as the Eastern Docklands and Western Docklands (on either side of Centraal Station). A vast new residential hub is springing up around the latter, with the construction of the Houthavens ('lumber ports') neighbourhood on seven artificial islands. Across the water, the previously industrial Amsterdam Noord area is also rapidly expanding. These are the new 'it' neighbourhoods for eye-popping, sustainably designed housing, offices and public buildings like the EYE Film Institute and A'DAM Tower.

Further east, there's IJburg, a new archipelago of artificial islands in the IJmeer lake. Six islands are now inhabited; following delays due to environmental concerns, construction on the last four (IJburg 2) begins in 2018.

Digging Down

The city's premium on space has not only seen its skyline rise: builders are also digging down. Underground projects include the North–South metro line, aka the Noord/Zuidlijn, linking Amsterdam Noord with the World Trade Centre in the south. Public transport company GVB is now calling for the Noord/Zuidlijn to be extended to Schiphol International Airport, and for the construction of an East–West cross-city metro line

(Oost/Westlijn) from IJburg to Schiphol via the Prinsengracht and Overtoom.

Another new project is the 600-space Albert Cuyp underground parking station below the Ruysdaelkade canal in De Pijp. It sees the removal of 300 car spaces from the streets above to allow better access for pedestrians and, especially, cyclists (the garage itself will have 60 bike spaces).

Bicycle spaces have long been a pressing issue in this cycling-oriented city, and in 2017 authorities approved plans to build an underground bicycle garage on the northern side of Centraal Station, which will provide parking for over 4000 bikes.

Ultimately, the goal is to build 50km of tunnels below the city centre with parking stations, sports facilities such as swimming pools, cinemas and supermarkets. Upon leaving Amsterdam's ring road, the A10, all traffic would be directed underground, with fumes filtered before reaching the surface.

Extended Hours

Nightlife in Amsterdam is undergoing major change. The city was the first in the world to appoint a night mayor (*nachtburgemeester*), to manage and promote its nocturnal economy and social life.

Since 2012, its inaugural night mayor, Mirik Milan, has established 24-hour club licences for selected venues that provide a contribution to the city's cultural offerings with creative (rather than profit-driven) events, and can also be used during the day.

New 'Square Hosts' at inner-city nightlife hubs like Leidseplein and Rembrandtplein identify and diffuse issues like excessive noise or littering before trouble arises, and ensure the city's residents and club goers coexist harmoniously. Infrastructure around nightlife hotspots has also been improved, such as increased lighting on the streets.

The five-year-term *nachtburgemeester* position is jointly funded by city government and the nightlife industry, and has a 20-person advisory council. The initiative has proven so successful that it's been adopted elsewhere – other cities with night mayors now include London, Paris and Zürich.

Looking Forward

Amsterdam consistently ranks as one of the world's leading start-up hubs. It's cheaper to run a business here than in places such as Silicon Valley, Beijing and New York City. There are plenty of English-fluent coders and programmers, a large university population, and state-of-the-art resources including the recently opened data centre, AM4, with 120,000 servers. And it's a creative environment, with a quality of life that attracts top international talent.

Their pioneering projects range from building a canal house and bridge by 3D printer, to offering networks where residents can trade surplus green energy with each other.

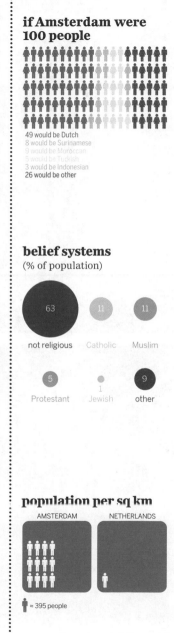

if Amsterdam were 100 people

49 would be Dutch
8 would be Surinamese
9 would be Moroccan
5 would be Turkish
3 would be Indonesian
26 would be other

belief systems
(% of population)

63 not religious
11 Catholic
11 Muslim
5 Protestant
1 Jewish
9 other

population per sq km

AMSTERDAM   NETHERLANDS

= 395 people

EWAIS/SHUTTERSTOCK ©

3

MUSEUMOFBAGSANDPURSES/TASSENMUSEUMHENDRIKJE ©

Tropenmuseum (p188)
e a huge collection of colonial booty at this gloriously quirky
useum.

Madame Tussauds (p69)
is Van Gogh wax figure is one of many focussing on local culture.

7. Tassenmuseum Hendrikje (p101)
The Museum of Bags & Purses holds a covetable collection of
arm candy.

4. NEMO Science Museum (p92)
Kids and adults alike enjoy the investigative mayhem at NEMO.

History

Amsterdam may have spawned one of the world's great trading empires, but this area was once an inhospitable patchwork of lakes, swamps and peat, at or below sea level; its contours shifted with the autumn storms and floods. The oldest archaeological finds here date from Roman times, when the IJ River lay along the northern border of the Roman Empire. Maritime trading, egalitarian attitudes and engineering ingenuity all paved the way for the modern city today.

From the Beginning

The mighty Romans – who had conquered the lands now known as the Netherlands in the 1st century – left behind no colosseums or magnificent tombs. In uncharacteristic style, they left practically no evidence, much less any grand gestures, of settlement. While the swampy, sea-level topography made the construction of grand edifices challenging, the Romans had been known to bypass such challenges before in other regions. In the end, they simply had other more important lands south of the Low Countries to inhabit and rule.

Around 1200, a fishing community known as Aemstelredamme ('the dam built across the Amstel') emerged at what is now the Dam, and the name Amsterdam was coined.

Early Trade

Farming was tricky on the marshland and with the sea on the doorstep, early residents turned to fishing. But it was commercial trade that would flourish. While powerful city-states focused on overland trade with Flanders and northern Italy, Amsterdam shrewdly levelled its sights on the maritime routes. The big prizes? The North and Baltic Seas, which were in the backyard of the powerful Hanseatic League, a group of German trading cities.

TIMELINE	1150–1300	1275	1345
	Dams are built to retain the IJ River between the Zuiderzee and Haarlem. A tiny community of herring fishermen settles on the banks of the Amstel river.	Amsterdam is founded after toll-free status is granted to residents along the Amstel. The city gains direct access to the ocean via the Zuiderzee, now the IJsselmeer.	The 'Miracle of Amsterdam' occurs and the city becomes an important place of pilgrimage, causing its population to grow considerably.

Ignoring the league's intimidating reputation, Amsterdam's clever *vrijbuiters* (buccaneers) sailed right into the Baltic, their holds full of cloth and salt to exchange for grain and timber. It was nothing short of a coup. By the late 1400s the vast majority of ships sailing to and from the Baltic Sea were based in Amsterdam.

By this time sailors, merchants, artisans and opportunists from the Low Countries (roughly present-day Netherlands, Belgium and Luxembourg) made their living here.

At the time, Amsterdam was unfettered by the key structures of other European societies. With no tradition of Church-sanctioned feudal relationships, no distinction between nobility and serfs, and hardly any taxation, a society of individualism and capitalism took root. The modern idea of Amsterdam – free, open, progressive and flush with opportunity – was born.

Independent Republic

The Protestant Reformation wasn't just a matter of religion; it was also a classic power struggle between the 'new money' (an emerging class of merchants and artisans) and the 'old money' (the land-owning, aristocratic order sanctioned by the established Catholic Church).

The Protestantism that took hold in the Low Countries was its most radically moralistic stream, known as Calvinism. It stressed the might of God and treated humans as sinful creatures whose duty in life was sobriety and hard work. The ascetic Calvinists stood for local decision-making and had a disdain for the top-down hierarchy of the Catholic Church.

Calvinism was key to the struggle for independence by King Philip II of Spain. The hugely unpopular Philip, a fanatically devout Catholic, had acquired the Low Countries in something of a horse trade with Austria. His efforts to introduce the Spanish Inquisition, centralise government and levy taxes enraged his subjects and awoke a sense of national pride.

In 1579 the seven northern provinces, with mighty Amsterdam on their side, declared themselves to be an independent republic, led by William of Orange: the seed that grew into today's royal family. William was famously dubbed 'the Silent' because he wisely refused to enter into religious debate. To this day, he remains the uncontested founder – and father – of the Netherlands.

Hans Brinker, who supposedly stuck his finger in a dyke and saved the Netherlands from a flood, is an American invention and unknown in the Netherlands. He starred in a 19th-century children's book.

1380	1452	1519	1543
Canals of the present-day Medieval Centre are dug. Amsterdam flourishes, winning control over the sea trade in Scandinavia and later gaining free access to the Baltic.	Following the second 15th-century fire to devastate the city, laws decree that brick and tile are the only building materials that can be used in the city.	Spain's Charles V is crowned Holy Roman Emperor. Treaties and dynastic marriages make Amsterdam part of the Spanish Empire, with Catholicism the main faith.	Charles V unites the Low Countries (roughly the area covering what is now the Netherlands, Belgium and Luxembourg) and establishes Brussels as the region's capital.

Golden Age (1580–1700)

In 1588, Den Haag was established as the seat of the Dutch Republic, but Amsterdam grew rapidly to become the largest and most influential city in the Netherlands.

By 1600 Dutch ships controlled the sea trade between England, France, Spain and the Baltic, and had a virtual monopoly on North

THE CURIOUS HISTORY OF TULIPMANIA

When it comes to investment frenzy, the Dutch tulip craze of 1636–37 ranks alongside the greatest economic booms and busts in history.

Tulips originated as wildflowers in Central Asia and were first cultivated by the Turks, who filled their courts with these beautiful spring blooms (the word tulip derives from 'turban' due to the petals' resemblance to the headwear). In the mid-1500s the Habsburg ambassador to Istanbul brought some bulbs back to Vienna, where the imperial botanist, Carolus Clusius, learned how to propagate them. In 1590 Clusius became director of the Hortus Botanicus in Leiden – one of Europe's oldest botanical gardens – and had great success growing and cross-breeding tulips in the Netherlands' cool, damp climate and fertile delta soil.

The more exotic specimens of tulip featured frilly petals and 'flamed' streaks of colour, which attracted the attention of wealthy merchants, who put them in their living rooms and hallways to impress visitors. Trickle-down wealth and savings stoked the taste for exotica in general, and tulip growers arose to service the demand.

A speculative frenzy ensued, and people paid top florin for the finest bulbs, many of which changed hands time and again before they sprouted. Vast profits were made and speculators fell over themselves to outbid each other. Bidding often took place in taverns and was fuelled by alcohol, which no doubt added to the enthusiasm.

Of course, this bonanza couldn't last, and when several bulb traders in Haarlem failed to fetch their expected prices in February 1637, the bottom fell out of the market. Within weeks many of the country's wealthiest merchants went bankrupt and many more of humbler origins lost everything.

However, love of the unusual tulip endured, and cooler-headed growers perfected their craft. To this day, the Dutch continue to be the world leaders in tulip cultivation and supply most of the bulbs planted in Europe and North America. They also excel in other bulbs such as daffodils, hyacinths and crocuses.

So what happened to the flamed, frilly tulips? They're still produced but have gone out of fashion, and are now known as Rembrandt tulips because of their depiction in so many 17th-century paintings.

For an informative read about the era, pick up a copy of *Tulipomania: The Story of the World's Most Coveted Flower* by Mike Dash.

1578	1580	1600s	1602
Amsterdam is captured in a bloodless coup. A Dutch Republic made up of seven provinces is declared a year later, led by William the Silent.	The Protestant Reformation picks up steam and Catholicism is outlawed, with clandestine worship permitted.	The Golden Age places Amsterdam firmly on the cultural map. While Rembrandt paints in his atelier, the grand inner ring of canals is constructed. The city's population surges to 200,000.	Amsterdam becomes the site of the world's first stock exchange when the offices of the Dutch East India Company trade their own shares.

Sea fishing and Arctic whaling. Jewish refugees taught Dutch mariners about trade routes, giving rise to the legendary Dutch East India and Dutch West India Companies. For a while, the Dutch ran rings around the fleets of great powers, which were too slow or cumbersome to react. In the absence of an overriding religion, ethnic background or political entity, money reigned supreme.

Two decades on, Dutch traders had gone global, exploring the far corners of the earth, and by the mid-17th century the Dutch had more seagoing merchant vessels than England and France combined. Half of all ships sailing between Europe and Asia belonged to the Dutch, and exotic products – coffee, tea, spices, tobacco, cotton, silk and porcelain – became commodities. Amsterdam became home to Europe's largest shipbuilding industry, and the city was veritably buzzing with prosperity and innovation.

In 1651, England passed the first of several Navigation Acts that posed a serious threat to Dutch trade, leading to several thorny, inconclusive wars on the seas. Competitors sussed out Dutch trade secrets, regrouped and reconquered the sea routes. In 1664 the Dutch lost the colony of New Netherland, including the provincial capital New Amsterdam (now New York City) to the British, in exchange for Suriname in South America (which the Dutch governed until 1954). Louis XIV of France seized the opportunity to invade the Low Countries two decades later, and the period of prosperity known as the Golden Age ended. While the city hardly went into decay or ruin, the embattled economy would take more than a century to regain its full strength.

Wealthy Decline (1700–1814)

While the Dutch Republic didn't have the resources to fight France and England head on, it had Amsterdam's money to buy them off and ensure freedom of the seas.

As the costs mounted, Amsterdam went from being a place where everything (profitable) was possible, to a lethargic community where wealth creation was a matter of interest rates. Gone were the daring sea voyages, the achievements in art, science and technology, and the innovations of government and finance. Ports such as London and Hamburg became powerful rivals.

The decline in trade brought poverty, and exceptionally cold winters hampered transport and led to serious food shortages. The winters of 1740 and 1763 were so severe that some residents froze to death.

The city's symbol, XXX, appears on its coat of arms, flag (two horizontal red stripes with a central black stripe with three diagonal white St Andrew's crosses), municipal buildings and merchandising everywhere. It originated in 1505 when Amsterdam was a fishing town (St Andrew is the patron saint of fishers).

1618	1636–37	1664	1688
World's first weekly broadsheet newspaper, the *Courante uyt Italien, Duytslandt, &c.,* is printed in Amsterdam.	Tulipmania sweeps the nation, when the flower bulbs are more valuable than a canal house. Tulip speculators get rich fast, but the market crashes and many are left bankrupt.	The Dutch infamously lose the colony of New Netherland (now the northeastern US), including New Amsterdam (now New York City), to the British.	William III of Orange repels the French with the help of Austria, Spain and Brandenburg. William then invades England, where he and his wife are proclaimed king and queen.

Amsterdam's support of the American War of Independence (1776) resulted in a British blockade of the Dutch coast, followed by British conquests of Dutch trading posts around the world, forcing the closure of the Dutch West and East India Companies.

Enter the French: in 1794 French revolutionary troops invaded the Low Countries. In a convenient act of nepotism, the Dutch Republic became a monarchy in 1806, when Napoleon installed his brother Louis Napoleon as king.

After Napoleon's defeat in 1813, Amsterdam's trade with the world recovered only slowly; domination of the seas now belonged to the British.

New Infrastructure (1814–1918)

In the first half of the 19th century, Amsterdam was a gloomy, uninspiring place. Its harbour had been neglected and the sandbanks in the IJ proved too great a barrier for modern ships. Rotterdam was set to become the country's premier port.

Things began to look up as the country's first railway, between Amsterdam and Haarlem, opened in 1839. Trade with the East Indies was the backbone of Amsterdam's economy, and a canal, later extended to the Rhine, helped the city to benefit from the Industrial Revolution under way in Europe.

Amsterdam again attracted immigrants, and its population doubled in the second half of the 19th century. Speculators hastily erected new housing beyond the Canal Ring – dreary, shoddily built tenement blocks.

The Netherlands remained neutral in WWI, but Amsterdam's trade with the East Indies suffered from naval blockades. Food shortages brought riots, and an attempt to bring the socialist revolution to the Netherlands was put down by loyalist troops.

Boom & Depression (1918–40)

After WWI, Amsterdam remained the country's industrial centre. The Dutch Shipbuilding Company operated the world's second-largest wharf and helped carry a large steel and diesel-motor industry. The harbour handled tropical produce that was processed locally, such as tobacco and cocoa (Amsterdam remains the world's biggest cocoa importer).

The 1920s were boom years. In 1920 KLM (Koninklijke Luchtvaart Maatschappij; Royal Aviation Company) began the world's

---

Amsterdam is the official (constitutional) capital of the Netherlands, but Den Haag is the seat of government and the site of the royal family's residence, Huis ten Bosch. All embassies are located in Den Haag, although some countries also have consulates general in Amsterdam.

1795	1806	1813–14	1830
French troops occupy the Netherlands and install the Batavian Republic. The fragmented United Provinces become a centralised state, with Amsterdam as its capital.	The Dutch Republic becomes a monarchy when Napoleon installs his brother Louis Napoleon as king.	The French are overthrown and William VI of Orange is crowned as Dutch King William I.	With French help, the southern provinces secede to form the Kingdom of Belgium. The country is not formally recognised by the Dutch government until 1839.

SIGHTS FOR HISTORY BUFFS

Amsterdam Museum (p70) Lift the veil on the city's storied past.

Stadsarchief (p120) Plumb the city's rich archives.

Anne Frank Huis (p104) See the annexe where the Frank family hid, and pages from Anne's poignant diary.

Verzetsmuseum (p91) Learn about Dutch Resistance efforts during WWII.

West-Indisch Huis (p107) Ponder the 17th-century building where the Dutch West India Company's governors authorised establishing New Amsterdam (now New York City).

first regular passenger air service between Amsterdam and London from an airstrip south of the city, and bought many of its planes from Anthony Fokker's factory north of the IJ. There were two huge breweries, a sizeable clothing industry and even a local car factory. The city hosted the Olympic Games in 1928.

The world Depression in the 1930s hit Amsterdam hard. Make-work projects did little to defuse the mounting tensions between socialists, communists and a small but vocal party of Dutch fascists. The city took in 25,000 Jewish refugees fleeing Germany; many were turned back at the border because of the country's neutrality policy.

WWII (1940–45)

The Netherlands attempted to remain neutral in WWII, but Germany invaded in May 1940. For the first time in almost 400 years, Amsterdammers experienced war first-hand. Few wanted to believe that things would turn really nasty (the Germans, after all, had trumpeted that the Dutch were of the 'Aryan brotherhood').

In February 1941, dockworkers led a protest strike over the treatment of Jews, commemorated as the 'February Strike'. By then, however, it was already too late.

The Dutch Resistance, set up by an unlikely alliance of Calvinists and communists, only became large-scale when the increasingly desperate Germans began to round up able-bodied men to work in Germany.

Towards the end of the war, the situation in Amsterdam was dire. Coal shipments ceased; many men aged between 17 and 50 had gone into hiding or to work in Germany; public utilities were halted; and the Germans began to plunder anything that could assist their war effort. Thousands of lives were lost to severe cold and famine

1865–76	1889	1914–20	1928
In a period of rapid economic and social change, the North Sea Canal is dug, the Dutch railway system is expanded and socialist principles of government are established.	Centraal Station makes its grand debut, and – in an instant – Amsterdam is connected by rail to the rest of Europe.	The Netherlands remains neutral in WWI. Food shortages cripple the country, leading to strikes, unrest and growing support for the Dutch Communist Party.	Amsterdam hosts the Olympic games during the 1920s boom years. The Olympic flame is lit for the first time since ancient Greece.

Canadian troops finally liberated the city in May 1945 in the final days of the war in Europe.

Postwar Growth (1945–62)

The city's growth resumed after the war, with US aid through the Marshall Plan.

Massive apartment blocks arose in areas annexed west of the city to meet the continuing demand for housing, made more acute by the demographic shift away from extended families. The massive

---

JEWISH AMSTERDAM

It's hard to overstate the role Jewish people have played in the evolution of civic and commercial life in Amsterdam. The first documented Jewish presence goes back to the 12th century, but it was expulsion from Spain and Portugal in the 1580s that brought a large number of Sephardic (Jews of Spanish, Middle Eastern or North African heritage) refugees.

As in much of Europe, Jews in Amsterdam were barred from many professions. Monopolistic guilds kept most trades firmly closed. But some Sephardim were diamond cutters, for which there was no guild. Other Sephardic Jews introduced printing and tobacco processing, or worked in unrestricted trades such as retail, finance, medicine and the garment industry. The majority, however, eked out a meagre living as labourers and small-time traders. They lived in the Nieuwmarkt area, which developed into the Jewish quarter.

Yet Amsterdam's Jewish people had some human rights unheard of elsewhere in Europe. They were not confined to a ghetto and, with some restrictions, could buy property. Although the Protestant establishment sought to impose restrictions, civic authorities were reluctant to restrict such productive members of society.

The 17th century saw more Jewish refugees arrive, this time Ashkenazim (Jews from Europe outside of Iberia), fleeing pogroms in Central and Eastern Europe. Amsterdam became the largest Jewish centre in Europe – some 10,000 strong by Napoleonic times. The guilds and all remaining restrictions on Jews were abolished during the French occupation, and Amsterdam's Jewish community thrived in the 19th century.

All that came to an end, however, with WWII. The Nazis brought about the near-complete annihilation of Amsterdam's Jewish community. Before the war about 140,000 Jews lived in the Netherlands, of whom about 90,000 lived in Amsterdam (comprising 13% of the city's population). Only about 5500 of Amsterdam's Jews survived the war, barely one in 16, the lowest proportion of anywhere in Western Europe.

Today there are approximately 30,000 Jews in the Netherlands, some half of whom live in Amsterdam.

1939	1940	1944–45	1966
The Dutch government establishes Westerbork as an internment camp to house Jewish refugees.	Germany invades the Netherlands. Rotterdam is destroyed by the Luftwaffe, but Amsterdam suffers only minor damage before capitulating.	The Allies liberate the southern Netherlands, but the north and west of the country are cut off from supplies. Thousands of Dutch perish in the bitter 'Hunger Winter'.	Crown Princess Beatrix marries German-born Claus von Amsberg (1926–2002). Despite violent protests on their wedding day he ultimately becomes one of the most popular Dutch royals.

Bijlmermeer housing project (now called De Bijlmer) southeast of the city, begun in the mid-1960s and finished in the 1970s, was built in a similar vein.

Cultural Revolution (1962–82)

For nearly a century leading up to the 1960s, Dutch society had become characterised by *verzuiling* (pillarisation), a social order in which each religion and political persuasion achieved the right to do its own thing, with its own institutions. Each persuasion represented a pillar that supported the status quo in a general 'agreement to disagree'. In the 1960s the old divisions were increasingly irrelevant and the pillars came tumbling down, but not the philosophy they spawned.

Amsterdam became Europe's *magisch centrum* ('magic centre'): hippies smoked dope on the Dam, camped in the Vondelpark and tripped at clubs such as the Melkweg, an abandoned dairy barn. In 1972 the first coffeeshop opened and in 1976 marijuana was decriminalised to free up police resources for combating hard drugs. With soaring housing prices, squatters began to occupy buildings left empty by speculators. In the process, they helped save several notable historical structures from demolition.

Since 2010, squatting has been illegal, and some former squats have become legitimate cultural centres.

New Consensus (1982–2000)

Twenty years after the cultural revolution began, a new consensus emphasised a decentralised government. Neighbourhood councils were established with the goal of creating a more liveable city, through integration of work, schools and shops within walking or cycling distance; decreased traffic; renovation rather than demolition; friendly neighbourhood police; a practical, non-moralistic approach towards drugs; and legal recognition of homosexual couples.

By the early 1990s, the families and small manufacturers that had dominated inner-city neighbourhoods in the early 1960s had been replaced by professionals and a service industry of pubs, coffeeshops, restaurants and hotels. The city's success in attracting large foreign businesses resulted in an influx of high-income expats.

Jewish inhabitants gave the city its nickname, Mokum, from the Yiddish for 'town' (derived from the Hebrew *makom*, meaning 'place'). The term is widely used today, and Amsterdam natives are known as Mokummers.

1976	1980	2001	2002
The Netherlands' drug laws distinguish soft from hard drugs; possession of small amounts of marijuana is decriminalised.	Queen Beatrix' investiture in Amsterdam is disrupted by smoke bombs and riots instigated by squatters rioting against the lack of affordable housing.	The Netherlands becomes the first country in the world to legalise same-sex marriage. Numerous nations follow suit in the years after.	Pim Fortuyn, a hard-line politician on immigration and integration, is assassinated. The ruling Dutch parties shift to the right after suffering major losses in the national election.

New Millennium (2000–Present)

Ups and downs have characterised the 21st century for Amsterdam. After smouldering for years, a noisy debate erupted over the Netherlands' policy towards newcomers, which quickly led to a tightening of immigration laws. The limits of tolerance, a core value of Dutch identity, were called into question. Pim Fortuyn, a right-wing politician, declared the country 'full' before he was assassinated in 2002.

Social tensions flared in the wake of the Fortuyn murder, and the number of people leaving the country reached a 50-year high, although most departed for economic and family reasons. The mood was edgy, like a cauldron about to boil over.

It finally did in the autumn of 2004, when filmmaker Theo van Gogh – known for his anti-Muslim views – was murdered on an Amsterdam street. The leading political parties in the Netherlands responded with a big shift to the right. In 2006 the government passed a controversial immigration law requiring newcomers – except those from countries with reciprocal arrangements or pre-existing treaties – to have competency in the Dutch language and culture before they could get a residency permit. This meant the policy mostly fell on immigrants from non-Western countries. Indeed, immigration from these countries slowed considerably after the law was enacted – but recently it began to tick upward again given the many refugees fleeing conflict in the Middle East. Immigration overall has been on the rise since 2008, thanks to newcomers from Eastern Europe.

In 2008, the Dutch government made waves – both locally and abroad – by announcing its plans to reduce the number of coffeeshops and legal brothels. The legal age of prostitutes was raised from 18 to 21 in 2013, and rules went into effect in 2014 to shut down coffeeshops operating near schools. Amsterdam's authorities are often at odds with the national government when it comes to such policies, especially those involving coffeeshops, and the city is loath to enforce the issue. Nonetheless, a number of coffeeshops have closed over the past few years, as have many Red Light District's windows.

A budget crisis over austerity measures as a result of the global financial crisis led to the fall of the Dutch government in 2012. Subsequent elections saw Prime Minister Mark Rutte retain the position of de-facto head of government and form a new coalition government with his liberal People's Party for Freedom and Democracy (VVD) and the centre-left Labour party. The latter is the faction of Amsterdam mayor Eberhard van der Laan, who has been at the job since 2010.

HISTORY NEW MILLENNIUM (2000–PRESENT)

Historical Reads: Fiction

Tulip Fever (Deborah Moggach)

Max Havelaar (Eduard Douwes Dekker)

The Coffee Trader (David Liss)

Rembrandt's Whore (Sylvie Matton)

In 2017, it was revealed that King Willem-Alexander, a qualified pilot, had been flying twice a month as a 'guest pilot' for Dutch airline KLM (and prior to that, Martinair) for 21 years. He has since stepped down from the part-time job.

2004	2008	2009	2010
Activist filmmaker Theo van Gogh, a fierce critic of Islam, is murdered, touching off intense debate over the limits of Dutch multicultural society.	The city announces Project 1012. The goal is to clean up the Red Light District and close prostitution windows and coffeeshops believed to be controlled by organised crime.	Amsterdam courts prosecute Dutch parliamentary leader Geert Wilders for 'incitement to hatred and discrimination'. (He is acquitted of all charges in 2011.)	Members of the Dutch government officially apologise to the Jewish community for failing to protect the Jewish population from genocide.

Royal Palace (p66) on National Tulip Day

Historical Reads: Nonfiction

....

Amsterdam: A History of the World's Most Liberal City (Russell Shorto)

....

The Embarrassment of Riches (Simon Schama)

....

Amsterdam: The Brief Life of a City (Geert Mak)

At the Royal Palace, Queen Beatrix stepped down after 33 years, abdicating in favour of her eldest son Willem-Alexander, who became king on 30 April 2013. His investiture took place in the Nieuwe Kerk. He is the first male to accede to the Dutch throne since 1890.

In the 2017 Dutch general election, Mark Rutte's VVD party defeated controversial far-right politician Geert Wilders' Party for Freedom (PVV), gaining 33 seats to the PVV's 20. Had the PVV garnered a majority of seats, Wilders would have been unlikely to govern, given no potential coalition parties expressed willingness to work with him in light of his extreme views (such as comparing the Quran to *Mein Kampf*) and policies (including his advocation for a 'Nexit' from the EU, and hardline anti-immigration stance).

2013	2015	2017	2017
After a 33-year reign, Queen Beatrix abdicates in favour of her eldest son, Willem-Alexander, who becomes the Netherlands' first king in 123 years.	Scores of prostitutes and their supporters take to the streets to protest the closure of roughly one-fifth of the Red Light District's windows.	Prime Minister Mark Rutte's People's Party for Freedom and Democracy (VVD) defeats Geert Wilders' Party for Freedom (PVV) in the Dutch general election.	Two paintings from the Van Gogh museum are discovered behind a toilet in an Italian farmhouse after being stolen in a 2002 heist. They are returned to the museum and put on display once again.

Dutch Painting

They don't call them the Dutch Masters for nothing. The line-up includes Rembrandt, Frans Hals and Jan Vermeer – these iconic artists are some of the world's most revered and celebrated painters. And then, of course, there's Vincent van Gogh, who toiled in ignominy while supported by his loving brother Theo, and 20th-century artists including De Stijl–proponent Piet Mondrian and graphic genius MC Escher. Understanding these quintessential Dutch artists requires a journey back into history.

15th & 16th Centuries (Flemish & Dutch Schools)

Above: *Merry Drinker* by Frans Hals

Prior to the late 16th century, when Belgium was still part of the Low Countries, art focused on the Flemish cities of Ghent, Bruges and Antwerp. Paintings of the Flemish School featured biblical and allegorical subject matter popular with the Church, the court and (to a lesser extent) the nobility, who, after all, paid the bills and called the shots.

Among the most famous names of the era are Jan van Eyck (c 1385–1441), the founder of the Flemish School, who was one of the earliest artists to use oils in detailed panel painting; Rogier van der Weyden (1400–64), whose religious portraits showed the personalities of his subjects; and Hieronymus (also known as Jeroen) Bosch (1450–1516), with his macabre allegorical paintings full of religious topics. Pieter Bruegel the Elder (1525–69) used Flemish landscapes and peasant life in his allegorical scenes.

In the northern Low Countries, painters began to develop a style of their own. Although the artists of the day never achieved the level of recognition of their Flemish counterparts, the Dutch School, as it came to be called, was known for favouring realism over allegory. Haarlem, just west of Amsterdam, was the centre of this movement, with artists such as Jan Mostaert (1475–1555), Lucas van Leyden (1494–1533) and Jan van Scorel (1495–1562). Painters in the city of Utrecht were famous for using chiaroscuro (deep contrast of light and shade), a technique associated with the Italian master Caravaggio.

17th Century (Golden Age)

When the Spanish were expelled from the Low Countries, the character of the art market changed. There was no longer the Church to buy artworks and no court to speak of, so art became a business, and artists were forced to survive in a free market. In place of Church and court emerged a new, bourgeois society of merchants, artisans and shopkeepers who didn't mind spending money to brighten up their houses and workplaces. The key: they had to be pictures the buyers could relate to.

Painters became entrepreneurs in their own right, churning out banal works, copies and masterpieces in factory-like studios. Paintings were mass-produced and sold at markets alongside furniture and chickens. Soon the wealthiest households were covered in paintings from top to bottom. Foreign visitors commented that even bakeries and butcher shops seemed to have a painting or two on the wall. Most painters specialised in one of the main genres of the day.

Rembrandt van Rijn

The 17th century's greatest artist, Rembrandt van Rijn (1606–69), grew up a miller's son in Leiden, but had become an accomplished painter by his early 20s.

In 1631 he went to Amsterdam to run the painting studio of the wealthy art-dealer Hendrick van Uylenburgh. Portraits were the studio's cash cow, and Rembrandt and his staff (or 'pupils') churned out scores of them, including group portraits such as *The Anatomy Lesson of Dr Tulp*. In 1634 he married Van Uylenburgh's niece, Saskia, who often modelled for him.

Rembrandt fell out with his boss, but his wife's capital helped him buy the sumptuous house next door to Van Uylenburgh's studio (the current Museum het Rembrandthuis). There Rembrandt set up his own studio, with staff who worked in a warehouse in the Jordaan. These were happy years: his paintings were a success and his studio became the largest in Holland, though his gruff manner and open agnosticism didn't win him dinner-party invitations from the elite.

Rembrandt became one of the city's biggest art collectors. He was a master manipulator, and not only of images: the painter was also known to have his own pictures bid up at auctions. He often sketched and painted for himself, urging his staff to do likewise. Residents of the surrounding Jewish quarter provided perfect material for his dramatic biblical scenes.

The Night Watch

In 1642, a year after the birth of their son Titus, Saskia died and business went downhill. Although Rembrandt's majestic group portrait

Female painters during the Dutch Golden Age were rare. Judith Leyster (1609–1660) was the only woman registered with the artists' guild during the time. She trained with Frans Hals, and his influence is seen in her fluid portraits. The Rijksmuseum has some of her works.

Great Rembrandt Paintings

The Night Watch (1642; Rijksmuseum)

Peter Denies Christ (1660; Rijksmuseum)

Self Portrait (1620; Rijksmuseum)

The Night Watch by Rembrandt, Rijksmuseum (p151)

The Night Watch (1642) was hailed by art critics (it's now the Rijksmuseum's prize exhibit, and there's a life-size bronze sculpture re-creation on Rembrandtplein), some of the influential people he depicted were not pleased. Each subject had paid 100 guilders, and some were unhappy at being shoved to the background. In response, Rembrandt told them where they could shove their complaints. Suddenly he received far fewer orders.

Rembrandt began an affair with his son's governess, but kicked her out a few years later when he fell for the new maid, Hendrickje Stoffels, who bore him a daughter, Cornelia. The public didn't take kindly to the man's lifestyle and his spiralling debts, and in 1656 he went bankrupt. His house and rich art collection were sold and he moved to the Rozengracht in the Jordaan.

Etchings

No longer the darling of the wealthy, Rembrandt continued to paint, draw and etch – his etchings on display in the Museum het Rembrandthuis are some of the finest ever produced. He also received the occasional commission, including the monumental *Conspiracy of Claudius Civilis* (1661) for the city hall, although authorities disliked it and had it removed. In 1662 he completed the *Staalmeesters* (The Syndics) for the drapers' guild and ensured that everybody remained clearly visible, though it ended up being his last group portrait.

Later Works

The works of his later period show that Rembrandt had lost none of his touch. No longer constrained by the wishes of clients, he enjoyed new-found freedom. His works became more unconventional, yet showed an ever-stronger empathy with their subject matter, as in *The Jewish Bride* (1667). The many portraits of Titus and Hendrickje, and his ever-gloomier self-portraits, are among the most stirring in the history of art.

The Damrak in Amsterdam by George Hendrik Breitner

A plague epidemic between 1663 and 1666 killed one in seven Amsterdammers, including Hendrickje. Titus died in 1668, aged 27 and just married; Rembrandt died a year later, a broken man.

Frans Hals
Another great painter of this period, Frans Hals (c 1582–1666), was born in Antwerp but lived in Haarlem. He devoted most of his career to portraits, dabbling in occasional genre scenes with dramatic chiaroscuro. His ability to capture his subjects' expressions was equal to Rembrandt's, though he didn't explore their characters as much. Both masters used the same expressive, unpolished brush strokes and their styles went from bright exuberance in their early careers to dark and solemn later on. The 19th-century Impressionists also admired Hals' work. In fact, his *Merry Drinker* (1628–30), in the Rijksmuseum's collection, with its bold brush strokes, could almost have been painted by an Impressionist.

Group Portraits
Hals also specialised in beautiful group portraits, in which the participants were depicted in almost natural poses, unlike the rigid line-ups produced by lesser contemporaries – though he wasn't as cavalier as Rembrandt in subordinating faces to the composition. A good example is the pair of paintings known collectively as *The Regents & the Regentesses of the Old Men's Almshouses* (1664) in the Frans Hals Museum in Haarlem. The museum is a space that Hals knew intimately; he spent his final years in the almshouse.

Johannes Vermeer
The grand trio of 17th-century masters is completed by Johannes (also known as Jan) Vermeer (1632–75) of Delft. He produced only 35 meticulously crafted paintings in his career and died poor with 10 children;

Great Frans Hals Paintings

The Merry Drinker (1628–30; Rijksmuseum)

Wedding Portrait (1622; Rijksmuseum)

Meagre Company (1637; Rijksmuseum)

Great Vermeer Paintings

Kitchen Maid (c 1660; Rijksmuseum)

Woman in Blue Reading a Letter (c 1663; Rijksmuseum)

Girl with a Pearl Earring (c 1665; Mauritshuis, Den Haag)

his baker accepted two paintings from his wife as payment for a debt of more than 600 guilders. Yet Vermeer mastered genre painting like no other artist. His paintings include historical and biblical scenes from his earlier career, his famous *View of Delft* (1661) in the Mauritshuis in Den Haag, and some tender portraits of unknown women, such as the stunningly beautiful *Girl with a Pearl Earring* (c 1665), also hanging in the Mauritshuis.

To comprehend Vermeer's use of perspective, study *The Love Letter* (1670) in the Rijksmuseum.

The Little Street (1658) in the Rijksmuseum's collection is Vermeer's only street scene.

Vermeer's work is known for serene light pouring through tall windows. The calm, spiritual effect is enhanced by dark blues, deep reds, warm yellows and supremely balanced composition. Good examples include the Rijksmuseum's *Kitchen Maid* (aka *The Milkmaid*) and *Woman in Blue Reading a Letter*.

Other Golden Age Painters

Around the middle of the century, the focus on mood and subtle play of light began to make way for the splendour of the baroque. Jacob van Ruysdael (c 1628–82) went for dramatic skies, while Albert Cuyp (1620–91) painted Italianate landscapes. Van Ruysdael's pupil Meindert Hobbema (1638–1709) preferred less heroic, more playful scenes, full of pretty bucolic detail.

The genre paintings of Jan Steen (1626–79) show the almost frivolous aspect of baroque. A good example is the animated revelry of *The Merry Family* (1668) in the Rijksmuseum; it shows adults having a good time around the dinner table, oblivious to the children in the foreground pouring themselves a drink.

Cuyp, Hobbema, Van Ruysdael and Steen all have main streets named after them in the South and De Pijp districts, and many smaller streets here are named after other Dutch artists.

Jan Steen was also a tavern keeper, and his depictions of domestic chaos led to the Dutch expression 'a Jan Steen household'.

18th Century

The Golden Age of Dutch painting ended almost as suddenly as it began when the French invaded the Low Countries in 1672. The economy collapsed and the market for paintings went south with it. Painters who stayed in business concentrated on 'safe' works that repeated earlier successes. In the 18th century they copied French styles, pandering to the fashion for anything French.

Cornelis Troost (1696–1750) was one of the best genre painters, and is sometimes compared to the British artist William Hogarth (1697–1764) for his satirical as well as sensitive portraits of ordinary people; Troost, too, introduced scenes of domestic revelry into his pastels.

Gerard de Lairesse (1641–1711) and Jacob de Wit (1695–1754) specialised in decorating the walls and ceilings of buildings – De Wit's trompe l'œil decorations (painted illusions that look real) in the Bijbels Museum are worth seeing.

19th Century

The late 18th century and most of the 19th century produced little of note, save for the landscapes and seascapes of Johan Barthold Jongkind (1819–91) and the gritty, almost photographic Amsterdam scenes of George Hendrik Breitner (1857–1923). They appear to have inspired French Impressionists, many of whom visited Amsterdam.

Jongkind and Breitner reinvented 17th-century realism and influenced the Hague School of the last decades of the 19th century. Painters such as Hendrik Mesdag (1831–1915), Jozef Israels (1824–1911) and the three Maris brothers (Jacob, Matthijs and Willem) created landscapes, seascapes and genre works, including Mesdag's impressive *Panorama Mesdag* (1881; located in Den Haag), a gigantic, 360-degree cylindrical painting of the seaside town of Scheveningen viewed from a dune.

Top: *Bluff-bowed Scheveningen Boats at Anchor* by Henrik Willem Mesdag

Bottom: *The Milkmaid* by Johannes Vermeer, Rijksmuseum (p151)

Vincent van Gogh

Van Gogh produced an astonishing output of art during his 10-year artistic career, of which 864 paintings and almost 1200 drawings and prints have survived.

Without a doubt, the greatest 19th-century Dutch painter was Vincent van Gogh (1853–90), whose convulsive patterns and furious colours were in a world of their own and still defy comfortable categorisation. (A post-Impressionist? A forerunner of expressionism?)

While the Dutch Masters were known for their dark, brooding paintings, it was Van Gogh who created an identity of suffering as an art form, with a morbid style all his own. Even today, he epitomises the epic struggle of the artist: the wrenching poverty; the lack of public acclaim; the reliance upon a patron – in his case, his faithful brother Theo; the mental instability; the untimely death by suicide; and, of course, one of the most iconic images of an artist's self-destruction, the severed ear.

The Artist's Legend

Vincent van Gogh may have been poor – he sold only one painting in his lifetime – but he wasn't old. It's easy to forget from his self-portraits, in which he appears much older (partly the effects of his poverty), that he was only 37 when he died. But his short life continues to influence art to this day.

Van Gogh Museum's Famous Five

········

Sunflowers (1889)
········
Wheatfield with Crows (1890)
········
Self Portrait with Felt Hat (1886–87)
········
Almond Blossom (1890)
········
The Bedroom (1888)

Born in Zundert in 1853, the Dutch painter lived in Paris with his younger brother Theo, an art dealer, who financially supported him from his modest income. In Paris he became acquainted with seminal artists including Edgar Degas, Camille Pissarro, Henri de Toulouse-Lautrec and Paul Gauguin.

Van Gogh moved south to Arles, Provence, in 1888. Revelling in its intense light and bright colours, he painted sunflowers, irises and other vivid subjects with a burning fervour. He sent paintings to Theo in Paris to sell, and dreamed of founding an artists colony in Provence, but only Gauguin followed up his invitation. Their differing artistic approaches – Gauguin believed in painting from imagination, Van Gogh painting what he saw – and their artistic temperaments, fuelled by absinthe, came to a head with the argument that led to Van Gogh lopping his ear (which he gave to a prostitute acquaintance) and his subsequent committal in Arles.

In May 1889, Van Gogh voluntarily entered an asylum in St-Rémy de Provence, where he painted prolifically during his one-year, one-week and one-day confinement, including masterpieces like *Irises* and *Starry Night*. While there, Theo sent him a positive French newspaper critique of his work. The following month, Anna Boch, sister of his friend Eugène Boch, bought *The Red Vines* (or *The Red Vineyard; 1888*) for 400 francs (less than €100 today). It now hangs in Moscow's Pushkin Museum.

Even Van Gogh's last words ring with the kind of excruciating, melancholic beauty that his best paintings express. With Theo at his side, two days after he shot himself in the chest, he's said to have uttered in French 'la tristesse durera toujours' (the sadness will last forever).

Legacy of a Tortured Genius

On 16 May 1890 Van Gogh moved to Auvers-sur-Oise, just outside Paris, to be closer to Theo, but on 27 July that year he shot himself, possibly to avoid further financial burden on his brother, whose wife had just had a baby son, named Vincent, and who was also supporting their ailing mother. Van Gogh died two days later with Theo at his side. Theo subsequently had a breakdown, was also committed, and succumbed to physical illness. He died, aged 33, just six months after Van Gogh.

It would be less than a decade before Van Gogh's talent would start to achieve wide recognition, and by the early 1950s, he had become a household name. In 1990 he broke the record for a single painting (*A Portrait of Doctor Gachet*) at Christie's, which fetched US$82.5 million. Accounting for inflation, it's still one of the highest prices paid at a public auction for art to this day.

20th Century & Beyond

During the 20th century, the standout De Stijl movement was a major influence on the arts, while abstract expressionism also made waves. In the 21st century, artistic endeavours have focused on Dutch design and tech innovations, but the works of up-and-coming Amsterdam artists can be seen in galleries and studios throughout the city.

De Stijl

De Stijl (The Style), also known as neoplasticism, was a Dutch design movement that aimed to harmonise all the arts by bringing artistic expressions back to their essence. Its major advocate was the magazine of the same name, first published in 1917 by Theo van Doesburg (1883–1931).

A major proponent of De Stijl was Piet Mondrian (originally Mondriaan; 1872–1944), who initially painted in the Hague School tradition. After flirting with cubism, he began working with bold rectangular patterns, using only the three primary colours (yellow, blue and red) set against the three neutrals (white, grey and black). He named this style neoplasticism and viewed it as an undistorted expression of reality in pure form and pure colour. His *Composition in Red, Black, Blue, Yellow & Grey* (1920), in the Stedelijk Museum's collection, is an elaborate example. Mondrian's later works were more stark (or 'pure') and became dynamic again when he moved to New York in 1940.

Throughout the 1920s and 1930s, De Stijl also attracted sculptors, poets, architects and designers. One of these was Gerrit Rietveld (1888–1964), designer of the Van Gogh Museum and several other buildings, but best known internationally for his furniture, such as the *Red Blue Chair* (1918) and his range of uncomfortable zigzag seats that, viewed side-on, formed a 'z' with a backrest.

Theo Van Doesburg produced works similar to Mondrian's, though he dispensed with the thick, black lines and later tilted his rectangles at 45 degrees, departures serious enough for Mondrian to call off the friendship.

MC Escher

One of the most remarkable graphic artists of the 20th century was Maurits Cornelis Escher (1898–1972). His drawings, lithographs and woodcuts of blatantly impossible images continue to fascinate mathematicians: a waterfall feeds itself; people go up and down a staircase that ends where it starts; a pair of hands draw each other. You can see his work at Amsterdam's Stedelijk Museum, and at the dedicated Escher in het Paleis in Den Haag.

CoBrA

After WWII, artists rebelled against artistic conventions and vented their rage in abstract expressionism. In Amsterdam, Karel Appel (1921–2006) and Constant (Constant Nieuwenhuys; 1920–2005) drew on styles pioneered by Paul Klee and Joan Miró, and exploited bright colours and 'uncorrupted' children's art to produce lively works that leapt off the canvas. In Paris in 1945 they met up with the Danish Asger Jorn (1914–73) and the Belgian Corneille (Cornelis van Beverloo; 1922–2010), and together with several other artists and writers formed a group known as CoBrA (Copenhagen, Brussels, Amsterdam). It has been called the last great avant-garde movement.

Their first major exhibition, in the Stedelijk Museum in 1949, aroused a storm of protest (with comments such as 'my child paints like that, too'). Still, the CoBrA artists exerted a strong influence on Dutch figurative painting, even after they disbanded in 1951. The Cobra Museum (p160) in Amstelveen, south of central Amsterdam, displays a good range of their works, including colourful ceramics.

Architecture in Amsterdam

The lovely canalscapes depicted in centuries-old paintings of Amsterdam remain remarkably unchanged. The city was spared from wartime destruction, and it has been careful about preserving its core from ham-fisted developers. In fact, the enchanting old centre contains no fewer than 7000 historical monuments interspersed between its humpback bridges and profusion of trees including leafy elms, plane trees, lime trees, poplars and willows along the canal banks.

A City Built on Freedom

Above: Magna Plaza shopping centre (p249)

Unlike many capitals, Amsterdam has few grand edifices to trumpet. There is hardly the space for a Louvre or a Westminster Abbey, which would be out of keeping with Calvinist modesty anyway. But you'll be pressed to find another city with such a wealth of residential architecture, and with an appeal that owes more to understated elegance than to power and pomp.

Amsterdam's beauty was built on freedoms – of trade, religion and aesthetics. Many of its gabled mansions and warehouses were erected by merchants in the Golden Age, with little meddling by city officials. Thus its leading citizens determined the look of the city, in what amounted to an early urban experiment.

Dutch architecture today is one of the country's most successful exports, with names such as Rem Koolhaas and Lars Spuybroek popping up on blueprints from Beijing to Seattle. Back home, rivalry can be intensely local as talents in Amsterdam and Rotterdam jostle for a spot in the architectural pantheon.

Middle Ages

Around the year 1200, Amsterdam was a muddy little trading post on the Amstel river. The soft marshland couldn't support brick, so the earliest houses were made of timber, often with clay and thatched roofs (similar to ones still standing in Amsterdam Noord today), but even these modest abodes would list into the soggy ground.

Two fires burned down much of the city centre in 1421 and 1452, and wood was subsequently outlawed as a main building material. There was plenty of clay to make brick, but this was too heavy, as was stone.

Engineers solved the problem by driving piles into the peat. Timber gave way to heavier brick, and thatched roofs were replaced by sturdier tile. Eventually brick and sandstone became de rigueur for most structures.

Dutch Renaissance

As the Italian Renaissance filtered north, Dutch architects developed a rich ornamental style that merged the classical and the traditional with their own brand of subtle humour. They inserted mock columns, known as pilasters, into facades and replaced old spout gables with step gables. Sculptures, columns and little obelisks suddenly appeared all over the Canal Ring. Red brick and horizontal bands of white were all the rage, too.

Without a doubt, the best-known talent of this period was Hendrick de Keyser (1565–1621), the city sculptor. He worked with Hendrick Staets, a canal ring planner, and Cornelis Danckerts, the city bricklayer, to produce some of Amsterdam's finest masterpieces, including magnificent canal architecture such as the Bartolotti House. De Keyser also designed several of Amsterdam's churches. His Zuiderkerk (p88), Noorderkerk (p136) and Westerkerk (p106) show off the style of the day with ornate steeples and layouts, and florid details enlivening the walls and roof lines.

Dutch Classicism

During the Golden Age of art in the 17th century, architects such as Jacob van Campen and brothers Philips and Justus Vingboons decided to stick to Greek and Roman classical design, dropping many of De Keyser's playful decorations.

Influenced by Italian architects, the Dutch made facades look like temples and pilasters like columns. All revolved around clever deception. Neck gables with decorative scrolls came into fashion, often crowned by a temple-like roof. Garlands appeared under

One of the city's signature buildings and a Rembrandt favourite, the Montelbaanstoren was built as a defensive tower in 1516. Its octagonal steeple was designed by master architect Hendrick de Keyser in 1606 to house a clock that's still in use today.

The most impressive example of Dutch Classicism is Jacob van Campen's town hall (now the Royal Palace). It was the largest town hall in Europe, and was given a precious shell of Bentham sandstone, and a marble interior inspired by the Roman palaces.

Amsterdam American Hotel (p121)

windows, and red brick, which was prone to crumbling, was hardened with dark paint.

The Vingboons designed the Bijbels Museum (p107) and the fine example at Keizersgracht 319. Don't miss Justus Vingboons' Trippenhuis (p88): it's about as austere as it gets. It was built between 1660 and 1664 for the wealthy Trip brothers, who made their fortune in metals, artillery and ammunition. The most striking hallmarks are up at roof level – chimneys shaped like mortars.

18th-Century 'Louis Styles'

The Gallic-culture craze proved a godsend for architect and designer Daniel Marot, a Huguenot refugee who introduced matching French interiors and exteriors to Amsterdam. Living areas with white

GABLES

Among Amsterdam's great architectural treasures are its magnificent gables – the roof-level facades that adorn the elegant houses along the canals. The gable hid the roof from public view, and helped to identify the house, until the French occupiers introduced house numbers in 1795. Gables then became more of a fashion accessory.

There are four main types of gable: the simple spout gable, with diagonal outline and semicircular windows or shutters, that was used mainly for warehouses from the 1580s to the early 1700s; the step gable, a late-Gothic design favoured by Dutch Renaissance architects; the neck gable, also known as the bottle gable, a durable design introduced in the 1640s; and the bell gable, which appeared in the 1660s and became popular in the 18th century.

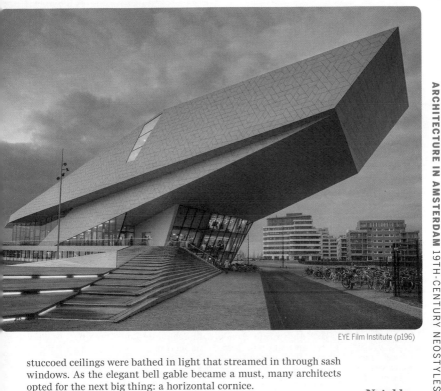

EYE Film Institute (p196)

stuccoed ceilings were bathed in light that streamed in through sash windows. As the elegant bell gable became a must, many architects opted for the next big thing: a horizontal cornice.

The dignified facades and statuary of the Louis XIV style hung on until about 1750. In rapid succession it was followed by Louis XV style – rococo rocks, swirls and waves – and Louis XVI designs, with pilasters and pillars making a comeback. The late-Louis-style Felix Meritis (p113), with its enormous Corinthian half-columns, is an exemplar of the genre.

19th-Century Neostyles

After the Napoleonic era, the Dutch economy stagnated, merchants closed their pocketbooks and fine architecture ground to a halt. Seen as safe and sellable, neoclassicism held sway until the more prosperous 1860s, when planners again felt free to rediscover the past.

The late 19th century was all about the neo-Gothic, harking back to the grand Gothic cathedrals, and the neo-Renaissance. It was around this time that Catholics regained their freedom to worship openly, and built churches like mad in neo-Gothic style.

A leading architect of the period was Pierre Cuypers, known for a skilful design of several neo-Gothic churches. Cuypers also designed two of Amsterdam's most iconic buildings: Centraal Station (p266) and the Rijksmuseum (p151), both of which display Gothic forms and Dutch Renaissance brickwork. A similar melange is CH Peters' General Post Office, now the **Magna Plaza** (Map p300; www.magnaplaza.nl; Nieuwezijds Voorburgwal 182; ⊘11am-7pm Mon, 10am-7pm Tue-Sat, noon-7pm Sun; 🚊1/2/5/13/14/17 Dam/Raadhuisstraat) shopping centre.

Notable Historic Buildings

Oude Kerk (Old Church; Red Light District)

Nieuwe Kerk (New Church; Medieval Centre)

Royal Palace (Medieval Centre)

Amsterdam American Hotel (Southern Canal Ring)

Rijksmuseum (the South)

HOISTS & HOUSES THAT TIP

Many canal houses deliberately tip forward. Given the narrowness of staircases, owners needed an easy way to move large goods and furniture to the upper floors. The solution: a hoist built into the gable, to lift objects up and in through the windows. The tilt allowed loading without bumping into the house front. Some houses even have huge hoist-wheels in the attic with a rope and hook that run through the hoist beam.

The forward lean also makes the houses seem larger, which makes it easier to admire the facade and gable – a fortunate coincidence for everyone.

Around the turn of the century, the neo-Goths suddenly fell out of favour as art nouveau spread its curvy plant-like shapes across Europe. Gorgeous relics of the era include the Amsterdam American Hotel (p121) and the riotous Pathé Tuschinskitheater (p130).

Berlage & the Amsterdam School

The Amsterdam School ushered in a new philosophy of city planning, given a boost by the 1928 Olympic Games held in Amsterdam. Humble housing blocks became brick sculptures with curved corners, odd windows and rocket-shaped towers, to the marvel (or disgust) of traditionalists.

The father of modern Dutch architecture was Hendrik Petrus Berlage (1856–1934). He criticised the lavish neo-styles and their reliance on the past, instead favouring simplicity and a rational use of materials.

In Berlage's view, residential blocks were a holistic concept rather than a collection of individual homes. Not always popular with city elders, Berlage influenced what became known as the Amsterdamse School (Amsterdam School) and its leading exponents Michel de Klerk, Piet Kramer and Johan van der Mey.

The titans of the Amsterdam School designed buildings of 'Plan South', an ambitious project mapped out by Berlage. It was a productive period: the Beurs van Berlage (p69) displayed the master's ideals to the full, with exposed inner struts and striking but simple brick accents.

Johan van der Mey's remarkable Scheepvaarthuis (p88) was the first building in the Amsterdam School style. It draws on the street layout to reproduce a ship's bow.

De Klerk's Het Schip (p139) and Kramer's De Dageraad (p175) are like fairy-tale fortresses rendered in a Dutch version of art deco. Their eccentric details are charming, but the 'form over function' ethic meant these places weren't always great to live in.

Functionalism

Must-See Canal Buildings

As the Amsterdam School flourished, a new generation began to rebel against the movement's impractical and expensive methods. In 1927 they formed a group called 'de 8', influenced by the German Bauhaus school, America's Frank Lloyd Wright and France's Le Corbusier.

Architects such as Ben Merkelbach and Gerrit Rietveld believed that form should follow function and advocated steel, glass and concrete. The Committee of Aesthetics Control didn't agree, however, which is why you'll see little functionalism in the Canal Ring.

After WWII, entire suburbs, such as the sprawling Bijlmermeer in Amsterdam-Zuidoost, were designed along functionalist lines. By the late 1960s, however, resistance had grown against such impersonal, large-scale projects.

Rietveld left Amsterdam the Van Gogh Museum (p154), where the minimalist, open space allows the artist's works to shine.

Top: Ornate bell-tower of Westerkerk (p106)

Bottom: Entrepotdok (p91), the former head-quarters of the Dutch East India Company

ARTUR BOGACKI/SHUTTERSTOCK ©

Kraanspoor (p196)

The Present

On the shores of the IJ just east of Centraal Station stands the Oosterdokseiland, a row of landmark buildings that includes the OBA: Centrale Bibliotheek Amsterdam (p92) and features a high-density mix of shops, restaurants, offices, apartments and a music conservatorium (p99).

Looking southeast from Centraal Station, you can't miss the green copper snout of the NEMO Science Museum (p92), a science museum designed by Renzo Piano that resembles the prow of a ship. The cube-like glass shell of the Muziekgebouw aan 't IJ (p92) stands not far to the north, on the IJ waterfront. In the Plantage district, a must-see is the huge Entrepotdok (p91). Sprawling half a kilometre along a former loading dock, the shipping warehouses have been recast as desirable apartments, studios and commercial spaces.

Heading east, the Eastern Islands and docklands were full of derelict industrial buildings until the 1980s and early '90s, when they got a new lease of life. Borneo, Java and KNSM islands are home to innovative residential projects as well as stylishly repurposed

Children's section, OBA: Centrale Bibliotheek Amsterdam (p92)

buildings. Striking Docklands' buildings include the residential and commercial complex dubbed the 'Whale'.

Further east is the burgeoning IJburg neighbourhood, on a string of artificial islands some 10km from the city centre. Some 45,000 residents are predicted to inhabit the islands by 2025. The curvaceous Enneüs Heerma Brug, dubbed Dolly Parton Bridge by locals, links it to the mainland.

Northwest of Centraal Station and also on the IJ, you'll find a flurry of construction in the Houthavens ('lumber ports') area, whose seven artificial islands are transforming into a new residential hub. One of the most striking sites in the area is the REM Eiland (p142), a 22m-high former pirate-broadcasting rig now housing a restaurant and bar.

Across the IJ River in Amsterdam Noord, housing blocks and office towers are springing up on a former industrial estate at the Overhoeks development, where the architectural centrepieces are the EYE Film Institute (p196) and A'DAM Tower (p196), along with the glass-box-topped Kraanspoor (craneway; p196).

Based in Amsterdam, influential architecture firm Concrete has designed projects around the globe, from London's Spice Market to Stuttgart's Mercedes-Benz Museum, Seoul's Hyundai finance outlets and New Jersey's Harborside Plaza skyscrapers. Locally, Concrete designed REM Eiland and the Van Gogh Museum's central hall, among many, many others.

EVAISLA/SHUTTERSTOCK ©

1. Bike hire (p29)
Do as the locals do and ride a bike.

2. Retro style
Just because you're riding a bike doesn't mean you can't travel in style.

3. Cycling (p29)
Amsterdam is one of the world's safest cities for cyclists.

4. Parks
Amsterdam's many parks are perfect for cyclists.

5. Bike parking
Amsterdam has more bicycles than cars.

Dutch Design

Contemporary Dutch design has a reputation for minimalist, creative approaches to everyday furniture and homewares products, mixed with vintage twists and tongue-in-cheek humour to keep it fresh. What started out as a few innovators has accelerated to become a movement that is putting the Netherlands at the forefront of the industry. Dutch fashion is also reaching far beyond the country's borders, with designs that are vibrant and imaginative, yet practical, too.

The Beginning of a Movement

The Dutch design movement today can be traced back to a handful of designers working in different materials and mediums around the same time, who started gaining respect at home and abroad.

Providing a key platform was Droog (p99), established in 1993. This design collective works with a community of designers to help produce their works and sell them to the world, with the partners to make it happen and the connections to facilitate collaborations with big brands. Signature Droog designs employ surreal wit, such as a chandelier made of 80-plus light bulbs clustered like fish eggs, or an off-centre umbrella inspired by the country's blustery weather.

Design Pioneers

Among the contemporary pioneers was Marcel Wanders, who first drew international acclaim for his iconic Knotted Chair, produced by Droog in 1996. Made from a knotted aramid-and-carbon-fibre thread and resin, Wanders' air drying technique meant it was ultimately shaped by gravity. It's now in the permanent collection of the Museum of Modern Art in New York. Wanders founded Moooi (p147) in 2001 – the name is a play on the Dutch word for 'beautiful', with an additional 'o' symbolising extra beauty and uniqueness. Now a world-leading design label, Moooi also showcases other pioneering designers such as Maarten Baas (best known for his Smoke series of charred timber furniture) and Studio Job (Job Smeets and Nynke Tynagel's neo-Gothic decorative arts).

Other pioneering designers include Droog designer Jurgen Bey, who has strong architectural links, working with interior and public-space design; Hella Jongerius, whose designs include porcelain plates and tiles using new printing techniques; Piet Hein Eek, who works with reclaimed wood; Scholten & Baijings (Stefan Scholten and Carole Baijings), who produce colourful textiles and kitchenware; sculptor Hans van Bentem, who produces dazzling chandeliers; and Ineke Hans, whose celebrated recyclable plastic Ahrend 380 chair incorporates a table.

Furniture, product and interior designer Richard Hutten has been involved with Droog since its foundation. Famed for his 'no sign of design' humorous, functional furniture, his works have been exhibited worldwide and are held in the permanent collections of museums including Amsterdam's Stedelijk Museum.

Dutch Design Events

FashionWeek Amsterdam (www.fashionweek.nl) Twice-yearly runway shows.

Design Icons (www.design-icons.com) Weekend-long festival in early April.

vt wonen&design beurs (www.vtwonen.nl) Six-day interior design fair in early October.

Gaining Momentum

The momentum that Wanders, Bey, Hutten and others generated inspired a new wave of young designers. This second generation focused not just on concept and function, but also on aesthetics. Often starting with traditional influences, their works tend to mix vintage and reclaimed materials, colour and form, resulting in something totally unique. Renowned second-wave makers include Wieki Somers, awarded for designs such as her Merry-go-round Coat Rack and rowboat-shaped Bathboat tub, and Marloes Hoedeman, who designed the interiors of retailer Scotch & Soda and who has more recently dipped into fashion design, with her lingerie brand Love Stories.

The Future of Dutch Design

Dutch designers to watch out for include: Lex Pott, working with raw materials including wood, stone and metal; Mae Engelgeer, a designer who incorporates tufts of colour and texture into towels, rugs and other textiles at her studio in the Eastern Islands; and Dirk Vander Kooij, who uses 3D printing to create furniture and lighting.

The waves of intrepid designers have also triggered an explosion of new design stores stocking innovative pieces by established and emerging artists, which continues to feed the industry. Not simply places to view the artistic designs, gain inspiration, or even pick up products for your own home or workplace (although they are all that), these accessible galleries frequently incorporate cafes where you can browse design magazines amid the wares (and where, often, even the chair you're sitting on is for sale).

Design & Fashion

As the Dutch furniture, product and interior designers were taking flight, so too was a generation of cutting-edge fashion designers.

Amsterdam fashion house Viktor & Rolf, founded by Viktor Horsting and Rolf Snoeren, is enjoying huge international success. From haute couture to ready-to-wear collections, their range now spans men's and women's apparel, shoes, accessories including eyewear, and fragrances. Collaborations such as with retail giant H&M have broadened their appeal.

Dutch retail brands making a global impact include Amsterdam success story **Scotch & Soda** (Map p302; www.scotch-soda.com; Huidenstraat 3-5; ☺10am-6pm Tue & Wed, to 9pm Thu, to 7pm Fri & Sat, noon-6pm Sun & Mon; ☐1/2/5 Spui), selling its own-label affordable designs for men, women and children, as well as the Amsterdams Blauw denim line and a vintage furniture collection. Amsterdam brand Denham the Jeanmaker (p114) is also making a name for itself in denim wear, both in the city and as far afield as Japan.

Lingerie label Undressed by Marlies Dekkers (p114) was hailed as a new approach in lingerie design; her spin-off lines include Undressed Men, Undressed Secrets (her vintage lingerie collection), Sundressed (beachwear and sunglasses) and Nightdressed (evening wear). Launched in 2014, Marloes Hoedeman's lingerie label Love Stories (p114) has been a runaway success that has seen her open boutiques across Europe and beyond.

Shoe and accessory designer **Hester van Eeghen** (Map p300; www. hestervaneeghen.com; Hartenstraat 1; ☺1-6pm Mon, 11am-6pm Tue-Sat, noon-5pm Sun; ☐13/14/17 Westermarkt) creates eye-catching leather shoes

DUTCH DESIGN GAINING MOMENTUM

Best Dutch Design Stores

Droog (Nieuwmarkt)

Moooi (Jordaan)

Frozen Fountain (Western Canal Ring)

Hutspot (De Pijp)

X Bank (Medieval Centre)

Raw Materials (Jordaan)

Edha Interieur (the South)

Best Boutiques for Dutch Fashion

Young Designers United (Southern Canal Ring)

By AMFI (Medieval Centre)

VLVT (the South)

Tenue de Nîmes (Western Canal Ring)

Van Ravenstein (Western Canal Ring)

and handbags in bright colours, fur, suede, and geometric patterns and prints.

Headed up by Anja Klappe, Agna K (www.agnak.com) teams up with changing young designers to build its classic, well-cut womenswear collections. Eline Starink, who founded her label Amatør (p114) in Amsterdam in 2011, creates clothing targeted at young, ambitious businesswomen. Her jackets, suits and dresses are sophisticated and cool, fusing colour and materials, but always practical enough to wear while cycling.

Other designers to keep an eye on include Daisy Kroon, who produces brightly coloured, minimally cut womenswear, and Jivika Biervliet, who seeks out and subverts boundaries in her conceptual, wearable menswear lines. Renowned stylist to the stars Danie Bles is earning recognition with ByDanie, her line of bohemian, retro-tinged clothing and accessories for women.

Designer Hotels

Dutch design has now moved beyond furnishings and fashion to become a lifestyle. This is evident at several hotels that have opened in recent years, where design is implicit to the brand.

Take Droog, the trailblazing collective. It expanded its concept to include Hôtel Droog (p99), a complex that houses the Droog store, along with a gallery and cafe, and a guest room (really an apartment, complete with a kitchen and separate bedroom) on the top floor.

Another inspired hotel intersecting the design and fashion spheres is the independent Hotel The Exchange (p214) in Amsterdam's former stock exchange. Created by Otto Nan and Suzanne Oxenaar, who also worked on Amsterdam's Lloyd Hotel (p215), Hotel The Exchange's 61 rooms are dressed 'like models' by young designers from the Amsterdam Fashion Institute. Decor ranges from details such as buttons or embroidery hoops on the walls to eye-popping whole-room concepts such as a gigantic knitted jumper or Rembrandt-esque collar.

Marcel Wanders put his talents to work on the Hyatt's fantastical Andaz Amsterdam (p216), in the city's former public library. Students from Eindhoven's Design Academy let their imaginations run wild creating the rooms at Hotel Not Hotel (p219).

Dutch design is at the heart of Mr Jordaan (p218) hotel, and the new W Amsterdam (p214), inside a former telephone exchange and bank that now also incorporates immense new design emporium X Bank (p83).

Dutch Design Online

Dutch Design Daily (www.dutchdesigndaily.com) Highlights a new idea daily.

Dutch Profiles (http://dutchdesign.submarinechannel.com) Short videos explain design concepts.

Amsterdam Next (www.amsterdamnext.com) Guide to local interior design.

Survival Guide

Directory A-Z

Customs Regulations

For visitors from EU countries, limits only apply for excessive amounts. Log on to www.belastingdienst.nl for details.

Residents of non-EU countries are limited to the following:

Alcohol 1L of spirits, 4L wine or 16L beer.

Coffee 500g of coffee, or 200g of coffee extracts or coffee essences.

Perfume Up to €430 in value.

Tea 100g of tea, or 40g of tea extracts or tea essences.

Tobacco 200 cigarettes, or 250g of tobacco (shag or pipe tobacco), or 100 cigarillos, or 50 cigars.

Discount Cards

Visitors of various professions, including artists, journalists, museum conservators and teachers, may get discounts at some venues if they show accreditation.

Students regularly get a few euros off museum admission; bring ID.

Seniors over 65, and their partners of 60 or older, benefit from reductions on public transport, museum admissions, concerts and more. You may look younger, so bring your passport.

I Amsterdam Card (www. iamsterdam.com; per 24/48/72/96 hours €57/67/77/87) Provides admission to more than 30 museums (though not the Rijksmuseum), a canal cruise, and discounts at shops, entertainment venues and restaurants. Also includes a GVB transit pass. Useful for quick visits to the city. Available at VVV I Amsterdam Visitor Centres and some hotels.

Museumkaart (www.museum kaart.nl; adult/child €59.90/ 32.45, plus one-time registration €5) Free and discounted entry to some 400 museums all over the country for one year. Purchase it at participating museum ticket counters and some hotels.

Holland Pass (www.holland pass.com; 3/4/6 attractions from €40/55/67.50) Similar to the I Amsterdam Card, but without the rush for usage; you can visit sights over a month. Prices are based on the number of attractions, which you pick from tiers (the most popular/expensive sights are gold tier). Also includes a train ticket from the airport to the city, and a canal cruise. Purchase it online; pick-up locations include Schiphol Airport and the city centre.

PRIOPASS

Priopass (www.priopass.com) is offered by many hotels. The pass – either a printed piece of paper or an electronic version on your mobile phone – provides fast-track entry to most attractions. It's not a discount card – you pay normal rates for museums and tours. But many visitors like it because it's convenient for queue-skipping, there's no deadline for use (so you don't have to scurry around and see several museums in a day to get your money's worth), and you only end up paying for what you use (ie it's not bundled with transit passes, canal cruises etc). The pass itself is free; you link it to your credit card and get charged as you go along.

Electricity

Type C
220V/50Hz

Type F
230V/50Hz

Emergency & Important Numbers

Police, fire, ambulance	♪112
Netherlands country code	♪31
International access code	♪00

Internet Access

➡ Free wi-fi is common in lodgings across the price spectrum; many places also have a computer or tablet on-site for you to use.

➡ Hotels will usually print boarding passes and tickets for guests on request.

➡ Most bars, *cafés* (pubs) and coffeeshops have free wi-fi. You may need to ask for the code.

➡ For free wi-fi hot spots around the city, check www.wifi-amsterdam.nl.

Legal Matters

Amsterdam *politie* (police) are pretty relaxed and helpful unless you do something clearly wrong, such as littering or smoking a joint right under their noses.

Police can hold offenders for up to six hours for questioning (plus another six hours if they can't establish your identity, or 24 hours if they consider the matter serious). You won't have the right to a phone call, but you can request that they notify your consulate. You're presumed innocent until proven guilty.

ID Papers

Anyone over 14 years of age is required by law to carry ID. Foreigners should carry a passport or a photocopy of the relevant data pages; a driver's licence isn't sufficient.

Drugs

➡ Technically, marijuana is illegal. However, possession of soft drugs (eg cannabis) up to 5g is tolerated. Larger amounts are subject to prosecution.

➡ Don't light up in an establishment other than a coffeeshop without checking that it's ÖK to do so.

➡ Hard drugs are treated as a serious crime.

➡ Never buy drugs of any kind on the street; deaths can and do occur.

Prostitution

Prostitution is legal in the Netherlands. The industry is protected by law, and prostitutes pay tax. Much of this open policy stems from a desire to undermine the role of pimps and the underworld in the sex industry.

In Amsterdam's Red Light District the streets are well-policed, but the back alleys are more dubious.

LGBT+ Travellers

The Netherlands was the first country to legalise same-sex marriage (in 2001), so it's no surprise that Amsterdam's gay scene is among the world's largest.

Five hubs of the queer scene party hardest: Warmoesstraat, Zeedijk, Rembrandtplein, Leidseplein and Reguliersdwarsstraat.

Top festivals include the music-rocking **Milkshake Festival** (www.milkshakefestival.com) in late July, **Amsterdam Gay Pride** (www.pride.amsterdam) in late July/early August and **Hartjesdagen Zeedijk** (Heart Day; www.stichtinghartjesdagen.nl) on the third weekend of August. Resources:

Gay Amsterdam (www.gayamsterdam.com) Lists hotels, shops and clubs, and provides maps.

Pink Point (♪020-428 10 70; www.facebook.com/pinkpointamsterdam; Westermarkt; ◷10.30am-6pm; 🚊13/14/17 Westermarkt) Located behind the Westerkerk, Pink Point is part LGBT information kiosk, part souvenir shop. It's a good place to pick up news about parties, events and social groups.

Reguliers (www.reguliers.net) Info on the Reguliersdwarsstraat scene, including current club openings and closings.

Gay & Lesbian Information and News Center (www.gaylinc.nl) Lists hotels, restaurants, nightlife and 'sexciting' events around town.

Medical Services

→ The Netherlands has reciprocal health arrangements with other European countries and Australia. If you're a citizen of the EU, Switzerland, Iceland, Norway or Liechtenstein, a European Health Insurance Card (EHIC) covers you for most medical care. If you qualify, make sure you arrange the paperwork in your home country prior to travelling to the Netherlands. You still might have to pay on the spot for medical services, but you should be able to claim it back at home.

→ Citizens of other countries are advised to take out travel insurance.

→ Worldwide travel insurance is available at www.lonelyplanet.com/travel-insurance. You can buy, extend and claim online anytime – even if you're already on the road.

Referrals

Contact the Centrale Doktersdiensten (Central Doctors Service; www.doktersdiensten.nl) for doctor, dentist or pharmacy referrals day or night.

Emergency Rooms

A number of hospitals have 24-hour emergency facilities, including:

Onze Lieve Vrouwe Gasthuis (020-599 91 11; www.olvg.nl; Oosterpark 9; 24hr; 3/14 Beukenweg) At Oosterpark, near the Tropenmuseum. It's the closest public hospital to the centre of town.

VU Medisch Centrum (020-444 44 44; www.vumc.com; De Boelelaan 1117; 24hr; 16/24 VU Medisch Centrum) Hospital of the Vrije Universiteit (Free University).

Pharmacies

Forget about buying flu tablets and antacids at supermarkets; for anything stronger than toothpaste you'll have to go to a pharmacy.

After hours, call **Informatie Dienstdoende Apotheken** (020-592 33 15) to find out which pharmacies are open nearest to you.

Money

The Netherlands uses the euro (€). Denominations of the currency are €5, €10, €20, €50, €100, €200 and €500 notes, and €0.05, €0.10, €0.20, €0.50, €1 and €2 coins (amounts under €1 are called cents).

ATMs

Automatic teller machines can be found outside most banks, at the airport and at Centraal Station. Most accept credit cards such as Visa and MasterCard, as well as cash cards that access the Cirrus and Plus networks. Check with your home bank for service charges before leaving.

ATMs are not hard to find, but in the city centre and at the airport they often have queues or run out of cash on weekends.

Cash

A surprising number of businesses do not accept credit cards, so it's wise to have cash on hand. (Conversely, many places only accept cards.)

Changing Money

Generally your best bet for exchanging money is to use GWK Travelex, which has several branches around town:

GWK Travelex Centraal Station (020-627 27 31; www.gwk.nl; Stationsplein; 8am-8pm Mon-Sat, 10am-5pm Sun; 1/2/4/5/9/13/16/17/24 Centraal Station)

GWK Travelex Leidseplein (0900 05 66; Leidsestraat 103; 9am-9pm Mon-Fri, from 10am Sat, 10am-8pm Sun; 1/2/5/7/10 Leidseplein)

GWK Travelex Schiphol Airport (0900 05 66; 6am-10pm)

Credit Cards

All the major international credit cards are recognised, and most hotels and large stores accept them. But a fair number of shops, restaurants and other businesses

---

PRACTICALITIES

Weights & Measures The metric system is used.

Smoking Forbidden inside all bars and restaurants, but permitted outdoors on venues' terraces.

Dutch newspapers *De Telegraaf,* the Netherlands' biggest seller; and *Het Parool,* Amsterdam's paper, with the scoop on what's happening around town.

English newspapers The *New York Times International Edition* and the *Guardian,* and weeklies such as the *Economist* and *Time,* are widely available on newsstands.

Listings magazines *Uitkrant* and *NL20* are free and you can pick them up around town.

(including supermarket chain Albert Heijn) do not accept credit cards, or only accept debit cards with chip-and-PIN technology. Be aware that foreign-issued cards (even chip-and-PIN-enabled foreign credit or debit cards) aren't always accepted, so ask first.

Some establishments levy a 5% surcharge (or more) on credit cards to offset the commissions charged by card providers. Always check first.

Consider getting a pre-loaded chip-and-pin debit card. Many banks provide such cards.

Tipping

Tipping is not essential, as restaurants, hotels, bars etc include a service charge on their bills. A little extra is always welcomed though, and common in certain instances.

Hotels porters €1 to €2 per bag

Restaurants 5% to 10% for a cafe snack, 10% or so for a meal

Taxis 5% to 10%

Opening Hours

Opening hours often decrease during off-peak months (October to Easter).

Cafés (pubs), bars & coffeeshops Open noon (exact hours vary); most close 1am Sunday to Thursday, 3am Friday and Saturday

General office hours 8.30am–5pm Monday to Friday

Museums 10am–5pm, though some close Monday

Restaurants 11am–2.30pm and 6–10pm

Shops 9am/10am–6pm Monday to Saturday, noon-6pm Sunday. Smaller shops may keep shorter hours and/or close Monday. Many shops stay open late (to 9pm) Thursday.

Supermarkets 8am–8pm; in the city centre some stay open until 9pm or 10pm.

Post

The national post office in the Netherlands is privatised and has gone through various name changes. The current operator is PostNL (www.postnl.nl). It has closed most city post offices and to mail a letter or package you'll need to go to a postal service shop which may be a supermarket or tobacco shop or something else. Use the website (available in English) to find a location near you.

Public Holidays

Most museums adopt Sunday hours on public holidays (except Christmas and New Year, when they close), even if they fall on a day when the place would otherwise be closed, such as Monday.

Nieuwjaarsdag (New Year's Day) 1 January

Goede Vrijdag (Good Friday) March/April

Eerste Paasdag (Easter Sunday) March/April

Tweede Paasdag (Easter Monday) March/April

Koningsdag (King's Day) 27 April

Dodenherdenking (Remembrance Day) 4 May (unofficial)

Bevrijdingsdag (Liberation Day) 5 May (unofficially celebrated annually; officially every five years, next in 2020)

Hemelvaartsdag (Ascension Day) 40th day after Easter Sunday

Eerste Pinksterdag (Whit Sunday; Pentecost) 50th day after Easter Sunday

Tweede Pinksterdag (Whit Monday) 50th day after Easter Monday

Eerste Kerstdag (Christmas Day) 25 December

Tweede Kerstdag (Second Christmas; Boxing Day) 26 December

Taxes & Refunds

See the Shopping (p57) chapter for information on claiming back tax on purchases.

Telephone

The Dutch phone network, KPN (www.kpn.com), is efficient, and prices are reasonable by European standards. It's free to make a collect call (*collect gesprek*; domestic ☏0800 01 01, international ☏0800 04 10).

Mobile Phones

Ask your home provider about an international plan. Alternatively, local prepaid SIM cards are widely available and can be used in most unlocked phones. The EU has abolished international roaming costs, but beware of high roaming charges from other countries.

Phone Codes

Drop the leading 0 on numbers if you're calling from outside the Netherlands.

Netherlands country code ☏31

Amsterdam city code ☏020

Free calls ☏0800

Mobile numbers ☏06

Paid information calls ☏0900, cost varies

Time

Amsterdam is in the Central European time zone (GMT/UTC plus one hour), but also observes daylight saving hours: clocks go forward one hour at 2am on the last Sunday in March and back again at 3am on the last Sunday in October.

Be aware that the Dutch use 'half' to indicate 'half before' the hour. If you say 'half eight' (8.30pm in many forms of English), a Dutch person will take this to mean 7.30pm.

Toilets

➡ Public toilets are not a widespread facility on Dutch streets, apart from the free-standing public urinals for men in places such as the Red Light District.

➡ Many people duck into a *café* (pub) or department store.

➡ The standard fee for toilet attendants is €0.50.

➡ The app HogeNood (High Need; www.hogenood.nu) maps the nearest toilets based on your location.

Tourist Information

I Amsterdam Visitor Centre (Map p290; ☑020-702 60 00; www.iamsterdam.com; Stationsplein 10; ⊘9am-5pm Mon-Sat; 🚊1/2/4/5/9/13/16/17/24 Centraal Station) Located outside Centraal Station.

I Amsterdam Visitor Centre Schiphol (www.iamsterdam. com; ⊘7am-10pm) Inside Schiphol International Airport at the Arrivals 2 hall.

Travellers with Disabilities

➡ Travellers with reduced mobility will find Amsterdam moderately equipped to meet their needs.

➡ Most offices and museums have lifts and/or ramps and toilets for visitors with disabilities.

➡ A large number of budget and midrange hotels have limited accessibility, as they occupy old buildings with steep stairs and no lifts.

➡ Restaurants tend to be on ground floors, though 'ground' sometimes includes a few steps.

➡ Most buses are wheelchair accessible, as are metro stations. Trams are becoming more accessible as new equipment is added. Many lines have elevated stops for wheelchair users. The GVB website (www. gvb.nl) denotes which stops are wheelchair accessible.

➡ Accessible Travel Netherlands publishes a downloadable guide (www.accessibletravelnl. com/blogs/new-city-guide-for-Amsterdam) to restaurants, sights, transport and routes in Amsterdam for those with limited mobility.

➡ Check the accessibility guide at Accessible Amsterdam (www. toegankelijkamsterdam.nl).

➡ Download Lonely Planet's free *Accessible Travel Online Resources* guide from http:// lptravel.to/AccessibleTravel.

Visas

Tourists from nearly 60 countries – including Australia, Canada, Israel, Japan, New Zealand, Singapore, South Korea, the USA and most of Europe – need only a valid passport to visit the Netherlands for up to three months. EU nationals can enter for three months with their national identity card or a passport.

Nationals of most other countries need a Schengen visa, valid within the EU member states (except the UK and Ireland), plus Norway and Iceland, for 90 days within a six-month period. Schengen visas are issued by Dutch embassies or consulates overseas and can take a while to process (up to two months). You'll need a passport that's valid until at least three months after your visit, and will have to prove you have sufficient funds for your stay and return journey.

The Netherlands Foreign Affairs Ministry (www. government.nl) lists consulates and embassies around the world. Visas and extensions are handled by the Immigratie en Naturalisatiedienst (Immigration & Naturalisation Service; www.ind.nl). Study visas must be applied for via your college or university in the Netherlands.

Women Travellers

In terms of safety, Amsterdam is probably as secure as it gets in Europe's major cities. There's little street harassment, even in the Red Light District, although it's best to walk with a friend to minimise unwelcome attention.

Transport

ARRIVING IN AMSTERDAM

Most visitors arrive by air at Schiphol International Airport or by train at Centraal Station.

Schiphol is among Europe's busiest airports and has copious air links worldwide, including many on low-cost European airlines. It's the hub of Dutch passenger carrier KLM.

National and international trains arrive at Centraal Station. There are good links with several European cities. The high-speed Thalys (www.thalys.com) runs from Paris (3¼ hours direct, 3¾ hours via Brussels) nearly every hour between 6.18am and 8.18pm. Eurostar (www.eurostar.com) runs from London (around five hours); it stops in Brussels, where you transfer onward via Thalys. A direct London–Amsterdam route is slated to be in regular service from spring 2018, and will cut travel time to four hours. German ICE trains run six times a day between Amsterdam and Cologne (2¾ hours); many continue on to Frankfurt (four hours). For more information on international trains (including ICE), see NS International (www.nsinternational.nl).

Bus travel is typically the cheapest way to get to Amsterdam; major bus companies Eurolines and FlixBus both serve the city.

Flights, cars and tours can be booked online at lonelyplanet.com/bookings.

Schiphol International Airport

Situated 18km southwest of the city centre, **Schiphol International Airport** (AMS; www.schiphol.nl) has ATMs, currency exchanges, tourist information, car hire, train-ticket sales counters, luggage storage, food and free wi-fi. It's easy to reach the city from Schiphol.

Train Trains run to Amsterdam's Centraal Station (€5.20 one way, 15 minutes) 24 hours a day. From 6am to 12.30am they go every 10 minutes or so; hourly in the wee hours. The rail platform is inside the terminal, down the escalator.

Shuttle bus A shuttle van is run by **Connexxion** (www.schipholhotelshuttle.nl; one way/return €17/27), every 30 minutes from 7am to 9pm, from the airport to several hotels. Look for the Connexxion desk by Arrivals 4.

Bus Bus 197/Amsterdam Airport Express (€5 one way, 25 minutes) is the quickest way to the Museumplein, Leidseplein or Vondelpark. It departs outside the arrivals hall door. Buy a ticket from the driver.

Taxi Taxis take 20 to 30 minutes to the centre (longer in

CLIMATE CHANGE & TRAVEL

Every form of transport that relies on carbon-based fuel generates CO_2, the main cause of human-induced climate change. Modern travel is dependent on aeroplanes, which might use less fuel per kilometre per person than most cars but travel much greater distances. The altitude at which aircraft emit gases (including CO_2) and particles also contributes to their climate change impact. Many websites offer 'carbon calculators' that allow people to estimate the carbon emissions generated by their journey and, for those who wish to do so, to offset the impact of the greenhouse gases emitted with contributions to portfolios of climate-friendly initiatives throughout the world. Lonely Planet offsets the carbon footprint of all staff and author travel.

TRAIN TRIPS FROM AMSTERDAM

NS (www.ns.nl), aka Dutch Railways, runs the nation's rail service. Trains are frequent from Centraal Station and serve domestic destinations such as Haarlem, Leiden and Delft several times per hour, making for easy day trips.

The main service centre to buy tickets for both national and international trains is on the station's west side.

Domestic Tickets

➡ Tickets can be bought at the NS service desk windows or at ticketing machines. The ticket windows are easiest to use, though there is often a queue.

➡ Pay with cash, debit or credit card. Visa and MasterCard are accepted, though there is a €0.50 surcharge to use them, and they must have chip-and-PIN technology.

➡ There is a €1 surcharge for buying a single-use disposable ticket. (Locals typically use a personalised, rechargeable plastic chip card, which exempts them from the fee.)

➡ Visitors can get a non-personalised rechargeable card at NS windows or at GVB public transport offices. It's not that useful unless you'll be travelling a lot by train. It costs €7.50 (non-refundable) and has a €20 minimum balance.

➡ If you want to use a ticketing machine and pay cash, bear in mind that they accept coins only (no paper bills). The machines have instructions in English.

➡ There's little difference in comfort between 1st and 2nd class, but if the train is crowded there are usually more seats in 1st class.

➡ There are two types of domestic train: Intercity (faster, with fewer stops) and Sprinter (slower, stops at each station).

➡ Taking your bike (or pet) on board costs €3.10. Bikes are only accepted on Sprinter services.

➡ Check both in and out with your ticket/card. Tap it against the card reader in the gates or free-standing posts. You'll hear one beep to enter, and two beeps when departing.

International Tickets

➡ NS International (www.nsinternational.nl) has separate windows to buy international tickets. Queues can be long. Upon entering, take a numbered ticket. When your number is called, you can proceed to the window.

➡ Unless you have a credit card with chip-and-PIN technology (even then, not all foreign chip-enabled cards will work), you'll need to use cash to buy your ticket on-site. There's a €7.50 to €22.50 booking charge for on-site purchases.

➡ An alternative is to buy tickets online at www.b-europe.com, which accepts foreign cards. You may need to print the tickets out.

➡ Be sure to reserve in advance during peak periods.

heavy traffic), costing around €37.50. The taxi stand is just outside the arrivals hall door.

Centraal Train Station

Centraal (Map p290; Stationsplein; ⬛1/2/4/5/9/13/16/17/24) is in the city centre, with easy onward connections. The station has ATMs, currency exchanges, tourist information, restaurants, shops, luggage storage (€6 to €11.50 per day), and national and international train ticket sales.

Bus Stations

Buses operated by Eurolines and FlixBus connect Amsterdam with all major European capitals and numerous smaller destinations.

Eurolines buses use **Duivendrecht station** (Stationsplein 3), south of the centre, which has an easy metro link to Centraal Station (about a 20-minute trip via metro numbers 50 or 54). The **Eurolines Ticket Office** (www.eurolines.nl;

Rokin 38a; ⏱9am-5pm Mon-Sat; 🚋4/9/14/16/24 Dam) is near the Dam.

FlixBus (www.flixbus.com) runs to/from **Sloterdijk train station**, west of the centre, linked to Centraal Station by metro number 50 (a six-minute trip). There's no ticket office; book online.

Car

If you're arriving by car, it's best to leave your vehicle in a park-and-ride lot near the edge of town. A nominal parking fee (around €8 for the first 24 hours and €1 per day thereafter) also gets you discounted public transport tickets. For more info see www.iamsterdam.com.

GETTING AROUND AMSTERDAM

Central Amsterdam is relatively compact and best seen on foot or by bicycle.

The GVB operates the public transport system, a mix of tram, bus, metro and ferry. Visitors will find trams the most useful option. There's a **GVB information office** (www.gvb.nl; Stationsplein 10; ⏱7am-9pm Mon-Fri, 8am-9pm Sat & Sun; 🚋1/2/4/5/9/13/16/17/24 Centraal Station) attached to the VVV I Amsterdam Visitor Centre across the tram tracks from Centraal Station. It has tickets, passes and transport maps.

The excellent 9292 Journey Planner (www.9292.nl) calculates routes, costs and travel times, and will get you for door to door wherever you're going in the city.

Bicycle

The vast majority of Amsterdammers get around town on fiets (bikes). Cycling is a big deal here. Bike-hire companies are located all over the city.

Boat

From late March to early November, the **Canal Bus** (📞02 0217 0501; www.canal.nl; day pass €21, cruises €15-20, pedaloes €8; ⏱10am-6pm; 📶) offers a unique hop-on, hop-off service among its 20 docks around the city and near the big museums.

Free ferries to Amsterdam Noord depart from piers behind Centraal Station.

Bus & Metro

➡ Amsterdam's buses and metro (subway) primarily serve outer districts.

➡ The GVB offers unlimited-ride passes for one to seven days (€7.50 to €34), valid on trams, some buses and the metro.

➡ Alternatively, buy a disposable OV-chipkaart (www.ov-chipkaart.nl; 1hr €2.90) from the GVB information office.

➡ *Nachtbussen* (night buses) run after other transport stops

(from 1am to 6am, every hour). A ticket costs €4.50.

➡ Note that Connexxion buses (which depart from Centraal Station and are useful to reach sights in southern Amsterdam) and the No 197 airport bus are not part of the GVB system. They cost more (around €5).

Car & Motorcycle

Amsterdam's narrow streets, unfenced canals and hundreds of thousands of cyclists mean driving is *not* recommended.

Parking

➡ Pay-parking applies in the central zone from 6am to midnight Monday to Saturday, and noon to midnight on Sunday. To use the parking machines you need a Dutch credit card; alternatively, go online at www.3377.nl to pay.

➡ Costs are around €5/30 per hour/day in most of the city

TRAVEL PASSES

➡ Travel passes are extremely handy and provide substantial savings over per-ride ticket purchases.

➡ The GVB offers unlimited-ride passes for one to seven days (€7.50 to €34), valid on trams, some buses and the metro.

➡ Passes are available at the GVB information office (p267) and VVV I Amsterdam Visitor Centres (p264), but not onboard.

➡ The I Amsterdam Card (www.iamsterdam.com; per 24/48/72/96 hours €57/67/77/87) includes a GVB travel pass in its fee.

➡ A wider-ranging option is the Amsterdam & Region Day Ticket (€18.50), which goes beyond the tram/metro system, adding on night buses, airport buses, Connexxion buses and regional EBS buses that go to towns such as Haarlem, Muiden and Zaanse Schans. The pass is available at the GVB office and at visitor centres.

➡ Another choice is the Amsterdam Travel Ticket (per one/two/three days €16/21/26). It's basically a GVB unlimited-ride pass with an airport train ticket added on. Buy it at the airport (at the NS ticket window) or GVB office.

centre and Canal Ring, and around €4/25 in the Jordaan, Museumplein area and around. Prices ease as you move away from the centre.

➔ Clampings are common and fines are steep.

➔ Parking garages include locations at Damrak, near Leidseplein and under Museumplein and the Stopera, but they're often full and cost more than street parking (per hour/day around €7/50).

➔ A park-and-ride deal near the edge of town is a much better bet.

Road Rules

➔ Drive on the right-hand side of the road.

➔ Seat belts are required for everyone in a vehicle.

➔ Children under 12 must ride in the back if there's room.

➔ Be alert for bicycles, and if you are trying to turn right, be aware that bikes going straight ahead have priority.

➔ Trams always have right of way.

➔ On roundabouts (traffic circles), approaching vehicles have right of way, unless there are traffic signs indicating otherwise.

➔ The blood-alcohol limit when driving is 0.05%.

Automobile Association

The ANWB (www.anwb.nl) is the Netherlands' auto association. Members of auto associations in their home countries (the AAA, CAA etc) can get assistance, free maps, discounts and more.

Rental

Requirements for renting a car in the Netherlands:

➔ Be able to show a valid driving licence from your home country.

➔ Be at least 23 years of age

(some companies levy a small surcharge – €10 or so – for drivers under 25).

➔ Have a major credit card.

RENTAL AGENTS

Note that most cars have manual transmission. If you need an automatic car, request it well in advance and be prepared for a hefty surcharge.

All the big multinational rental companies are here; many have offices on Overtoom, near Vondelpark. Rentals at Schiphol Airport incur a surcharge. Companies include the following:

Avis (www.avis.nl)

Enterprise (www.enterprise.nl)

Europcar (www.europcar.nl)

Hertz (www.hertz.nl)

Sixt (www.sixt.nl)

Taxi

➔ Taxis are expensive and not very speedy given Amsterdam's maze of streets.

➔ You don't hail taxis on the road. Instead, find them at stands at Centraal Station, Leidseplein and other busy spots around town. You needn't take the first car in the queue.

➔ At Centraal Station the queue is near the front entrance toward the west side.

➔ Another method is to book a taxi by phone. **Taxicentrale Amsterdam** (TCA; ☑020-777 77 77; www.tcataxi.nl) is the most reliable company.

➔ Fares are meter-based. The meter starts at €2.95, then it's €2.17 per kilometre thereafter. A ride from Leidseplein to the Dam costs about €12; from Centraal Station to Jordaan is €10 to €15.

Tram

➔ Most public transport within the city is by tram. The vehicles

are fast, frequent and ubiquitous, operating between 6am and 12.30am.

➔ Tickets are not sold on board. Buy a disposable OV-chipkaart (www.ov-chipkaart.nl; 1hr €2.90) or a day pass (one to seven days €7.50 to €34) from the GVB information office (p267).

➔ When you enter *and* exit, wave your card at the pink machine to 'check in' and 'check out'.

➔ Of Amsterdam's 15 tram lines, 10 stop at Centraal Station, and then fan out to the rest of the city. For trams 4, 9, 16, 24 and 26, head far to the left (east) when you come out the station's main entrance; look for the 'A' sign. For trams 1, 2, 5, 13 and 17, head to the right (west) and look for the 'B' sign.

➔ The GVB Information Office, across the tram tracks from Centraal Station, attached to the VVV I Amsterdam Visitor Centre, has tickets, passes and transport maps.

COMMON TRAM ROUTES

Jordaan & Western Canal Ring	Tram 1, 2, 3, 5, 10, 13
Southern Canal Ring	Tram 1, 2, 5 for Leidseplein; 4, 9 for Rembrandtplein
Vondelpark & the South	Tram 1, 2, 3, 5, 12
De Pijp	Tram 3, 4, 16, 24
Nieuwmarkt & Plantage	Tram 3, 7, 9, 10, 14, 26

TOURS

Guided tours are a great way to get to grips with the city, especially if you're short on time.

Walking tours abound, including themed tours covering subjects such as history, architecture or food. Cycling tours and boat tours are also ubiquitous. Many tours led by specialist guides offer a behind-the-scenes glimpse into various aspects of the city, such as the Red Light District or immigration.

➡ **Mee in Mokum** (Map p294; www.gildeamsterdam.nl; Gedempte Begijnensloot; tours adult/child €7.50/5; ⏰11am & 2pm Tue-Sun; 🚊1/2/5 Spui) Mee in Mokum's low-priced walkabouts are led by volunteers of all ages who often have personal anecdotes to add. Tours last between two and three hours and depart from the cafe in the **Amsterdam Museum** (p70). Reserve at least a day in advance and pay cash on the day.

➡ **Hungry Birds Street Food Tours** (📞06 1898 6268; www.hungrybirds.nl; day/night tour per person €79/89; ⏰11am Mon-Sat) Guides take you 'off the eaten track' to chow on Dutch and ethnic specialities. Tours visit around 10 spots over four hours in De Pijp, Utrechtsestraat, Rembrandtplein and the Spui, from family-run eateries to street vendors. Prices include all food. The meet-up location is given after you make reservations.

➡ **With Locals** (📞020-261 34 77; www.withlocals.com; ⏰tours from €20) The huge range of tours offered by locals through this outfit covers things like street art, markets, coffeeshops, food, craft beer and breweries, and shopping.

Most are walking tours but there are also several by bike. Tours generally last around two to three hours. Cheaper 90-minute introductory tours start from €8.

➡ **Amsterdam Underground** (Map p290; 📞020-261 34 77; www.amsterdamunderground.org; tour €12.50; 🚊1/2/4/5/9/13/16/17/24 Centraal Station) These 90-minute tours of the Red Light District are run by formerly homeless people and offer a different perspective on the city. A minimum of four people (or a minimum payment of €50) is required. Tours start at Prins Hendrikkade 50 and end at nearby socially-minded **Brouwerij de Prael** (Map p290; www.deprael.nl; Oudezijds Armsteeg 26; ⏰noon-midnight Mon-Wed, to 1am Thu-Sat, to 11pm Sun; 🚊1/2/4/5/9/13/16/17/24 Centraal Station).

➡ **Randy Roy's Redlight Tours** (Map p290; 📞06 4185 3288; www.randyroysredlighttours.com; tours €15; ⏰8pm Sun-Fri, 8pm & 10pm Sat; 🚊1/2/4/5/9/13/16/17/24 Centraal Station) Fun guides provide in-the-know anecdotes about the city's sex life and celebrity secrets on Randy Roy's lively 90-minute tour. The jaunt ends at a local bar with a free drink. Meet in front of the Victoria Hotel (Damrak 1–5), opposite Centraal Station, rain or shine. Reservations required.

➡ **Drugs Tour** (Map p290; 📞06 1528 2688; https://drugstour.com; tours by donation; ⏰6pm Fri; 🚊4/9/16/24 Dam) Reserve to take a two-hour tour exploring the myths and reality of Amsterdam's drug culture. The tour includes

'smart shops', a 'user room' (the tour doesn't go inside) and a look at fake drugs being sold on the street. Tours depart by the Oude Kerk. Private tours (€40 per four people) also can be arranged in multiple languages.

➡ **Prostitution Information Centre Red Light District Tour** (Map p290; www.pic-amsterdam.com; Enge Kerksteeg 3; tours €17.50; ⏰5pm Wed, Fri & Sat; 🚊4/9/16/24 Dam) The non-profit Prostitution Information Centre (p75) offers insightful 90-minute tours of the Red Light District, where guides explain the details of how the business works and take you into a Red Light room. Profits go to the centre; reservations are not necessary.

➡ **Sandeman's New Amsterdam Tours** (Map p294; www.neweuropetours.eu; tours by donation; ⏰up to 8 tours daily; 🚊4/9/16/24 Dam) Energetic young guides working on a tip-only basis lead a 2½-hour jaunt past the city centre's top sights. Meet at the **Nationaal Monument** (Map p294; Dam; 🚊4/9/16/24 Dam) on the Dam, regardless of the weather. The tour is first come, first served; to guarantee a spot, make a reservation.

➡ **Architectuur Tours** (Map p296; 📞06 3014 0945; www.architectuurtoursamsterdam.nl; Dijkstraat 55; tours €12.50-25; Ⓜ Nieuwmarkt) Architectural historian Alex Hendriksen offers highly recommended tours, which include walking tours exploring the buildings of Nieuwmarkt and architectural boat tours along the IJ River that fascinatingly expose the layers of history and development. Schedules for English-language tours and departure points are online.

Language

Dutch has around 20 million speakers worldwide. As a member of the Germanic language family, Dutch has many similarities with English.

The pronunciation of Dutch is fairly straightforward. It distinguishes between long and short vowels, which can affect the meaning of words, for example, *man* (man) and *maan* (moon). Also note that aw is pronounced as in 'law', eu as the 'u' in 'nurse', ew as the 'ee' in 'see' (with rounded lips), oh as the 'o' in 'note', öy as the 'er y' (without the 'r') in 'her year', and uh as in 'ago'.

The consonants are pretty simple to pronounce too. Note that kh is a throaty sound, similar to the 'ch' in the Scottish *loch*, r is trilled and zh is pronounced as the 's' in 'pleasure'. This said, if you read our coloured pronunciation guides as if they were English, you'll be understood just fine. The stressed syllables are indicated with italics.

Where relevant, both polite and informal options in Dutch are included, indicated with 'pol' and 'inf' respectively.

BASICS

Hello.	*Dag./Hallo.*	dakh/ha·*loh*
Goodbye.	*Dag.*	dakh
Yes./No.	*Ja./Nee.*	yaa/ney
Please.	*Alstublieft.* (pol)	al·stew·*bleeft*
	Alsjeblieft. (inf)	a·shuh·*bleeft*
Thank you.	*Dank u/je.* (pol/inf)	dangk ew/yuh

WANT MORE?

For in-depth language information and handy phrases, check out Lonely Planet's *Dutch Phrasebook*. You'll find it at shop.lonelyplanet.com, or you can buy Lonely Planet's iPhone phrasebooks at the Apple App Store.

| You're welcome. | *Graag gedaan.* | khraakh khuh·*daan* |
| Excuse me. | *Excuseer mij.* | eks·kew·*zeyr* mey |

How are you?
Hoe gaat het met u/jou? (pol/inf) — hoo khaat huht met ew/yaw

Fine. And you?
Goed. — khoot
En met u/jou? (pol/inf) — en met ew/yaw

What's your name?
Hoe heet u/je? (pol/inf) — hoo heyt ew/yuh

My name is ...
Ik heet ... — ik heyt ...

Do you speak English?
Spreekt u Engels? — spreykt ew *eng*·uhls

I don't understand.
Ik begrijp het niet. — ik buh·*khreyp* huht neet

ACCOMMODATION

Do you have a ... room?	*Heeft u een ...?*	heyft ew uhn ...
single	*éénpersoons-kamer*	eyn·puhr·sohns·*kaa·muhr*
double	*tweepersoons-kamer met een dubbel bed*	twey·puhr·sohns·*kaa·muhr* *mel* uhn *du·*buhl bet
twin	*tweepersoons-kamer met lits jumeaux*	twey·puhr·sohns·*kaa·muhr* met lee zhew·*moh*

How much is it per ...?	*Hoeveel kost het per ...?*	hoo·*veyl* kost huht puhr ...
night	*nacht*	nakht
person	*persoon*	puhr·*sohn*

Is breakfast included?
Is het ontbijt inbegrepen? — is huht ont·*beyt* in·buh·*khrey·*puhn

bathroom	badkamer	bat·kaa·muhr
bed and breakfast	gasten-kamer	khas·tuhn·kaa·muhr
campsite	camping	kem·ping
guesthouse	pension	pen·syon
hotel	hotel	hoh·tel
window	raam	raam
youth hostel	jeugdherberg	yeukht·her·berkh

DIRECTIONS

Where's the ...?
Waar is ...?   waar is ...

How far is it?
Hoe ver is het?   hoo ver is huht

What's the address?
Wat is het adres?   wat is huht a·dres

Can you please write it down?
Kunt u dat alstublieft opschrijven?   kunt ew dat al·stew·bleeft op·skhrey·vuhn

Can you show me (on the map)?
Kunt u het mij tonen (op de kaart)?   kunt ew huht mey toh·nuhn (op duh kaart)

at the corner	op de hoek	op duh hook
at the traffic lights	bij de verkeers-lichten	bey duh vuhr·keyrs·likh·tuhn
behind	achter	akh·tuhr
in front of	voor	vohr
left	links	lingks
near (to)	dicht bij	dikht bey
next to	naast	naast
opposite	tegenover	tey·khuhn·oh·vuhr
straight ahead	rechtdoor	rekh·dohr
right	rechts	rekhs

EATING & DRINKING

What would you recommend?
Wat kan u aanbevelen?   wat kan ew aan·buh·vey·luhn

What's in that dish?
Wat zit er in dat gerecht?   wat zit uhr in dat khuh·rekht

I'd like the menu, please.
Ik wil graag een menu.   ik wil khraakh uhn me·new

Delicious!
Heerlijk/Lekker!   heyr·luhk/le·kuhr

Cheers!
Proost!   prohst

Please bring the bill.
Mag ik de rekening alstublieft?   makh ik duh rey·kuh·ning al·stew·bleeft

KEY PATTERNS

To get by in Dutch, mix and match these simple patterns with words of your choice:

When's (the next bus)?
Hoe laat gaat (de volgende bus)?   hoo laat khaat (duh vol·khun·duh bus)

Where's (the station)?
Waar is (het station)?   waar is (huht sta·syon)

I'm looking for (a hotel).
Ik ben op zoek naar (een hotel).   ik ben op zook naar (uhn hoh·tel)

Do you have (a map)?
Heeft u (een kaart)?   heyft ew (uhn kaart)

Is there (a toilet)?
Is er (een toilet)?   is uhr (uhn twa·let)

I'd like (the menu).
Ik wil graag (een menu).   ik wil khraakh (uhn me·new)

I'd like to (hire a car).
Ik wil graag (een auto huren).   ik wil khraakh (uhn aw·toh hew·ruhn)

Can I (enter)?
Kan ik (binnengaan)?   kan ik (bi·nuhn·khaan)

Could you please (help me)?
Kunt u alstublieft (helpen)?   kunt ew al·stew·bleeft (hel·puhn)

Do I have to (get a visa)?
Moet ik (een visum hebben)?   moot ik (uhn vee·zum he·buhn)

I'd like to reserve a table for ...	Ik wil graag een tafel voor ... reserveren.	ik wil khraakh uhn taa·fuhl vohr ... rey·ser·vey·ruhn
(two) people	(twee) personen	(twey) puhr·soh·nuhn
(eight) o'clock	(acht) uur	(akht) ewr

I don't eat ...	Ik eet geen ...	ik eyt kheyn ...
eggs	eieren	ey·yuh·ruhn
fish	vis	vis
(red) meat	(rood) vlees	(roht) vleys
nuts	noten	noh·tuhn

Key Words

bar	bar	bar
bottle	fles	fles
breakfast	ontbijt	ont·beyt
cafe	café	ka·fey
cold	koud	kawt
dinner	avondmaal	aa·vont·maal

LANGUAGE MEAT & FISH

drink list	drankkaart	drang·kaart
fork	vork	vork
glass	glas	khlas
grocery store	kruidenier	kröy·duh·neer
hot	heet	heyt
knife	mes	mes
lunch	middagmaal	mi·dakh·maal
market	markt	markt
menu	menu	me·new
plate	bord	bort
pub	kroeg	krookh
restaurant	restaurant	res·toh·rant
spicy	pikant	pee·kant
spoon	lepel	ley·puhl
vegetarian (food)	vegetarisch	vey·khey·taa·ris
with/without	met/zonder	met/zon·duhr

Meat & Fish

beef	rundvlees	runt·vleys
chicken	kip	kip
duck	eend	eynt
fish	vis	vis
herring	haring	haa·ring
lamb	lamsvlees	lams·vleys
lobster	kreeft	kreyft
meat	vlees	vleys
mussels	mosselen	mo·suh·luhn
oysters	oester	oos·tuhr
pork	varkensvlees	var·kuhns·vleys
prawn	steurgarnaal	steur·khar·naal
salmon	zalm	zalm
scallops	kammosselen	ka·mo·suh·luhn
shrimps	garnalen	khar·naa·luhn
squid	inktvis	ingkt·vis
trout	forel	fo·rel
tuna	tonijn	toh·neyn
turkey	kalkoen	kal·koon
veal	kalfsvlees	kalfs·vleys

QUESTION WORDS

How?	Hoe?	hoo
What?	Wat?	wat
When?	Wanneer?	wa·neyr
Where?	Waar?	waar
Who?	Wie?	wee
Why?	Waarom?	waa·rom

Fruit & Vegetables

apple	appel	a·puhl
banana	banaan	ba·naan
beans	bonen	boh·nuhm
berries	bessen	be·suhn
cabbage	kool	kohl
capsicum	paprika	pa·pree·ka
carrot	wortel	wor·tuhl
cauliflower	bloemkool	bloom·kohl
cucumber	komkommer	kom·ko·muhr
fruit	fruit	fröyt
grapes	druiven	dröy·vuhn
lemon	citroen	see·troon
lentils	linzen	lin·zuhn
mushrooms	paddestoelen	pa·duh·stoo·luhn
nuts	noten	noh·tuhn
onions	uien	öy·yuhn
orange	sinaasappel	see·naas·a·puhl
peach	perzik	per·zik
peas	erwtjes	erw·chus
pineapple	ananas	a·na·nas
plums	pruimen	pröy·muhn
potatoes	aardappels	aart·a·puhls
spinach	spinazie	spee·naa·zee
tomatoes	tomaten	toh·maa·tuhn
vegetables	groenten	khroon·tuhn

Other

bread	brood	broht
butter	boter	boh·tuhr
cheese	kaas	kaas
eggs	eieren	ey·yuh·ruhn
honey	honing	hoh·ning
ice	ijs	eys
jam	jam	zhem
noodles	noedels	noo·duhls
oil	olie	oh·lee
pastry	gebak	khuh·bak
pepper	peper	pey·puhr
rice	rijst	reyst
salt	zout	zawt
soup	soep	soop
soy sauce	sojasaus	soh·ya·saws
sugar	suiker	söy·kuhr
vinegar	azijn	a·zeyn

Drinks

beer	*bier*	beer
coffee	*koffie*	ko·fee
juice	*sap*	sap
milk	*melk*	melk
red wine	*rode wijn*	roh·duh weyn
soft drink	*frisdrank*	fris·drangk
tea	*thee*	tey
water	*water*	waa·tuhr
white wine	*witte wijn*	wi·tuh weyn

EMERGENCIES

Help!
Help! help

Leave me alone!
Laat me met rust! laat muh met rust

Call a doctor!
Bel een dokter! bel uhn *dok*·tuhr

Call the police!
Bel de politie! bel duh poh·*leet*·see

There's been an accident.
Er is een ongeluk uhr is uhn *on*·khuh·luk
gebeurd. khuh·*beurt*

I'm lost.
Ik ben verdwaald. ik ben vuhr·*dwaalt*

I'm sick.
Ik ben ziek. ik ben zeek

It hurts here.
Hier doet het pijn. heer doot huht peyn

Where are the toilets?
Waar zijn de toiletten? waar zeyn duh twa·*le*·tuhn

I'm allergic to (antibiotics).
Ik ben allergisch voor ik ben a·*ler*·khees vohr
(antibiotica). (an·tee·bee·*yoh*·tee·ka)

SHOPPING & SERVICES

I'd like to buy ...
Ik wil graag ... kopen. ik wil khraakh ... *koh*·puhn

I'm just looking.
Ik kijk alleen maar. ik keyk a·*leyn* maar

Can I look at it?
Kan ik het even zien? kan ik huht *ey*·vuhn zeen

Do you have any others?
Heeft u nog andere? heyft ew nokh *an*·duh·ruh

How much is it?
Hoeveel kost het? hoo·*veyl* kost huht

That's too expensive.
Dat is te duur. dat is tuh dewr

Can you lower the price?
Kunt u wat van de kunt ew wat van duh
prijs afdoen? preys *af*·doon

SIGNS	
Ingang	Entrance
Uitgang	Exit
Open	Open
Gesloten	Closed
Inlichtingen	Information
Verboden	Prohibited
Toiletten	Toilets
Heren	Men
Dames	Women

There's a mistake in the bill.
Er zit een fout in de uhr zit uhn fawt in duh
rekening. rey·kuh·ning

ATM	*pin-automaat*	pin·aw·toh·maat
foreign exchange	*wisselkantoor*	wi·suhl·kan·tohr
post office	*postkantoor*	post·kan·tohr
shopping centre	*winkel-centrum*	wing·kuhl·sen·trum
tourist office	*VVV*	vey·vey·vey

TIME & DATES

What time is it?
Hoe laat is het? hoo laat is huht

It's (10) o'clock.
Het is (tien) uur. huht is (teen) ewr

Half past (10).
Half (elf). half (elf)
(lit: half eleven)

am (morning)	*'s ochtends*	sokh·tuhns
pm (afternoon)	*'s middags*	smi·dakhs
pm (evening)	*'s avonds*	saa·vonts

yesterday	*gisteren*	khis·tuh·ruhn
today	*vandaag*	van·daakh
tomorrow	*morgen*	mor·khuhn

Monday	*maandag*	maan·dakh
Tuesday	*dinsdag*	dins·dakh
Wednesday	*woensdag*	woons·dakh
Thursday	*donderdag*	don·duhr·dakh
Friday	*vrijdag*	vrey·dakh
Saturday	*zaterdag*	zaa·tuhr·dakh
Sunday	*zondag*	zon·dakh

January	*januari*	ya·new·waa·ree
February	*februari*	fey·brew·waa·ree
March	*maart*	maart
April	*april*	a·pril
May	*mei*	mey
June	*juni*	yew·nee
July	*juli*	yew·lee
August	*augustus*	aw·khus·tus
September	*september*	sep·tem·buhr
October	*oktober*	ok·toh·buhr
November	*november*	noh·vem·buhr
December	*december*	dey·sem·buhr

TRANSPORT

Public Transport

Is this the ... to (the left bank)?	*Is dit de ... naar (de linkeroever)?*	is dit duh ... naar (duh ling·kuhr·oo·vuhr)
ferry	*veerboot*	veyr·boht
metro	*metro*	mey·troh
tram	*tram*	trem
platform	*perron*	pe·ron
timetable	*dienstregeling*	deenst·rey·khuh·ling

NUMBERS

1	*één*	eyn
2	*twee*	twey
3	*drie*	dree
4	*vier*	veer
5	*vijf*	veyf
6	*zes*	zes
7	*zeven*	zey·vuhn
8	*acht*	akht
9	*negen*	ney·khuhn
10	*tien*	teen
20	*twintig*	twin·tikh
30	*dertig*	der·tikh
40	*veertig*	feyr·tikh
50	*vijftig*	feyf·tikh
60	*zestig*	ses·tikh
70	*zeventig*	sey·vuhn·tikh
80	*tachtig*	takh·tikh
90	*negentig*	ney·khuhn·tikh
100	*honderd*	hon·duhrt
1000	*duizend*	döy·zuhnt

When's the ... (bus)?	*Hoe laat gaat de ... (bus)?*	hoo laat khaat duh ... (bus)
first	*eerste*	eyr·stuh
last	*laatste*	laat·stuh
next	*volgende*	vol·khun·duh

A ticket to ..., please.	*Een kaartje naar ... graag.*	uhn kaar·chuh naar ... khraakh
What time does it leave?	*Hoe laat vertrekt het?*	hoo laat vuhr·trekt huht
Does it stop at ...?	*Stopt het in ...?*	stopt huht in ...
What's the next stop?	*Welk is de volgende halte?*	welk is duh vol·khuhn·duh hal·tuh
I'd like to get off at ...	*Ik wil graag in ... uitstappen.*	ik wil khraak in ... öyt·sta·puhn
Is this taxi available?	*Is deze taxi vrij?*	is dey·zuh tak·see vrey
Please take me to ...	*Breng me alstublieft naar ...*	breng muh al·stew·bleeft naar ...

Cycling

I'd like ...	*Ik wil graag ...*	ik wil khraakh ...
my bicycle repaired	*mijn fiets laten herstellen*	meyn feets laa·tuhn her·ste·luhn
to hire a bicycle	*een fiets huren*	uhn feets hew·ruhn
I'd like to hire a ...	*Ik wil graag een ... huren.*	ik wil khraakh uhn ... hew·ruhn
basket	*mandje*	man·chuh
child seat	*kinderzitje*	kin·duhr·zi·chuh
helmet	*helm*	helm

Do you have bicycle parking?	*Heeft u parking vóór fietsen?*	heyft ew par·king vohr feet·suhn
Can we get there by bike?	*Kunnen we er met de fiets heen?*	ku·nuhn wuh uhr met duh feets heyn
I have a puncture.	*Ik heb een lekke band.*	ik hep uhn le·kuh bant
bicycle path	*fietspad*	feets·pat
bicycle pump	*fietspomp*	feets·pomp
bicycle repairman	*fietsenmaker*	feet·suhn·maa·kuhr
bicycle stand	*fietsenrek*	feet·suhn·rek

GLOSSARY

bibliotheek – library
bier – beer
biertje– glass of beer
bitterballen – small, round meat croquettes
broodje – bread roll (with filling)
bruin café – brown cafe; traditional Dutch pub
café – pub, bar; also known as *kroeg*
coffeeshop (also spelt *koffieshop* in Dutch) – cafe authorised to sell cannabis
CS – Centraal Station
drop – salted or sweet liquorice
dwarsstraat – street connecting two (former) canals
eetcafé – *café* serving meals
fiets – bicycle
frites – French fries; also known as *patat*
gezellig – convivial, cosy
gezelligheid – conviviality/cosiness
gracht – canal

Grachtengordel – Canal Ring
GVB – Gemeentevervoerbedrijf; Amsterdam municipal transport authority
GWK – Grenswisselkantoor; official currency exchanges
hof – courtyard
hofje – almshouse or series of buildings around a small courtyard or garden, such as the Begijnhof
jenever – Dutch gin; also spelled *genever*
kaas – cheese
kade – quay
kerk – church
koffiehuis – coffee house (distinct from a *coffeeshop*)
koninklijk – royal
kroketten – croquettes
markt – town square, market
NS – Nederlandse Spoorwegen; Dutch railway company
OV-chipkaart – fare card for Dutch public transit

pannenkoeken – pancakes
paleis – palace
plein – square
proeflokaal – tasting house
Randstad – literally 'rim city'; the urban agglomeration including Amsterdam, Utrecht, Rotterdam and Den Haag
stamppot – potatoes mashed with another vegetable (eg sauerkraut or kale), served with bacon bits and a smoked sausage
stedelijk – civic, municipal
steeg – alley, lane
straat – street
stroopwafel – thin, syrup-filled waffle
toren – tower
VVV – tourist office
waag – old weigh house
De Wallen – Red Light District
zaal – hall

Behind the Scenes

SEND US YOUR FEEDBACK

We love to hear from travellers – your comments keep us on our toes and help make our books better. Our well-travelled team reads every word on what you loved or loathed about this book. Although we cannot reply individually to your submissions, we always guarantee that your feedback goes straight to the appropriate authors, in time for the next edition. Each person who sends us information is thanked in the next edition – the most useful submissions are rewarded with a selection of digital PDF chapters.

Visit **lonelyplanet.com/contact** to submit your updates and suggestions or to ask for help. Our award-winning website also features inspirational travel stories, news and discussions.

Note: We may edit, reproduce and incorporate your comments in Lonely Planet products such as guidebooks, websites and digital products, so let us know if you don't want your comments reproduced or your name acknowledged. For a copy of our privacy policy visit lonelyplanet.com/privacy.

OUR READERS

Many thanks to Fiona Fraser, Nancy Reagin and John van de Werken, who used the last edition and wrote to us with helpful hints, useful advice and interesting anecdotes.

WRITER THANKS

Catherine Le Nevez

Hartelijk bedankt first and foremost to Julian, and to everyone throughout Amsterdam and the Netherlands who provided insights, inspiration and good times during this update and over the years. Huge thanks, too, to Destination Editor Daniel Fahey and co-author Abigail Blasi, and everyone at LP. As ever, a heartfelt *merci encore* to my parents, brother, *belle-sœur* and *neveu*.

Abigail Blasi

Huge thanks to Daniel Fahey for commissioning me, and Catherine Le Nevez for her support. A massive *dank je* to Jo Dufay for sharing her city knowledge and books, to Wouter Steenhuisen and Geerte Udo at iAmsterdam, to Esther Nelsey for local recommendations, and to Luca, Gabriel, Benjamin and Alessia for coming along for the ride.

ACKNOWLEDGEMENTS

Cover photograph: Typical Dutch houses along the Damrak Canal, Amsterdam, Richard Taylor / 4Corners ©

Amsterdam Transport Network Map © GVB Amsterdam. Map designed by Carto Studio, Amsterdam.

THIS BOOK

This 11th edition of Lonely Planet's *Amsterdam* guidebook was researched and written by Catherine Le Nevez and Abigail Blasi. The previous two editions were also written by Catherine, with Karla Zimmerman. This guidebook was produced by the following:

Destination Editor
Daniel Fahey

Product Editors
Hannah Cartmel, Genna Patterson

Senior Cartographer
Mark Griffiths

Book Designer
Jessica Rose

Assisting Editors Sarah Bailey, Judith Bamber, Alexander Knights,

Kristin Odijk, Charlotte Orr, Tamara Sheward, Gabrielle Stefanos, Ross Taylor

Cover Researcher
Naomi Parker

Thanks to Kate Chapman, Shona Gray, Kate James, Kate Kiely, Alison Lyall, Anne Mason, Claire Naylor, Karyn Noble, Lauren O'Connell, Lyahna Spencer, Tony Wheeler

See also separate subindexes for:

✕ **EATING P281**

🍷 **DRINKING & NIGHTLIFE P282**

☆ **ENTERTAINMENT P283**

🔒 **SHOPPING P283**

🏃 **SPORTS & ACTIVITIES P284**

🛏 **SLEEPING P284**

Index

⭐ **ENTERTAINMENT**

🛌 SLEEPING

Amsterdam Maps

Sights

- Beach
- Bird Sanctuary
- Buddhist
- Castle/Palace
- Christian
- Confucian
- Hindu
- Islamic
- Jain
- Jewish
- Monument
- Museum/Gallery/Historic Building
- Ruin
- Shinto
- Sikh
- Taoist
- Winery/Vineyard
- Zoo/Wildlife Sanctuary
- Other Sight

Activities, Courses & Tours

- Bodysurfing
- Diving
- Canoeing/Kayaking
- Course/Tour
- Sento Hot Baths/Onsen
- Skiing
- Snorkelling
- Surfing
- Swimming/Pool
- Walking
- Windsurfing
- Other Activity

Sleeping

- Sleeping
- Camping
- Hut/Shelter

Eating

- Eating

Drinking & Nightlife

- Drinking & Nightlife
- Cafe

Entertainment

- Entertainment

Shopping

- Shopping

Information

- Bank
- Embassy/Consulate
- Hospital/Medical
- Internet
- Police
- Post Office
- Telephone
- Toilet
- Tourist Information
- Other Information

Geographic

- Beach
- Gate
- Hut/Shelter
- Lighthouse
- Lookout
- Mountain/Volcano
- Oasis
- Park
- Pass
- Picnic Area
- Waterfall

Population

- Capital (National)
- Capital (State/Province)
- City/Large Town
- Town/Village

Transport

- Airport
- Border crossing
- Bus
- Cable car/Funicular
- Cycling
- Ferry
- Metro station
- Monorail
- Parking
- Petrol station
- S-Bahn/Subway station
- Taxi
- T-bane/Tunnelbana station
- Train station/Railway
- Tram
- Tube station
- U-Bahn/Underground station
- Other Transport

Routes

- Tollway
- Freeway
- Primary
- Secondary
- Tertiary
- Lane
- Unsealed road
- Road under construction
- Plaza/Mall
- Steps
- Tunnel
- Pedestrian overpass
- Walking Tour
- Walking Tour detour
- Path/Walking Trail

Boundaries

- International
- State/Province
- Disputed
- Regional/Suburb
- Marine Park
- Cliff
- Wall

Hydrography

- River, Creek
- Intermittent River
- Canal
- Water
- Dry/Salt/Intermittent Lake
- Reef

Areas

- Airport/Runway
- Beach/Desert
- Cemetery (Christian)
- Cemetery (Other)
- Glacier
- Mudflat
- Park/Forest
- Sight (Building)
- Sportsground
- Swamp/Mangrove

Note: Not all symbols displayed above appear on the maps in this book

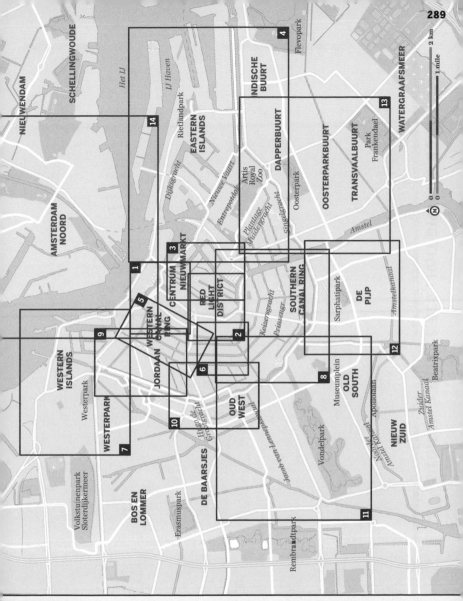

MAP INDEX

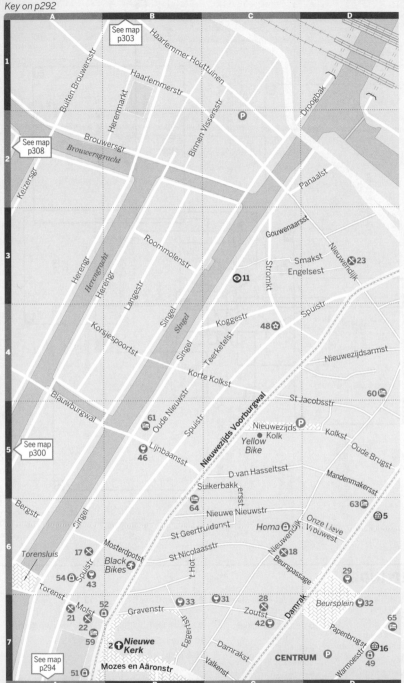

Key on p292

See map p303

See map p308

See map p300

See map p294

Haarlemmer Houttuinen

Haarlemmerstr

Buiten Brouwerssstr

Herenmarkt

Binnen Vissersstr

Brouwersgr

Brouwersgracht

Keizersgr

Droogbak

Panaalst

Gouwenaarsst

Herengr

Herengracht

Herengr

Langestr

Roommolenstr

Korsjespoortst

Singel

Singel

Singel

Singel

Stromkt

Smakst

Engelsest

Nieuwendijk

⊙11

23

Koggestr

Teerketelst

48 ☆

Spuistr

Korte Kolkst

Nieuwezijdsarmst

Blauwburgwal

Oude Nieuwstr

Spuistr

St Jacobsstr

60

61

Lijnbaansst

46

Nieuwezijds Voorburgwal

Nieuwezijds

Yellow Bike

Kolk

Kolkst

Oude Brugst

D van Hasseltsst

Mandenmakersst

Suikerbakk

ersst

Bergstr

Singel

64

Nieuwe Nieuwstr

63

5

St Geertruidonst

Homa

Onze Lieve Vrouwest

Torensluis

17

Mosterdpotst

St Nicolaasstr

Nieuwendijk

18

29

Black Bikes

54

Spuistr

43

't Hot

Beurspassage

Torenst

52

Gravenstr

33

31

28

Zoutst

Damrak

Beursplein

32

42

21

Molst

22

59

Eggertstr

Damrakst

65

2 Nieuwe Kerk

Valkenst

CENTRUM

16

Mozes en Aäronstr

49

51

Warmoesstr

Papenbrugst

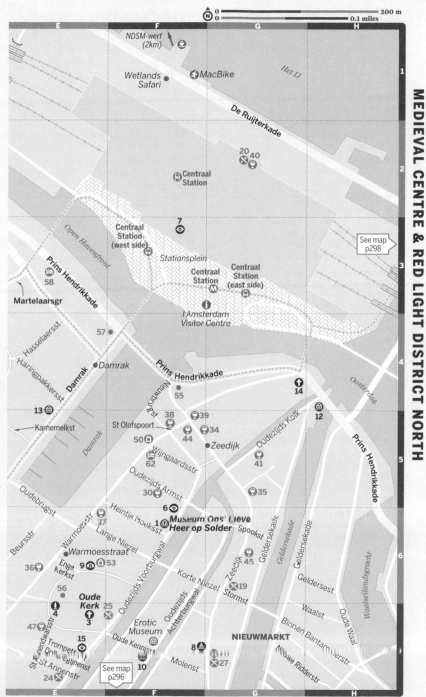

N 0 — 200 m
0 — 0.1 miles

NDSM-werf
(2km)

Wetlands
Safari

MacBike

Het IJ

De Ruijterkade

20 40

Centraal
Station

7

Open Havenfront

Centraal
Station
(west side)

See map
p298

Stationsplein

Prins Hendrikkade

58

Centraal
Station

Centraal
Station
(east side)

Martelaarsgr

M

57

I Amsterdam
Visitor Centre

Hasselaersst

Damrak

Damrak

Prins Hendrikkade

Oosterdok

Prins Hendrikkade

Haringpakkersst

Karnemelkst

13

Damrak

55

14

38 39

St Olofspoort

44 34

50

Zeedijk

Oudezijds Kolk

12

Wijngaardsstr

62

41

Oudezijds Armst

30

35

Heintje Hoekst

6

Oudebrgst

Beursstr

Warmoesstr

37

Lange Niezel

1 Museum Ons' Lieve
Heer op Solder

Spookst

Geldersekade

Geldersekade

Geldersekade

Oudezijds Voorburgwal

Warmoesstraat

Enge
Kerkst

9 53

45

Zeedijk

Geldersest

36

56

Oude
Kerk

25

Korte Niezel

Oudezijds Achterburgwal

19
Stormst

Waalst

Binnen Bantammerstr

Oude Waal

Waalseilandsgracht

4

3

47

St Jansstr

Trompettersteeg

15

Erotic
Museum

Oude Kennis

8

NIEUWMARKT

Nwe Ridderstr

St Annenstr

St Annenstr

24

See map
p296

10

Molenst

27

Dollebijnenst

Nwe Ridderstr

MEDIEVAL CENTRE & RED LIGHT DISTRICT NORTH *Map on p290*

MEDIEVAL CENTRE & RED LIGHT DISTRICT SOUTH *Map on p294*

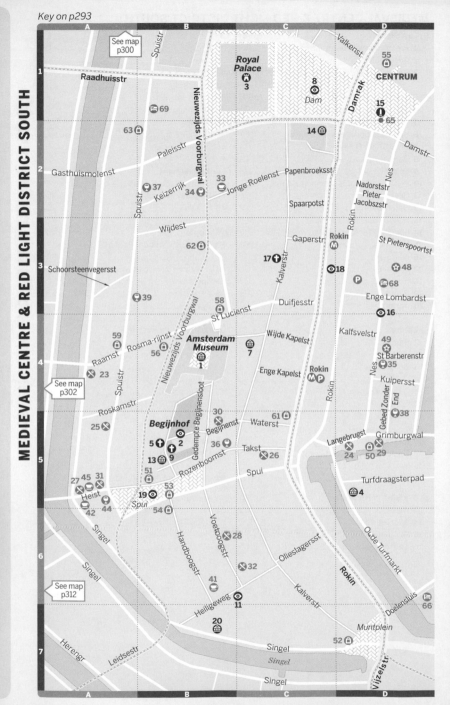

Key on p293

MEDIEVAL CENTRE & RED LIGHT DISTRICT SOUTH

See map p300

Raadhuisstr

Spuistr

Nieuwezijds Voorburgwal

Royal Palace
3

8
Dam

Valkenst

55

CENTRUM

Damrak

15
65

Damstr

69

63

Paleisstr

Gasthuismolenst

Keizerrijk

Spuistr

37

34

33

Jonge Roelenst

Papenbroeksst

14

Nes

Nadorststr
Pieter Jacobszstr

Spaarpotst

Wijdest

62

Gaperstr

Rokin

Rokin

St Pieterspoortst

48

Schoorsteenvegersst

17

Kalverstr

18

P

68

Enge Lombardst

39

58

St Lucienst

Duifjesst

16

Rosma-rijnst

Nieuwezijds Voorburgwal

Amsterdam Museum
1

Wijde Kapelst

Kalfsvelstr

49

59

56

7

St Barberenstr

35

Raamst

23

Spuistr

Roskamstr

Enge Kapelst

Rokin

Nes

Kuipersst

Gebed Zonder End

38

25

Gedempte Begijnensloot

Begijnhof

30

Begijnenst

61

Waterst

Langebrugst

Grimburgwal

5

2

Rozenboomst

36

Takst

24

50

29

13

9

26

Spui

51

53

Turfdraagsterpad

27 45 31

Heist

19

4

42

44

54

Spui

Handboogstr

Voetboogstr

28

Oude Turfmarkt

Olieslagersst

Rokin

32

Singel

Singel

See map p312

41

Heiligeweg

11

Kalverstr

Doelensluis

66

20

Muntplein

52

Herengr

Leidsestr

Singel

Singel

Vijzelstr

See map p302

0   200 m
0   0.1 miles

See map p290

See map p296

See map p304

E   F   G   H

Warmoesstr
St Jansstr
Leidekkersstr
Stoofstr
Oudezijds Voorburgwal
Oudezijds Achterburgwal
Monnikenstr
Bloedstr
Zeedijk
Geldersekade
Koningsstr
Nieuwmarkt
Barndest
Koestr
Bethaniënstr
NIEUWMARKT
Dijkstr
Nieuwmarkt
St Antoniesbreestr
Nieuwe Hoogstr
Snoekjesstr
Jodenbreestr
Oude Doelenstr
Prinsenhofst
Oude Hoogstr
Boe...enstr
Oudezijds Voorburgwal
Steenhst
St Agnietenstr
Oudezijds Achterburgwal
Spinhuisstr
Rusland
Slijkstr
Kloveniersburgwal
Zandstr
Zanddwarsstr
Raamgracht
Raamgr
Oudemanhuispoort
Kloveniersburgwal
Groenburgwal
Groenburgwal
Verversstr
Zwanenburgwal
Zwanenburgwal
Waterlooplein
Binnen Gasthuisstr
Nieuwe Doelenstr
Staalstr
Gravelandse Veer
Staalkade
Stopera
Amstel
Binnen Amstel
Amstel
Bakker...
Paardenstr

46 Pijlst
64
47
6
12
57
10
43
22
21
60
40
67

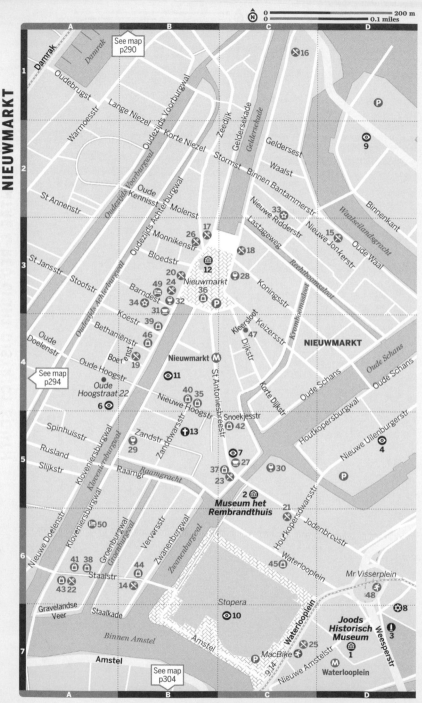

NIEUWMARKT

See map p290

0 200 m
0 0.1 miles

Damrak

Oudebrugst

Lange Niezel

Warmoesstr

Korte Niezel

Oudezijds Voorburgwal

Oude Kennisst

Molenst

Oudezijds Achterburgwal

Oudezijds Monnikenstr

St Annenstr

St Jansstr

Stoofstr

Bloedstr

Barndest

Koestr

Bethaniënstr

Oude Doelenstr

Oude Hoogstr

Oude Hoogstraat 22

Spinhuisstr

Rusland

Slijkstr

Kloveniersburgwal

Kloveniersburgwal

Nieuwe Doelenstr

Gravelandse Veer

Nieuwmarkt

Nieuwmarkt

Zandstr

Zanddwarsstr

Raamgr

Raamgracht

Groenburgwal

Groenburgwal

Ververstr

Staalstr

Staalkade

Zeedijk

Geldersekade

Geldersekade

Stormst

Binnen Bantammerstr

Nieuwe Ridderstr

Lastageweg

Koningsstr

Kleersloot

Keizersstr

Kromboomssloot

Dijkstr

St Antoniesbreestr

Snoekjesstr

Korte Dijkstr

Nieuwe Hoogstr

Zwanenburgwal

Zwanenburgwal

Houtkopersdwarsstr

Jodenbreestr

Waterloopleirn

Amstel

Amstel

Nieuwe Amstelstr

Gelderst

Waalst

Binnenkant

Binnen Bantammerstr

Nieuwe Jonkerstr

Oude Waal

Waalseilandsgracht

Rechtboomssloot

NIEUWMARKT

Oude Schans

Oude Schans

Oude Schans

Houtkopersburgwal

Nieuwe Uilenburgerstr

Mr Visserplein

Weesperstr

Boer

Nieuwe Hoogstr

Museum het Rembrandthuis

Stopera

Binnen Amstel

Stopera

MacBike

Joods Historisch Museum

Waterlooplein

See map p294

See map p304

See map p290
See map p294
See map p304

PLANTAGE & THE EASTERN ISLANDS

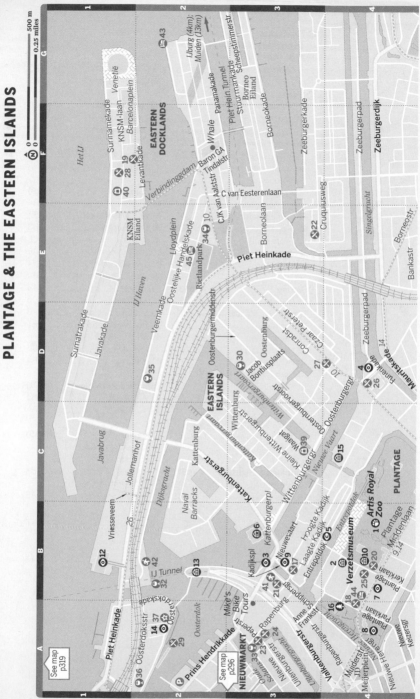

500 m
0.25 miles

See map p319

Piet Heinkade

Het IJ

KNSM Eiland

Surinamekade
KNSM-laan
Venetië
Barcelonaplein

43

19
28
40

Levantkade

EASTERN DOCKLANDS

Verbindingsdam
Baron GA Tindalstr
Whale
Panamakade
Piet Hein Tunnel
Sturmankade
Scheepstimmerstr
Borneo Eiland
Borneokade

IJburg (4km);
Muiden (13km)

CJK van Aalststr
C van Eesterenlaan

Zeeburgerkade
Zeeburgerpad
Zeeburgerdijk

Borneolaan

Cruquiusweg

22

Borneostr
Bankastr

Singelgracht

IJ Haven

Sumatrakade
Javakade

Veemkade
Oostelijke Handelskade
Lloydplein
Rietlandpark

34
45
10

Piet Heinkade

Zeeburgerpad

Oostenburgermiddenstr

Oostenburg

Czaar Peterstr

Zeeburgerpad

14

EASTERN ISLANDS

35

Javabrug

Dijksgracht

Jollemanhof

Vrieseveem

26

Naval Barracks

Kattenburg
Kattenburgerstr

Kattenburgergracht
Wittenburg
Wittenburgerstr
Kleine Wittenburgerstr
Waalgat

Jacob Bontiusplaats
Corradsstr

30

27
10

4
26

Funenkade
Mauritskade

PLANTAGE

15

Oostenburgervoorstr
Oostenburgergr

39

Nieuwe Vaart

Kattenburgerpl

6

Hoogte Kadijk
Laagte Kadijk
Entrepotdok

5

Burgpoort

Artis Royal Zoo

1

Plantage Middenlaan

9 14

Nieuwekeizersgracht

IJ Tunnel

IJ Tunnel

32

13

Kadijkspl

3

Nieuwevaart

17

9

41
21

Mike's Bike Tours

Oosterdok

Oosterdoksstr
14 37
Oosterdok
36
29

Oosterdokskade

Prins Hendrikkade

Valkenburgerstr

Rapenburg
Anne Frankstr
Schippersgr

Entrepotdok

2

18
44
25

7

Verzetsmuseum

10
20

Plantage Kerklaan

Plantage Parklaan

16

8

Meijerplein
Mr Visserplein
Nieuwe Herengracht
Muiderstr
Plantage Parklaan

Nieuwe Kerkstraat

See map p296

NIEUWMARKT

33
23
24

Nieuwe Uilenburgerstr
Nieuwe Batavierstr
Oudeschans

Rapenburgergr

PLANTAGE & THE EASTERN ISLANDS

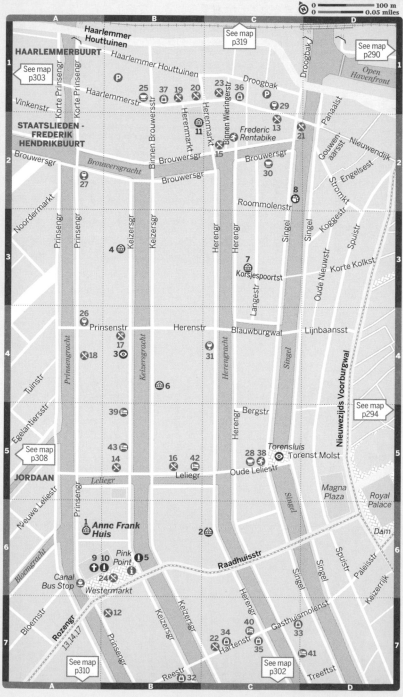

0 100 m
0 0.05 miles

See map p319

See map p290

Haarlemmer Houttuinen

HAARLEMMERBUURT

See map p303

Haarlemmer Houttuinen

Open Havenfront

Droogbak

Vinkenstr

Korte Prinsengr

Korte Prinsengr

Haarlemmerstr

25 37 19 20 23 36

29

STAATSLIEDEN - FREDERIK HENDRIKBUURT

Binnen Brouwersstr

Herenmarkt

Herenstr

Binnen Wieringerstr

Droogbak

Panaalst

Gouwen-aarsst

Nieuwendijk

11

Frederic Rentabike

13

21

Engelsest

Brouwersgr

Brouwersgracht

27

Brouwersgr

Brouwersgr

15

Brouwersgr

30

Stromkt

Koggestr

Roommolenstr

8

Spuistr

Noordermkt

Prinsengr

Prinsengr

Keizersgr

Keizersgr

Herengr

Herengr

Singel

Singel

Singel

4

Roommolenstr

7

Korsjespoortst

Oude Nieuwstr

Korte Kolkst

Langestr

26

Prinsenstr

Herenstr

Blauwburgwal

Lijnbaansst

Tuinstr

17

3

18

31

Herengracht

See map p294

Keizersgracht

6

Egelantiersstr

39

Bergstr

Herengr

Singel

Nieuwezijds Voorburgwal

See map p308

43

14

16 42

Leliegr

28 38

Torensluis

Torenst Molst

JORDAAN

Nieuwe Leliestr

Prinsengr

Leliegr

Oude Leliestr

Singel

Magna Plaza

Royal Palace

1 Anne Frank Huis

2

Dam

Bloemgracht

9 10

Pink Point

5

Raadhuisstr

Singel

Spuistr

Paleisstr

Canal Bus Stop

24

Westermarkt

Herengr

Keizerrijk

Bloemstr

12

Keizersgr

Herengr

Gasthuismolenst

33

Rozengr

22 34

40

41

13,14,17

Reestr

35

Hartenstr

Treeftst

See map p310

32

See map p302

WESTERN CANAL RING NORTH

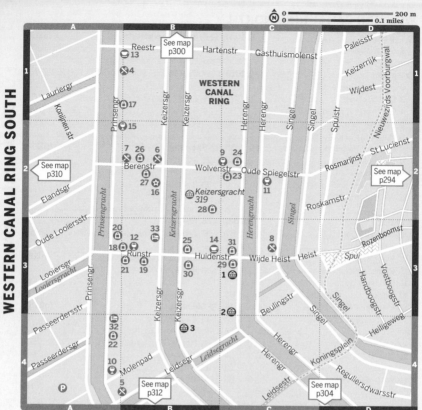

Sights (p106)
1 Bijbels Museum...C3
2 Het Grachtenhuis.......................................C3
3 Huis Marseille...B4

Eating (p108)
4 Café Restaurant van Puffelen.................B1
5 Casa Perú..B4
6 De Struisvogel...B2
7 Pancakes!...B2
8 Singel 404...C3

Drinking & Nightlife (p111)
9 Brix Food 'n' Drinx....................................C2
10 Café Het Molenpad..................................A4
11 De Admiraal..C2
12 De Doffer...B3
13 Koffiehuis De Hoek...................................B1
14 Pâtisserie Pompadour.............................B3
15 Vyne..B2

Entertainment (p113)
16 Felix Meritis..B2

Shopping (p113)
17 360 Volt..B1
18 Amatør..B3
19 De Kaaskamer..B3
20 Denham the Jeanmaker Men's
   Store...A3
21 Denham the Jeanmaker Women's
   Store...B3
22 Frozen Fountain...A4
23 Laura Dols...C2
24 Love Stories..C2
25 Marie-Stella-Maris....................................B3
26 Marlies Dekkers..B2
27 Mendo..B2
28 Negen Straatjes..B2
29 Scotch & Soda...C3
30 Van Ravenstein..B3
31 Zipper...C3

Sleeping (p216)
32 Andaz Amsterdam.....................................A4
33 Dylan..B3

THE WEST

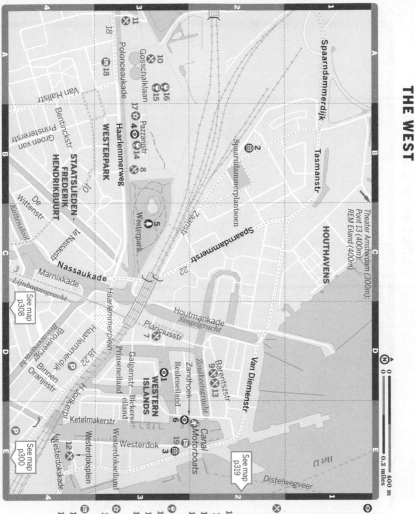

N

0   400 m
0   0.2 miles

Key on p306

SOUTHERN CANAL RING

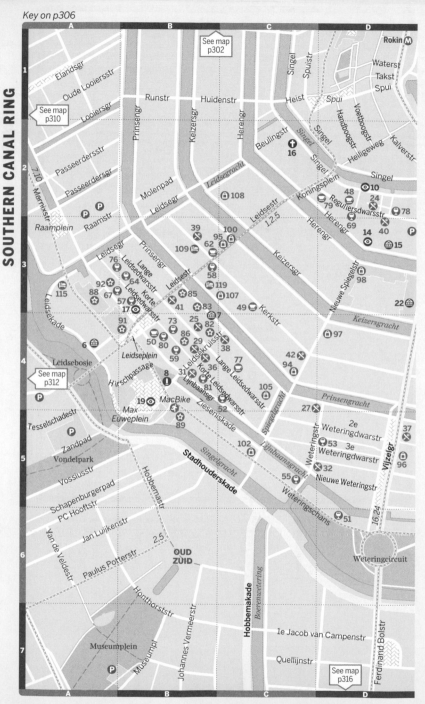

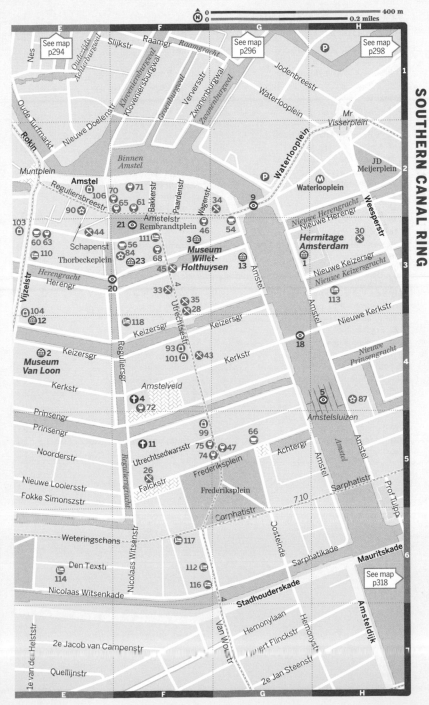

SOUTHERN CANAL RING *Map on p304*

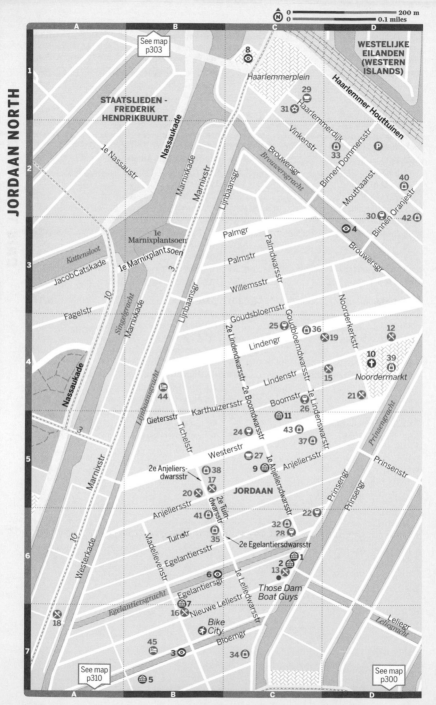

0   200 m
0   0.1 miles

See map
p303

WESTELIJKE
EILANDEN
(WESTERN
ISLANDS)

STAATSLIEDEN -
FREDERIK
HENDRIKBUURT

Haarlemmerplein

Haarlemmer Houttuinen

8

29

31 Haarlemmerdijk

Vinkenstr

33

40

Binnen Oranjestr

42

30

4 Brouwersgr

1e Nassaustr

Marnixkade

Nassaukade

Marnixstr

Lijnbaansgr

Brouwersgr
Brouwersgracht

Mouthaanst

Binnen Dommersstr

P

Kattensloot

1e
Marnixplantsoen

1e Marnixplantsoen

JacobCatskade

Fagelstr

Singelgracht

Marnixkade

Lijnbaansgracht

Palmgr

Palmstr

Palmdwarsstr

Willemsstr

Goudsbloemstr

25 Goudbloemdwarsstr 36 19

Lindengr

2e Lindendwarsstr

Lindenstr

15

Noorderkerkstr

12

10

39

Noordermarkt

2e Boomdwarsstr

Boomstr

26 1e Lindendwarsstr

21

Nassaukade

Karthuizersstr

11

24 43

37

Gietersstr

Tichelstr

Westerstr

27

9

Anjeliersstr

Prinsengracht

Prinsenstr

2e Anjeliers-
dwarsstr

38

17

20 JORDAAN

41

2e Tuindwarsstr

Anjeliersstr

22

Tuinstr

32

28

35

Madelievenstr

2e Egelantiersdwarsstr

Egelantiersstr

Prinsengr

1

6

2

13

Those Dam
Boat Guys

Egelantiersgr

1e Leliedwarsstr

Nieuwe Leliestr

7

16

Bike
City

Bloemgr

Leliegr
Leliegracht

Egelantiersgracht

18

45

3

34

See map
p310

5

See map
p300

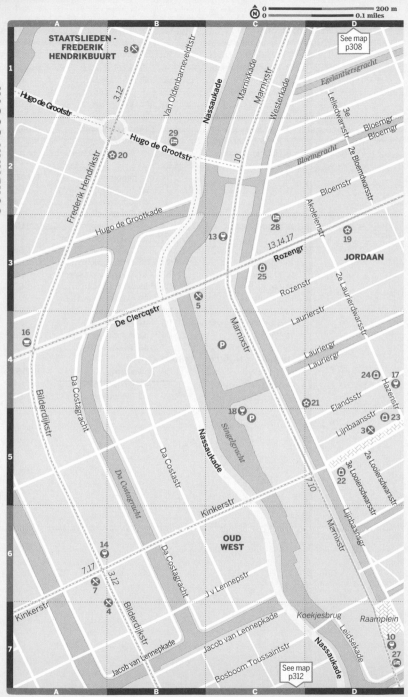

◎ **Sights** **(p136)**
1 Houseboat Museum.............E4
2 Johnny Jordaanplein...........E4

🍴 **Eating** **(p139)**
3 Balthazar's Keuken..............D5
4 Mastino V.............................B7
5 Moeders..............................B3
6 Pazzi...................................E5
7 Seoul Food...........................A6
8 Yam Yam.............................B1

🍸 **Drinking & Nightlife** **(p142)**
9 Café de Jordaan....................E5
10 Café de Koe..........................D7
11 Café de Laurierboom...........E3
12 Café Pieper..........................E7
13 Cafe Soundgarden..............C3
14 De Trut...............................A6
15 La Tertulia...........................E5
16 Monks Coffee
Roasters...........................A4

17 Saarein.................................D4
18 Waterkant............................C5

⭐ **Entertainment** **(p146)**
19 Boom Chicago.....................D3
20 De Nieuwe Anita.................B2
21 Maloe Melo..........................D4

🛍 **Shopping** **(p147)**
22 Antiekcentrum
Amsterdam.......................D5
23 Arnold Cornelis....................D5
24 Cats & Things.......................D4
25 Raw Materials......................C3

🛏 **Sleeping** **(p218)**
26 Amsterdam Wiechmann
Hotel.................................E5
27 BackStage Hotel..................D7
28 Christian Youth Hostel
'The Shelter Jordan'..........C3
29 Morgan & Mees....................B2

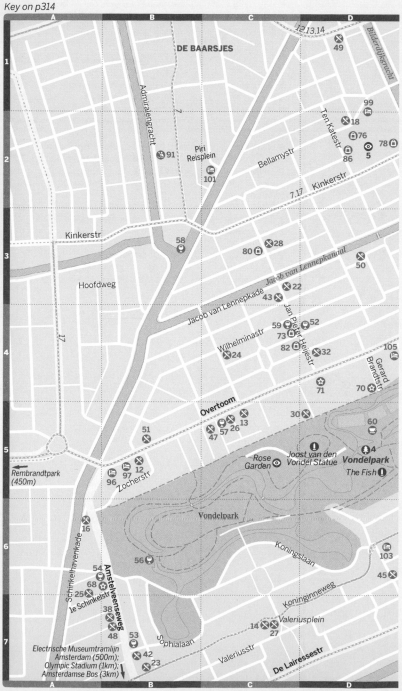

Key on p314

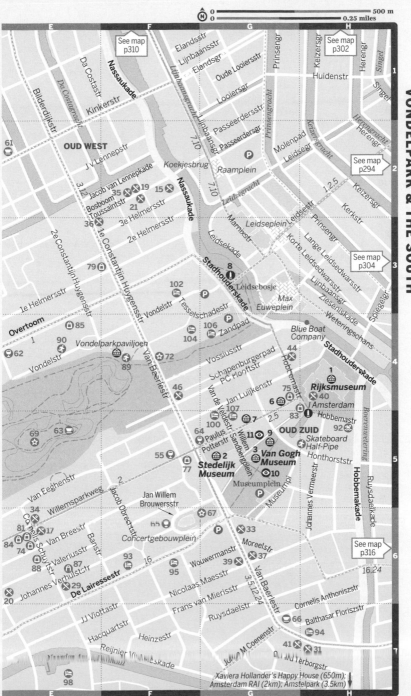

0   500 m

0   0.25 miles

See map p310

See map p302

See map p294

See map p304

See map p316

OUD WEST

Elandsstr

Lijnbaansstr

Elandsgr

Oude Looiersstr

Looiersgr

Huidenstr

Singel

Herengr

Keizersgr

Prinsengr

Da Costakade

Nassaukade

Kinkerstr

Bilderdijkstr

Da Costastr

Passeerdersstr

Passeerdersgr

Molenpad

Leidsegr

Herengr

Kerkstr

J v Lennepstr

Koekjesbrug

Raamplein

Keizersgr

Prinsengr

Leidsegracht

Jacob van Lennepkade

Bosboom Toussaintstr

1e Constantijn Huygensstr

3e Helmersstr

2e Helmersstr

Nassaukade

Marnixstr

Leidsekade

Leidseplein

Leidsestr

Lange Leidsedwarsstr

Korte Leidsedwarsstr

Lijnbaansgr

Zieseniskade

Weteringschans

Spiegelgr

2e Constantijn Huygensstr

79

1e Helmersstr

Stadhouderskade

Leidsebosje

Max Euweplein

Overtoom

85

Vondelstr

Tesselschadestr

Zandpad

Blue Boat Company

Stadhouderskade

90

Vondelparkpaviljoen

Vondelstr

Van Baerlestr

Vossiusstr

Schapenburgerpad

PC Hooftstr

Hobbemastr

Rijksmuseum

i Amsterdam

Hobbemastr

Boerenwetering

Jan Luijkenstr

Van de Veldestr

Willem Sandbergplein

Paulus Potterstr

OUD ZUID

Skateboard Half-Pipe

Honthorststr

Stedelijk Museum

Van Gogh Museum

Museumpl

Hobbemakade

Ruysdaelkade

Van Eeghenstr

Willemsparkweg

Jacob Obrechtstr

Jan Willem Brouwersstr

Museumplein

Johannes Vermeerstr

De Lairessestr

Concertgebouwplein

Wouwermanstr

Moreelsstr

Nicolaas Maesstr

Frans van Mierisstr

Van Baerlestr

Ruysdaelstr

Cornelis Anthoniszstr

JJ Viottastr

Hacquartstr

Heinzestr

Reijnier Vinkeleskade

Balthasar Florisztr

Johannes Verhulststr

Johannes Vermeerstr

Valeriusstr

JM Coenenstr

Ruysdaelstr

Xaviera Hollander's Happy House (650m);
Amsterdam RAI (2km); Amstelpark (3.5km)

VONDELPARK & THE SOUTH *Map on p312*

DE PIJP *Map on p316*

Key on p315

DE PIJP

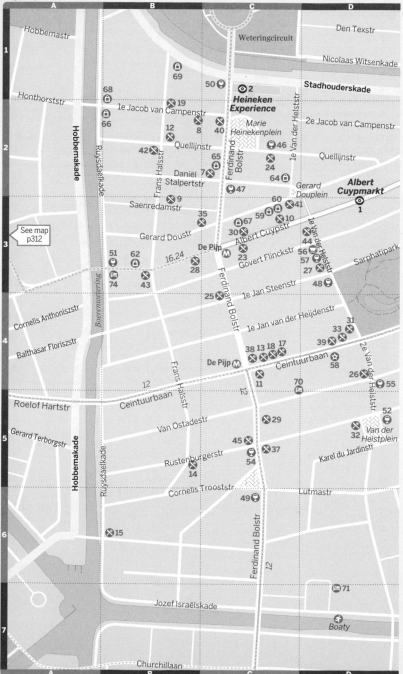

Hobbemastr

Weteringcircuit

Den Texstr

Nicolaas Witsenkade

Honthorststr

Stadhouderskade

◎ 2
Heineken
Experience

69

50

68

66

1e Jacob van Campenstr

19

12

8

40

Marie
Heinekenplein

2e Jacob van Campenstr

Hobbemakade

Ruysdaelkade

Quellijnstr

42

65

7

46

24

64

Quellijnstr

Daniël
Stalpertstr

47

Frans Halsstr

Saenredamstr

9

35

60

59

67

10

41

Albert
Cuypmarkt

1

Gerard
Douplein

See map
p312

Gerard Doustr

51

62

16.24

De Pijp

30

23

44

56

57

27

Sarphatipark

Albert Cuypstr

Govert Flinckstr

74

43

28

25

1e Jan Steenstr

48

1e Van der Helststr

Cornelis Anthoniszstr

Balthasar Floriszstr

1e Jan van der Heijdenstr

31

33

39

38 13 18 17

De Pijp

Ceintuurbaan

58

26

55

12

Ceintuurbaan

Frans Halsstr

11

70

Roelof Hartstr

Van Ostadestr

29

52

Gerard Terborgstr

45

32

Van der
Helstplein

37

54

Rustenburgerstr

14

Karel du Jardinstr

Cornelis Trooststr

Lutmastr

49

15

Ferdinand Bolstr

71

Jozef Israëlskade

Boaty

Churchillaan